CRIME & POLITICS

Ted Gest

CRIME & POLITICS

Big Government's Erratic Campaign for Law and Order

OXFORD
UNIVERSITY PRESS

2001

OXFORD
UNIVERSITY PRESS

Oxford   New York
Athens   Auckland   Bangkok   Bogotá   Bombay   Buenos Aires   Kolkata
Cape Town   Chennai   Dar es Salaam   Delhi   Florence   Hong Kong   Istanbul
Karachi   Kuala Lumpur   Madrid   Melbourne   Mexico City   Mumbai
Nairobi   Paris   São Paulo   Shanghai   Singapore   Taipei   Tokyo   Toronto   Warsaw

and associated companies in
Berlin   Ibadan

Copyright © 2001 by Ted Gest

Published by Oxford University Press, Inc.
198 Madison Avenue, New York, New York 10016

Oxford is a registered trademark of Oxford University Press

Library of Congress Cataloging-in-Publication Data
Gest, Ted.
Crime & politics : big government's erratic campaign for law and order / by Ted Gest.
p. cm.
Includes bibliographical references and index.
ISBN 0-19-510343-2
1. Crime—Government policy—United States. 2. Criminal justice, Administration
of—Political aspects—United States. 3. Crime prevention—United States. 4. United
States—Politics and government—20th century. I. Title
HV6789 .G47 2001
364.4'0973—dc21
00-065214

1 3 5 7 9 8 6 4 2
Printed in the United States of America
on acid-free paper

ACKNOWLEDGMENTS

This book is based on my reporting over three decades as a writer and editor for the *St. Louis Post-Dispatch* and *U.S. News & World Report*, as well as interviews with dozens of key policymakers and observers and a survey of the academic and popular literature on the fight against crime.

Among primary sources, special thanks go to those who directed the federal anticrime funding agencies. Laurie Robinson, the assistant attorney general for justice programs during the Clinton administration, provided considerable background information and invited me to observe an unusual 1997 conference that gathered most of her predecessors and their senior advisers over 30 years in one room to discuss where the program had gone right and wrong.

Whether or not they attended the session, many leaders of the federal program and officials in the main Justice Department agreed to interviews discussing their experiences. In addition to Ms. Robinson, they included Shay Bilchik, Robert Diegelman, Gerald Caplan, Henry Dogin, Andrew Fois, J. Price Foster, Nancy Gist, James Gregg, Jimmy Gurule, Lois Herrington, Charles Lauer, Jerris Leonard, Thomas Madden, Kent Markus, Patrick V. Murphy, Charles Rogovin, Donald Santarelli, John Schmidt, Daniel Skoler, James K. Stewart, Jeremy Travis, Craig Uchida, Richard (Pete) Velde, and James Wootton.

Edwin Meese and Janet Reno, the modern-day attorneys general with the most experience in state and local crime-fighting, contributed their reminiscences and analysis.

Important sources in interest groups who followed anticrime policy closely included Gwen Holden of the National Criminal Justice Association, Nolan Jones of the National Governors Association, Donald Murray of the National Association of Counties, and Laura Waxman of the U.S. Conference of Mayors. Key members of Congress who were most helpful included Senator Joseph Biden of Delaware (and aides Mark Gitenstein and Cynthia Hogan), Senator Edward Kennedy of Massachusetts (and aides Kenneth Feinberg and Ronald Weich), Representative Dan Lungren of California (and aide Kevin Holsclaw), Representative Bill McCollum of Florida (and aide Paul McNulty), Representative William Hughes of New Jersey (and aides Hayden Gregory and Eric Sterling), Representative Don Edwards of California (and aides James X. Dempsey and Virginia Sloan), Representative Neal Smith of Iowa, and Representative Harold Sawyer of Michigan.

Others whose contributions I particularly valued were Alfred Blumstein of Carnegie Mellon University, Roger Conner of the Justice Department, Philip Heymann of Harvard Law School, George Kelling of Rutgers University, Gary Kleck of Florida State University, youth advocate Marion Mattingly, Marc Mauer of the Sentencing Project, Bruce Reed and Jose Cerda of President Clinton's domestic policy staff, Josh Sugarmann of the Violence Policy Center, Jeffrey Roth of the Urban Institute, Lawrence Sherman of the University of Pennsylvania, Mary K. Shilton of the International Community Corrections Association, Michael Tonry of the University of Minnesota Law School (later Cambridge University), attorney and Police Corps advocate Adam Walinsky, Robert Weiner of the Office of National Drug Control Policy, Gordon Witkin of *U.S. News & World Report*, and David Yassky of Brooklyn Law School.

A list of people too long to name here gave their time and expertise to help inform me about criminal justice practices during visits everywhere from the public defender's office in Seattle to the prosecutor's office in Brooklyn to a community policing station in San Diego to a juvenile judges' organization in Reno.

Thanks to my agent, Gail Ross, for helping me get started on what turned out to be a lengthy project, and Dedi Felman, my editor at Oxford University Press, for considerable advice on how to shape a book that she inherited long after its conception, and Richard Gage for preparing graphics material.

Special appreciation goes to my wife, Kathy, one of the best editors in Washington and an astute observer of government and politics.

Washington, D.C.
December 31, 2000

CONTENTS

Introduction   1

1   When National Politics Met Crime   5

2   The Rise and Fall of LEAA   17

3   The "Get-Tough" 1980s   41

4   Making a Federal Case of It   63

5   Not Getting Them Young   83

6   Drugs: Is the War Winnable?   109

7   Guns Don't Kill?   133

8   A Cop On Every Corner?   157

9   Three Strikes: Baseball to Crime   189

10 Capitol Crime Extravaganza 219

11 Smarter Ways to Fight Crime 249

Notes 277

Bibliography 287

Index 290

INTRODUCTION

American politicians always seem to be waging a war on crime. Whether the latest problem is drive-by shootings, open-air drug markets, or child molesters, a solution usually is at hand. It may come in the form of enacting new gun controls, sweeping loiterers into police vans, or requiring longer prison terms.

Such crime controls once were purely local issues in the United States. Over the twentieth century, however, they became national concerns. Federal law enforcement powers in important areas like drug and gun control grew steadily, as did the amount of money Washington spent on anticrime programs run by states, counties, and cities. By the dawn of the twenty-first century, the Justice Department alone was handing out more than $5 billion in such aid each year. Lower levels of government came to depend on it for much of their justice system expansion and innovation.

How did crime policy become federalized and how much good has it done? The first chapters of this book trace how politicians made crime a national issue, often with little more than simplistic debate. In the late 1960s, for example, Congress rejected any notion of federal taxpayer money going to hire local police officers. Thirty years later, hardly anyone raised objections to Washington's paying for as many as 100,000 community officers, about one fourth of the nation's police forces. On the criminal sentencing front, a system that had given federal and state executive branch officials considerable leeway to decide when convicts were released from custody was largely scrapped. New and sometimes overlapping sets of "sentencing guidelines" and mandatory terms generated a huge prison expansion that had policymakers worried about not only the high operating costs but also what would happen when the inmates were released.

Meanwhile, many important policy questions were mired in simplistic debate in Congress over tangential issues. For many years, lawmakers had talked about updating a 1974 federal law that helped guide state policies on handling juvenile offenders. But that long-pending overhaul remained stalled in Congress in 2000 in a largely symbolic dispute over regulating sales at gun shows, not a prime source of firearms used in crime, particularly juvenile offenses. Congress spent many years debating the rules for federal appeals of state death-penalty convictions, an important and highly charged issue but not one that has much effect on crime rates.

The second part of the book examines how federal policymakers and bureaucrats, and their counterparts at lower levels, dealt with the major crime issues of the latter twentieth century: drugs, guns, policing, juvenile crime, and penalizing criminals. In large part, high-pitched political rhetoric has drowned out serious public discussion of crime's root causes on a national level. That has discouraged the kind of consistent high-powered leadership starting in the White House, and Congress that, for example, has fostered striking gains in medical treatment.

Crime rates dropped in the late 1990s, but they remained high enough to frighten much of the public, especially senior citizens. A lack of sustained scientific evaluation in Washington and elsewhere meant that no one could prove that crime's fall had been caused by government policies. Even as federal aid for state and local crime-fighting grew rapidly, lawmakers ignored an executive branch request to reserve a paltry 1 percent for determining whether the spending was effective.

This book tells the inside story of how shallow partisan politics has largely determined how policies are made on a problem that consistently ranks among the top concerns of Americans. It is a story of personal idiosyncrasies and ideological biases that played major roles in decisionmaking.

The story concentrates on federal policy, which has a ripple effect in states and localities, where most anticrime laws are enforced. When President George W. Bush and a new Congress took office in January 2001, they inherited a Justice Department whose Federal Bureau of Investigation devoted a growing portion of its resources to street crime as well as an Office of Justice Programs with a $5 billion budget. This spending, largely driven by a wide-ranging law enacted in 1994, was likely to continue unabated, no matter how crime rates changed.

Just as candidates for the White House and Congress have felt impelled to ratchet up their pronouncements on the latest sensational crime, political operatives and bureaucrats have scrambled to invent ways of sending taxpayer dollars back to localities, often for small-gauge programs that might just as easily have been financed locally. How much of this has reduced crime or significantly improved the criminal-justice system? The lack of evaluation made it hard to tell.

Of course, the picture was not all bleak. Plenty of local anticrime programs showed promise, if not proved success. Many of them sprouted up from the grassroots level, where they may or may not have gained recognition and support from federal funders. The last chapter discusses many of these programs.

A word about terminology: this book is concerned with what is typically called "street crime," a phrase that has come to encompass not only violence in public places but domestic strife as well. White-collar offenses like bribery, embezzlement, and cybercrime also beset the nation, but they are mostly not the province of the policymaking that is discussed here.

Chapter 1

WHEN NATIONAL POLITICS
MET CRIME

BARRY Goldwater started it. The 1964 Republican presidential candidate was the first to put crime on the national agenda in response to soaring rates of violence in the 1960s. It probably was inevitable that contenders for the White House would transform what had long been regarded as primarily a local concern into a national issue. After all, political leaders respond to the public's worries, and crime was headed to the top of the list. So the conservative senator from Arizona vowed during his acceptance speech at the Republican national convention to make "enforcing law and order" a campaign issue. He railed against "violence in the streets" and said he would "do all that I can to see that women can go out on the streets of the country without being scared stiff."[1]

Goldwater failed miserably at the ballot box against incumbent Lyndon Baines Johnson, but LBJ and his advisers did not fail to notice the resonance of the Arizonan's stinging demands for law and order. "It was understood," said Gerald Caplan, the U.S. Justice Department's crime-research chief in the early 1970s, "that the effect of Senator Goldwater's lopsided defeat was not to bury crime as an issue, but merely to transfer the official responsibility to the Democratic administration."[2]

The essential message from either major political party would be the same: a larger role for the federal government in local crime issues. Johnson's response to Goldwater's anticrime pronouncements was to appoint a blue-ribbon commission on law enforcement and the administration of justice. At the time of the panel's creation, agencies around the nation that dealt with crime and criminals—police, courts, probation officers, jails, and prisons—for the most part operated independently, with little coordination or overall crime-fighting strategy. "Practically no data on the criminal justice system existed," said Henry S. Ruth, Jr., deputy staff director of the LBJ panel. "Not much police data existed. Court data were a mess."[3] The last national panel to examine crime had been the 1931 Wickersham Commission, a Herbert Hoover-era project whose calls for reform went mostly unheeded.

On July 23, 1965, LBJ's 19 commissioners, later joined by 63 staff members and 175 consultants, drew up the first national blueprint to fight crime in more than three decades.[4] The president wanted his commission to "deepen our understanding of the causes of crime and of how society should respond. . . ." The eventual study was pathbreaking because it would summarize the nation's accumulated knowledge about crime and justice—along with its shortcomings—in one volume, *The Challenge of Crime in a Free Society,* that would define an issue that occupied the country for the next 30 years and beyond.

Johnson hoped that a bipartisan commission would provide the impetus for a coordinated national attack on crime. As it evolved, however, the panel's work was flawed by behind-the-scenes power politics in Washington, foretelling the course of erratic anticrime policymaking for decades to come.

In the case of the Johnson crime commission, a key obstacle was J. Edgar Hoover. Having spent four decades building the FBI's image as the nation's premier law enforcement agency, Hoover had little interest in a new commission's taking a prominent role in crime-fighting. The FBI's actual jurisdiction covered a narrow sliver of offenses, not many of them common street crimes, but the so-called G-men had become adept at handling many prominent kidnappings and bank robberies. For 40 years, Hoover was the nation's top crime solver—and he wanted to keep it that way.

Hoover maintained a strong public association with the ups and downs of local violence by issuing the Uniform Crime Reports every year, thus giving the impression that he was somehow the nation's top cop. He took no responsibility for the crime rate, of course, but Hoover's annual pronouncements of gloom contributed to the incorrect perception that the FBI was the main agency responsible for fighting violence on the street.

The White House was forced to deal with Hoover, not only because of his immense power over federal cases and his agency's secret files on Washington power brokers, but also because the commission would have to rely on the FBI for data and perhaps staff assistance.

Hoover would continue to cast a shadow over the commission's work. Before Johnson appointed his panel, seeds for a beefed-up federal involvement in local crime fighting had been planted by another prominent Democrat as well. In 1964, Attorney General Robert Kennedy—who had taken office during his brother's presidency but continued under LBJ—created an Office of Criminal Justice within his Justice Department that would study crime problems and potential solutions. Kennedy's deputy, Nicholas Katzenbach, tapped Harvard law professor James Vorenberg to head the new unit. Vorenberg tried but failed to establish a relationship with Hoover, whose backstage battles with the Kennedy family were legion. "I called every day, but was told he was busy," Vorenberg said. When Vorenberg eventually invoked Kennedy's name, Hoover passed word through an aide that he would grant Vorenberg an audience "when the civil-rights problems were over," a reference to the widespread and growing strife in the South over integrating public facilities.[5] Correctly foreseeing that the FBI would be embroiled in the civil rights furor for many years, Vorenberg gave up on seeing Hoover.

The Vorenberg-Hoover rift did not bode well when the crime commission was created, and Vorenberg became the panel's staff director. LBJ's first impulse was to try forging a bipartisan consensus on crime. "He wanted to bring every-one together—to 'reason together' was the phrase of the times," said historian Isidore Silver.[6]

In the zeal to make the study a bipartisan one, the Johnson administration wanted a prominent Republican to help lead it. A logical choice was onetime prosecutor, former New York governor, and 1948 presidential candidate Thomas Dewey. "We wanted someone with a crimebuster reputation," said Katzenbach, who was given the task of recruiting Dewey.[7]

Once again the problem was J. Edgar Hoover. Johnson hoped the FBI director would talk Dewey into taking the job. Katzenbach made a pitch to Hoover, who was noncommittal, and then visited Dewey. The Republican elder statesman seemed interested at first; Katzenbach recalled a "warm and cordial meeting." But in a second session in which LBJ's men hoped to seal the deal, "not only was he not interested, he was hostile to the idea," said Vorenberg, who also attended. Because Dewey's newfound skepticism reflected Hoover's, Vorenberg concluded that Hoover must have advised Dewey against taking the job. The attempt to strike a bipartisan note in crime fighting had failed. (Vorenberg said the FBI chief considered the commission a "nuisance" that "didn't understand anything about law enforcement.")

A reluctant Katzenbach eventually accepted the chairmanship himself. Filling out the panel was a largely establishment group dominated by white male law-yers, with a smattering of persons with other backgrounds represented, including civil rights leader Whitney Young and two women, Genevieve Blatt, of the Penn-sylvania state pardon board, and Julia Stuart, president of the League of Women Voters. Katzenbach, who worked with Johnson aide Joseph Califano to find members from varying geographical areas, defended the abundance of lawyers as inevitable, to avoid teaching basic legal principles to panel members.

Still, many commissioners were ignorant of criminal justice issues. Members like Yale University President Kingman Brewster, New York City Mayor Robert Wagner, and Los Angeles newspaper publisher Otis Chandler had little relevant experience. Those actually working in the justice system belonged to what Silver termed the "law enforcement establishment" and were unlikely to support bold changes. They included Boston prosecutor Garrett Byrne, San Francisco Police Chief Thomas Cahill, and California Attorney General Thomas Lynch.

With a dearth of knowledge on its subject, the crime commission largely depended on its staff for the hard task of research. Vorenberg recruited a cadre of aides (most in their 30s or younger), but the full crew was not in place until December 1965, six months after the panel had been appointed and only a year before its report was due. That was not enough time to study a complex social and legal problem that had not been scrutinized in the same depth for decades.

The panel and its staff divided into task forces to consider major subjects, including police, courts, prisons, organized crime, juvenile delinquency, and technology. Some field studies were extensive. The police unit, for example, questioned 2,200 departments nationwide looking for promising new practices. Similar surveys were conducted among courts, delinquency-prevention agencies, and other areas of the justice process.

Commission researchers "rode in police cars, sat in courtrooms, visited prisons, walked the streets of city slums," said the commission's final report. They studied all the literature and talked to all the experts they could. "Consultants and advisers from every relevant discipline and agency"—more than 400 in all—were called in to help, noted Deputy Director Henry Ruth.

The commission may have weakened the battle against crime by attempting too much. One big diversion was debates over the legal rights of suspects, prompted by Supreme Court rulings under Chief Justice Earl Warren to overhaul criminal procedure, like the 1966 *Miranda* decision on suspects' right to legal counsel. Traditionalists argued that the high court was tilting the justice process too far in the direction of defendants and hamstringing police officers at a time when they should become more aggressive. The commission finally avoided taking a stand on the wisdom of the high court decisions; seven panel members issued what amounted to a dissent, calling for a constitutional amendment to overturn the court rulings and "strengthen law enforcement."

The core study was ambitious enough. It was divided into seven categories: preventing crime, attempting to rehabilitate offenders, eliminating unfairness in the justice system, training police and other personnel better, expanding research on crime, spending more money on the justice apparatus, and getting more citizens, businesses, and social service agencies involved in anticrime work. What Deputy Staff Director Henry Ruth estimated at more than two and one-half million words of material had to be absorbed in 18 months, with the full panel meeting only seven times for two or three days each.

The final report included more than 200 recommendations—explained over more than 300 pages—and it covered not only the central issues surrounding the causes and spread of street crime but everything from public drunkenness to the tenure of local judges.

Almost lost in the morass of material were some of the key issues. One central theme that political leaders so conspicuously failed to address in later years was the call to "keep delinquents and youthful offenders from settling into lives of crime." Another key recommendation that gained only perfunctory recognition until many years later was the idea of dealing with offenders in community-based programs rather than locking them up. Still, the panel contributed to the lack of attention given to the issue by devoting only a small part of its report to the "corrections" system, even while complaining about the subject's "invisibility."

The commission's attempt to cover the waterfront was a conscious strategy. Echoing the catch phrase of the 1960s debate over national defense priorities, historian Silver said Johnson wanted both "guns and butter" out of the crime commission at the same time. That helped explain the scattershot approach. "Johnson was running for cover—he wanted no enemies on the right," said Silver. "So he decided to get out in front, partly to help his poverty program." The idea was that if the panel offered suggestions that would appeal to many points on the political spectrum, conservatives who rallied around a strong anticrime agenda might pull their punches on criticizing LBJ's liberal inner-city repair proposals.

Still, the commission's lengthy discussion of social problems as contributors to the crime plague—reflecting the Johnson-era Great Society emphasis—gave it a predominantly liberal cast. That characterization was correct, at least from the vantage point of those who emphasize criminal justice remedies like aggressive arrests and long prison sentences rather than social solutions like education, job training, and recreation.

The group started with a conservative interpretation of its mandate, said staffer Lloyd Ohlin, later a distinguished criminologist, on the ground that "radical attempts" to deal with crime would be "unlikely to gain wide acceptance." Ohlin said a "progressive liberalization" occurred "from the necessity to confront the facts of crime and the relative ineffectiveness of the criminal justice system."

In essence, a staff more liberal than its commissioners eventually persuaded the panel to make recommendations that Ohlin says "went far beyond incremental reform" of the justice system "and instead addressed basic inadequacies in the allocation of the resources of American society."[8]

In the end, the commission watered down many recommendations and shied away from anything that would resemble a highly aggressive attack on street crime that conservatives might welcome. The result was an equivocating document full of "pious hopes," said Silver. One example was the debate over how to discipline police officers whose strong-arm tactics in many cities were brutalizing suspects and increasing public mistrust as much as they were cracking down on criminals. Staffers favored strong civilian complaint review boards, but commissioners like San Francisco Police Chief Cahill disagreed. So the group failed to take a bold stand.

Even if the crime commission did not succeed in focusing on high-priority issues, it made several landmark contributions that transcended ideology.

Perhaps most prominent was its detailed dissection of the criminal-justice system that would serve as a framework for reforms. At the time, few Americans appreciated how criminal cases proceeded, from arrest to a final sanction. The commission produced a flow chart that traced how a large number of crimes reported to the police were winnowed by the legal process. The chart, often compared to a funnel, showed graphically how only a small fraction of crimes eventually resulted in findings of guilt, and later in prison terms. It helped to educate the nation about how criminal procedure actually operated and to show pressure points at which the system could operate more effectively to control crime.

Another notable accomplishment was the commission's focus on the wildly varying quality of American law enforcement. Although it was widely known that many individual police officers were ignorant, brutal, untrained, or some combination, the crime commission laid out the problem vividly. The report led to decades of efforts to improve police officers' education and draw up standards of accreditation for police forces. The report was circulated so widely that Katzenbach said he "got a tremendous kick when a small town police chief" praised the "bible" he had helped produce.

The commission also focused attention on victims of crime by helping to start a massive federal survey to determine how many Americans had been victimized in the previous year. The study established that only a small fraction of crime besides homicide actually is reported to law enforcement agencies. The survey evolved in an unorthodox way. In 1963, the National Aeronautics and Space Administration (NASA) started a project on "social indicators." One participant was Albert Biderman, a sociologist at the private Bureau of Social Research in Washington, who had noticed for many years a perfunctory mention

What is the sequence of events in the criminal justice system?

Entry into the system   **Prosecution and pretrial services**   **Adjudication**   **Sentencing and sanctions**   **Corrections**

Crime

Reported and observed crime

Investigation

Unsolved or not arrested

Arrest

Released without prosecution

Charges filed

Released without prosecution

Charges dropped or dismissed

Initial appearance

Preliminary hearing

Bail or detention hearing

Charges dropped or dismissed

Felonies

Grand jury

Refusal to indict

Information

Arraignment

Charge dismissed

Guilty plea

Trial

Acquitted

Convicted

Sentencing

Appeal

Probation

Revocation

Intermediate sanctions

Prison

Revocation

Parole

Revocation

Habeas corpus

Pardon and clemency

Capital punishment

Out of system (registration, notification)

Out of system

Misdemeanors

Unsuccessful diversion

Information

Arraignment

Charge dismissed

Reduction of charge

Guilty plea

Trial

Acquitted

Convicted

Sentencing

Jail

Revocation

Probation

Revocation

Out of system

Out of system

Diversion by law enforcement, prosecutor, or court

Juvenile offenders

Nonpolice referrals

Police juvenile unit

Prosecution as a juvenile

Intake hearing

Released or diverted

Formal juvenile or youthful offender court processing

Waived to criminal court

Informal processing diversion

Released or diverted

Adjudication

Released

Disposition

Probation or other nonresidential disposition

Revocation

Residential placement

Revocation

Aftercare

Revocation

Out of system

Note: This chart gives a simplified view of caseflow through the criminal justice system. Procedures vary among jurisdictions. The weights of the lines are not intended to show actual size of caseloads.

Source: Adapted from The challenge of crime in a free society. President's Commission on Law Enforcement and Administration of Justice, 1967. This revision, a result of the Symposium on the 30th Anniversary of the President's Commission, was prepared by the Bureau of Justice Statistics in 1997.

of crime victims by J. Edgar Hoover in the FBI's annual compilation of reported crimes.

Biderman viewed the Hoover reference as a "phony ploy" because the FBI compilation did not reflect the true extent of crime victimization in America.[9] All the FBI did was to publish data supplied by thousands of local police agencies. Some of the reports at best were sloppy and at worst were manipulated by politicians or police chiefs who wanted to hide crime increases. Many victims did not call the police, because they feared retaliation by the assailant or lacked confidence that the authorities would or could do anything.

As part of the NASA project, Biderman wrote a paper on the inadequacy of the FBI report and suggested that the Census Bureau ask a representative sample of Americans if they had been victimized by crime in the previous year, thus taking into account the many crimes that had gone unreported. Biderman passed on the suggestion to staffer Lloyd Ohlin at the crime commission, which endorsed it.

(The Richard Nixon team's fear of losing the 1972 election prompted both the Watergate scandal and the crime survey. In the proposal's early years, resistance from the FBI and elsewhere was so sharp that Biderman felt "trampled by the bureaucracy." It was saved during a key round of budget cuts when Nixon's advisers expressed fear that the FBI might report in 1972 that crime was rising. Knowing that the victimization survey was in the works, the White House wanted to promise that the new report would give a more accurate picture of crime trends. As it happened, a drop in reported property crimes brought the FBI "index" of serious crime down in 1972, and the first victimization survey was not published until after the election.)

The crime commission also focused attention on the primitive state of law enforcement technology. "It was in a quill pen era," said technology director Alfred Blumstein.[10] It was obvious that technological leaps were necessary for the justice process to operate more like a well-coordinated system, but staff director Vorenberg and his colleagues "were concerned that we would highlight sexy-looking gadgets that would attract attention away from their policy concerns," Blumstein said. It was a legitimate worry that later would play a large part in derailing the huge federal anticrime-aid program of the 1970s. As a result, the commission did not stress technical issues, a wise choice considering the flak taken by federal anticrime officials later when money was handed out for police helicopters and tanks (delicately called "armored personnel carriers").

But the report had a strong impact in a few key areas. Consider the 911 phone system. Blumstein knew of the 999 emergency number used in Great Britain and wanted the commission to push for a similar approach in the United States. First, he had to fend off a protest from the Chesapeake and Potomac Telephone Company, which served the Washington area and had gotten wind of the commission's plan. A phone company official feared that if a 911 system were created, everyone else—from the FBI to Sears Roebuck—would want their own single national number.

The company relented after it realized that it could charge the government for its services. Blumstein was angry at the turnaround, telling the Chesapeake and Potomac executive, "You son of a bitch—after the big fight you put up, you're adopting our recommendation to benefit your organization." Eventually, 911 became a standard feature of reporting crimes.

Although a strong believer in his mission to improve technology, Blumstein did heed Vorenberg's warning and restrained some colleagues, including one who studied whether police officers could shoot suspects with a sticky substance that would immobilize them and avoid the need for bullets. That and a few other ideas deemed too unorthodox failed to make the final report, although in later years, other entrepreneurs came up with items like Mace, pepper spray, and bean bags to accomplish the same goal.

Once the commission made its final decisions, it was time to get its message out. But the panel had become involved in so many controversial issues tangential to street crime, most prominently federal policy on wiretapping, that delivery of its final volume in 1967 was endangered by a side controversy. When Vorenberg advised Johnson aide Joseph Califano that the report was ready, Califano stunned the staff director by declaring that the president would not accept it. Califano explained that Johnson had heard that the panel was recommending that wiretapping be expanded. LBJ was adamantly opposed to such an idea.

The proposal had been toned down to avoid taking a firm position, Vorenberg reported. But Califano balked, saying that LBJ believed the rumor he had heard and wanted to avoid having anything to do with the study.

Vorenberg's response was "I have a mandate to deliver the report by the end of the day today. Either I will bring it over properly, or hold a press conference and throw it over the White House fence." When Califano said, "You wouldn't do that," Vorenberg responded, "Joe, you know I would." A few minutes later, Califano called and relented. (Vorenberg later was told that Johnson had been misinformed by a commission member about the wiretapping issue and was "quite pleased" with the report.)

The commission didn't simply publish its report and go home. Rather, it "made an enormous implementation effort," said Deputy Director Ruth. Staff members prepared the first draft of legislation that, as passed by Congress in the landmark anticrime law of 1968, required each state to set up a justice-system planning agency. Letters were sent to every state governor explaining the plan.

It didn't work like clockwork. The FBI, which maintained current addresses for local police departments, ostensibly agreed to help the commission send its report to the agencies. But the bureau reported at the 11th hour that it was unable to find the address labels, a failure that commission staffers were convinced was a last-ditch Hoover attempt to thumb his nose at the panel.

The report did get wide circulation, and it was cited for years to come. Still, its attempt to cover every subject with dozens of recommendations that were difficult for the public and policymakers to absorb quickly limited its effectiveness. "We probably should have prioritized," chairman Katzenbach lamented years later. Isidore Silver declared in the paperback edition of the panel's report that it "disappoints the impatient believer in miraculous nostrums by offering little more than complex and confused data about the 'causes' of crime [and] not much more...."

Some of the blame for the commission's muted impact can be traced to an important 1966 personnel shift. Midway through the panel's deliberations, its chairman, Nicholas Katzenbach, who had succeeded Robert Kennedy as attorney general, was persuaded by Johnson to take the number two job at the State Department. Insiders said Katzenbach's absence as a driving force significantly hampered the effort to publicize and implement the commission's findings. It was an early example of the lack of consistent leadership that would plague the federal anticrime program for years.

As the main federal law enforcement agency, the Justice Department was key to the fate of the crime commission's recommendations. The change at the top was a blow to their success because it was not just a substitution of one LBJ loyalist for another. Ramsey Clark, a Texan in his late 30s and son of Supreme Court Justice Tom Clark, was a civil-rights advocate whom journalist Tom Wicker called "the most revolutionary public voice in America today."[11] When it came to anticrime policy, Clark's interests differed sharply from Katzenbach's. Clark stressed crime's social causes, favored gun control, opposed capital punishment, and denounced both police brutality and Hoover's "excessive domination" of the FBI.

As recounted by Gerald Caplan, a commission staff member and later the Justice Department's anticrime research chief, Clark "seemed obsessed by the fear that the public alarm over crime might express itself in repressive laws and vigilante actions ... [he] worried that there might be a military takeover of the government." This unorthodox view "plunged the Crime Commission's recommendations into controversies that might otherwise have been avoided," Caplan said.[12]

Any LBJ idea of a bipartisan truce on crime was illusory. In the 1968 presidential campaign, Richard Nixon gave 17 speeches on law and order, by the count of Richard (Pete) Velde, who helped advise the Republican nominee. Nixon's themes were not those expressed by the crime commission, but rather,

in Velde's words, focused on "painting Ramsey Clark as the bad guy for supporting the soft, liberal Warren Court."[13]

As flawed as the commission's report was, it marked a significant point in
the shift to a national anticrime policy, setting a baseline for analyzing many of
the nation's most vexing modern crime problems. But the volatile politics of
the era meant that its short-term impact fell far short of its leaders' hopes.
Instead, an election-year struggle to put some of the panel's conclusions into
action handed the problem off to a new bureaucracy in the Justice Department,
a part of the federal executive branch ill-suited to direct a war against local
violent crime.

Chapter 2

THE RISE AND FALL OF LEAA

INDIANA Avenue in Washington, D.C., lacks the renown of "state" streets that crisscross the city, like Pennsylvania Avenue—which links the White House and the Capitol—and Massachusetts Avenue, with its string of embassies. But among law enforcers nationwide, Indiana Avenue is infamous for the capital's brand of crime and justice. The three-block-long Indiana was the birthplace of the federal agency that disbursed billions of dollars in anticrime funds all over the nation.

In a nondescript 12-story office building at 633 Indiana Avenue, a succession of political appointees and civil servants tried to follow several generations of marching orders on fighting crime that changed at the whim of whoever controlled the Capitol, six blocks to the east, the main Justice Department, three blocks to the west, or the White House, about ten blocks away.

Over three decades, a bewildering array of agencies, programs, and task forces handed out money in the hope that large chunks of federal aid, supplemented by money from state capitals, county courthouses, and city halls, could stem crime or at least improve the justice system.

But the political ups and downs of the nation's war on crime produced as many misfires as hits on the target. By the year 2000, no one knew for sure how much of the billions of taxpayer dollars that had been dispensed had a significant impact on crime and justice—or were simply wasted.

The money machine on Indiana Avenue started with a tiny program during Lyndon Johnson's presidency called the Office of Law Enforcement Assistance (OLEA). While Nicholas Katzenbach and James Vorenberg were setting up the president's crime commission in 1965, they hired Courtney Evans, a former aide to J. Edgar Hoover, and Daniel Skoler, director of a national juvenile judges' organization, to award about $7 million each year for innovative state and local anticrime programs.[1]

As had happened with the commission, the fledgling unit's tension with Hoover, the powerful FBI director, was palpable. Hoover long had anointed himself Washington's main conduit to local police chiefs. The last thing he wanted was a program inspired by Attorney General Robert Kennedy providing federal largesse to his constituents. "All those years, Hoover had been in the catbird's seat," said Patrick Murphy, who worked in the grant office and later served as police chief in Washington, New York City, and Detroit. "He did not like the idea of an Office of Law Enforcement Assistance."[2]

Sometimes Murphy would find himself explaining the office's ways to local officials who stopped by at the suggestion of their representatives in Congress. Later, police chiefs would call Murphy and report that a local FBI agent-in-charge had warned that it was necessary for them to clear grant applications with the FBI. That "was absolutely not the case," Murphy had to explain, making it clear that it was the main Justice Department—not the FBI—that decided which cities would get federal money.

Hoover seethed about RFK's dealing directly with mayors and local police chiefs. The FBI director's low opinion of Evans, his former underling who now directed the Kennedy Justice Department aid unit, was apparent in a marginal note the FBI chief made on an Evans speech text that crossed his desk. Hoover complained that Evans "didn't do anything while he was with the FBI—now he's [supposedly] the world's greatest expert."

Considering that state and local criminal justice systems spent billions of dollars each year, OLEA's budget was tiny. So it could issue only paltry grants—some of which became fodder for critics. In Washington, D.C., which federal officials constantly hoped could serve as a national model, small grants became an excuse to micromanage.

One early federal award went for repainting Washington's undistinguished black-and-white police cars to make them more noticeable. That idea annoyed Representative John Rooney, a Brooklyn Democrat and perennial nitpicker, who headed the committee controlling Justice Department appropriations.

"Has anybody complained about the colors?" asked Rooney at one hearing. OLEA's Murphy replied patiently that "the white cars are difficult to see in the daytime." Rooney reminded Murphy that most people could be expected to recognize a police car by the distinctive red light on top. "That would be what

I would look for," admitted Murphy, who then was pressed to disclose that OLEA had made money available for repainting the previous spring. "A year ago?" the annoyed congressman asked, demanding to know why "you can't decide on the colors of the squad cars?" So it went, with Rooney asking sarcastically during a discussion of motor scooters whether Murphy planned to give officers "ice skates for bad weather?"[3]

The exchange was characteristic of Rooney, whose dim view of federal anticrime aid was a prime reason the program got off to a bad start. (At one hearing, the Brooklynite said that all the anticrime office needed "was somebody to see to it that the checks are sent to the right addresses and that one of the people knows how to run a checkwriter.")

Amid debates over petty pork barrel spending, officials largely ignored more fundamental reforms. One was the idea of putting more police officers in neighborhoods, which became a political winner for President Bill Clinton nearly 30 years later. It wasn't that no one had thought of it. OLEA Director Skoler recalled talking about "wonderful British tradition of the bobby who said hello to everybody."[4] The Johnson crime commission promoted a different approach: "community service officers" who would help spot neighborhood problems like uncollected garbage and decrepit housing or recreation facilities that could serve as breeding grounds for crime.

Instead of enacting a broad anticrime strategy, members of Congress who took an interest in anticrime work sought isolated projects for their districts, in the pork barrel tradition. Key members of the Senate on crime policy were mostly moderates or conservatives whose notions differed starkly from those of the liberal-dominated presidential crime commission. They included Judiciary Committee Chairman James Eastland, a conservative Mississippi Democrat; senior Republican Roman Hruska of Nebraska; and Democrat James McClellan of Arkansas, who held perhaps the most powerful position by serving both as a Judiciary Committee member and as head of the panel that decided on Justice Department appropriations. The House Judiciary Committee was headed by liberal Democrat Emanuel Celler of New York City, whose panel was to the left of the House as a whole.

Armed with the crime commission's report and with a national election on the horizon, Congress was bent on creating some kind of anticrime program in 1968. It would be the first in a series of omnibus federal laws that influenced state and local policy by putting conditions on how money from Washington could be spent.

A racial issue could have derailed it. Richard (Pete) Velde, an aide to Senator Hruska who later would head the anticrime grant agency, recalled a fierce fight between conservatives and liberals on the Senate Judiciary Committee in a private markup session over the scope of the employment antidiscrimination rules that federal aid recipients would be required to heed.[5] It took Senate Majority Leader Mike Mansfield to mediate the squabble that allowed the aid program to emerge with fairly strong antibias clauses. In the mid-1970s, civil libertarians and black police officers charged in a lawsuit that federal officials were not enforcing the law's civil rights provisions vigorously enough. Velde found himself as the main defendant. After two trips to the Supreme Court, the case finally was settled.

The 1968 crime bill was embroiled in side issues with important civil liberties implications, like wiretapping and "preventive detention"—the power of judges to jail suspects they believed dangerous. Congress paid thorough attention. The bill was debated on the Senate floor for more than three weeks in the spring of 1968, more time than most subsequent crime legislation would get.

What got short shrift—less than a day—were the important sections on how federal money could be spent. It would set the stage for a long battle for control over the program. Congress came up with a scheme known as "block grants" that would allow states to spend the money with only a few strictures from Washington. The idea was that under broad guidelines, governors, mayors, and county executives would be able to use federal funds for whatever they pleased.

Executive branch money monitors were not pleased. James Gregg, an Office of Management and Budget staff member who later would succeed Velde as interim head of the anticrime program, helped prepare a memo urging the Johnson administration to veto the bill. "We were skeptical about the concept," Gregg recalled. "It was a Rube Goldberg kind of management structure."[6] Attorney General Ramsey Clark pondered his recommendation but decided to urge the president's approval, Gregg said. Given LBJ's determination to get the Democrats ahead on the crime issue, that may have been a foregone conclusion.

Congress made another fateful decision that plagued the program for several key years. J. Edgar Hoover's growing unpopularity at the FBI had underscored fears of a national police force; many lawmakers were wary of giving the Justice Department significant control over local law enforcement agencies via regulations on the use of federal funds. Moreover, conservative members of Congress distrusted the liberal attorney general. (Arkansas's McClellan, in particular, "despised" Clark, said OLEA's Murphy.)

So legislators put the decisionmaking power of the new aid-dispensing agency known as the Law Enforcement Assistance Administration (LEAA) in the hands of a bipartisan troika of three administrators, at least two of whom would have to agree on any decision. This unusual arrangement, modeled after regulatory units like the National Transportation Safety Board, was to prove awkward at best and, in the end, unworkable.

Even though the new agency probably would be overhauled if the Republicans won the presidential election later in 1968, the Democratic incumbents got off to a fast start. Murphy, the same official who had tangled with Congressman Rooney over the police-car painting, was named to head the first troika, along with Northern California sheriff Wesley Pomeroy and a researcher named Ralph Siu. ("We knew it didn't make any sense administratively, but we respected and liked each other," said Pomeroy.[7])

Clark apparently made the selections with no strong sense of partisanship. By Pomeroy's account, after the attorney general had chosen Murphy and Siu, whom he knew were Democrats, he asked Pomeroy—who worked in the attorney general's office organizing conferences for police chiefs on riot control—to recommend a Republican experienced in law enforcement as the third member. Pomeroy disclosed that he himself was a Republican and promptly got the job.

Because Congress had decided that the federal funds should be funneled through state governments, the troika began helping states create agencies to administer the aid. They soon plunged into the debate over purse strings: how much should Washington control state and local anticrime ventures? One way to help decide was to have each state prepare a long-term plan. That would ensure that at least some of the money wouldn't be spent according to the whim of whatever local politician or bureaucrat happened to obtain it. "Comprehensive planning became the holy grail," said Skoler, the official from Robert Kennedy's first anticrime unit, who stuck around to help get the expanded program going.[8]

Congress required states to prepare anticrime plans even though a similar rule in a federal aid program called "Model Cities" was not necessarily working well. Still, the prospect of more planning in the chaotic justice process created what LEAA leader Murphy recalled as "a lot of enthusiasm about what this program could do. We had the feeling that we were starting to systematize things, that crime could be brought under better control."

An urban crisis gave a cry for police equipment priority over a management overhaul. Violent and property crime totals continued rising in the late 1960s, but what made law enforcement officials most fearful was not random muggings. Rather, it was a wave of unrest in what developed into the memorably violent summer of 1968. "What seemed to concern the majority of voters most in 1968," said Richard Harris, whose book *Justice* chronicled the rough transition between the Justice Departments of Ramsey Clark and John Mitchell, Richard Nixon's attorney general, "were the black riots that had engulfed a hundred cities across the nation and that, to many white people, were the most flagrant and frightening kind of criminal activity."[9]

Under pressure from liberal big-city mayors as well as conservatives, Clark, who became attorney general after Nicholas Katzenbach departed for the State Department, allowed federal funds to be spent on riot-suppression gear. One infamous purchase was an armored personnel carrier nicknamed "Big Bertha" purchased by New Orleans officials. Thomas Madden, a lawyer who joined the Justice Department anticrime grants office in 1969 and stayed nearly a decade, said congressional pressure to spend money immediately after the 1968 riots "caused grief for LEAA in later years," when officials were called on the carpet by Congress to defend the grants.[10] It was not hardliner Richard Nixon but the urban-oriented Johnson administration that began this long-running headache for 633 Indiana Avenue.

The horror stories abounded, but many were exaggerated as they were retold. One state official recalled arguing with South Carolina Senator Ernest Hollings—a fixture on the committee that decided Justice Department appropriations—to disabuse the senator of the notion that federal anticrime money had gone to purchase a submarine.

At the time, fighting riots was a bipartisan concern. Liberal Michigan Senator Philip Hart, a Democrat, called for helping officials of battle-scarred cities like Detroit in his home state. Clark responded promptly, with GOP aide Pomeroy leading the way. "Everyone was short of equipment," said Pomeroy, whose "top priority was to get hand-held radios into every cop's hands."

After Democrats initiated spending for most disputed equipment, it was the Nixon administration that found itself on the hot seat by the time Congress got around to holding hearings.

Nixon won the White House in November 1968, and word went out that the short-lived LEAA leadership would be replaced. It didn't take long. On the new administration's first day in office, January 20, 1969, Deputy Attorney General Richard Kleindienst called in Murphy and Pomeroy (the third troika member; Siu, was out of town) and announced that "it gives me great pleasure to ask for your resignation." Kleindienst seized immediate authority over decisions to award grants.

The change in administration accentuated the lack of vision for the new agency. The management shift wasn't just a partisan matter. Charles Rogovin was a moderate Democrat who headed the LBJ crime commission's study of organized crime. When the panel neared its shutdown, Elliot Richardson, then attorney general of Massachusetts, came looking for someone to help him delve into his state's organized crime and hired Rogovin. Richardson later joined the Nixon administration and recommended Rogovin for a job in Washington. Attorney General John Mitchell tapped him to head LEAA, which Rogovin accepted in the hope that he could "influence the direction of criminal justice."[11]

Rogovin was designated head of the troika, but Velde, the Hruska aide who had helped write the law establishing LEAA, was installed in one of the two subsidiary jobs. Leadership might have been strengthened considerably if the third position had been filled by an outspoken Los Angeles police official, Daryl Gates, who had come to the attention of Rogovin and Velde. But Gates demurred, anticipating correctly that he would be named police chief in his home town.

With Gates out of the picture, Clarence Coster, a little-known police chief from Bloomington, Minn., got the job at the recommendation of Clark Mc-Gregor, a Republican congressman from Minnesota with a strong interest in LEAA. In the meantime, Rogovin and Velde were not getting along. The two came from different backgrounds—Rogovin, a prosecutor with liberal leanings, Velde a conservative ex-congressional staffer whose father had been a leading member of the House Un-American Activities Committee. It wasn't a total gridlock; both men, for example, backed more funds for helping states improve their prisons, and they fought off efforts from the main Justice Department to seize money they did not get around to spending in a particular fiscal year.

But overall, the need to achieve unanimity was "murderous," Rogovin said. Case in point: Rogovin wanted to hire Henry Ruth, who had been deputy director of the LBJ crime commission, for the important job of LEAA research director. Velde preferred a business executive he knew, a man with no criminal justice experience. Rogovin had to lobby Attorney General Mitchell to get his choice. The two troika members feuded over how much authority Ruth should be given to award grants. The result, Rogovin said, was that some grants were "held up interminably."

Another dispute erupted over a plan to accomplish one of the crime commission's main goals—improving the education of police officers. Rogovin viewed many courses listed by institutions that sought funding as "sheer crap—vocational training in the guise of higher education." He believed that skills like analyzing blood and ballistics were too routine to be considered worthy of federal aid, but Minnesota chief Coster disagreed. "I thought we were talking apples and oranges," Rogovin said.

On that issue and many others, Rogovin found that "Velde and Coster were on one side, I was on the other, and I had only one vote." At one point, Rogovin wrote a proposal that LEAA campaign to encourage more blacks to enter law enforcement, where they were underrepresented. Velde resisted, noting that few blacks had voted for Nixon. "My response was 'who the hell cares?' " said Rogovin. Velde, who said the troika might have succeeded if the trio had been more congenial, attributed most of the strife to conflicts between Rogovin and Coster, who "got along like oil and water."

The three finally decided to try coming to a meeting of the minds, holding an all-day session at a hotel in a Virginia suburb of Washington. Velde came away believing that things had been worked out to Rogovin's satisfaction. Rogovin had a completely different view. "We didn't solve anything," he said, recalling an argument with Coster over whether federal funds should go to police for analyzing blood samples. Coster considered such instruction basic education;

Rogovin thought it was vocational training that Washington should avoid. Within a week, Rogovin announced he would resign after only about 16 months in office.

The clashes at the top were not the only big problems that bedeviled the new agency. One of its main goals was to improve the justice system, and thereby help reduce crime, but at the outset the spending was very unbalanced.

Police departments—not courts, prisons, and the myriad other criminal-justice agencies—predominantly sought aid. "When police perceive something is in their interest," said Rogovin, "they are paramilitary—they bring people in and say, 'get this done.' Cops were best able to utilize the money—but the question was, to utilize it for what?" To complicate the picture, Congress had said no more than one-third of the funds could go to hiring, presumably another way to avoid a national police force.

That meant that training and hardware got most of the money, encouraging criticism that federal tax dollars were being poured into police radios and vo-cational classes. "The equipment manufacturers descended like locusts on the local police," said Richard Harris, who headed Virginia's criminal justice plan-ning agency.[12] Many police chiefs, inexperienced with federal paperwork re-quirements, found that "filling out grant applications drove them crazy," Harris said. So vendors obliged by writing the requests themselves and just having the police chiefs, in effect, sign a blank check. Harris and some counterparts in other states tried to keep the buying spree under control, to little avail. "We knew that the most politically dangerous thing we could do was to spend lots of money on equipment," he said later. "It came back to haunt us."

The new spending program also spawned a conflict between governors and mayors. Congress insisted that the federal funds be delivered through state cap-itals. Washington had provided direct aid to cities during the troubled 1960s, and mayors assumed that LEAA "was going to be another bonanza," Rogovin said. Instead, governors won the upper hand when the LEAA legislation was written, and "some states never developed any capacity to do planning." Pressure to get the money fast prompted some governors to hire consulting firms to write their plans. The idea of making what were termed "state planning agen-cies" the central point for the anticrime money flow "could have worked, but in an imperfect world it didn't, because nobody was prepared to wait and see the necessary expertise generated," said Rogovin.

The statewide plans were deeply flawed. Echoing the lack of information available to the crime commission a few years earlier, some states did not even know how many law enforcement agencies existed within their boundaries. Pennsylvania, for example, counted 900 the first time around and 1,150 when its second plan was filed.

One big shortcoming of the state agencies was that they became miniature versions of the bureaucracy in Washington doling out money, but they often did not have much real-world savvy. In the view of Donald Murray, who spent many years watching federal anticrime spending for the National Association of Counties, many states and localities committed the crucial mistake of failing to have elected officials play an important part in the process. More "politicians should have been involved," said Murray, because they had a broad view of what citizens want from a wide array of government services.[13] Instead, what typically happened was that the basic decisions were made solely by justice-system officials like police chiefs, judges, and jail wardens, often with little knowledge of how their actions would affect other social services.

That helped build LEAA's reputation as an agency that allowed local bureaucrats to feather their nests. And the lack of significant involvement by local politicians hurt LEAA during its tailspin in the late 1970s, when Congress heard few voices in its defense.

But the immediate problem for the embryonic LEAA in 1970 was Rogovin's departure. Attorney General Mitchell made an unorthodox choice by tapping Jerris Leonard, a former Wisconsin state senator who had compiled a solid record in school desegregation cases as the Justice Department's civil-rights chief. Leonard had sent signals that he was growing bored in the civil-rights job and might welcome a move to the White House counsel's office. The order to take over LEAA was "a terrible shock," Leonard recalled. Knowing about the troika arrangement, Leonard "thought the agency was worthless" as a career move. Mitchell explained that Congress had amended the law to give the administrator more power, but Leonard anticipated that the remaining troika members—Velde and Coster—were "going to create nothing but problems . . . I knew the place was a mess."[14]

Mitchell told the resistant Leonard that Nixon wanted him in the job, so Leonard decided that "you don't contest the president" and went to speak to Nixon. When Leonard asked about his mission, Nixon was blunt: "Get the crime rate down by the 1972 election." As Nixon perceived it, Leonard said, "Joe Public was scared to death and we weren't responding to it. He was saying, basically, that people are afraid, so do something about it."

Leonard was no crime expert, but he quickly decided that he had better start thinking about a new thrust for the sagging agency. One immediate problem was the state criminal-justice plans, many of which Leonard regarded as "not plans at all, but packages of goodies, like a Christmas tree." Yet the law required the LEAA administrator to sign them. After he was confirmed by the Senate, Leonard arrived at 633 Indiana Avenue and found his office loaded with thick red books. He first thought it was a mistake—that bureaucrats had decided to use the administrator's vacant space as a library. "Why do you have to store all this stuff in my office?" he snapped to an aide, who responded, "No, boss, you've got to sign these."

Leonard made one of his first executive decisions: "I'm not going to sign these because I'm not going to read them, and I don't sign anything I don't read." He told the aide that his name could be rubber-stamped on the documents. After learning that he also was required to review the telephone bills, rent, and postage costs of his agency's various regional headquarters, Leonard declared that he wanted as much bureaucracy removed from the administrator's office as possible.

That was only the first of many challenges. Word of LEAA's initial missteps, like the spending on tanks, had spread. As Virginia's Harris had feared, critics were beginning to harp on the abundance of police equipment being ordered. Among local newspaper stories cited by political scientist Thomas Cronin in a review of the early LEAA: "Government squanders $2.3 million of your money on new police cars that are too small for most cops" and "Indiana Governor used plane bought with U.S. crime fund."[15]

It was perfect fodder for congressional hearings, and Representative John Monagan, a Connecticut Democrat with oversight authority over LEAA, jumped in. He called a string of witnesses, including officials from Congress's General Accounting Office, to two 1971 hearings that featured tales of state and local officials' questionable expenditures.

To promote his cause, Monagan got CBS television's popular "60 Minutes" magazine program interested. The newly appointed Leonard understandably wanted to avoid being forced to make a public defense of spending begun under his predecessors' regime. ("I didn't want to go on the program, but Mitchell insisted," he said.)

Leonard was forced to defend Congress's decision to give anticrime-spending leeway to state and local officials generally according to population, meaning that tax money wasn't necessarily going to the nation's most serious crime problems. East coasters found spending in low-crime areas difficult to understand. Off the air, CBS reporter Mike Wallace pressed Leonard about money going to fight cattle rustling in Wyoming. Leonard said, "I told him that's because there are cattle rustlers in Wyoming, not in New York City."

Such logic didn't protect Leonard from a devastating "60 Minutes" account. The program showed case after case of cities using LEAA funds for riot equipment and police radios that went unused. Louisiana invested LEAA money not in anticrime projects but in federal securities instruments, earning $53,000 in interest. An Arkansas official pleaded on the air for ideas on how to spend $484,000 in leftover funds so that the state wouldn't have to return the money to Washington. Monagan asserted that only 25 percent of LEAA appropriations actually had made their way to localities, and Leonard's predecessor, Rogovin, came on the air to charge that the agency he had left in disgust did not know how its money was being spent.

Leonard promised reforms, but he was on the defensive. Asked for an example of an LEAA success, he cited the "fine, safe" city of Washington, D.C., where crime had declined. But Rogovin told the "60 Minutes" audience that the capital's apparent good fortune was the result not of LEAA but rather of a huge increase in police manpower that effectively gave Washington "wall to wall" protection.

After his television exposure, the LEAA director hardly relished the idea of appearing before Monagan's committee. "His sole purpose in life was to embarrass LEAA, but he wasn't going to embarrass me," Leonard recalled thinking. He even protested to Democratic Majority Leader Hale Boggs that Monagan was being unfair by criticizing someone who had arrived at the agency only recently. Leonard was angry that Monagan picked out a few examples of supposedly outlandish spending, such as the LEAA money used for a tank in Birmingham, Ala. (Leonard called the vehicle a "personnel unit," although he did not defend the purchase.)

The damage had been done. Buttressed by several reports issued by a liberal watchdog organization under the title "Law and Disorder," the public image of LEAA was on the wane. The Monagan panel concluded in May 1972 that after $1.4 billion in federal spending, LEAA had had "no visible impact on the incidence of crime in the U.S."[16] (The story didn't turn out well for Monagan, either. Behind the scenes, Leonard urged police chiefs in Monagan's Connecticut district to back another candidate, arguing that the congressman wasn't doing them any favors. Monagan was ousted in the 1972 election.)

This was not the way the "law and order" Nixon administration wanted its anticrime program portrayed as it prepared for a reelection campaign. CBS's Wallace had reminded viewers of the president's promise to the 1968 Republican national convention in Miami Beach that "the wave of crime is not going to be the wave of the future in the United States of America." As the 1972 election campaign grew closer, everyone from Nixon and Mitchell to top White House domestic policy aides John Ehrlichman, H. R. Haldeman, and Egil Krogh "were demanding that LEAA show results," said agency lawyer Thomas Madden.

To get his beleaguered agency—and Nixon's political fortunes—back on track, Leonard brought in three officials who had worked with him in Wisconsin and ordered them to design a scheme to reduce crime.

They came up with an idea called "high impact." Cities in each of LEAA's ten regions would get $20 million each to reduce violent crimes committed by strangers, as well as burglary, by 5 percent within two years and 20 percent within five years. Where did those goals originate? "I just made them up; it sounded good," Justice Department Research Director Martin Danziger was quoted in a report by the Twentieth Century Fund.[17]

Leonard believed cities "didn't want to have Washington telling them what to do. Each city had its own plan of how it was going to reduce specific types of crimes." Indeed, "crime-specific planning" became a mantra for Leonard, who believed previous efforts had been flawed by attempts to attack crime too broadly.

LEAA regional administrators assessed the level of cooperation that they could expect from mayors who might participate, target cities were chosen, and the program was announced by Vice President Spiro Agnew.

High impact was a departure for LEAA in several important ways. In its short history, the agency had essentially given out money to police departments and other criminal-justice agencies on the assumption that the crime rate would be affected indirectly. Leonard's plan was unheard of: set a bold goal that an infusion of funds would cut crime by a fairly dramatic figure within a year. The program went directly to cities and largely bypassed the state bureaucracies that had been set up to process federal funds.

Atlanta's designation as a target city did not sit well with the governor of Georgia, Jimmy Carter, who would have used his state's money for other projects. Leonard had no way of knowing it, but his action would bode ill for LEAA five years later, when Carter was elected president. (The other winning cities were Baltimore, Cleveland, Dallas, Denver, Newark, Portland, Ore., and St. Louis.)

For the most part, the selection seemed to go smoothly. But a flareup in Pennsylvania showed how federal anticrime funds could be mired in politics. Before Leonard came on the scene, his predecessor, Rogovin, ran into trouble with a $100,000 plan to fight juvenile crime in Philadelphia. Police Commissioner Frank Rizzo, a flamboyant Democrat, wanted the money, as did District Attorney Arlen Specter, a Republican. When the police department was designated the recipient, Rogovin got a call from a distressed Deputy Attorney General Kleindienst. "What are you doing to Hugh Scott?" he demanded, citing the Senate Republican leader, a Pennsylvanian. Rogovin had been unaware that Scott was taking Specter's side in the competition. Kleindienst fumed, "Jesus Christ. Hugh Scott is all over me about some goddamned juvenile gang grant. What's the matter with you? He's the majority leader. . . ." Rogovin maneuvered to find a way for Specter to get some of the money.[18]

Now it was Leonard's turn. Philadelphia had lost out in the competition for impact money, but Chief Rizzo wouldn't take no for an answer. So Leonard made an exception and created a "mini version" of the program for Rizzo. That angered Pennsylvania Governor Milton Shapp in the same way Georgia's Carter had been offended because it was another pot of money he could not control.

The FBI's Uniform Crime Reports said that reported crime totals actually

dipped in 1972—the one year during that era that such a national decline occurred. Violent crime did not drop, but property offenses like burglaries, auto
thefts, and larcenies went down. As for the impact cities, an analysis for the
National Academy of Sciences concluded that even if crime did go down, "there
was no way to prove that this was the result of the Impact Program rather than
of a host of unrelated factors."[19]

In Leonard's view, the high impact program had some effect through
"friendly intimidation." LEAA would give money to improve the criminal justice
system across the board, but only if leaders like police chiefs and probation
officials took an active part in the planning. Courts were a sticking point. If
judges wanted aid, Leonard believed, "they shouldn't be able to dictate the terms
and say 'I'm the chief judge of the criminal court, and I'll run my court the
way I want to.' Our message was, 'Judge, you don't do that anymore ... the
system has to improve.' We forced people to work together through the carrot
and stick approach."

The high impact program was condemned in 1977 by a distinguished group
of academics convened by the National Academy of Sciences, which concluded
that its tying the crime rate to changes in the justice system amounted to a
"total lack of realism." The panel noted that the "impact" cities had been "chosen for political reasons," and declared that the effort was "wrongheaded ...
crime cannot simply be purged from society by committing massive government
resources."

As it evolved, crime was not a crucial issue in the presidential race. Nixon
trounced George McGovern, while the Watergate affair remained a menacing
cloud on the horizon. At LEAA, Leonard believed that in nearly two years at
the helm, he had turned the focus of the agency from improving the justice
system to reducing crime. He decided that his job essentially was done and that
he wanted to leave soon after Nixon's second term began.

As Nixon's first term neared its end, an extraordinary new study of anticrime
tactics was getting underway. It was run by a federal panel known by the clunky
name of the National Advisory Commission on Criminal Justice Standards and
Goals. It was conceived largely by Associate LEAA Administrator Pete Velde,
who hoped to put policy flesh on the bones of what he viewed as the wishy-
washy Johnson crime commission by honing in on specific ways the justice
system could be reformed.

Velde, as a member of the LEAA's ruling troika, was getting "sick and tired"
of reading the states' annual versions of the "comprehensive" anticrime plans
required so that they could dip into the federal money well. A staunch Republican who believed the Johnson commission had veered too far to the left, Velde
was galled by finding the LBJ panel's conclusions "regurgitated and recited over
and over" by state officials to support their applications.[20]

By the early 1970s, in Velde's view, "a lot of [the crime commission's report] was out of date and very superficial." He wanted a new commission, but his idea was fought by top Justice officials like William Rehnquist, later U.S. chief justice but then in charge of policy issues for Attorney General Mitchell.

One day, Mitchell's office called LEAA seeking material for a speech he planned at a prison dedication. Velde slipped in his idea for a "standards and goals" commission. "Doggone if he didn't use it," a surprised Velde discovered later. The mid-level official had successfully outmaneuvered the attorney general's senior advisers. The panel operated in two phases, the first headed by Delaware Governor Russell Peterson, the second by New Jersey Governor Brendan Byrne.

The standards and goals commission came out with a few recommendations that were radical compared with the Johnson panel's six years earlier. In its initial report, issued during the first summer of Nixon's second term while the Watergate scandal dominated the news, the commission called on the nation to aim for a 25 percent drop in homicide and a 50 percent decrease in robberies in the next decade—paralleling Leonard's impact city approach. Many of its proposals were more specific than those of the LBJ group.[21]

The most far-reaching proposal was a call for eliminating the manufacture, sale, and private possession of handguns by 1983. The provision was advocated by Commission Vice Chair Peter Pitchess, sheriff of Los Angeles County and one of the first major law enforcement officials to support gun control publicly. Nixon administration officials were outraged, and the proposal never went anywhere. But it did have political consequences for Republicans. Indianapolis Mayor Richard Lugar, a commission member, lost a bid for the U.S. Senate partly because Democrat Birch Bayh labeled him a gun control advocate. (Lugar later won a Senate seat that he held for many years.)

An important subtext was the commission's skepticism about the role of the justice system in the war on crime. New York criminologist Isidore Silver, who had criticized Lyndon Johnson's crime panel, found it significant that the new group admitted that criminal-justice agencies might operate in "counterproductive" and "criminogenic" ways. It was a rare instance in modern crime politics in which a a Republican-appointed panel embraced the liberal critique that punishing some criminals without trying to rehabilitate them might produce even worse offenders.

As the new panel wrapped up its work, back at LEAA Jerris Leonard was gone by mid-March 1973. His successor was Donald Santarelli, a young former prosecutor in Washington. Leonard thought he had "established LEAA in such a way that no one could screw it up," but the aggressive Santarelli promptly removed all ten of Leonard's regional administrators. "He destroyed the leadership in a matter of months," Leonard said later. The shakeup was all too typical of the anticrime agency's erratic path.

In his relatively brief career, Santarelli became one of LEAA's more controversial figures. He had started his career in crime policy by working for a liberal Democrat, House Judiciary Chairman Emanuel Celler, but he concluded that the Democrats were too "bogged down in poverty and civil rights" to be very interested in fighting crime effectively.[22] So he switched to the Republican side, drafting a "white paper" on crime for Nixon's 1968 campaign. After the election, Santarelli managed to create a job for himself at the Justice Department, taking charge of crime-policy issues.

Having observed the 1968 crime law being drafted from his congressional staff perch, Santarelli knew the main thrust of the men most responsible for writing the new statute: Washington would help but not intrude. "The conservative Democrats who were in control couldn't stand Ramsey Clark and the civil-rights revolution," he said. "They could see how dangerous that was to federalism, and they didn't want that to happen to law enforcement."

Santarelli was eager to move into private law practice in 1973. But Nixon, with the backing of Arkansas Senator McClellan, leaned on him to head LEAA. At the time, Santarelli likened the agency to "a large, fat whale in the water, with a lot of blubber." He worried that "unless it moves very quickly, a shark will eat it." He wanted to sharpen LEAA's sense of priorities and to resist politicians who wanted to use the agency as just another source of pork barrel spending. His strategy was to devote his time to "aggressive marketing" and to leave the details to Velde, the surviving member of the original Nixon troika, and another deputy, Charles Work.

The Leonard-to-Santarelli transition was notable for another of the many shifts in the Justice Department's mission regarding state and local crime-fighting that had plagued the program from the outset. Santarelli was not enthralled with Leonard's crime-specific planning or high impact concepts. The impact program may have encouraged some improvements, like cutting the average police department response time to a citizen's call for help, Santarelli believed, but that wasn't necessarily a cost-effective way to cut crime.

Rather, the new administrator wanted to avoid LEAA's being "seen as directly responsible for reducing crime." That was tricky, because it left the main alternative as improving the justice system, not necessarily a good justification to spend what was approaching $1 billion a year in federal funds. Nevertheless, Santarelli recalled, "Every speech I gave, I said, 'Don't look to the criminal justice system to solve the problem.' "

It was this uncertainty over the basic purpose of the program, on top of the flak over spending on police equipment, that most contributed to LEAA's eventual downfall. Local officials who were responsible for drawing up the long-term plans to seek federal aid were confused. One veteran of the process was Ernest Allen, who had worked on anticrime programs in Louisville for two decades before heading the national agency that dealt with the problem of missing children. Allen said that the rhetoric from officials like Leonard during LEAA's formative years "was crime reduction, but the purpose of the [1968] law was justice system improvement."[23] Although Allen believed that LEAA had a positive impact, he said "the problem was that an awful lot of what was being done in the name of crime reduction had nothing whatever to do with crime."

Another paradox was that the more anticrime advocates did to focus on better ways to combat a particular offense—rape, for example—the more those violations would tend to be reported, making it seem, falsely, that the supposed remedy actually had created crime. Allen routinely advised elected officials in Louisville that "one of the worst things you can do is to take credit for crime reports going down, because that probably has very little to do with the real incidence of crime; the most important thing we can do is improve reporting and have the crime numbers go up."

Back at the 633 Indiana Avenue headquarters of LEAA in 1973, Donald Santarelli had more than crime rates on his mind. As he attempted to change the main subject on his agenda to criminal justice, he found himself constantly fighting against pressure from ideological conservatives to concentrate on reversing the Supreme Court cases that had expanded defendants' rights. It was a constant theme over the years, as typified by a supplement to the Johnson crime commission report written by LBJ ally Leon Jaworski of Texas and six others. Santarelli sympathized with such criticism, but he believed it "would be a can of worms" to spend much time addressing it.

There was no doubt that many Warren Court rulings were highly debatable, like the *Miranda v. Arizona* holding that barred police officers from questioning suspects without an attorney present and the exclusionary rule, which kept illegally seized evidence out of trials. But Santarelli knew that the vast majority of criminal cases did not turn on these rulings. "They were marginal and symbolic," Santarelli said, adding, "I knew we would founder on them, both constitutionally and politically."

One Santarelli tactic was changing the subject to the rights of crime victims. He argued that the purpose of paying more attention to victims was not to diminish defendants' rights but to balance them with the interests of victims on a case-by-case basis. So LEAA awarded funds to local prosecutors for new units that would deal with victims a thrust Santarelli viewed, at least philosophically, as an extension of Nixon's "free market" policies. The offices were known as "victim-witness agencies" on the assumption that most victims were also key witnesses whom prosecutors would want to testify.

Now that the criticism over local spending excesses had receded, Santarelli could more easily defend another new Nixon policy, "revenue sharing," or sending federal dollars directly back to the states. The president would say in private meetings that "we can't stop the goddamned Internal Revenue Service from collecting taxes but we can stop the goddamned Congress" from spending them, Santarelli said.

But Santarelli found, as his predecessors had discovered, that the states were far from equal in their ability to devise rational plans to spend the money. "There was no cadre of sophisticated criminal justice planners," he said. "That's America—this is not a monolithic country."

It's hard to say where Santarelli would have taken the agency, but he never really had the chance. In early 1974, the always outspoken administrator told a journalist, in what he believed was an off-the-record comment, that Nixon—then in the throes of what would become the height of the Watergate scandal—should think about resigning. When the remark was publicly attributed to him, Santarelli found himself out of a job only a few months before Nixon himself left office.

After years of waiting in the wings, it was now Pete Velde's turn to take the helm of the rapidly growing federal anticrime program. There was no doubt about Velde's depth of knowledge. After all, as a congressional aide, he had written much of the authorizing language of the program he now headed. But Velde's appointment was another demonstration of LEAA's erratic leadership. Jerris Leonard had arrived with no expertise in the crime field, and he proceeded to invent programs as he went along. Pete Velde knew every detail of the program, but he lacked front-line experience, either as an elected officeholder or as a criminal justice practitioner.

To make matters worse, Velde had to operate in a rapidly changing political atmosphere. The departure of Nixon and Mitchell during Watergate had brought in new leaders to the executive branch. President Gerald Ford's attorney general, Edward Levi, a legal scholar from the University of Chicago, had little interest in one of Velde's principal thrusts at LEAA, the development of law enforcement technology. In the aftermath of Watergate and the spectacle of an attorney general of the United States going to prison for obstruction of justice, Ford's priority for Levi was to return integrity and luster to a tarnished department.

Levi did work behind the scenes with Massachusetts Senator Edward Kennedy and others on issues like imposing criminal sentences more fairly and reining in excesses by federal law enforcement agencies. Kennedy and some of the others wanted to "depoliticize the crime debate and develop the kind of bipartisanship that was the hallmark of post–World War II foreign policy," said Kenneth Feinberg, a former federal prosecutor who served as Kennedy's chief aide on crime issues.[24]

But those discussions had little impact on where federal dollars were being spent on state and local anticrime work. Just as the LEAA troika had failed in the early 1970s, so did the relationship between Levi and LEAA chief Velde mid-decade. Perhaps the low point was Velde's excitedly displaying to Levi at a Justice Department meeting a reinforced tire that LEAA had helped develop for police vehicles. After the show-and-tell had ended and Velde had left the main Justice Department building for his office at 633 Indiana Avenue, a disgusted Levi—who had no interest in tires—told an aide that he never wanted to see Velde again. Nevertheless, LEAA continued growing, reaching a budget peak of $900 million in 1975.

But there was not much more opportunity for Velde to promote his gadgets. Ford lost the White House in 1976, and Jimmy Carter, the Georgia governor who had been annoyed when Atlanta received direct federal aid in Jerris Leonard's impact anticrime program years earlier, won the presidency. Crime was not a major issue in the campaign. Paul Wormeli, one of Velde's deputies, prepared a speech for Ford calling for police officers to become more involved in community life and was told by a Ford campaign aide that the draft was "far too thoughtful for this president."[25]

The Carter victory was widely considered a product of voter revulsion over Watergate. Even though Levi had begun to restore the Justice Department's reputation damaged in the scandal, it was clear that even more changes lay ahead under his successor, Griffin Bell, a prominent federal appeals judge and longtime Carter adviser.

Bell and Levi had in common a deep interest in strictly legal matters—after all, the Justice Department's primary task—and an equally deep lack of interest in the department's role in fighting street crime, which had become a very costly and very public adjunct to the department's main mission of handling federal cases and determining the government's legal policy. In one important way, Bell picked up where Levi left off, disdaining his own department's seeming emphasis on police technology.

Bell would delight in telling meetings of the Carter cabinet about the supposed technological excesses of LEAA. After he complained about what he understood to be a prototype police vehicle that had been transformed into a tank, LEAA officials brought the invention—actually a converted minivan—over to the Justice Department's courtyard for the attorney general to inspect. Because improvements like a more efficient fuel system had not changed the van's outward appearance, Bell was left muttering, "Where's the big tank?"

It was clear that the days of longtime Republican operative Velde as head of LEAA were over. But instead of choosing a prominent Democrat to take the reins, Bell was satisfied to leave the program in the hands of a bureaucrat, James Gregg. As a onetime federal budget officer handling crime issues and a former official in a Nixon antidrug unit, Gregg knew about many of the basics. But Gregg lacked Velde's extensive contacts on Capitol Hill, a problem that the Carter administration faced generally. "They didn't understand how Washington works," complained Wormeli, who said that the Carter aides ignored important niceties like informing members of Congress when funds were awarded for projects in their districts. Because they did not benefit from any public association with the program, it wasn't surprising that lawmakers then slighted LEAA at budget time.

As the Carter administration struggled to put its stamp on a sprawling federal executive branch, LEAA was becoming lost in the shuffle. One of the few high-level observers who spanned the Ford-Carter transition was Walter Fiederowicz, who had become an assistant to Levi while a White House Fellow and was assigned to watch LEAA. Continuing in his job when the Carter administration took over, he advised the new team that the agency had become something of a dumping ground for political hacks. It was not familiar territory for Judge Bell. "The notion of a soiled grants agency grafted on to the Justice Department, and the need to deal down and dirty with governors about budgets, was not his schtick," said Fiederowicz.[26]

In a controversial move soon after taking office, Bell closed down LEAA's regional offices, including one in Atlanta that had not always enjoyed smooth relations with Carter's Georgia administration. But that change might have happened by accident. The attorney general may have intended first to eliminate the "state planning agencies"—often known by the initials SPA—which prompted Bell to demand an explanation at one meeting for why LEAA was sending people to "spas." By one account, Bell mistakenly told a news reporter during an in-flight interview that he planned to close the regional offices, and astonished aides believed that they were required to follow through to avoid embarrassing the boss, even though it seemingly made little sense to run details of the sprawling program from 633 Indiana Avenue. After all, Jerris Leonard had done the reverse—delegating power to the regions.

Acting Administrator Gregg heard repeated rumblings that the Carter administration was cool to LEAA, but Bell was cordial in direct dealings. The attorney general appointed a task force of insiders to study the agency, which admitted that overblown rhetoric about its work had led to "inflated public expectation that the provision of limited federal funds and technical assistance was going to solve a problem for which state and local governments have the primary responsibility."[27]

But the group concluded that "there must be some federal government response to the problems of crime and the inefficient administration of justice," urging that LEAA be overhauled but not eliminated. Eventually, Bell overcame his deep skepticism and decided, as he told a congressional hearing in 1978, that

"I had a duty to try to make it into a better agency." Later, in a book on his experiences as attorney general, Bell assailed LEAA's pork barrel spending but defended its "meritorious" programs like the one that encouraged prosecution of career criminals.[28] And despite the fact that he had been lukewarm about the federal aid program, he criticized politicians who denounce crime "in emotional speeches and then seek public approval by cutting the money needed for programs to reduce crime."

Bell had occasion to impose his own prejudices on the agency. For years, court leaders had complained that they had been slighted when LEAA money had been handed out to police and, to a lesser extent, prisons. Before the 1976 election, Velde aide Wormeli had worked with Senator Edward Kennedy, a Judiciary Committee member, to arrange for a special $50,000 grant for each state to plan court improvements. But Bell, who as a judge might have been expected to applaud the idea, surprised and angered insiders by vetoing it, saying that the "state judges should get their own money," Wormeli said.

With all of LEAA's ups and downs, it was hardly surprising that Bell was having trouble finding anyone to head the agency. "It was perceived as unmanageable," Fiederowicz said. "It was not something people were jumping to do." Eventually, Bell departed from tradition and reached into academia for an LEAA administrator. He chose Norval Morris, like Levi, a University of Chicago legal scholar but, unlike Levi, a prolific criminologist well equipped to get LEAA into the business of tackling tough crime problems.

It soon turned out Bell had misfired. It seemed that Morris had been far too blunt in expressing his liberal views for Washington's political tastes in 1978. Gun control may have been acceptable to a Republican crime commission five years earlier, but it was not palatable to Senate Republicans when Morris's name was raised. In a 1969 book called *The Honest Politician's Guide to Crime Control*, the Chicagoan had issued a call for a "disarmed populace"—no handguns in private hands and limitations even on gun use in hunting.[29] Whatever his considerable merits as a scholar, it became obvious that Morris would not be confirmed by the Senate. The nomination was dropped, but not until the Carter administration had completed half of its term and lost much of its initial momentum.

Once again, LEAA seemed a lost cause as far as any prominent policy measures were concerned. Henry Dogin, a former deputy LEAA regional director and New York State criminal justice official, was elevated to succeed Gregg as acting administrator. Dogin worked to expand successful programs like prosecution of repeat criminals, and he started a campaign against the rising threat of arson. But LEAA had gone through so many upheavals that it failed to capitalize on its successes. Crime problems were back on the rise in Newark, for example, years after Jerris Leonard's high impact program there had faded.

On the surface, LEAA was chugging along, but in the back rooms of Washington, serious trouble was brewing. The agency had failed to build much support in Congress, and accumulated complaints from local officials over various real and imagined indignities over grants were getting attention in important places. As the agency grew larger, critics pointed to the difficulties of running a bureaucracy whose main purpose was to give out money but whose important other programs—to gather statistics and do research about crime and justice—were sometimes neglected.

Still, Congress spent much of 1979 restructuring the agency. Led by Senators Joseph Biden and Edward Kennedy (who said "major surgery" was needed), the plan created a new super-agency called the Office of Justice Assistance, Research, and Statistics (OJARS), which incorporated LEAA but split off the research and statistics-gathering functions into separate units. The Senate version authorized $825 million for anticrime work, a high total for the time. The debate was much more contentious in the House, which established a complex formula for distributing aid according to either a state's population or a four-part procedure that took crime totals, criminal-justice spending, and local tax rates into account. The debate was punctuated with criticism that the anticrime grants had gotten out of hand and that the agency should be abolished.

A crucial figure in LEAA's fate the following year was Neal Smith, a Democratic congressman from Iowa who had risen to the chairmanship of the subcommittee that controlled the Justice Department's appropriations. Smith concluded that by handing out funds to local agencies with few restrictions, LEAA was becoming a "a bad example of federal administration."[30] Smith began to accumulate horror stories like that of the Iowa town that used LEAA money to buy radio equipment even though it didn't even have a "base station" that would allow it to broadcast. Other cities justified using federal funds to purchase patrol cars if they were a different color from the existing ones. Then there were the consultants who earned fat fees by offering municipal officials their services to obtain money from 633 Indiana Avenue.

Smith discussed the problem with Joseph Early, a fellow appropriations panel member from Massachusetts, who reported similar abuses. "Joe and I said, 'let's put a stop to this,' " Smith recalled. "It was a waste. There was no way to set it up so that it was only good programs and not wasted programs. So we just decided to defund it."

Meanwhile, with crime generally a less prominent national issue than it had been during the Nixon days or that it would become later, the federal anticrime program was lost in the executive branch shuffle. As Carter pursued various government reorganization projects, it was becoming "apparent that LEAA was the agency that the Justice Department was going to contribute to the cause," said Bell adviser Fiederowicz.

Presidential politics played a role. One of LEAA's main defenders was Kennedy, a principal rival to Carter for the 1980 Democratic nomination. There was no reason for the president to save one of his competitor's prize programs. "Kennedy fought a fairly lonely fight to save LEAA," said Kenneth Feinberg, his aide handling crime issues at the time. "But it was tilting at windmills. The die was cast, and the political momentum was all the other way."

In the end, LEAA leaders got an unwelcome bolt out of the blue. In 1980, Acting Administrator Dogin was in Seattle to give a speech when Benjamin Civiletti, who had succeeded Bell as attorney general, called with startling news: the Carter administration would propose to eliminate LEAA. As the official story went, the White House was desperately seeking ways to reduce the growing federal budget deficit as the election campaign geared up. The White House gave each cabinet department orders to cut, and cut fast. The Justice Department needed to continue its core functions of enforcing the law, representing the federal government in litigation, and advising the entire executive branch on legal matters. One obvious place to start trimming was a troubled program that had little constituency. "It came out of nowhere—a shocker," said Dogin, who later lamented his "failure to read the tea leaves properly."[31] Dogin and Civiletti met with James McIntyre, Carter's budget director, to appeal the closure, but they were told that "we cannot turn this around."

In fact, it was the powerful Office of Management and Budget (OMB) that sealed LEAA's fate. It is a long Washington tradition that OMB plays the decisive backstage role in knifing controversial or moribund programs. One OMB insider recalled years later that the decision on LEAA didn't seem particularly difficult: "There were not program evaluations that established its impact, management, or ability to reduce crime." That LEAA played at least some part in improving the criminal-justice system—the alternative goal espoused by many of its early leaders—carried little weight in the agency's dying days.

In retrospect, Carter and his senior aides never had been enthralled with the program, and the uncertain leadership underscored by the failure to win Norval Morris's confirmation had taken a big toll. Another nail in the coffin had been Bell's departure. Even though he was unenthusiastic about LEAA, as a certified member of the "Georgia Mafia" he was an important link to OMB chief McIntyre and might have been able to preserve the agency in reduced form.

After its many years of handing out federal aid sought by members of Congress, LEAA's almost complete lack of support on Capitol Hill was stunning. The agency was openly criticized by key members who otherwise favored big federal spending. Michigan Representative John Conyers, a liberal Democrat, cited LEAA's "bureaucratic failures . . . compounded by cynicism and arrogance." In an interview long after LEAA had ended, Senator Kennedy admitted that with "very little oversight," the agency had "lost public confidence" as it failed to deliver federal anticrime money to the places where it was most needed.[32] By the late 1970s, with the crime problem relatively quiescent, "there was a general sense that there were other priorities," Kennedy said.

The rise and fall of LEAA was summed up years later by Paul Michel, who helped give it a "decent burial" as a top Justice Department official under Carter: "It was a typical Washington phenomenon. We get all excited about a problem, start up a big program, and throw a lot of money at it. There are some excesses, some newspaper exposes, and then there is some revulsion against it. Then the overreaction: 'let's kill this thing.' Both excesses are bad. LEAA in its heyday became excessive, wasteful, and dumb, but the total annihilation of LEAA was equally dumb."[33]

It was left to yet another interim LEAA director, a bureaucrat named Robert Diegelman, to phase out the agency, a complicated task that involved monitoring more than 1,000 grants totaling $750 million over the next two and one half years. The staff of 800 began to wither, although through skillful use of the federal personnel process, Diegelman managed to prevent the indignity of forcing out on the street all but an amazingly small total of 18 people. Those who left when they saw the end coming included some of the "youngest and brightest," in Diegelman's estimation.[34] If he was correct, the government was robbed of a brain trust that might have kept the national anticrime campaign on something of an even keel until it was abruptly resurrected in the 1990s.

As Jimmy Carter's 4 years in the White House neared an end, so did Washington's 12-year effort to reduce local crime through large infusions of federal aid—a strategy that would be reinvented when the Democrats next captured the presidency in 1992.

The 1980s marked an abrupt shift in the way the federal government tried to cope with street violence. An executive branch dominated for three presidencies by ideological conservatives changed the thrust from spending money to a largely untested one of manipulating the justice system to get tough on criminals.

Chapter 3

THE "GET-TOUGH" 1980s

I T did not begin that way, but 1980 marked the start of a watershed decade in the modern debate over crime policy. Violence on America's streets was not a major campaign issue in Ronald Reagan's successful challenge to Jimmy Carter. The crime rate in the late 1970s had seemed relatively stable, not producing outcries of public concern. Democratic incumbent Jimmy Carter was consumed by other worries, most prominently a wavering economy, a plague of gasoline shortages, and the taking of American hostages in the U.S. Embassy in Tehran.

Despite the invisibility of crime as an issue at the beginning of the decade, the 1980s would bring a burst of federal legislation as Republicans and Democrats battled for dominance of the issue. Unlike the 1970s and 1990s, the main crime issues of the 1980s did not revolve around spending more money and enlarging local police forces. Rather, a broad conservative thrust to turn the criminal law to the right ended up crystallizing into a highly debatable campaign to extend prison terms, especially for drug-law violations.

The new laws helped fill federal prisons with drug offenders but seemingly did little about the nation's overall crime problem, which worsened during the decade, especially in its second half.

Any fleeting chance that the 1980s might begin with anticrime policy in Washington made amicably on a bipartisan basis was dashed fairly quickly. One reason was that the crime numbers themselves suggested a new sense of urgency.

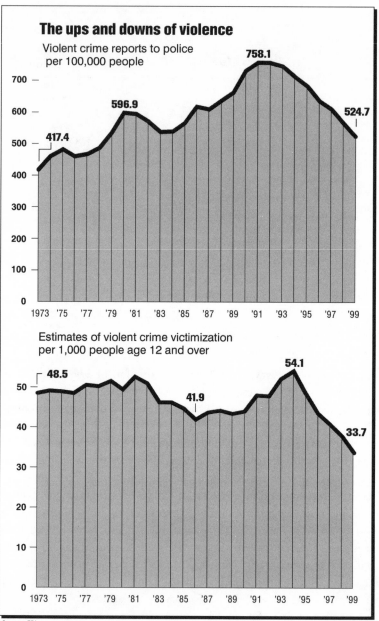

The ups and downs of violence

Violent crime reports to police
per 100,000 people

758.1

596.9

524.7

417.4

700
600
500
400
300
200
100
0

1973 '75 '77 '79 '81 '83 '85 '87 '89 '91 '93 '95 '97 '99

Estimates of violent crime victimization
per 1,000 people age 12 and over

54.1

48.5

41.9

33.7

50
40
30
20
10
0

1973 '75 '77 '79 '81 '83 '85 '87 '89 '91 '93 '95 '97 '99

Source: FBI
Source: U.S. Bureau of Justice Statistics

When the totals for 1980 were reported, it turned out that the election year had set a modern record of more than 23,000 homicides. This set the stage for what typically passed for a debate on crime: "get-tough" Republicans versus defendants' rights-oriented Democrats. It was a contest that would produce few effective measures.

Those who had followed the career of Ronald Reagan, the former movie actor and California governor who defeated Carter, expected him to take a hard-line tack. Much of his support came from a conservative wing of the Republican Party that had been unhappy both about court rulings that expanded defendants' rights and about two consecutive presidencies after Nixon that did not make a big issue of street crime.

Reagan's first move, the appointment of an attorney general, did not accurately signal his administration's course on crime. Like presidents before him, Reagan chose a personal friend, in this case Los Angeles civil lawyer William French Smith, who had little expertise in criminal justice. Behind the scenes, Edwin Meese—longtime Reagan adviser on crime, veteran of LEAA grants from his days in California government, and now a White House counselor—was destined to play a major role.

After only a few weeks in office, Smith appointed a task force on violent crime and asked it to report within 120 days—almost record speed for Washington. The panel conducted a vastly more focused study than had Lyndon Johnson's crime commission a decade and a half earlier.[1] The Reagan group confined its mission to studying violence, avoiding wide-ranging inquiries like those of the LBJ commission, which had delved into areas like public drunkenness and criminal court schedules. The new task force stuck to the role of the federal government, making it clear that it would not seek to expand Washington's reach over state and local justice systems and shortchange federal resources against organized crime and white-collar violations.

The task force superficially resembled the Johnson panel in bipartisanship and representation from various segments of the criminal justice system. Carter's original attorney general, Griffin Bell, was recalled to service, co-chairing the group with Republican federal prosecutor Jim Thompson of Chicago. The six other members included a city police chief, a public defender, a local prosecutor, a state law enforcement director, Harvard crime scholar James Q. Wilson, and, in a departure for the time, Frank Carrington, a Virginia lawyer who had made his mark as a crusader for the rights of crime victims.

The panel's report, delivered on August 17, 1981, bore little resemblance to the Johnson crime commission's. Its 64 recommendations were largely confined to beefing up the federal role in many kinds of cases, from arson to juvenile crime. Other planks included some changes in the law that had been sought for many years by Republican anticrime theorists, including limitations on bail releases and on the insanity defense—both of which ended up being included in a wide-ranging federal crime law passed in 1984—and curbing habeas corpus appeals in death penalty cases, which took 15 more years and Republican control of both houses of Congress to accomplish.

The Republicans who dominated the Reagan panel did not call for a massive infusion of federal funds—with one glaring exception: $2 billion to help states build prisons. The GOP favored more incarceration, but party leaders were even more emphatic about not spending federal tax dollars to help states do the job. So the prison plan went nowhere during Reagan's presidency. (States expanded their prison populations without help from Washington; a much larger version of federal support for prison construction ended up in the big federal anticrime law of 1994.)

While the Reagan administration's task force was laying out its opening marker on crime policy—get tough but don't spend much money doing it— key members of Congress were regrouping their own forces after years of frustration. During the Carter presidency, the Democratic-controlled legislative branch had produced little on crime. A prime reason was that a group of lawmakers had been working through the 1970s on a massive rewrite of the federal criminal code—a project that had consumed countless hours of hearings and drafting sessions amid sharp debates over seemingly intractable issues such as the permissible extent of wiretapping and disclosure of government secrets by whistle-blowers. The well-meaning effort to update a hodgepodge of federal laws that had been assembled piecemeal over many decades sparked little public interest.

The dynamic shifted radically in the early 1980s. Republicans seized control in November 1980 of both the White House and the Senate. In Washington, those simultaneous turnovers signaled dramatic changes, although liberal Democrats retained key chairmanships in the House Judiciary Committee and would try to bottle up attempted conservative reforms. Instead of low-key backroom tiffs over important but sometimes esoteric criminal law questions, the public debate evolved into a partisan battle over basic crime and punishment issues.

An unwieldy pattern developed. Every two years, the Senate would put together a massive anticrime bill, with controversial and innocuous provisions jammed into a huge document. (A 1984 bill, for example, included far-reaching provisions on criminal sentencing and bail reform along with a measure on "livestock fraud.") The House, meanwhile, would consider legislation piecemeal. Eventually, a bill would be thrown together by a difficult-to-manage "conference committee" of members from both houses, where provisions would be added or struck according to the whims of various members. Then the full membership of each chamber would be confronted with election-year up or down votes. Anyone who opposed an anticrime bill risked the voters' wrath.

Details differed in each round, but the proceedings rarely resembled the "how a bill becomes a law" scenario laid out in textbooks on legislation. As law making had evolved, conference committees tended to meet at odd hours to consider documents largely put together by staff members that included pet provisions of majority party members, often inserted without any hearings or open-committee drafting known as "markups." It might take years for courts, prosecutors, and future legislative committees to determine their implications or to correct errors and inequities that may have resulted. This phenomenon wasn't limited to crime bills, but it did ensure the enactment of popular-sounding but ill-conceived measures that have marked anticrime politics for many years.

While the newly empowered Republicans plotted their strategies in 1981, a few Democrats also were ready to plunge in. On the Senate side, the lead was taken by Joseph Biden of Delaware, who had been jockeying with Edward Kennedy for leadership of his party's anticrime forces. After the Republican takeover, Kennedy decided to shift his focus to the Labor Committee and to leave the senior Democratic spot on Judiciary to Biden. Democratic leader Robert Byrd of West Virginia asked Biden to assemble a task force that would reassess the party's stance on crime.

Biden had belonged to a special Senate committee in the 1970s headed by Frank Church of Idaho that reviewed excesses and shortcomings in the government's intelligence apparatus. The experience convinced him that crime should be viewed as a form of domestic security. So Biden's first effort at an expansive anticrime bill was titled the National Security and Violent Crime Control Act of 1981. His attempt to put crime in a defense context—getting the armed forces involved in drug interdiction, for example—attracted some moderates but repelled others like Georgia's Sam Nunn, a rising power on the Armed Services Committee, who was dubious about the military's role in the fight against crime.

Biden's aggressive manner did not win him universal admiration, especially among liberals, but many appreciated his determination to make crime a winning issue for Democrats, the party that had been tagged as "soft" since the Goldwater days. "Give me the crime issue," the senator would plead repeatedly to Democratic Party caucuses, one staff member recalled, "and you'll never have trouble with it in an election."

How did so much crime legislation pass during the partisan 1980s? A key element was important personal relationships in the Capitol, especially between Biden and the new Senate Judiciary Committee chairman, Strom Thurmond of South Carolina. The conventional wisdom was that the then 78-year-old Thurmond was a dyed-in-the-wool conservative who would have little interest in working with Democrats to pass anticrime bills.

But the enthusiastic Biden, 40 years junior to Thurmond, visited the South

Carolinian and made him a pitch. "Mr. Chairman, no one expects this relationship to work," Biden said. "But there are a lot of things we agree on and a lot we don't. Why don't we agree on what we can and leave aside what we can't? If you do that, I promise that I will never embarrass you by publicly taking you on."[2] Thurmond said he would think it over. A week later, he called Biden and agreed. By Biden's account, Thurmond lived up to the deal, frequently reining in conservative GOP members when they were reluctant to compromise.

A moderate coalition also was taking shape in the House. William Hughes, a middle-of-the-road former New Jersey prosecutor, was building his credentials as head of the subcommittee on crime. Hughes played a role somewhat similar to Biden's as a pragmatist, but his challenge was different: to bring into the fold liberal Democrats who supported big government in other contexts but were skeptical about expanding the federal role in the battle against street crime. Hughes's Republican counterpart was Harold Sawyer, a civil lawyer-turned-prosecutor who had won Gerald Ford's former House seat in Michigan. Sawyer, who had no strong ideological agenda, would find himself outflanked by Republican colleagues who did.

Reestablishing a strong federal narcotics policy was the first area where Biden and Hughes wanted to make a mark. Their main goal was to reverse the Democrats' perceived weakness on drugs. The Carter White House was best known for proposing to decriminalize marijuana, an idea that wilted under heavy opposition. Hughes was more interested in enforcement measures. One of his early forays was known jokingly among insiders as the "pee in the bottle" bill because it would expand mandatory urine tests for defendants in federal drug cases.

In another sharp departure from the Carter regime, Hughes also wanted Congress to continue effective programs begun under the dying LEAA. He called for a new Office of Justice Assistance that would provide up to $150 million a year for state and local agencies—a far cry from LEAA in its $900 million-per-year heyday but enough to maintain a notable federal influence.

In the Senate, Biden took a broader tack. Based on what he had learned about intelligence and foreign affairs and on reports from Congress's watchdog General Accounting Office, Biden became convinced that federal antidrug policy was a mess. One Justice Department unit, the Drug Enforcement Administration (DEA), was the single largest agency handling drug cases, but authority was diffused throughout the executive branch.

The parent Justice Department had a huge influence on policy through its supervision of federal prosecutors spread out over more than 90 judicial districts. But two of the major law-enforcement agencies within the department— the FBI and DEA—were rivals. The FBI tended not to cooperate with DEA even when it turned out that organized-crime figures and other lawbreakers it was pursuing had ties to the drug trade. A host of other cabinet and subcabinet agencies, from the State, Treasury, and Defense departments to the Customs Bureau and the Marshals Service, played roles in the war on drugs.

It seemed clear to Biden that narcotics was rapidly increasing as a part of the overall federal criminal caseload but that "the conventional criminal justice apparatus did not handle the drug issue well," said Mark Gitenstein, Biden's chief aide on crime legislation for a decade beginning in 1977.[3] One problem was that drug trafficking had become a highly complex business, but DEA lacked the expertise to penetrate the financial transactions characteristic of major drug deals.

Then there were the international aspects. Biden, also a member of the Foreign Relations Committee, "began to see that there was very little coordination" between the Justice and State departments in dealing with narcotics problems in source countries, Gitenstein said. A Biden trip to the Mediterranean and a major speech on the "Sicilian connection" in the drug trade called attention to America's need to focus more on international narcotics enforcement. To coordinate the many moving parts of the U.S. drug policy, Biden became convinced that the government needed a cabinet-level director of narcotics policy (soon nicknamed the "drug czar").

As Biden, Hughes, and other members of Congress were writing legislation to embody their crime-fighting ideas, the Reagan Justice Department task force headed by Jim Thompson and Griffin Bell held hearings to gather material for its report due out that summer. It was becoming evident that the priorities of the different government branches were not in sync.

Moving on to a new anticrime agenda meant that the longstanding squabbles over the criminal code would have to be resolved. Capitol veterans assumed that the code would be the centerpiece of any anticrime legislation. The problem was that by 1981, the draft had amassed opponents on both the left and the right. Civil libertarians were outraged, for example, over provisions like one they believed would unduly penalize government employees for disclosing "official secrets," an important question that had nothing to do with crime in the streets.

Other liberals had more basic objections. Michigan's John Conyers figured that the criminal code essentially would result in much harsher treatment of defendants than was warranted. As chairman of the Criminal Justice Subcommittee, he was in a position to keep parts of the bill tied up. Much of the drafting work was assigned to a panel headed by Representative Robert Drinan of Massachusetts. Conyers ignored most of the initial Drinan sessions but, said Republican Sawyer, "after two years, [Conyers] arrived and started objecting to everything. I thought, 'what the hell is *he* doing here?' "[4] Conyers was influential with committee chairman Peter Rodino, which Sawyer attributed partly to a reported threat by Conyers to recruit black candidates against the white chairman in his predominantly minority Newark district.

A group of conservative senators elected in 1980 also began to criticize the criminal code plan. They charged that the bill would allow obscene material to be mailed and would hamper prosecution of pornography offenses. Justice Department and Judiciary Committee lawyers disputed the accusations, but it was becoming clear that the criminal code reform plan was too controversial to pass. Biden, the Democrats' leader on crime policy, concluded that many of the suggested code revisions were "well intended, but basically a way to emasculate the civil rights of Americans."

By late April 1981, it was clear that the code overhaul would not survive a threatened filibuster in the Senate, so it was abandoned. Biden, Thurmond, and others decided to try assembling a much more modest crime bill that could survive a wide range of opposition. Congressional leaders managed to agree on a limited measure, but the first omnibus anticrime law in 14 years included what proved to be two "killer" provisions.

One was the drug czar. Opponents, mainly those representing cabinet departments that anticipated locking horns with the new office, argued that far from providing more coordination, the drug policy director had the potential to create more confusion. If the czar could overrule cabinet secretaries at the same level, it was hardly a model of efficient government. But if the new office was not granted that power, it could end up as a superfluous bureaucratic layer.

A powerful opponent was Meese, who acted as Reagan's senior adviser on law enforcement. Meese believed that the drug czar was a "lousy idea" that amounted to creating "a White House bureaucrat."[5] A better model, Meese argued, was the one that Reagan adopted: a cabinet-level council on drug policy, parallel to the National Security Council and headed by the attorney general, who was in charge of the department with the most muscle in the antidrug fight.

The other major stumbling block was a provision promoted by Arlen Specter, the former Philadelphia district attorney who now was a freshman senator from Pennsylvania. Specter, convinced that many local prosecutors were not successfully pursuing cases against career criminals who were responsible for a disproportionate amount of violence, made it his top priority to pass the Armed Career Criminal Act. The idea was to permit federal prosecutors to charge people with two state convictions on their record who were suspected of using a gun in a third felony. Essentially, Specter wanted to make a federal crime out of state offenses.

Specter was in the vanguard of two major anticrime trends in the 1980s: creating new federal offenses and imposing mandatory minimum prison sentences, in this instance 15 years. Specter worked hard to win passage, no easy task for a freshman with a controversial bill. He was able to lobby President Reagan personally in a White House meeting, and he made a vital compromise with his former constituency, leaders of the National District Attorneys Association. Local prosecutors feared "grandstanding" federal counterparts who would invoke the law mainly in celebrated cases that might win them notoriety (thus taking away some bragging points from the local officials, who often were embroiled in hotly contested elections). So Specter agreed that district attorneys would need to sign off before a typically local case could be taken into federal court. That provision offended the Reagan White House, which believed it an inappropriate limit on federal power.

After the bill passed, its main sponsors arranged a meeting with Reagan in the White House Treaty Room to argue their case for the president's backing. With Biden on one side of the president and Thurmond on the other, the senators spoke. When the presentations got a bit long-winded for Edwin Meese, the presidential aide pointed to his watch and announced that Reagan had to leave. The president began to rise, but Thurmond startled the group by grabbing Reagan's arm and pulling him back down in his chair, a bold act that only the elderly senator could get away with. "When you get as old as I am and you've been around as long, you know you've got to compromise on some of these things," Thurmond told the president.

Knowing that the drug czar measure could bring down the bill, Thurmond offered to rewrite it to satisfy the White House. Reagan was reluctant to reject the first major anticrime bill to come to him, but he had the advantage of being able to act after the 1982 congressional election. The administration figured that the election "had just taken place, and it would be two years until another one—time to pass crime legislation more to the administration's liking," said Charles Wise, a political scientist who studied Congress's twists and turns on crime in the early 1980s.[6] Largely because of the drug czar provision, Reagan vetoed the bill in January 1983.

Reagan's action set the stage for biennial battles over crime bills in the 1980s. Instead of trying to forge a sensible compromise, sponsors of both disputed provisions refused to give up on their pet ideas. Specter inserted his armed career criminal legislation into an even bigger crime bill that Reagan could not afford to veto two years later. The drug czar idea took longer, but Biden finally won passage as Reagan was leaving office in 1988.

The demise of the 1982 bill disappointed congressional conservatives and moderates who had hoped to make a major mark on anticrime policy for the first time since 1968. But another group was pleased that the bill had fallen on its face. Liberals in the House, including Michigan's Conyers, New Jersey's Rodino, and California's Don Edwards saw themselves as the bulwarks against misguided attempts to make the federal government into an intrusive, punitive force against small-time local crime suspects (many of them members of minority groups).

Liberals believed they could continue using their positions as committee and subcommittee chairs to bury legislation they opposed. But several other forces were coalescing that would overwhelm them and enact what many Democrats considered to be draconian anticrime policies, step by step, every two years during the rest of the 1980s.

One of them was a growing lobby of victims. Anticrime policy in the past almost always had been debated with the perpetrator in mind. Hard-liners wanted to put lawbreakers behind bars longer, and liberals focused on trying to rehabilitate them. Crime victims were mostly afterthoughts. Local prosecutors had obtained LEAA grants for victim-witness units, but the aim was as much to encourage testimony against defendants as to improve the victims' welfare. Some crime victims had formed local support organizations, most prominently women's rape crisis centers that were opened in the 1970s.

The 1981 Reagan violent crime task force report encouraged a new outlook by recommending that the attorney general lead the way "in ensuring that the victims of crime are accorded proper status by the criminal justice system." That modest proposal would help accelerate a profound change in the way criminal cases were handled, starting with the Reagan administration's appointment of a high-level task force to study the problem.

The group was headed by Lois Herrington, a former prosecutor in the same Oakland, Calif., office where Edwin Meese and Lowell Jensen, who later became deputy U.S. attorney general, had worked. Oakland's district attorney had been one of the first to establish a unit for victims, and Herrington—one of its former directors—was a natural choice to head the Reagan panel. Not only did she have the proper professional credentials, but she boasted important personal connections as well. Herrington's husband, John, headed Reagan's personnel office (later serving as energy secretary and chairman of the California Republican Party), and she was a friend of Meese and of Meese's wife, Ursula.

Like some of the earlier crime commissions, the victims' task force drew members from various segments of the justice system. One well-known member was the Reverend Pat Robertson. Herrington said that she "started from the ground up."[7] She worked night and day, organizing hearings around the country in the fall of 1982 and then "locking myself in the house for three weeks" to take the lead in writing the final report.

Even as a veteran prosecutor who had worked with crime victims, Herrington was stunned to hear tale after tale of their poor treatment in the justice system. "Police would drive a rape victim to the hospital, take her clothes [as evidence], send her home in a cab, and send her a bill for the rap sheet that they would need to prosecute," she said. "These things really did happen."

When it seemed unlikely that the task force would devote much energy to dealing with men's attacks on their wives and girlfriends, crusaders against domestic violence picketed the panel's hearing in San Francisco. Herrington surprised the protesters by agreeing with them and advising, "Don't stop picketing." She promised a separate task force on domestic violence, which was named later in Reagan's presidency. (On the victims' panel, Pat Robertson first expressed the classic male view that domestic strife usually did not amount to a crime, but he changed his mind after hearing the evidence, Herrington said.)

The task force's report went far beyond the conclusions on crime victims that had been expressed by the earlier federal crime commissions. It called for a constitutional amendment to guarantee victims' rights throughout the justice process (which later was adopted by many states but not by Congress) and a laundry list of major legal changes that were hallmarks of the get-tough movement. These included eliminating parole, requiring criminals to provide restitution to victims—both later enacted—and abolishing the "exclusionary rule" that barred the use in trials of improperly gathered evidence.

Herrington's enthusiastic rallying to the cause of crime victims was not a guaranteed success even in the sympathetic Reagan administration. One of her priorities was to improve financial compensation for victims, but that idea was anathema to David Stockman, Reagan's stingy budget director. When Herrington got the chance to brief Reagan's cabinet, Stockman surprised Herrington by protesting that her idea could turn into a budget buster. "This is an entitlement, Mr. President," he said. Stockman outranked the feisty Herrington, but that did not stop her from challenging the budget director by saying, "Mr. President, people don't go out and get themselves knocked over the head and robbed so that they can get to the hospital and get money."

Presenting her case as if she were a prosecutor appealing to a jury, Herrington worried that she would lose out when other cabinet members failed to support her against Stockman's blast. But Reagan saved the day, telling the cabinet that he understood Herrington to be arguing that "if we treat victims better, they will participate in the system, help hold criminals accountable, and there will be fewer victims because they'll be fewer people preying on them." Herrington won the president's approval for a fund, later created by Congress, that devoted fines and penalties paid to federal courts—sometimes huge sums from white-collar-crimes—to victim-compensation programs.

Another high-profile segment of the victims' movement emerged from one terrible case. Six-year-old Adam Walsh was snatched from a shopping center in Hollywood, Fla., on July 27, 1981, after his mother left him alone briefly. The boy's body was found two weeks later in a ditch 100 miles away. Child advocates, along with the Walsh family, used the case in a campaign that hyped the child-kidnapping problem far out of proportion.

News accounts using dubious estimates implied that anywhere from 4,000 to 50,000 youngsters each year were being plucked by strangers and then molested or murdered. The proved cases indeed were horrifying, but studies in later years established that the actual number of abductions by strangers was only about 100 each year; most of the others involved runaways or divorce-custody squabbles.[8]

That didn't stop Congress from setting up a National Center for Missing and Exploited Children that spent several million tax dollars (and more in private contributions) each year to encourage steps like printing notices of missing children on milk cartons.

Lois Herrington's crusades on behalf of crime victims made such an impression on the Reagan administration that she was named assistant attorney general for justice programs—the equivalent, during the 1980s and beyond, of heading LEAA. That put her in charge of handing out federal anticrime grants. Despite Herrington's expanded duties, she continued to devote a large percentage of her time to victims issues. Critics faulted her for paying little attention to other major areas under her domain, such as a controversial juvenile crime unit that the Reagan administration was trying to kill.

Herrington's single-minded focus played a large part in elevating the victim issue to the high plane that it would occupy for years. Eventually, victims became an influential lobbying force both in Congress and in state capitals on reshaping the nation's crime laws against defendants' interests—for example, allowing evidence of a crime's impact on victims and their families to be used in death penalty trials.

But the victims issue was just one in a raft of issues that conservatives were pushing in what would become the surprisingly sweeping federal anticrime law of 1984. While most of the prominent crime-fighting pronouncements were coming from the White House and the Justice Department, important Reagan allies were working quietly on Capitol Hill. Republicans in the House were so badly outnumbered that few paid attention to most of their proposals on crime or much else. While GOP leaders like House Minority Leader Bob Michel of Illinois played the loyal opposition and occasionally prevailed on an issue, victory came only rarely. Some conservative back benchers like Newt Gingrich of Georgia, frustrated that their views were being routinely trampled, organized a Conservative Opportunity Society and resolved to seek more visibility for their core goals.

When Gingrich's group sorted out the assignments, the crime issue ended up with Dan Lungren, a Long Beach, Calif., lawyer (and the son of Richard Nixon's physician), who had joined the House in 1979 at the age of 33. Lungren had not practiced criminal law, but the conservative Republican got something of a forced introduction to the subject when he was assigned to the subcommittee then headed by Drinan of Massachusetts that had inherited the job of rewriting the federal criminal code. In dozens and dozens of drafting sessions, Lungren jousted with Drinan, a Catholic priest whom he complained was "about as liberal as you can get." Critics complained that markups on the criminal code were Drinan's equivalent of a social life.

Although the massive recodification eventually landed in the trash heap, when the Republicans gained strength in the 1980 elections, Lungren warmed to the idea of an omnibus crime law that would incorporate much of the GOP wish list. What he didn't want was the kind of limited approach that Reagan ended up vetoing in 1982. Ardent conservatives "knew that we'd probably get one chance to have fundamental change in the federal system," Lungren said.[9] In fact, Lungren had recommended the Reagan veto. The Californian viewed the bill as containing only about "three pieces of the 47 we wanted."

But Lungren saw the same doomed scenario developing in early 1983, when Reagan called a bipartisan meeting at the White House to rev up a new crime bill. After the president delivered his pitch on the importance of the crime issue, Senate Judiciary Chairman Thurmond promised quick action. By 1984, the Senate had come through with a bill much more extensive than the one that Reagan had rejected.

Thurmond's House counterpart, liberal Peter Rodino, who had made it his business to bury conservative crime bills, had warned Reagan in 1983 that the House did things differently. It would consider each issue, piece by piece, Rodino said, a strategy the conservatives recognized as a way to kill controversial proposals in hostile subcommittees.

It was time for Gingrich's Conservative Opportunity Society to spring into action. The group was beginning to capitalize on the one-minute statements House members were entitled to deliver on any subject. They decided to organize groups of lawmakers to speak on a single theme. Another tactic was to make pleas for unanimous consent to pass major legislation. They knew these motions would fail, but they forced the Democrats to protest popular proposals like plans to balance the budget. Lungren and others raised the crime issue constantly in 1983 and 1984. "If we ever got a chance to have it [debated] on the floor," he explained, "the argument could not be made that we had a hidden agenda, that it had never been discussed, that it had to go back to the Judiciary Committee for consideration."

By happenstance, 1984 was the first year that the cable television network C-SPAN began broadcasting House proceedings, a development that allowed the Republican minority to get its message out nationwide, bypassing the congressional leadership. "We had to learn to tame that creature of C-SPAN," Lungren said. "We very consciously decided how we would pitch our arguments on the floor differently" to appeal to a lay television audience rather than solely to fellow House members.

A leading example was one of the crime bill's most far-reaching sections, which would create "sentencing guidelines" for all federal judges in criminal cases. Some liberals favored the idea to reduce inequities in penalties handed out by judges in different courts for the same crimes. But conservatives wanted the change for a different reason: to prevent the courts from allowing the release of convicts long before the scheduled end of their prison terms.

The phrase "sentencing guidelines" was hardly likely to stir the passions of C-SPAN watchers, so Lungren decided to use the phrase "truth in sentencing" to embody the criticism that many lawbreakers "were being sentenced to time that they never served." Lungren and his followers cited cases in which convicts were sentenced, say, to 30 years but were paroled in only 8. Under the GOP proposal, 30 years meant 30 years. "Truth in sentencing" soon became a watchword. (Lungren did not invent the slogan, which had been used by insiders at least since sentencing reform had been debated starting in the late 1970s, but he and his colleagues did popularize it.)

Among other items that the Republicans sought were cutbacks in federal habeas corpus appeals filed by death row inmates—which could keep appeals going for a decade or more—and a tightening of both pretrial bail releases and use of the insanity defense, a high-profile issue after John Hinckley's acquittal in the 1981 shooting of Ronald Reagan. The GOP also wanted to eliminate or greatly restrict the "exclusionary rule," the court-imposed directive that prohibited use in criminal trials of evidence that police officers had obtained illegally. The rule was invoked in only a small percentage of criminal cases. Critics charged that although it had been conceived more than a half-century earlier to deter police misconduct, more recently it had led to dismissal of solid criminal cases just because well-intentioned officers had misinterpreted complicated evidentiary doctrines that had confused even some judges.

The conservative Republicans really didn't expect to see a crime bill enacted. Instead, they hoped to create so much publicity around the issue that Democratic candidates would be forced to take a stand during their 1984 election campaigns. To keep the pressure on, the Republicans held rump hearings on crime, irking the Democrats by announcing that the sessions were necessary because the majority had refused to hold official hearings. (Republican Sawyer, for example, had repeatedly pressed Rodino to move on the bail reform issue, but the stubborn New Jerseyan had rebuffed him.)

To help build grass-roots support for the GOP platform, Lungren aide Kevin Holsclaw recruited crime victims to testify, which generated local news stories. Republicans also made it their business to lobby editorial boards of newspapers in their districts.

Then, lightning struck in the fall of 1984. In a scenario that became routine in later years, as the October 1 start of the new federal fiscal year approached, Congress had not enacted all of the 13 appropriations bills necessary to keep the government running.

The solution was a "continuing resolution" that would maintain current spending levels while Congress mulled over the remaining appropriations measures. It had become common for lawmakers to try attaching substantive legislation to those catchall bills because they were sure to reach the president's desk. Leaders in both parties tried to keep controversial riders to a minimum.

The gatekeeper in the House was the Rules Committee, which decided which amendments were suitable for debate. In late September 1984, the Democratic-dominated panel voted to allow a few substantive issues to reach the floor. Lungren proposed a "sense of the House" resolution that the Senate-passed crime bill should be voted on, too, but he was rejected both in the Rules panel and on the floor. He returned disappointed to a meeting of a conference committee on a major immigration-reform bill, another subject of his deep interest.

But Lungren soon got a call from Bill Pitts, an aide to House Republican Leader Michel. Pitts had studied the House rules and determined that by allowing some major provisions of substantive legislation to be added to the appropriations bill, the Democrats had opened the door to a vote on the crime issue on what was known as a "motion to recommit." In the meantime, the campaign committee that supported GOP House candidates circulated press releases singling out each member who had voted against bringing the crime measure to the floor, building the pressure on any jittery lawmakers.

Lungren believed Pitts's idea was brilliant, but Lungren had a problem. Motions to recommit normally would be made by the senior party member handling the bill, in this case the ranking member of the appropriations panel, moderate Silvio Conte of Massachusetts. Lungren had criticized Conte for other legislation he had backed, and Lungren had tried to change GOP rules to prevent Conte and any other Republican from taking charge of legislation on the floor if they disagreed with the GOP position on any of its provisions. It was a slap in the face to moderates like Conte who wanted freedom to express their views while retaining leadership positions. Slights like Lungren's typically ended any chance of cooperation among lawmakers, even those in the same party.

But after a Massachusetts newspaper had picked up on the dispute, the polite Lungren called Conte to apologize. Conte was so appreciative that the two became friendly, to the point that Conte asked Lungren's son to serve as bat boy of the Republican baseball team that he managed. With the crime bill now at a crucial juncture, Conte gave his blessing for Lungren to offer the motion (thus annoying other Appropriations Committee members, because Lungren was not even a member of their panel).

Lungren delivered an emotional speech on the House floor, telling members that finally, they would be required to take a stand on a crime bill that had passed the Senate without a single Democratic vote against it. "It's put up or shut up time," Lungren said, warning colleagues that they would have to defend their views on the campaign trail within a month.

Now the Democrats were worried. Issues they thought had been buried suddenly were being debated on the House floor. New Jersey's Hughes, chairman of the crime subcommittee, urged a "no" vote, saying that the bill was too extreme—much more far-reaching than the one vetoed by Reagan two years earlier.

Given that the Democratic leadership, including the liberal subcommittee chairmen who were being outmaneuvered, were fighting hard against the bill, Lungren, whose party had been firmly in the House minority for decades, remained pessimistic. At least, he thought, "We finally got a vote that people can't hide from, so come November it will be an [election] issue."

Lungren and his allies anxiously watched the electronic board where ongoing votes were tallied. It was nip and tuck. The bill was ahead, then behind, then ahead again. "It was like watching the last 24 seconds of a professional basketball game in slow motion," Lungren recalled. Eventually, the Republicans reached the magic 218 vote majority needed to win, and some Democrats changed their votes to yes. In the end, 89 Democrats voted "aye," bringing the total to 243. Reconstructing his triumph later, Lungren learned that many Democrats, fearing that they would not be able to explain to voters why they had opposed a crime bill, went to then-Speaker Thomas (Tip) O'Neill and said, "Tip, I know this is a 'party vote,' but I've got to vote my district."

The victory was so unexpected that the Republicans had no game plan. In fact, they worried that Reagan, who had wanted a "clean" continuing resolution without controversial issues attached, would not appreciate the significance of the crime bill's passage and would veto the spending bill that contained it. Lungren quickly called Paul Laxalt, the Nevada senator with longstanding ties to Reagan who often served as a go-between between Congress and the president. Laxalt agreed to run interference with the White House. Deborah Owen, a former staffer for House Republicans who now worked for Senate Judiciary Chairman Thurmond, spread the word among sympathetic Senate staffers, who would encourage their bosses to fight for the measure.

Because of the unorthodox way the crime bill had been passed, the outcome was far from clear. Normally, the Senate-House conference committees, where final details of legislation were worked out, were made up, logically, of panel members who had initiated the legislation, in this case the appropriations panels. But the crime bill was a huge, complex piece of legislation that had been written mainly by Senate Judiciary Committee members. By the time a conference committee meeting was called in early October, after Reagan had ordered a partial government shutdown because the spending bill had not been enacted, it was clear that the appropriators were going to need help.

At first, Lungren was told that Judiciary members would be barred from the crucial meeting of conferees, so he headed home to a Catholic Mass he held periodically with several other couples. Democratic Senator Biden, a prime architect of the crime bill in the Senate, took his usual train home to Delaware.

Liberal opponents hoped they could kill the crime bill in conference. But in modern-day American government, key policy decisions tend to be made during the appropriations process. That proved to be the case in 1984. Neal Smith, the Iowan heading the subcommittee that handled Justice Department appropriations, told his Senate counterpart, Ernest Hollings of South Carolina, "let's just add a crime bill this year."[10]

The Democratic appropriations leaders realized that they had better call in their Judiciary colleagues who had been working on the substance of anticrime legislation. So they summoned allies like New Jersey's Hughes, who started trying to undermine provisions objectionable to liberals in the Republican-inspired bill. Robert McConnell, the Reagan Justice Department's chief lobbyist, observed the scene and called Lungren at home, saying, "You've got to come down here and save us." The Californian returned to the Capitol at 10 P.M. and spent the rest of the night arguing with Hughes and others to preserve the main points of the crime legislation, which, after all, had been approved by both Houses. "We saved 98 percent," Lungren boasted.

As Iowa's Smith recalled it, "We went section by section . . . in a few hours, we had a 600-page bill." Democrats did manage to knock out a few provisions. Smith, a moderate who shared few of the reservations of his liberal Judiciary Committee colleagues, defended the unwieldy process, saying that "with as big a country as we have, sometimes you have to do things that way as a matter of efficiency."

Efficient or not, when the dust had settled, it became clear that the 1984 crime law was a landmark, and not only because the Republicans finally had found a way to outmaneuver the Democratic House liberals. Some of the GOP's prize issues, including the exclusionary rule and habeas corpus reform, had been lost in the shuffle. But moderates like Biden and Specter were able to slip in important provisions like a reinstatement of LEAA-like state and local anticrime aid programs—"a major coup," said Biden aide Scott Green.[11]

One unfortunate by-product was that because the law was passed in such an unusual way—with key Democrats essentially blindsided—many key sections were slapped summarily on the federal law books with little consideration of their implications. Because the significant legal changes were not subject to the detailed scrutiny that should be part of the normal legislative process, they became embedded in the federal law-enforcement process whether or not they were wise.

To take just one: a far-reaching "forfeiture" scheme made it much easier for federal agents to seize the property of accused criminals as well as convicted ones. In theory, the law merely shifted the balance a bit more toward the prosecution and away from defendants, who supposedly could enjoy the fruits of their crimes while their cases languished in court.

In practice, however, the law skewed the priorities of law enforcers at all levels because it gave their budgets a direct cut of forfeiture proceeds. In many cases it was true that the statute allowed authorities to obtain the ill-gotten gains of guilty drug dealers earlier than they could have in a clogged court system under the law as it stood previously. But critics in later years cited a string of horror stories in which overzealous agents, seeing a way to pad their coffers, seized the homes and vehicles of suspects who turned out to be innocent.

Conservatives and liberals agreed later that the law permitted too many abuses. Among those who had second thoughts was Victoria Toensing, an official in the Reagan Justice Department, who backed the law initially but realized once she became a defense attorney after leaving the government how innocent suspects could be harmed. Similar concerns were expressed by Republican Henry Hyde of Illinois. But despite the fact that in 1995 Hyde became chairman of the powerful House Judiciary Committee, that idea got scant attention. Finally, a version of forfeiture reform was enacted in 2000—16 years after its origin.

Another provision with an unexpectedly wide impact created a fund for programs that aid crime victims, using fines and other penalties paid in federal cases. Few disputed the basic impulse. But the law's result was to create an "off-the-books" pot of money that might or might not be used wisely.

In its early years, the fund had a modest $70 million to spend each year. Then, in 1996, a huge fine in a white-collar crime case produced a sudden $500 million influx; the fund plummeted next year to $363 million, still a hefty amount but a fluctuation that didn't lend itself to good planning. In 2000, antitrust fines paid by vitamin makers caused the fund to balloon to $1.26 billion. Insiders worried that in years of plenty, victim-aid groups might squander the windfall on frivolous projects. Congress angered victim-rights advocates by putting a $537 million cap on annual expenditures from the fund for fiscal year 2001.

Perhaps the most far-reaching section of the 1984 crime law set into motion a process of drawing up sentencing guidelines that would set the parameters for penalties for all federal crimes. Again, the impulse was well intended: to reduce the number of cases in which judges in different courts imposed widely varying sentences, even though the offense and the criminal's background were essentially the same. It wasn't difficult to see how that could happen, with hundreds of judges on the bench and largely open-ended penalties on the books.

Reform efforts began at a dinner organized by Senator Edward Kennedy in the mid-1970s to draw sentencing experts into a discussion with Marvin Frankel, a federal judge from New York City, whose 1972 book calling attention to the problem, *Criminal Sentences: Law Without Order*, had attracted attention in judicial circles.[12] The dinner meeting led to a lengthy drafting process involving congressional aides and outside specialists. The driving force from the Democratic side was that "the downtrodden—people who couldn't afford a lawyer—got heavier penalties," said Kennedy aide Kenneth Feinberg. Kennedy "saw guidelines as a way to level the playing field."[13]

In the meantime, a similar process was occurring in a few states, most prominently Minnesota. There, riots by prison inmates in the mid-1970s had led legislators to conclude that one major trigger had been "indeterminate" terms that gave convicts little idea of when they would be released. Some lawmakers favored flat terms until they realized that they likely would be forced to build expensive new prisons to accommodate those serving additional time.

Several years of negotiation ensued, during which the concept emerged of guidelines giving maximum and minimum penalties for each offense. Dale Parent, a criminologist who took part in the process as a staffer on the governor's crime commission, recalled a process of "imprecise guesswork . . . adding to some terms, subtracting from others" until lawmakers came up with a plan that might keep the prison population stable.[14] Unlike the normal process in Congress, Parent said, the two major political parties in Minnesota "did not engage in a contest to see which could appear most fierce on crime."

Minnesota's rules, which became effective in 1980, are generally regarded as successful in limiting racial, ethnic, and gender differences in sentencing, a national survey led by Parent concluded in 1996. But the Minnesota experience did not create a national stampede. Fewer than a dozen other states had enacted required sentencing guidelines at the time of Parent's survey.

While Minnesota put its experiment into action, drafts of a federal sentencing code went back and forth. The proposal was revised a bit, but because it was just one small part of the huge appropriations package, it received little attention as the 1984 bill sped through. Federal judges, who later would object strongly to their loss of discretion, took little part in the debate; neither did House liberals, who figured that the measure was unlikely to pass.

Superficially, staffer Feinberg saw the outcome as a "win-win for everybody." Conservatives, mindful of the opinion surveys that consistently showed the public believing judges to be insufficiently harsh, saw the scheme as a way to prevent "soft" judges from letting defendants off too easily. Liberals, heavily influenced by the leadership of Kennedy, viewed it as a way to reduce inequities in the way justice was meted out in the federal system.

The eventual result satisfied mostly the conservative side. The law said that a seven-person commission would write the guidelines. Initial members, chosen mostly by a conservative Justice Department and the federal judiciary, turned out to be not mere technicians but rather a group of highly charged, somewhat partisan personalities who feuded over seemingly every detail like "a bunch of political hacks," sniffed a staff member for the judicial branch.

The commissioners included Stephen Breyer, a future Supreme Court justice, who had worked on Kennedy's Judiciary staff, and Chairman William Wilkins, a federal judge from South Carolina, whose patron was Senate Judiciary Chairman Thurmond. (Wilkins also yearned to be on the high court, but his embattled tenure on the sentencing panel might not have helped.)

Operating in a politically frenzied anticrime atmosphere in Washington, the commission was forced to tackle immensely complicated issues in a relative hurry. Wilkins noted that the Minnesota guidelines writers had to deal with only 251 crimes but the federal commissioners coped with 800, including complex violations like extortion and racketeering. The mammoth task was finished on time, Wilkins said.[15]

But not without rancor. The commission "adopted no sentencing philosophy" and ordered up no studies to guide its work, complained one of its first members, law professor and former prosecutor Paul Robinson, the only dissenter from the original guideline proposal. Instead of devising an innovative, well-thought-out new system, Robinson said, his colleagues merely instructed judges to use the mathematical average of overall sentences imposed by the judiciary in recent years, a formula he believed might have made sentencing practices worse than before.

Robinson received his own share of complaints for proposing what critics charged was a hopelessly complicated alternative scheme. (Robinson would have created 360 levels of sentences compared with the 43 the panel finally proposed.)

The guideline-writing process took nearly three years, during which Congress embarked on a frenzy of passing mandatory minimum sentences in drug cases that ignored or contradicted much of the guideline structure. Wilkins complained privately to key lawmakers that Congress and his commission were "going in different directions." The typical response was that the guidelines would require several years to take hold, but the mandatory minimums would have an immediate effect. Wilkins believed that the commission's ongoing work was able to "stop the flood" of new mandatory minimums, but the panel could not repeal those passed before it was able to formulate its plan.

When there was a choice, the guidelines themselves tended to make sentences more severe. For example, the commission "apparently made a conscious decision to ensure that a [convict's] criminal record would 'dramatically affect' the severity of a sentence," said Kate Stith of Yale Law School and federal appeals Judge Jose Cabranes in Fear of Judging, a study of the guidelines published in 1998.[16] The average time served by federal convicts jumped to 43 months after the guidelines went into effect from 13 months before, and fewer than 15 percent of convicts were put on probation compared with half earlier.

As they played out over their first decade, the federal guidelines may have brought a bit of order out of the chaos that had pervaded the justice system. But in other ways, the cure may have been as bad as the disease. Many judges complained that the law allowed too little leeway for reasonable exceptions. It's easy to declare that certain offenses should get specified penalties. The problem was that the level of offense often was determined through a complicated plea bargaining process in which the prosecutor effectively set the penalty. The most egregious new disparities were evident in narcotics cases. Mid-level participants in drug-sales conspiracies pled guilty to lesser offenses in exchange for fingering higher-ups, while drug couriers in the same ring who had no such bargaining chips ended up getting harsher sentences.

A Sentencing Commission study in 1991 asserted that its work had resulted in a "dramatic reduction" in sentencing disparity. It highlighted the example of bank robbers, whose typical sentences had ranged from 4 to 40 months before the guidelines and from 21 to 38 months afterward.[17] But that narrowed range hardly proved that unwarranted disparities were eliminated. After a year-long investigation, the *Washington Post* concluded in October 1996 that "a system meant to impose uniformity is still riddled with disparity, from region to region and even from courtroom to courtroom."[18] The newspaper devoted long articles over five days to detailing the system's vagaries, including the finding that judges and probation officers had interpreted the guidelines differently in half of 79,000 cases the newspaper checked.

For his part, former commission chairman Wilkins argued that even if the guidelines system had not eliminated disparity, at least judges had to express the reasons for their actions publicly, and extreme sentences were not being imposed "for unknown, inappropriate reasons."

If the sentencing guidelines pleased conservatives by serving as a vehicle for racheting up terms, they disappointed moderates and outraged liberals. Kennedy aide Feinberg faulted the commission for "micromanagement," arguing that Democrats did not intend the commission to delve in so much detail into what judges could and could not do. The guidelines "should have been much more generic," he contended. Kennedy, in a symposium held shortly before the guidelines' tenth anniversary in 1997, said that the rules "clearly . . . have fallen well short" of their goals. The most serious problem, he declared, was Congress, which "continues to enact ill-advised, costly, mandatory minimum sentences that undermine the guidelines."

Even though he had been a driving force behind the guideline system, Kennedy's voice was not very influential in the Republican-dominated Congress of the late 1990s. Utah Senator Orrin Hatch, by then Judiciary Committee chairman, told the *Washington Post* that the guidelines were working well: "We don't want to go back to the days where the liberal judges let everyone off and the conservative ones hang everyone. I've come to the conclusion that we can't be tough enough." It was the Republican rallying cry on crime.

The get tough theme permeated anticrime policy in the 1980s. Whether it was Washington's extended reach in drug control, the rise of the victim-rights movement, or the spread of sentencing guidelines, it seemed that a policy could survive only if it could be portrayed as more punitive. The flurry of major federal anticrime laws during the decade reflected a drive to federalize criminal law that gained strength relentlessly as crime dominated the national agenda.

Chapter 4

MAKING A FEDERAL CASE OF IT

H E seemed like a mixed-up kid who decided to bomb his mother's car. Because the vehicle was used in a Pittsburgh-area catering business, and it occasionally crossed state lines, the case could be prosecuted either by the U.S. attorney's office or a local district attorney. The feds stepped in, and the young man was named in a federal charge of malicious destruction of property.

The prosecution was perfectly within the limits of the law, but U.S. District Judge D. Brooks Smith "had the nagging sense that this case didn't belong in federal court." After all, the U.S. attorney's manual—the Justice Department's official guide for its prosecutors across the nation—requires a "substantial federal interest" for them to take on a case. Because such phrases are far from precise, decisions on where to file cases like the Pittsburgh car bomb episode may boil down to questions of an incident's prominence or a prosecutor's convenience. Was the violation so notorious that the U.S. attorney decided to pull rank over a local prosecutor and file it in federal court? Or, as may have been true of Judge Smith's case, did the investigating agency—the federal Bureau of Alcohol, Tobacco, and Firearms (ATF)—want to stay within its familiar bailiwick and make sure that someone pursued the case, instead of merely hoping that a state district attorney would put the federal agents' work to use in a prosecution?

For most of the nation's history, violent crime has been considered a state and local affair. More than 90 percent of criminal cases historically have landed in local courts, with federal courts most often handling complex white-collar cases and those involving exclusively federal laws. But the line has become increasingly blurred in recent decades, to the point that it often seems a tossup where a prominent case will end up. "There is a mere 5 percent chance of being prosecuted federally—and no clue about how that 5 percent is selected," complained Scott Wallace of the National Legal Aid and Defender Association.[1]

The creeping federalization of local crime prosecutions raises significant questions: Are government resources being allocated wisely? Are defendants treated fairly if they have little idea where their case will be heard? Can taxpayers feel assured that the federal criminal justice system handles cases better than do state courts?

There's no doubt that the scope of federal jurisdiction has widened. The number of federal criminal offenses jumped from 17 when the country was founded to several thousand by the late 1990s. An American Bar Association (ABA) task force attempted to bring the count up-to-date in 1998, but gave up poring through all of the overlapping statutes and concluded only that a widely cited estimate of 3,000 was out of date. The task force did find that more than 40 percent of all federal criminal provisions enacted since the Civil War had gone into the law books since 1970.[2]

Of course, the feds long have had the authority to prosecute cases involving people or objects that crossed state lines, including kidnapping and auto theft. Wallace of the defense lawyers' group traces the origin to an 1872 mail fraud law—based on the fact that the federal government delivers the mail—and the turn-of-the-twentieth-century Mann Act, which made it a crime to take a woman to another state to "give herself up to debauchery." Over the years, most drug offenses and many firearms crimes have been included as automatic or optional federal cases. That covers a lot of territory, but until recent years, federal, state, and local investigators divided up their respective caseloads without much rancor and confusion.

But starting in the 1970s and increasingly in the 1980s and 1990s, Congress enacted a seemingly endless parade of laws to expand the reach of federal law. Some of it makes good sense. Large-scale, organized criminal conspiracies usually do cross state lines and sometimes may be cracked only with the kind of national and international resources that the federal government can command. Task forces that include federal, state, and local prosecutors and agents now are commonplace, and a national working group meets periodically to sort out priorities among the Justice Department, state attorneys general, and state prosecutors, who usually work at the county level.

Even if such high-level meetings work out operational problems, many local prosecutors are disdainful of the trend. Federalization is politically popular in

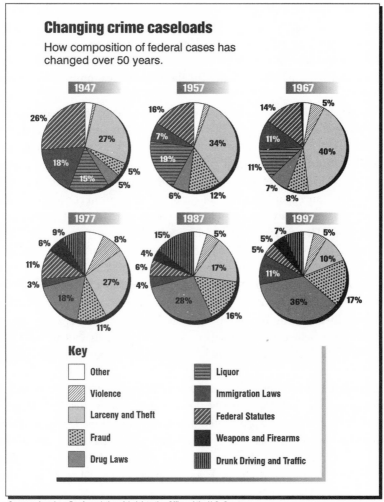

Changing crime caseloads

How composition of federal cases has changed over 50 years.

1947
26%
27%
18%
15%
5%
5%

1957
16%
7%
19%
6%
12%
34%

1967
14%
5%
11%
11%
7%
8%
40%

1977
9%
6%
11%
3%
18%
11%
27%
8%

1987
15%
5%
4%
6%
4%
28%
16%
17%

1997
7%
5%
5%
5%
11%
36%
17%
10%

Key

☐	Other	▨	Liquor
▨	Violence	■	Immigration Laws
▨	Larceny and Theft	▨	Federal Statutes
▨	Fraud	■	Weapons and Firearms
▨	Drug Laws	▥	Drunk Driving and Traffic

Sources: American Bar Association, Administrative Office of the U.S. Courts

Congress, but "reduction of crime—particularly violent crime—has been adversely affected," chief prosecutor Harry Shorstein of Jacksonville, Florida, told a House committee in 1999. He explained that the list of traditionally local crimes that federal authorities increasingly are prosecuting "significantly overlaps and duplicates" local dockets, sometimes diffusing the fight against crime rather than enhancing it.

Much expansion of the federal criminal law has stemmed from political impulses. Under the notion popularized by Barry Goldwater in the 1960s that crime is a national problem, it's easy for the White House and Congress to assume, or at least pretend, that federal authorities do better than their state and local counterparts at investigating many categories of offenses. Whenever some type of crime reaches national prominence, whether it is abortion clinic bombings, church burnings, or stalking, so do demands to bring in federal agents. "We federalize everything that walks, talks, and moves," observed Delaware Senator Joseph Biden, a Democrat, who headed the Judiciary Committee between 1986 and 1994.

Enacting federal laws, however, does not necessarily mean reducing street crime. Surveying the spate of legislation, the ABA task force concluded in 1999 that "increased federalization is rarely, if ever, likely to have any appreciable effect on the categories of violent crime that most concern Americans, because in practice federal law enforcement can only reach a small percent of such activity." The panel spanned the ideological spectrum, from conservative former Attorney General Edwin Meese to liberal Democrat and former Deputy Attorney General Philip Heymann of Harvard Law School.

Because it's possible to identify some interstate nexus with virtually any crime, just about anything goes when it comes to making a theoretical federal case of some category of violations. Noting the tendency of legislators to over-react after single "horrendous" crime incidents, the reasons they typically offer for federal involvement are "pretty spurious," in Meese's view. Congress tends to "pass a law whether it's necessary or not, if it's politically salient," said Meese, who chaired the ABA task force and has taken part in an informal alliance of conservatives and liberals who try to fight against the trend, often in vain.

Consider pharmacy robberies. In the early 1980s, after a wave of holdups by persons seeking illegal drugs, the National Association of Retail Druggists demanded that such cases be prosecuted in federal court. If the Drug Enforcement Administration had the basic authority to go after narcotics cases, why shouldn't pharmacy robbery be included in the federal mandate, the theory went. Illinois Republican Representative Henry Hyde proposed such a law in 1982, but it attracted little interest at first.

When the anticrime political stakes were raised two years later, it was a different story. In 1984, Republicans were threatening to make street crime a major issue in that fall's congressional elections, and Democrats were under pressure to appear more concerned about violent crime. As recounted by journalist Dan Baum, in an atmosphere of intensified political-party competition, the pharmacy proposal that had been largely ignored two years earlier now passed within a matter of a few weeks. "We can look tough and become heroes to the pharmacists," Baum quoted Democratic Representative William Hughes of New Jersey, chairman of the House crime subcommittee, who championed Republican Hyde's idea.[3] Even though the Justice Department promised to review pharmacy cases before rushing into court, the message was clear: Washington cares.

The Armed Career Criminal Act, which was also enacted in 1984 after a relentless campaign by Republican Pennsylvania Senator Arlen Specter, is a prime example of federalization. Inserted into that year's omnibus anticrime law over Justice Department skepticism, the law later became a staple of federal firearms prosecutions. Suddenly, the feds could bring local hoodlums into court if they had a local rap sheet with three felonies. By the late 1990s, the law had helped put more than 2,000 convicts in federal prison for an average of 18 years. Before the law went on the books, agents say that suspects with similar records would have received only three or four years behind bars. Enforcing the law, a project that goes by the name Project Achilles, has become "a very significant piece of what we do," said a senior agent of the ATF. (The project owes its name to the idea that illegal possession of firearms under federal law can be the Achilles heel of legal vulnerability for street criminals.)

If the 2,000 prosecution total sounds unimpressive in the context of a national count of serious crimes that reaches about 13 million reported crimes each year, ATF has tried to disabuse anyone of such a notion. Extrapolating from estimates that the typical career criminal commits 160 offenses each year and that each crime costs about $2,600 to victims and the general public (in police and court processing costs, for example), the bureau said that as of 1998, the armed career criminal law has "saved" $764 million in crimes that were prevented while the convicts sat behind bars (even after subtracting the $45,000 annual government cost of housing the prisoners). The claim of saving more than three quarters of a billion dollars sounds considerably more impressive than just 2,000 prosecutions.

The problem is that the massive "savings" total ignores the fact that many of the same defendants probably would have received long prison terms if they had ended up in state courts, which also have toughened their sentencing practices in the years since Congress expanded federal criminal-prosecution authority dramatically in 1984. In other words, ATF's fancy calculations may not justify the Armed Career Criminal Act's blatant federalization.

If the armed career criminal law is a most prominent example of modern-day federalization of local crime, Specter, in an interview long after his legislative triumph, was "glad to accept the responsibility" for escalating the trend. As district attorney in Philadelphia, Specter recalled being continually frustrated in his attempts to put a group of 500 career criminals behind bars for long stretches. Defense lawyers were able to "shop" for local judges who would issue lenient sentences to the attorneys' clients.[4]

Once he entered Congress, Specter was determined to help his former colleagues in the district attorney's office and others across the country. Even if many eligible cases didn't end up in federal court, he reasoned, the spectacle of just a few defendants getting very long sentences would persuade suspects in both federal and state courts to enter guilty pleas with relatively high terms, like 7 to 15 years for robbery, instead of the year or 2 that they formerly would have received.

Federalization of anticrime laws is resisted by some at both ends of the ideological spectrum. "I had a hell of a time getting it passed," Specter recalled, in large part because conservatives like then Senate Judiciary Chairman Strom Thurmond of South Carolina were notorious states' righters who resisted extending the reach of the federal criminal law.

Specter never gave up. In 1993, for example, he introduced a Drive-By Shooting Act, declaring that once rare drive-by shootings by then were plaguing "urban centers and small towns alike." Citing the bill's proposed penalty of up to 25 years in prison, Specter said it "will be an effective deterrent because once these hoodlums know a drive-by shooting is a federal offense they will be less inclined to commit the crime."

While the Pennsylvania senator has been a leader in the federalization trend, it has been a bipartisan affair. Auto theft once was restricted almost entirely to unoccupied vehicles. But the 1990s saw a rise in carjacking—the hijacking of an auto directly from a driver. The successor to New Jersey's Hughes as senior Democrat on the House crime subcommittee, Charles Schumer of Brooklyn, led the campaign for a 1992 law that made carjacking a federal crime.

At first, the bill had nothing to do with carjacking. One week, Schumer returned from New York in a dither because his car had been stolen from Kennedy Airport. An aide recalled Schumer's declaring, "We need to do something about auto theft," retreating to his private office, and slamming the door. Police had made some progress against auto thieves by requiring that each vehicle bear a hard-to-remove identification number, but the Schumer aides came up with a way to extend the concept and require that key auto parts be individually numbered.

The problem was that the auto industry didn't want to go to the considerable expense such a plan would entail. They had a powerful ally, veteran Democratic Representative John Dingell of Michigan, who headed the Commerce Committee and had the power to block legislation related to his official bailiwick. With Dingell standing in the way, Schumer's idea went nowhere.

But Dingell didn't count on one egregious crime that was widely publicized in the capital in 1992. Of course, it helped that not only was it an election year but also that the case occurred in a Maryland suburb in Washington's media market. Pamela Basu, 34, had just left home on September 8, 1992, driving her 2-year-old daughter, Sarina, to her first morning of preschool when two men pulled Pamela Basu from the car and drove off. In her attempt to rescue Sarina, Pamela Basu became tangled in a seat belt and was dragged to her death.

Quickly, Schumer saw an opening: amend his auto theft bill to make carjacking a federal crime. No one denied that the crime was horrible. The only question was why federal intervention in cases like Basu's was warranted. Said Schumer, "Those who just say 'keep it the way it is' are forgetting that the state and local systems don't do a very good job."[5] Behind the scenes, congressional staffers figured that not many carjackings would become federal cases. Instead, the Basu tragedy was a way for Schumer to defeat Dingell on the parts question. With the carjacking issue suddenly in the forefront, the measure passed within a month, including a negotiated version of the parts-marking requirement.

The law came too late to bring Basu's case into federal court, but did it make a difference? Basu's assailants were prosecuted in state court, and both were sentenced to life prison terms. That prompted the National Conference of State Legislatures to ask whether congressional action really was necessary. Observed criminologists Franklin Zimring and Gordon Hawkins of the University of California at Berkeley: "There is no reason to suppose that current federal law enforcement resources are better suited to the apprehension of carjackers" than are state and local officers.[6]

As is typical of federal anticrime legislating, Congress is fond of passing statutes first and getting the facts later. The first official federal estimate of the extent of carjacking, published by the U.S. Bureau of Justice Statistics in 1994, estimated that about 35,500 such attempted or completed crimes occur each year, a disturbing number but only a tiny fraction of the nearly 2 million auto thefts. (The estimate was revised to 49,000 in 1999.)[7] Victims were seriously injured in only 4 percent of cases. Assuming that federal investigators entered only a small number of those cases in which local authorities were deemed inadequate, that might amount to a few hundred a year nationwide.

The carjacking statute was followed in short order by laws that gave the FBI jurisdiction over "deadbeat dads" who cross state lines, as well as certain cases of stalking, terrorism involving abortion clinics, and "animal terrorism" incidents aimed at research laboratories.

New York Senator Alfonse D'Amato, a Republican, set off alarm bells in the federal judiciary and elsewhere throughout the early 1990s when he kept up a campaign to give federal agents authority to make arrests in virtually every category of gun crime. Defending such an expansion, Texas Senator Phil Gramm, a conservative Republican who otherwise tends to support limits on federal power, asserted, "When you have violent predators, the public doesn't care whether the local police or the FBI apprehends them. They want something done."[8]

The D'Amato bill was not enacted, after repeated denunciations by the federal judiciary—including Chief Justice William Rehnquist—and others. But one supposedly lax prosecution of a local gun crime might put it back on center stage. D'Amato lost his Senate seat in 1998, but the victor was fellow federalizer Schumer.

Judges occasionally slow the federalization trend. One of the most prominent public fears about crime has involved guns in schools, a worry highlighted by the 1989 massacre of elementary-school students in Stockton, California. The next year, Congress overwhelmingly passed a measure called the Gun-Free School Zones Act. The law, which made it a federal offense to possess a gun within 1,000 feet of a school, sailed through with hardly a murmur of dissent. Any objection, after all, might be interpreted as favoring guns on school grounds. (Some self-defense advocates did argue after a spate of school shootings in later years that allowing teachers and other staffers to possess guns might have stemmed the violence.)

Sponsors assumed that the statute would be safe from legal attack on the same basis that supports other federal firearms laws: that most guns travel in interstate commerce. But a five-justice Supreme Court majority unexpectedly struck down the law in 1995, holding that lawmakers had failed to justify why federal jursidiction was necessary. The ruling, in a case known as *U.S. v. Lopez*, prompted some legal pundits to predict that the high court's conservative majority would begin regularly striking down congressional efforts expanding federal jurisdiction.[9] But such turnarounds usually do not occur quickly, and the guns-in-schools aberration may have been due more to sloppy legislative drafting than to some watershed in constitutional theory.

When a couple in Sacramento, California, allegedly burned down their home to get a $4 million insurance payment, they were charged in federal court with arson on the ground that some of their natural gas came from another state. The U.S. Ninth Circuit Court of Appeals threw out the case in 1995, saying that such an arson "has only a remote and indirect effect on interstate commerce."[10] Five years later, the Supreme Court reached a similar conclusion in an Indiana case.

The 1994 Violence Against Women Act provoked another high court backlash. Part of that year's federal anticrime law converted many assaults against women into potential federal crimes. Again, the federal judiciary expressed fears about the prospect of domestic disputes by the tens of thousands landing on their dockets. The law's language was narrowed as a result of consultations between Delaware's Biden, the prime mover in the Senate, and federal Judge Stanley Marcus of Miami, representing the U.S. Judicial Conference.

One case that did make it to court involved Christy Brzonkala of Washington, D.C. As a freshman at Virginia Tech University in 1994, Brzonkala allegedly was raped in her dorm room by two members of the school's football team. She sued the institution under the Violence Against Women Act, seeking damages for an alleged security failure. Although it was not a criminal case, it put the players (who were not charged with a crime outside the university discipline system) through a costly federal civil proceeding accusing them of violating her rights.

A federal district judge tossed the case out in a ruling that relied partly on the high court's decision on the Gun-Free School Zones Act. The court essentially held that a rape case couldn't be sustained as an interstate act under the Constitution's Commerce Clause. The entire 11-member U.S. Court of Appeals for the Fourth Circuit in Richmond studied the issue for a year before issuing a 7-to-4 decision in March 1999 striking down the provision of the law that allowed civil suits by sexual-assault victims. A 214-page opinion by Judge Michael Luttig called the statute "a sweeping intrusion" by Congress into state authority. By a 5-to-4 vote, the Supreme Court agreed in May 2000, the majority saying that upholding the law would "obliterate the distinction between what is national and what is local."

The razor-thin high court majority may not stop the federalization trend. A juvenile delinquency bill that Congress may consider in 2001, for example, could convert many crimes by local street gangs into potential federal cases. One version of the proposal would give federal prosecutors more authority to handle juvenile crime charges that otherwise would be pursued in state courts. The prosecutors would not have much of a chance to build up expertise in handling teen crimes. Jacksonville, Florida, prosecutor Harry Shorstein told members of Congress considering the issue that even if the bill were enacted, he would "prosecute in a day more cases than you will prosecute in all the federal courts . . . in a year."

A proposed federal Hate Crimes Prevention Act carries the prospect of making many local offenses into federal crimes if they involve some element of racial bias. (A notorious Texas case in which a black man was dragged to his death by several whites was prominently cited by advocates of the federal law in 1998 even though state authorities were successful in obtaining the death penalty against at least one of the defendants.) The hate crime bill was shelved by Republican leaders as Congress struggled to adjourn for the 2000 election campaign.

The expansion of federal crimes is partly legislative grandstanding. But it also has a real impact in budgetary terms. The FBI and other federal law enforcement agencies face constant pressure to shift resources in line with congressional mandates. The FBI has grown rapidly in the last two decades, from an annual budget of a little over $2 billion just eight years earlier to more than $3.2 billion in 2001. Overall, federal justice system expenditures increased at twice the rate of state and local justice spending between 1982 and 1993: 317 percent in the federal sector compared with 163 percent in state and local agencies. During the same period, the number of employees in the federal justice system rose by 96 percent compared with a 42 percent state and local increase. (That includes a rise in the ranks of federal prosecutors from 3,000 to 8,000 in three decades.)

Much of this growth was due to routine caseload increases, but federalization also played a significant part.

To keep the trend in perspective, the federal share of America's criminal prosecution forces remains small. The FBI, for example, employs some 11,600 agents compared with about 600,000 local police officers. There is a similar disparity in the courts, with 1,250 federal trial judges—including lower-level magistrates—and about 29,000 comparable state jurists. Federal prisons hold only about 120,000 of the 2 million in custody nationwide.

And some federalization amounts to empty threats from Washington—what the ABA task force termed new crimes "enacted in [a] patchwork response to newsworthy events." Not a single prosecution was filed in 1997 under the 1994 federal drive-by shooting and interstate domestic violence provisions. Ditto with laws on odometer tampering and failure to report child abuse. The "animal enterprise terrorism" statute produced a mere three cases.

But if those provisions were paper tigers, a trickier problem was that federal agents and courts might suddenly be required to handle a major case not because of some rational decisionmaking process but because a U.S. attorney general or one of the 93 presidentially appointed U.S. attorneys wants to demonstrate that he or she is on the job. "By 'cherry picking' high-profile cases, the involvement of the federal government in too many areas of the fight against crime only leads to a very poor utilization of resources," said Stephen Saland, a New York State senator critical of the practice.[11] Scott Harshbarger, who served as Massachusetts attorney general during much of the 1990s, said he "spent a lot of my time putting out brush fires" between federal and local prosecutors arguing over who should pursue a case. When the feds "want to come in," Harshbarger said, "it's a one-way street" that may be based on "turf issues and a search for publicity."

Jumping into a local carjacking case, for example, might divert the time of FBI agents from work that is uniquely federal—counterintelligence or background checks on major candidates for federal office, for example. In a 1993 speech warning that "rapid, unchecked federalization of criminal activity could overwhelm the limited resources of federal law enforcement agencies," FBI Director Louis Freeh estimated that 30 percent of the FBI agents assigned to criminal matters were working on violent crime cases—presumably including many that could be handled just as well by local cops. Janet Reno, attorney general in the Clinton administration, generally supported the federalization trend but worried that "many cases may be brought in the federal system . . . because we have adequate [prison] cell space."

As is true of much criminal justice policymaking generally, the available data do not prove the case either way. No one really knows how much of a hindrance federalization may pose to effective prosecutions on a federal level. For example, if states took on many of the garden-variety criminal cases now piling up on federal dockets, it's not clear how many more white-collar crime cases that spanned state lines could be brought in federal court. The number of federal criminal cases filed each year has steadily increased, including a major jump of 70 percent—to about 47,500—between 1980 and 1992. Still, the total was much higher during the peak of the Prohibition era in the early 1930s. The modern-day figure neared the 60,000 mark in 1999. That did not include more than 55,000 civil cases filed each year by prisoners, most of them state inmates challenging their convictions under habeas corpus laws or complaining about confinement conditions.[12]

Divided among the federal judiciary, the criminal caseload amounts to about 93 per judge each year. That might not sound like much, but an increasing number of federal cases are highly complex, multidefendant indictments that may require several weeks of trial, if they get that far. In 1997, federal criminal cases amounted to 16 percent of the total, but they accounted for nearly 40 percent of the trials—and 62 percent of those trials lasted for 20 or more days. The median time period taken to handle a case has crept up, too, from 5.4 months in 1993 to 5.8 months 3 years later.

Because criminal matters almost always take precedence, some civil cases take

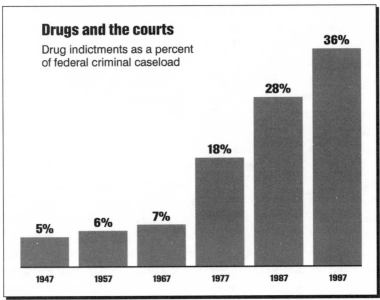

Drugs and the courts

Drug indictments as a percent
of federal criminal caseload

5% 1947
6% 1957
7% 1967
18% 1977
28% 1987
36% 1997

Sources: American Bar Association, Administrative Office of the U.S. Courts

many years to resolve, especially in border-area courts that often are overwhelmed with drug charges. "The federal criminal justice system was never designed for, and is not capable of, being the criminal court of primary resort," Richard Arcara, a federal trial judge in Buffalo, New York, and a former state prosecutor, told the Senate Judiciary Committee in 1998.

Arcara was expressing the federal judiciary's opposition to the proposed hate crime law. Among other things, the measure would permit federal prosecution of anyone who causes an injury motivated by the actual or perceived race, color, religion, or national origin of another person—a rather breathtaking range of possibilities.

The reigning theory behind federalization is that the federal courts will take on the most serious cases, whether hate crimes, drug running, or racketeering, leaving the run-of-the-mill matters to their state counterparts. But the elitism of federal judges and lawmakers doesn't necessarily give them the wisdom to be the best to decide how to handle routine crimes. That does not stop Congress from trying to set an example. In the final stages of debate on the controversial 1994 crime law, for example, the House slipped in a section proposed by Republican Representative Susan Molinari of Staten Island, New York, that in cases of sexual assault or child molestation, all evidence of similar previous accusations could be introduced in court.[13]

It wasn't literally a case of federalizing state offenses because Molinari's measure applied only to federal cases. But by liberalizing the evidence rules in those cases, the law would likely encourage more women to file them in federal courts. The law reversed the longstanding rule that barred unsubstantiated earlier charges from court. A mere arrest on a drug charge that failed to lead to a conviction, for example, usually may not be used against a suspect who is arrested years later.

Women's rights advocates argued that the innocent-until-proved-guilty notion wasn't appropriate for domestic violence cases, which supposedly were so different from the usual crime that it should be possible to use any charge from the past to prove a pattern of conduct.

Leaders of the federal judiciary tried to persuade Molinari that her provision was misguided, but their timing was particularly poor. The Staten Islander was among a bloc of moderate Republicans whose votes the White House needed during tense negotiations in August 1994 to pass that year's massive anticrime law and its beloved 100,000 cops program. Although key members of the House Judiciary Committee had scuttled the Molinari proposal, when President Clinton called to ask the price of her support for the crime law, the answer was White House backing for the rape-evidence clause. Clinton went along, and the Molinari measure was home free.

Congress did make one slight concession to critics, who argued that legal experts assembled by the U.S. Judicial Conference, which administers the federal courts, should be asked to assess the plan. Lawmakers asked two advisory panels of judges, practicing lawyers, and academics to review the issue after the bill was enacted. The groups both said overwhelmingly that the change in the rape-evidence rules was unwarranted, but Congress ignored them and let it remain in the law, at least for now.

Molinari's vote helped Clinton win a big political victory by passing the omnibus 1994 law, but it ended up making life more difficult for the president four years later. When he was required to testify by deposition in the Paula Jones sexual-harassment case, the Jones forces cited the Molinari provision when they surprised Clinton with a series of detailed questions about his relationship with former White House aide Monica Lewinsky to show Clinton's pattern of conduct. Clinton's answers—misleading or false, depending on one's interpretation—set the stage for the year-long special prosecutor's investigation and impeachment proceedings that put a cloud over the remainder of his presidency. The Molinari clause specifically applied to criminal cases, not to a damage suit like Jones's, and Clinton might have been required to answer the questions anyway under the federal rules of civil procedure. But Jones's lawyers reminded the president during the deposition that he had signed the bill containing the measure that included a definition of "sexual relations" used in the question-and-answer session in Jones's complaint about his behavior in an Arkansas hotel room.

The new evidence rules applied to a tiny number of federal cases, but supporters hoped they would serve as a model. Federal Judge D. Brooks Smith of Pennsylvania called it the "height of arrogance" for federal lawmakers to assume that they should provide guidance for states in sex cases. Still, the dominant theory in Washington is that no matter what the crime type, the feds are supreme. In the words of a senior U.S. firearms agent: In law enforcement, "the federal government has to demonstrate leadership—to set the pace and tone."

In the case of the Molinari provision, some opponents of the evidence-rule change vowed to seek a reversal after her departure from Congress. But the Clinton case was so politically charged that it seemed unlikely that the law would be changed soon.

Beyond the unresolved debate over whether creeping federalization would prove a true threat to the federal justice apparatus, significant federal inroads into basic local law enforcement took place rapidly via executive action and congressional acquiescence.

The stage was set in the early 1980s. Street crime was on the rise, but the federal Law Enforcement Assistance Administration was being shut down, and

Ronald Reagan arrived at the White House with somewhat conflicting impulses: to clamp down hard on crime while not allowing Washington to usurp local prerogatives.

The solution was for the Justice Department to create Law Enforcement Co-ordinating Committees that included representatives of federal, state, and local investigating and prosecuting authorities. The panels, set up in most of the 93 federal judicial districts, met periodically to work out procedures for handling overlapping cases. To the extent that this change resulted in a synergy of re-sources and eliminated duplication, it was welcome. But when it made the lines between the various levels of government so murky that no one could tell when federal jurisdiction ended and state authority began, it may have been a disservice.

The evolving theory of federal-state law enforcement relationships largely abandoned the traditional idea that the feds should take on only the enforcement jobs that local authorities were incapable of doing. William Webster, FBI direc-tor between 1978 and 1987, was wary, as was J. Edgar Hoover in earlier decades, of the agency developing into one that would amount to a national police force. Webster favored beefing up the bureau's forensic laboratory capabilities and units like the FBI office that employed behavioral science experts who specialize in profiles of serial murderers. Few local agencies would have the need to main-tain such expertise, he reasoned. Louis Freeh, who became FBI chief in 1993, spoke in the same vein, promising a group of mayors two years later that he would create a "critical incident response group" that would "respond instantly and aggressively to child kidnappings and serial murders."[14]

Unlike Hoover, who tried to accumulate high totals of stolen car recoveries to impress the FBI's congressional funders, Webster and his direct predecessor, Clarence Kelley, tried to change the FBI culture to one that stressed quality over quantity. Webster occasionally had to fend off pressure to broaden the FBI's scope. During the Reagan administration, he was summoned to a White House meeting with religious organizations that wanted the FBI to check motion pic-tures for obscenity violations.

Webster, a straight-arrow Republican, nevertheless found himself on the de-fensive as the group waited for the president to arrive, explaining to Cardinal John Krol of Philadelphia and other religious leaders that while he, too, was offended by obscenity, it did not threaten people's lives and that the FBI would not be comfortable assuming the role of censors by deciding which movies were worthy of federal investigations.

The FBI director was saved by some classic Reagan storytelling. The president began his remarks to the visitors by musing about how times had changed. In his earlier days as an actor, Reagan said, he would not be allowed to be filmed in bed with Doris Day. "To kiss her," he recalled, "I had to get out of bed, walk around, and give her a kiss on the other side." The story diverted the group from the FBI-enforcement issue—either deliberately or inadvertently—and Reagan then brought the session quickly to a close by suggesting that the attendees pose for pictures, getting Webster off the hook.

Meese did set up a controversial commission to study obscenity, but it did not result in the creation of new federal crimes. The Justice Department created a unit to concentrate on the subject, but it did not require a large commitment of FBI resources.

In more mainstream cases involving urban street criminals, however, the involvement of federal investigators continued to grow steadily. A major official step was the designation in 1989 of violent crime as one of the FBI's major priorities, enabling agents to be assigned to more cases previously viewed as local. (Of course, the agency long had had jurisdiction over certain potentially violent crimes, like kidnapping and bank robbery.)

Then in 1991, the Justice Department launched a program called Operation Triggerlock, which built on the ATF's Project Achilles that coordinated cases under the 1984 armed career criminal law. Now federal prosecutors in each judicial district were assigned to handle gun cases and to report their statistics to Washington periodically. "Everyone loved Triggerlock," wrote journalists Jim McGee and Brian Duffy in *Main Justice*, a book that documented its origin. "It required almost no additional funding, and it had the potential to run up big, impressive numbers of convictions."[15]

The Clinton administration was less enthralled, viewing Triggerlock as something of a gimmick started by its Republican predecessors, and the Justice Department put less emphasis on it after Janet Reno became attorney general in 1993. That led to a 46 percent drop in the number of federal firearms cases, which gave Republicans another basis on which to criticize the Clinton anticrime effort. The shift had two major causes: a routine change of priorities by a new administration and a sharp drop in the number of federal firearms agents, from about 2,200 to 1,700. At the same time, many states had toughened up their own firearms-prosecution programs, reducing the pressure for the feds to take action.

Republican Senator Jeff Sessions of Alabama, a former U.S. attorney himself, charged that Reno had "allowed Project Triggerlock to languish." But Justice Department officials stood their ground at a March 1999 hearing called by Sessions. They said that much of the decline in cases involved low-level offenders, who were getting sentences ranging from probation to three years in prison. The department also presented figures showing that state prosecutions of weapons offenders had increased, "more than offsetting the federal decline."

The administration of George H. W. Bush in its final year launched another major expansion of the federal role in street crime. On January 9, 1992, the FBI announced a "Safe Streets Violent Crimes Initiative" that encouraged the agents in charge of the bureau's 56 field offices to set up "proactive" task forces to deal with violence related to gangs and drugs. At the time, an estimated 200 gangs such as the Crips and the Bloods were operating in at least 35 states. Many gang members reportedly had migrated from East and West Coast cities to the heartland, thus arguably giving federal authorities some cause to act under their jurisdiction over interstate crime.

One way the FBI could quickly "reprogram" many of its agents was to take some 300 off of counterintelligence duty, given that the Cold War had come to an end, and shuffle the work force so that the same number could be added to local violence cases. This was not necessarily what FBI agents had joined the bureau to do, and there was some grumbling in the ranks, but most went along with the change.

Another productive task for federal agents, albeit not a very glamorous one, was to help track down large numbers of fugitives who had skipped court dates or otherwise eluded capture in previous years. Relatively little effort had been made to locate many of these defendants, even though they included career criminals. Fugitive task forces in the Washington, D.C., area, Newark, and Chicago were successful in reining in dozens of suspects.

The fugitive chases were widely publicized and successful at first, but the FBI later quietly shut down several of the task forces when they found that as many as three out of four fugitives in some areas could be easily located by merely sending agents to their home addresses or workplaces listed on their original arrest warrants. FBI officials concluded that such elemental police work was not worth their agents' time. Whether overburdened local authorities would decide to pick up the slack was problematic.

The Clinton administration was not content to limit its involvement in local crime to the initiative of the FBI, which after all could launch investigations but had to depend on federal prosecutors to bring the cases into court. Besides, the FBI was only one agency, if an important one. Under the federal government's diffuse law enforcement structure, separate agencies—most prominently ATF and the Drug Enforcement Administration—were heavily involved in violent-crime cases.

Based on proposals from career prosecutors that were vetted by top Justice Department political hands, on March 21, 1994, Attorney General Reno upped the ante in an announcement made from the White House's Oval Office. With Clinton, FBI Director Freeh, and other top law enforcers in attendance, Reno directed the 93 U.S. attorneys each to draw up a plan, in consultation with their local counterparts, to attack the worst violent crime problems in their districts. Authorities set up projects with handy code names. One such effort in New York, for example, was named JRAT—the Joint Robbery Apprehension Team.

Using federal racketeering laws and court-ordered wiretapping, among other techniques, the feds racked up an impressive series of cases. (The racketeering law, known as RICO, allowed prosecution of gang leaders in federal courts for conspiring to commit various crimes that, considered singly, might only be violations of state law.) In a report to Clinton issued during the 1996 presidential campaign, Reno said that the number of racketeering cases against gangs had increased 58 percent since 1990. She implied that this federal attack on violent crime was largely responsible for the national decline in violence reported by the FBI in 1994 and 1995, a rather extravagant claim in view of many other competing theories. The report did caution that "statistics alone cannot measure these successes."[16]

Few would quarrel with the merit of some major individual cases against gangs with colorful names, such as the 1995 "Bottoms Boyz" prosecution in Shreveport, Louisiana, or the "Short North Posse" roundup in Columbus, Ohio, the same year. Some cases were based on unusual uses of longstanding federal statutes, such as the Hobbs Act, which prohibits interference with interstate commerce. One prosecution in the Dallas area put two men in prison for 30 years for robberies that included fast-food chains. An FBI agent reflected that it felt odd to be pursuing a probe highlighted by a stickup at a McDonald's outlet.

The new federal thrust was no doubt politically popular, but some veteran enforcers worried that other kinds of cases suffered when federal agents went after guns and gangs. One of the leading skeptics was Harvard's Philip Heymann, who headed the Justice Department's criminal division in the administration of Jimmy Carter and served as Janet Reno's deputy in the early Clinton years before resigning in a falling out over policy and working style. Heymann believed that federal investigators should be devoting their full efforts to such issues as international crimes and technological developments that are beyond the scope of state and local police. "There is a very strong argument that the federal government should not be using its law enforcement capacities to deal with street crimes, even when the public is gravely concerned about that problem," Heymann wrote with Harvard colleague Mark Moore.[17]

In this belief, Heymann agreed with Reagan's attorney general Meese, who noted that the "principal progress against crime has not been the result of any federal effort." Meese yearned for the day when "real statesmen" in Congress will stand up and say, "Let's not make a federal case of it."

Meese's hope is probably unrealistic. The trend of members of Congress leaping on the "crime du jour" seems too well established to reverse. As one Justice Department insider noted, "This is not only a 1990s phenomenon—most of the federal drug and gun laws were passed between the 1930s and the 1960s. That's where the [major] prosecution numbers are." From their vantage point,

Justice Department career prosecutors agreed with many of their supervisors who held political appoinments that the critics of federalization had vastly overstated their case and that most criminal cases in overlapping jurisdictions were being handled responsibly.

After studying the issue, the ABA task force—which included representatives from all government levels as well as academia—concluded in its 1999 report that increasing federalization posed some subtle but important problems that could not be measured with statistics and anecdotes. Chief among them were fears that the gradual shift to federal authorities would discourage private citizens from believing that they had much impact on the crime problem and that the justice system overall would increasingly be perceived as unfair, as various levels of prosecutors made arbitrary and unappealable decisions about what cases to pursue. "Inappropriately federalized crime causes serious problems to the administration of justice in this country," concluded the task force.

Despite the certainty that some high-profile local crimes would continue to provoke congressional demands for federal action, there were some signs in the late 1990s that more rational policies were in prospect. One impetus was the increased skepticism among both civil libertarians and conservatives about some uses of federal police power. The Branch Davidian conflagration at Waco, Texas, and the killing of Vicki Weaver at Ruby Ridge, Idaho—both of which began as federal firearms cases—intensified the questioning of federal capabilities in handling explosive situations.

A federal commission chaired by former FBI Director Webster and created by Congress in light of the Waco and Ruby Ridge incidents weighed in on federalization in early 2000. The panel concluded that the trend poses "enormous practical burdens" for federal law enforcers and courts, "distracts federal law enforcement agencies from more serious criminal activity involving national interests, and may even bring the system of criminal justice into disrepute."[18] Despite the commission's strong language, some of its other recommendations were viewed as unrealistic in turf-conscious Washington, particularly one that would give ATF's firearms-investigation authority to the FBI.

Within the bureaucracy itself, the trends were mixed. In the FBI, formation of the "Safe Streets" units escalated rapidly after the Clinton administration overlaid its own violent-crime plan on the FBI's. One supervisor was alarmed to find that in 1994–95, he was given just 60 days to expand the concept in each of the bureau's 56 field offices—far too quickly for a national program to develop efficiently. On paper, the number of task forces exploded from 80 to 120 in just a few months.

Since then, the program has grown steadily if not spectacularly, reaching 174 task forces involving 805 FBI agents as of March 31, 2000. The number of cases generated was remarkably consistent over the 1993 to 1999 span—roughly 24,000 arrests that produced between 7,000 and 9,500 indictments and convictions each year. The FBI could boast of many breakthroughs, not all of them in the largest urban areas. An investigation of the Murder Town Gangster Crips in an Omaha public housing project, for example, resulted in a 70-year prison term for a gang leader and sentences of 3 to 7 years for 15 other members on drug charges.

Some other diversions have been more problematic. The Washington, D.C., area always has been a major enforcement hot spot, not only because of its undeniably high crime rate but also because of its high political visibility. Much of D.C.'s high-crime area adjoins Prince George's County, Md., where Police Chief John Farrell pleaded with Attorney General Reno, with whom he had worked in Miami, for help in dealing with Washington's crime overflow.

In March 1997, the Justice Department responded by assigning 50 FBI agents to Farrell's department for a two-month "blitz" against murderers, drug dealers, and armed robbers. "They're flying in agents from all over the country to work side by side with detectives," said Lynne Battaglia, the U.S. attorney for Maryland.[19]

The growth has not been unabated. FBI officials say that they have reined in some units that were straying too far into routine local crimes and have closed some task forces that have accomplished their main tasks. In addition, the widely hailed 1994 Justice Department prosecution initiative, which never had much special funding to begin with, had largely exhausted it by the middle of Clinton's second term.

As both major political parties continued competing to appear the toughest on crime, federal retrenchment on prosecuting violent crime seemed unlikely. In fact, the FBI issued a long report on its safe streets task forces in 2000, saying it was pursuing the "street gangs and other loosely knit groups [that] are responsible for a substantial portion of the increase in violent crime in the United States."

Washington's attack on local crime has gone far beyond prosecuting gang members. Since the early 1970s, Congress has staked out a federal role in dealing with the violent teenagers who are responsible for some of the nation's most heinous offenses.

Chapter 5

NOT GETTING THEM YOUNG

A horrific series of shooting sprees by public school students in the late 1990s had politicians and bureaucrats in Washington scurrying for solutions to the latest high-profile juvenile crime problem. But the remedies seemed just as elusive as they had a quarter-century earlier, when the capital was embroiled in another struggle over how best to fight violence committed by teenagers.

Policymakers split then and now over the tension between trying to stop crime-prone kids before they started and holding accountable those who already had broken the law. This prevention versus punishment debate played itself out in Congress and the federal bureaucracy, with the result that neither was pursued very consistently.

From the beginning, authority over the two basic elements of the juvenile crime problem was diffused in both government branches. That spawned a bureaucratic morass of duplication and confusion. "The national effort against juvenile delinquency was notably uncoordinated," concluded political scientist Thomas Cronin.[1] By the 1970s, he counted at least seven federal cabinet departments, dozens of subcabinet units, and thousands of federally subsidized state and local programs with some part in the fight against juvenile crime.

The mess was obvious as long ago as 1968, when the first major federal anticrime law was enacted. The Law Enforcement Assistance Administration (LEAA) created to aid states and localities did not devote much attention to juvenile violence. A separate law on youth crime gave the job of administering it to the cabinet department then known as Health, Education and Welfare (HEW), later called Health and Human Services (HHS).

Because Congress generally reflects the executive branch structure, different committees dealt with the juvenile crime programs in departments they oversaw. In the House of Representatives, the Judiciary Committee had oversight responsibility over most of the Justice Department. But the part of Justice assigned to fight juvenile crime reported to a different panel, Education and Labor.

The confused reporting lines were solidified in a landmark 1974 law that Congress had not managed to overhaul by the start of the twenty-first century. The statute established a pot of federal money that was aimed at giving Washington considerable influence in steering states toward the rehabilitative approach to juvenile crime. Drafted principally by liberal senators Birch Bayh of Indiana and John Culver of Iowa, the law imposed strict eligibility requirements for states to get their aid.

One of the most prominent was "sight and sound" separation of accused juveniles and adults. On the assumption that one of the worst things that could happen to impressionable youths would be to lock them up with adult career criminals, Congress stipulated that to receive federal aid, states and localities would have to provide separate lockups. The theory was defensible, given the long record of abuse suffered by juveniles in custody, but the rule stuck in the craw of rural sheriffs whose tiny lockups did not allow them to keep teens and adults completely apart. Sheriffs who wanted to jail teen suspects might be required to drive them long distances to find a jail that complied with the rules.

Another major goal of the new law was to do away with incarceration for "status offenses," criminal charges against teenagers that could not be filed against adults, such as breaking curfews, skipping school, or running away from home. Critics maintained that authorities too often used such charges unwisely and unfairly to punish youths in ways that encouraged them to commit more, not less, crime. In some places, going to jail became a badge of honor for young gang members. As with separating teens from adult criminals, states that continued to imprison status offenders would be denied help from Washington.

The 1974 law's progressive philosophy was prevalent in an era when crime rates had not yet increased dramatically. The big question was a bureaucratic one: Who would administer the new law? Even though HEW had been given the lead, by 1974 the senators who had oversight authority over the Justice Department flexed their political muscles and prevailed over House members who favored HEW. The new law shifted the power to Justice, where a unit was created under the unwieldy name of the Office of Juvenile Justice and Delinquency Prevention (OJJDP) to direct the federal battle against juvenile crime.

Despite its presumed importance in crime policy, OJJDP for much of its existence functioned as a poorly funded, largely neglected political stepchild of the federal anticrime apparatus. Senator Bayh wanted the office to get well over $100 million annually in its start-up years. But the administration of Gerald Ford, which inherited a law that had been written in the waning days of the Nixon presidency, persuaded Congress to approve only about $25 million, a minuscule sum for a national program trying to deal with a major social problem.

OJJDP's budget gradually increased, and the 1974 law ended up having a significant impact on the way states handled many routine juvenile crimes via its rules on separate youth jails and status offenders. OJJDP—which functioned as a largely independent unit in the Justice Department's 633 Indiana Avenue building that dealt with states and localities—was hobbled by having to operate under a long series of political patronage heads who had sharply different ideas about how to do business.

Like most federal anticrime agencies that aided states and cities, OJJDP was something of an anomaly. It was headed by a presidential appointee starting in the late 1970s, but it never was given authority over anti-teen crime programs governmentwide. OJJDP administered most of Washington's aid for states and localities, but other cabinet agencies, particularly HHS and the Labor Department, remained free to develop their own programs. Some complemented the Justice Department's; others didn't. "There is no federal youth policy—there never has been," said law professor Peter Edelman of Georgetown University, a juvenile delinquency expert who tried to cope with the problem as a senior HHS official during the early years of the Clinton administration. "Even if you add up every federal program targeted to adolescents, it's pitiful."[2]

OJJDP operated mostly in the bureaucratic backwater during the presidency of Jimmy Carter, which paid relatively little attention to the problem of street crime. Ira Schwartz, a University of Pennsylvania social work expert who headed OJJDP in the late 1970s, did succeed in getting legislation passed to improve jail conditions for accused juveniles.

By the time the Reagan administration took office in 1981, OJJDP was viewed with disdain by Republican ideologues who came into office determined to get tough on crime. Conservatives pegged the small agency as one that would reflexively favor a lax, rehabilitative approach to crime rather than promoting ideas that promised to hold dangerous teens accountable for their heinous acts through long terms in custody.

It wasn't long before the Reagan White House, looking for fat to trim in what it regarded as a bloated federal bureaucracy, zeroed in on the juvenile crime unit. Reagan budget cutters viewed OJJDP as yet another example of a superfluous federal agency that performed functions duplicating those that should be done by state and local governments.

It wasn't that the administration didn't want to fight youth violence. Edwin Meese, a senior Reagan aide from Reagan's days as governor of California who followed him to the White House, knew the federal program well from his service on the juvenile justice program's advisory committee in California. The official Reagan line was that federal aid for efforts against youth crime wouldn't end; it would remain an option for states to allocate within "block grants" of allocations for social services from Washington.

Insiders quickly realized that the total amount that would be available to the states from federal coffers was far from enough to maintain going at full strength all the programs like OJJDP that the Reagan Republicans were trying to consolidate. It was obvious to anyone who could do the math that something would have to give.

Most vulnerable were small agencies that lacked strong backers. At first glance, it seemed likely that a popular new Republican president, in tandem with a newly elected GOP Senate majority, would work its will and eliminate OJJDP, which probably would not be able to produce much evidence to justify the nearly $100 million it was spending each year. After all, the much larger LEAA had just been killed by Democrats who might have been expected to support federal largesse in an attack on a social problem like street crime.

But Reagan's budget cutters didn't count on Arlen Specter. The one-time Philadelphia prosecutor, who won a Senate seat in 1980, decided to capitalize on his background and focus on crime legislation during his freshman term. Specter's main cause was the Armed Career Criminal Act, which would make it possible for prosecutors to convert a succession of state-level offenses into potential federal crimes.

It was possible in 1981 for a new senator in the unexpected Republican majority to snag his own subcommittee. Specter pressed to be named chairman of the Senate Judiciary Subcommittee on juvenile crime, which he then used as a platform for a national campaign against crime. He worked to link his two major interests—youth crime and repeat offenses—by arguing for an approach that would include both prevention and punishment. Specter believed that "we should try to identify early those who would be career criminals," recalled one adviser. "Some juveniles could be saved, and at the other end of the spectrum were three-time losers."

Specter, who prided himself on being one of the few federal lawmakers who had served as a big-city prosecutor, saw the progression of criminal behavior as a "seamless web." He calculated that a typical pattern was "truancy at ages 7 and 8, vandalism at 9 and 10, larceny and auto theft by 14, burglary of vacant houses at 15, then armed robbery, and murder."[3] Unlike some of his more conservative colleagues who aimed to eliminate federal aid programs, Specter arrived in Washington believing that the federal government could have an impact on youthful violence. He hoped to be able to save OJJDP so that it would pay for innovative programs and studies that local agencies would not have the resources to initiate, just as LEAA had done during Specter's tenure as district attorney in Philadelphia.

Certainly, Specter's budding career as a legislator would suffer if the primary crime-fighting agency under his Senate jurisdiction were eliminated. And the unit had won support among state officials that received its funds. Pennsylvanians, who were among OJJDP's strongest backers, began pressuring their new senator to take on the White House.

Other interest groups that supported the agency's mission took up the campaign. Under the federal juvenile-crime law, each state maintains an advisory committee of citizens and justice-system officials who monitor youth-crime issues. With the federal aid program in jeopardy, many supporters sprang into action. One of them was Marion Mattingly, a longtime member of the Maryland advisory panel. Mattingly was a Republican who lived in the Washington, D.C., suburbs and was well positioned to jump into the fray.

Mattingly had served on the transition team that got Reagan administration programs going in the law enforcement area, so she was familiar with the key players. Mattingly knew that Herbert Ellingwood, an assistant to Reagan confidant Edwin Meese, was the man to see as Meese's liaison to criminal-justice interests. Mattingly asked for an appointment and ended up spending nearly three hours arguing the case for the federal program. With OJJDP's emphasis on getting volunteers involved to supplement government handouts, she said, the agency should be popular among Republicans.

But Mattingly received a striking example of the difference a conservative Republican administration would bring in Washington when it came to shaping anticrime policy. Ellingwood insisted that under the president's budget-cutting plans, there wasn't enough available in the Justice Department budget to keep the juvenile crime office going. Ellingwood, a fundamentalist Christian activist, said that preacher Jerry Falwell would help make up for the loss of the federal program by getting his adherents involved in the fight against crime. And the Meese adviser stunned Mattingly by telling her that the new administration had another way to fight youth violence: Reagan had met with actor Sylvester Stallone, whose Rocky and Rambo movies would serve as inspirations to teenagers that would dissuade them from taking up lives of crime. "I didn't know whether to laugh or cry," Mattingly said later. "But he seemed absolutely serious."[4]

Seeing that she wasn't getting anywhere, Mattingly decided that she had better try rallying support outside the Washington beltway. She identified organizations like the American Legion that had backed the agency and had the conservative credentials to be respected by the Reagan administration. Operating from OJJDP's office (where such lobbying by federal employees would violate the law), she asked leaders of those groups to write letters to the White House and Congress pleading that OJJDP be spared from the budget-cutting ax.

Mattingly's activism was aimed at supporting what became an annual ritual orchestrated by the aggressive Specter in the early 1980s. The Reagan White House would announce in its annual budget proposal that it wanted to eliminate OJJDP. Then Specter would schedule hearings of his Juvenile Justice panel to produce testimony about the agency's accomplishments. To make matters worse from the administration's view, Specter also held a seat on the Appropriations Committee and thus had a direct voice in determining the executive branch's budget.

Specter ended up keeping OJJDP in business, but it was no easy task for a lone freshman senator. One Specter staffer said his boss decided "almost out of the air" that $70 million would make a good annual budget total to seek for the threatened agency. As an experienced legal negotiator, Specter knew that the figure would seem a reasonable compromise that could lower the program under the White House Office of Management and Budget's radar screen of major targets that exceeded $100 million.

Specter wasn't above horse trading; he suggested that some of the funds needed to keep OJJDP alive be taken out of another program under the Judiciary panel's jurisdiction—a federal office that dealt with patents and trademarks. He was able to win support from other moderate Republicans like New Mexico's Pete Domenici. The White House came to realize that it would be difficult to shut down an agency that had attracted supporters nationwide by handing out money for nearly a decade.

Another moderate Republican who helped to thwart the Reagan shutdown effort was Connecticut's Lowell Weicker, who headed the Senate subcommittee that funded the Justice Department. The Reagan administration had asked Charles Lauer, a career government lawyer, to tend OJJDP as the battle was fought over closing it. Knowing he would be asked by Weicker in the annual appropriations hearing what would happen if states were asked to pick up the slack, Lauer did a survey and found that only a small handful vowed to keep juvenile justice programs going at their same level if OJJDP shut its doors. Weicker commended Lauer for giving him the honest answer that was not uttered by Reagan political appointees, who insisted that programs would not suffer by being converted to block grants.

The Reagan administration did succeed in some efforts to close agencies, but in the case of juvenile justice, they came up dry. It was easy for critics to round up protests from groups whose funds would be cut off by a closure, but it was tough for the Reagan team to find knowledgeable advocates for zeroing out OJJDP. Lamented one Justice Department political appointee, "There is no constituency for nothing."

Some key Reagan advisers may have been less hostile to OJJDP than the administration's official stance implied. At one point, Acting Director Lauer briefed William French Smith, the corporate attorney from Los Angeles who served as Reagan's first attorney general but who had no experience in the anticrime war, about the basic purposes of the juvenile crime law. When Lauer explained the federal aim of persuading states to separate youthful suspects from adults and restrict status offenses, Smith was incredulous that teens and hardened adult criminals would be thrown into the same cells. "Why would states do that?" he asked. Lauer then informed Smith that in many cases it was only because of the requirement to obtain federal aid that states were changing their practices.[5]

When Specter, Weicker, and other lawmakers refused to close OJJDP, the Reagan administration found itself in the awkward position of having to operate an agency that it wanted to eliminate. For two years while it did battle on Capitol Hill, the White House left OJJDP in career official Lauer's hands. When it became clear that the agency could not be killed, the administration devised another strategy: appoint an iconoclast to head it. It tapped Alfred Regnery, the son of a conservative publisher who had been working in the Justice Department's lands and natural resources unit and who had no background in dealing with juvenile crime.

Regnery had the correct instinct from the White House's point of view: advocate hard-line tactics against young criminals. Confident of confirmation because he had worked for powerful Nevada senator and Judiciary Committee member Paul Laxalt, Regnery announced to OJJDP's staff his support for stiffening punishments of juvenile offenders even before the Senate voted on his nomination. Violent 16-year-olds "are criminals who happen to be young, not children who happen to commit crimes," he was quoted by author Rita Kramer, whose book criticized juvenile courts for focusing on "youths who stole cars, picked off fruit stands or carried zip guns."[6]

Liberal organizations that long had supported OJJDP quickly put out the word to amass any derogatory information that might scuttle Regnery's nomination. The tips ranged from a supposed bumper sticker on Regnery's car that advocated corporal punishment to reports (which he denied) that he had been accused of domestic violence and had acted bizarrely while observing the birth of one of his children. Regnery eventually was confirmed by a 69 to 22 vote—a surprisingly high opposition total for a subcabinet nominee.

The new OJJDP chief faced strong obstacles in his attempts to change the direction of a federal law that had been on the books for the better part of a decade. As described in a sympathetic account published in a compendium of Reagan administration efforts to overhaul the bureaucracy called "Steering the Elephant; How Washington Works," Regnery was challenged at every turn by an "iron triangle" of bureaucrats, lawmakers, and lobbyists for organizations that received OJJDP grants. "I would make a decision and within half an hour be called by one of Senator Specter's staffers, wondering, in amazement, if I had really done what she had heard," Regnery said. "Then I would be called by a grantee in California to tell me what a bad decision I had made."[7]

The new chief hired as his deputy a conservative Virginia lawyer named James Wootton, who also was convinced that the juvenile courts were too lax. As a defense attorney for juvenile crime suspects, Wooton had been "struck by the cavalier attitude the defendants had about coming in contact with the juvenile justice system—they seemed to know that nothing much was going to happen to them."[8]

The two Reagan appointees moved to reassign careerists they viewed as hostile to the conservative cause. Regnery then began canceling tens of millions of dollars in grants that had been awarded by his predecessors to what he regarded as liberal groups he believed were wasting federal dollars on programs with goals like trying to finance jobs for delinquents or filing lawsuits to vindicate young offenders' rights. One unfortunate grantee on the West coast lost out after a visiting Regnery aide noticed its staffers using a photograph of Ronald and Nancy Reagan as a dart board.

When Regnery tried to shift the agency's $70 million budget to conservative recipients, liberals often contested his new grants as inconsistent with the 1974 law that established the program. But Regnery pronounced the statute so vague that he was permitted to change course, invoking a provision that allowed him to award discretionary funds on a noncompetitive basis. The Reagan conservatives viewed the struggle as nothing less than an ideological war. Liberals were so alarmed at Regnery's raiding the "piggy bank for the left," said deputy Wootton, that they tried to amend the law "to make the only people qualified to get the grants the people who were in their network."

From Regnery's vantage point, he merely was putting a conservative slant on what liberals had done for years. After listening to Ohio's liberal Senator Howard Metzenbaum and Pennsylvania's Specter "rant and rave about all the awful things we were doing," Regnery said, "that just confirmed to me that we were doing the right thing." One of the first beneficiaries of shifting OJJDP's focus was a former aide to George Deukmejian, Reagan's successor as California governor, who got $3 million to set up a National School Safety Center at California's Pepperdine University.

One signature thrust of the Regnery regime was an attack on young chronic lawbreakers. It started with a veteran bureaucrat named Robert Heck, who, in 1974, had begun a Justice Department program called ICAP (Integrated Criminal Apprehension Program) to go after adult career criminals. Crime records were often so poorly collected that law enforcers were oblivious to the rap sheets of those they picked up for relatively minor crimes. Under ICAP, federal funds went to police departments that would compile lists of those with long records and try to ensure that the book was thrown at them when they got into trouble again.

After the program had scored several successes over the years, a Wisconsin official asked Heck in the late 1970s, "What are you going to do about the little bastards who are junior career criminals?"[9] So he designed a version of ICAP for repeat juvenile criminals, but higher-ups in Jimmy Carter's Justice Department were not interested in pursuing it.

The Reagan hardliners were more receptive, so Heck worked between 1983 and 1986 to create two models with typically bureaucratic names—SHOCAP (Serious Habitual Offender Criminal Apprehension Program) and SHODI (Serious Habitual Offenders, Drug Involved). Heck persuaded 5 of the 17 local law enforcement agencies that were receiving funds for the adult ICAP to test the juvenile version.

The basic idea was the same: come down hard on youths with long records, a technique that sometimes included stepping up police surveillance on those with extended rap sheets. Wootton said liberal critics "resisted every step of the way" because SHOCAP ran counter to the longstanding liberal "ideology that kids really weren't responsible for what they did." More troubling to some detractors was the idea that a record of past infractions was sufficient evidence to justify officers' keeping watch over youths on public streets in what the critics regarded as a kind of Orwellian surveillance.

SHOCAP encountered some difficulty getting off the ground because of the traditional secrecy of juvenile-crime records, which were excluded even from some computerized systems available to police officers. To conservatives like Wootton, not keeping records on kids was a "fiction that they're essentially innocent." Wootton conceded that most youths who get into trouble with the law do so only once, but he argued that having rap sheets available on all of them was necessary to narrow the pool to the truly dangerous.

SHODI, the program for young drug offenders, had its own problems. Police officers found that judges, instead of sentencing youths to long terms behind bars, were putting them in drug treatment agencies. That may have been fine in theory, but in practice the teens tended to be among the worst offenders. They were so disruptive that they "were tearing up the programs," said Heck. Eventually, many didn't bother to appear for treatment, and those running the agencies were glad not to see them.

Heck kept working during the 1980s to fine-tune his inventions. The lack of record-sharing among the main components of the justice system proved a constant problem. "Everyone—cops, judges, and prosecutors—blamed each other," Heck recalled. As a hardliner in sync with the Reagan administration's views, Heck eventually concluded that the "juvenile justice system was a farce," in large part because officials refused to exchange data on many of the most dangerous offenders in their jurisdictions.

What Heck was encountering was the strong tradition of the juvenile court, the institution created in Chicago before the turn of the twentieth century and later replicated nationwide to hear cases, behind closed doors, against youths arrested before their 18th birthday. Advocates of juvenile courts insist that special treatment for teen delinquents, focused on preventing future crimes, offer the best chance of steering young troublemakers back on the right course. Hardliners argue that by the second half of the twentieth century, such a "social-work" approach was ill equipped to cope with teens they believed were becoming hardened criminals at younger and younger ages. Critics pointed to kids barely into their teens who seemed to have no remorse about killing and maiming others.

The essential theory behind juvenile courts was that the accused were too immature to appreciate fully the difference between right and wrong. The juvenile court and corrections system supposedly would have the flexibility to deal with teen troublemakers without exposing them to hardened adult criminals. If the juveniles did straighten out their lives, their records of lawbreaking would be sealed forever, as if nothing had happened.

That was the theory. In reality, juvenile courts were taking on more trappings of the adult justice system. The Supreme Court ruled in 1967 that juvenile suspects could invoke essentially the same legal protections as could adult defendants. Many needy defendants got little significant legal help, but the potential existed for an adversarial proceeding.

As the field of juvenile rights was evolving, crime fighters were struggling with a more basic question: how to identify and bear down on the highly concentrated universe of young perpetrators. Those who prey on victim after victim are primarily boys in their teens or early 20s, and the chronic offenders make up only a small fraction of that age group. This target population was highlighted in a pioneering 1972 study led by Marvin Wolfgang of the University of Pennsylvania.[10] Although a surprisingly high 35 percent of Philadelphia's young men had been arrested for something more serious than a traffic infraction, only about 6 percent of youths born around the same time were responsible for well over half of serious crimes. Later studies had arrived at a similar conclusion: anywhere from 5 to 15 percent of youths commit up to 80 percent of violent offenses.

The fact that most of America's serious crime problem can be traced to a few people begs the questions of how best to identify those offenders and what to do with them if they are caught. Harvard criminologist David Kennedy framed the issue this way: "If we know who they are; if they offend frequently; if they are frequently arrested and often convicted; if they are frequently on

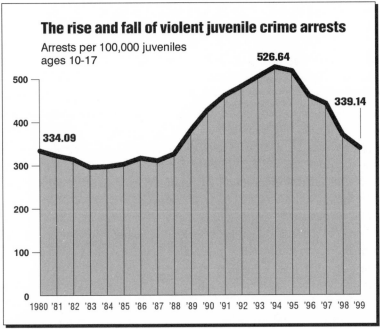

The rise and fall of violent juvenile crime arrests

Arrests per 100,000 juveniles
ages 10-17

526.64

339.14

334.09

Source: National Center for Juvenile Justice

probation, in jail and prison, and on parole; why are we not able to stop them from reoffending? It is a good question."[11]

Reagan administration officials in the juvenile justice agency groped for ways to go after young career criminals. The theories seemed endless. Some social scientists blamed family factors, primarily the absence of child-rearing fathers in many inner-city families. Others cited a shortage of jobs, poor education, inadequate housing, and a general lack of hope among many teens. Those may all have contributed, but it was simplistic to single out only one cause, because only a minority of youths who faced these problems turned to crime. It seemed that youths' reaction to other hard-to-measure elements, from violence on television to levels of neighborhood social cohesion, also played a part.

Wolfgang's studies in Philadelphia had established the appropriate precedent for research: follow "birth cohorts" of children born in particular years, carefully comparing those who got into trouble with the law with those who did not. Logical as that may sound, such studies rarely are undertaken because they are expensive and labor-intensive. By definition, a long-term federally financed effort would not yield results until well after whatever presidential administration had started it was long gone. Announcing an immediate crackdown on young murderers was much easier.

It was the determination of one official in the Reagan administration that succeeded in getting an extensive longitudinal study off the ground. James (Chips) Stewart was a former police officer in Oakland, Calif., who served as a White House Fellow in 1981 and then moved to the Justice Department, where he was put in charge of the research agency, the National Institute of Justice (NIJ).

Stewart recognized that a long-running juvenile-crime study could pay big dividends, but he also understood that his unit lacked the resources to fund it. Anticrime research long had suffered at budget time. NIJ typically got about $20 million each year, a pittance by Washington standards. Criminologists were fond of complaining about the anomaly that federal funds to study tooth decay, a problem long since brought under control, far exceeded that allocated to the control of crime—presumably one of the public's main concerns. It was something of a vicious circle. Crime, unlike dental disease, was perceived as such an amorphous problem of human behavior that it had not proved very conducive to scientific research. But when the public and its elected politicians would seemingly demand instant answers to crime, the research rarely was there to support one remedy or another, so policymakers were even more skeptical about investing in studies.

A few private foundations had devoted resources to crime studies. The Chicago-based MacArthur Foundation, for one, had expressed interest in a longitudinal project after criminologist Norval Morris of the University of Chicago held a series of meetings with foundation officials to refine the idea. But MacArthur had not gone forward amid disagreement among other experts over how best to proceed. After observing several of these fruitless sessions, Stewart approached MacArthur director James Furman with an unusual proposal: the federal government would enter into a partnership with MacArthur to conduct a long-running, comprehensive study of the contributors to delinquency.[12]

Furman was dubious. The Justice Department, especially under the conservative Reagan administration, seemed highly unlikely to put a large chunk of its limited research funds into a study that would cover problems far beyond its mandate, such as how mothers cared for their children before birth. If anything, the Reagan forces were known for a get-tough policy that favored less, not more, federal spending on subjects related to juvenile crime. Even if Washington contributed some start-up money, Furman recalled later, "We feared that the federal government would get out and we wouldn't have ongoing support."[13]

Furman consulted with one of his board members, Dr. Jonas Salk, who affirmed that "cohort studies" had been valuable in the development of a polio vaccine and might work in the analysis of delinquency, too. For his part, Justice's Stewart went to his own friends who knew Salk and could vouch for his good intentions. Other backing came from Murray Gell-mann, a Nobel Prize-winning physicist on the MacArthur board. Still, Furman "could not in his wildest imagination imagine the Justice Department supporting" the idea. Indeed, Stewart found that he was virtually alone among major figures in the Reagan Justice Department. Others, including those at the assistant attorney general level, took a dim view of the potential MacArthur partnership. One called it "idiocy," and another labeled it "sort of communist."

But Stewart was persistent. By the time the study proposal had reached the decisionmaking stage, Edwin Meese had taken over for William French Smith as attorney general. Although Meese was generally known as more of an anti-crime hardliner than the civil-law expert Smith, unlike his predecessor, Meese had spent most of his career in the criminal-justice system, mostly as a prosecutor in Stewart's former home of Oakland. The two had not worked together—by the time Stewart joined the police force, Meese was advising then-California Governor Reagan. But they had plenty of mutual acquaintances, and Stewart felt comfortable approaching Meese directly on important issues.

So Stewart appealed to the attorney general on the longitudinal study issue. To the surprise of many, Meese approved it. When Stewart reported back to the MacArthur director, Furman said, "You're kidding—my board won't believe this." The foundation promptly agreed to co-sponsor the project, and the Justice Department committed itself to spending $5 million each year for the next decade. This would have been a tiny sum for a military-weapons project, but it was a huge amount for a chronically starved crime-research program.

Stewart stayed behind after Meese was replaced by former Pennsylvania Governor Richard Thornburgh, doing everything he could to keep the project going. Thornburgh did nothing to disturb it, although he did make it clear that Stewart had no chance of a higher position in the anticrime agency because he lacked a law degree. Stewart later resigned to become a law enforcement consultant.

The complex study took many years to get underway. One early issue was where to conduct it. The final choices ended up being Baltimore, Chicago, and Los Angeles, with Chicago getting the nod partly because its structure of distinct neighborhoods more easily allowed the study of a wide range of socioeconomic classes and ethnic/racial groups in small areas.

By the late 1990s, the project involved interviews with more than 8,800 people in 80 neighborhoods chosen among Chicago's 343 identifiable living areas. Not surprisingly, the urban teens had considerable exposure to violence: More than one in five 15-year-olds had seen someone shot, and 87 percent had witnessed some kind of serious fighting.

Analyzing the data will take well into the twenty-first century, but in their preliminary findings, the social scientists directing the study theorized that the level of social cohesion in a neighborhood had a lot to do with its crime rate. "By far the largest predictor of the violent crime rate was collective efficacy," project leaders said in 1997. "Collective efficacy" referred generally to the extent to which neighborhood residents got involved in dealing with delinquents' problems like truancy and joining gangs. Such citizen action had long been talked about, but the Chicago study may end up proving the importance of community participation.

Furman, who after leaving the MacArthur staff continued to monitor the project as a board member, recalled having had to overcome opposition from experts who expressed "the fear that it could be used to isolate the underclass," presumably by giving ammunition to a policy of denying welfare aid to those with criminal tendencies. The project stirred other opposition after the *Chicago Tribune* published a series in 1993 and 1994 on genes and aggression. A letter to the editor charged that the human development study's unstated aim was to find a "violence gene," and a coalition was formed to work against the project. The study's managers deflected the attack by hiring a public relations consultant and meeting with community leaders to explain that they were not seeking to link crime and genetics.

While the Chicago project was gaining momentum during the 1980s, back at OJJDP in Washington, money continued flowing to a few programs that attacked serious juvenile crime. But tiny experiments in a few cities had mixed results, none of which could be viewed as definitive. Overall, compared with efforts to research health problems like cancer and heart disease, the crime projects were woefully limited during a period when juvenile violence began a sharp climb in the midst of a crack cocaine epidemic in many big cities.

The many years of conservative attacks on the federal juvenile crime program during the Reagan and Bush administrations hardly inspired the bureaucrats running it to take chances on innovative programs, so the agency largely limped along for 12 years. Regnery himself departed after about three years, before the crack problem reached full strength. The conservative ideologue was hounded by critics who pounced on an $800,000 grant he approved for a researcher at The American University in Washington, D.C., to study how magazines like *Playboy, Penthouse,* and *Hustler* depicted children in order to determine how the portrayals may have contributed to crime. Regnery defended the project, even after the university itself attempted to stop it, but he conceded that it became an "albatross" around his administration, blunting his own criticism of grants awarded by his liberal predecessors.

The conservative Reagan appointees heading OJJDP were unpopular with the liberal-leaning careerists. Some of them criticized Wootton, Regnery's deputy, for channeling what they considered a dubious $1 million grant to an organization called the Partnership for a Drug-Free America. After Regnery and Wootton left, the Bush administration continued the practice of naming ideological conservatives with scant crime-fighting records to head the juvenile justice program, perpetuating OJJDP's erratic record. But the new administrators could not agree on which policies they wanted to pursue, as the story of Robert Heck's SHOCAP program demonstrates.

Heck had funneled money to several medium-sized cities, most prominently Oxnard, California, which had become convinced that SHOCAP helped to reduce violent juvenile crime. But like many other federal anticrime programs over the years, it never was subjected to a rigorous national evaluation (one OJJDP official, asked by a reporter to cite evidence of SHOCAP's worth, pointed to a favorable article in the *Reader's Digest*).

Robert Sweet, a conservative activist who had been tapped to head OJJDP in the Bush administration, was asked by higher-ups in the Justice Department to shift SHOCAP funds to a new effort called "Weed and Seed," named for its goal to weed out lawbreakers from inner-city neighborhoods and plant the seeds leading toward community improvements. The program had been conceived and nicknamed by Andrew McBride, an aide to William Barr, who had risen to deputy attorney general and later attorney general after Thornburgh left. Despite its hokey name, Weed and Seed was a reasonably well-thought-out notion that was continued by the Clinton administration, which increased the number of weed and seed sites from 23 to more than 200.

Start-up funds were another matter. After Sweet balked at yielding his agency's funds for the new program, a messy internal fight led to his resignation under pressure. Critics cited the episode as an example of why small agencies like OJJDP should not be headed by presidential appointees confirmed by the Senate. With support from Capitol Hill, they could run what amounted to independent bureaucratic fiefdoms within a cabinet department.

It fell to another OJJDP director, Gerald Regier, to end federal funding for SHOCAP. Regier, whose main claim to fame had been starting a private group called the Family Research Council to promote government policies to help preserve families, told Heck that the $1 million needed each year to administer his program was needed to help Weed and Seed. Regier also complained that SHOCAP's administrative costs were too high.

SHOCAP joined the long list of arguably effective government anticrime programs that have risen and fallen with the political tides. A program begun and then hobbled by conservative Republicans ended up being praised during the 1990s by appointees of President Clinton who were under pressure from a Republican-dominated Congress to show what OJJDP had done to be tough on juvenile crime. In fact, the Clinton administration ended up providing several hundred thousand dollars each year to the International Association of Chiefs of Police to train members in SHOCAP procedures.

SHOCAP and many other federal programs aimed at juvenile crime suffered from a more fundamental problem in the eyes of Michael Agopian, a California criminologist who served as OJJDP deputy director during the George H. W.

Bush years. In their zeal to run what amounted to an "ATM for grant money,"[14] Agopian believed agency officials devoted too much effort to pleasing small cities and counties and their juvenile court judges, who were adept at lobbying through a national organization that often was headed by rural jurists.

Despite criminologist Wolfgang's uncontested finding that only a few teen thugs were responsible for most serious crimes, big cities—where the problem was most concentrated—were not prominently represented when policy was made and federal money was allocated. For many years, Agopian argued, "OJJDP has been in denial that we have a violent juvenile crime problem."

As the 1992 presidential election approached and it seemed that Clinton had a good chance of prevailing—partly on the strength of the crime issue—a few longtime career officials in OJJDP devised a plan they believed might serve as a bridge to revitalize the agency in a Democratic era. Led by John Wilson, who had joined the agency as a young lawyer from Michigan in the 1970s and had risen to become general counsel and later deputy director, OJJDP issued in mid-1993 what it billed as a blueprint for dealing with delinquents of all stripes.

Picking up on Arlen Specter's "seamless web" notion, the bureaucrats suggested that instead of choosing between concentrating only on first offenders or on hardened criminals, the juvenile justice system should devise a graduated approach that would impose successively harsher penalties as teens were arrested for new offenses. While hardly a revolutionary idea (to the Bush era's Agopian, "graduated sanctions was a catchy phrase for what juvenile-justice officials have been doing for 25 years"), the plan had the virtue of appealing to both ends of the ideological spectrum on youth crime.

Low-level offenses could continue to be handled by juvenile courts, mostly avoiding putting delinquents in custody. At the more serious end, the Wilson report asserted that research during the Reagan era had "demonstrated that most violent juvenile offenders could be successfully rehabilitated through intensive treatment in small, secure facilities"—a conclusion that some experts believed was far too optimistic.

After Clinton took office, Attorney General Janet Reno put a trusted former lieutenant from her former Miami prosecutor's office, Sheldon (Shay) Bilchik, in charge of OJJDP. Although sometimes eclipsed by political operatives in the White House and the Justice Department who believed that he was too cautious, he did preside over programs with names like "comprehensive communities" and "safe futures" that attempted to widen the federal reach. They experimented with solutions to juvenile crime in local areas that used the graduated sanctions model and sought to get local residents more involved. Some insiders faulted Bilchik's skills as a bureaucratic infighter, but his reign was marked by a huge increase in his agency's budget.

In the political arena, community-based anticrime efforts championed by the juvenile-justice agency often were ignored during the 1990s as critics focused on another long-discussed "solution" to the problem of violent juvenile crime: sending youths for trial as adults. The conventional wisdom of conservatives and even some moderates and liberals was that juvenile courts, whatever the merits of the ways they had dealt with young toughs in bygone eras, were incapable of handling modern teens who were seemingly beyond redemption.

Such teens were dubbed "superpredators" by political scientist John DiIulio;[15] the term was roundly criticized by liberals, who argued that it grossly exaggerated the problem of violent teens. Although only a minuscule number of juveniles would commit such heinous crimes that they would be featured in the lead stories on television and radio newscasts and front-page accounts in newspapers, many citizens would assume that they were typical of a broad stratum of youths who deserved to be hit hard by "adult courts." Because the authority of most juvenile court systems expired when offenders reached the cutoff age of 18, critics huffed that the arbitrary dividing line was preventing the justice system from giving them the long prison sentences that adults could get.

Part of the logic seemed correct: that traditional juvenile courts had largely failed to deal with the chronically violent. Success stories were rarely heard, and certainly for some youths, during the few years that they would shuttle in and out of "training schools," many would become more schooled in the ways of crime. Few experts seriously argued that the short periods of a few months or possibly years that most young criminals were in custody provided enough time and resources to rehabilitate them.

But the notion that the adult courts somehow would do better was badly flawed. For one thing, it lacked an internal logic in the conservative critique of a permissive justice system. The supposedly tough adult tribunals where they wanted the superpredators sent often were the very same ones that the hardliners had long assailed as inefficient and soft on criminals.

And even in places where the courts did run well, it didn't stand to reason that judges would be particularly tough on older teens. A jurist faced, for example, with a 25-year-old who had been convicted of a dozen crimes and a 17-year-old who had "only" a half dozen offenses on his rap sheet naturally would treat the older defendant more harshly.

Clearly, the main motive for trying youths as adults was the potential for longer sentences behind bars. But that was all relative. In a justice system that typically handed out terms of fewer than ten years in prison for murder, the difference between a long sentence for an old teenager in adult court and a shorter term in a juvenile facility was usually not very much. In fact, in many cases, the terms of imprisonment handed out to juveniles were even longer than those given to defendants charged with similar crimes who had been certified for trial as adults and then entered into a plea bargain to a crime that could not be treated very seriously under the prevailing sentencing rules.

Among the meager research findings on the issue were the conclusions of several Florida criminologists in the mid-1990s that teens who had been tried as adults actually had higher repeat-crime rates than those who stayed in the juvenile justice system.[16] Of course, that does not mean that the transfer to adult court caused more crime. Rather, it may suggest that the transfer system was largely successful in identifying the worst of the young criminals. At least, it raises questions about whether trying juveniles as adults was necessarily an effective tactic.

Some authorities tried to get around the either-or choice between flawed juvenile and adult justice systems. A prominent example was chief Jacksonville, Fla., prosecutor Harry Shorstein, who frequently sent juveniles to adult trials under a state policy that allows prosecutors to decide the court level. But Shorstein set up a system of keeping the convicted youths in a local jail, where they could enroll in classes, counseling, or drug rehabilitation. Since the program began in 1993, juvenile arrests in Jacksonville dropped more sharply than in Florida and the nation as a whole.[17]

Few places have adopted the Jacksonville approach, preferring to focus on trying more teens as adults. The studies that showed the shortcomings of that tactic should have given pause to state policymakers who rapidly changed their juvenile-crime laws, but more than half of the states amended their crime codes during the 1990s to require certain accused violent teens to be shipped automatically to adult courts at younger and younger ages.

In the late 1990s, it appeared that some of the states that acted on the adult-court issue would be rewarded by getting preference for federal anticrime funds through a plan pushed by conservative Republicans in Congress and not opposed by the Clinton administration, which wanted to demonstrate its toughness against youth crime. But a wide-ranging juvenile crime bill that would embed the trial-as-adult policy in federal law stalled in Congress. So the Republicans who controlled Capitol Hill continued to enact less stringent versions of their plan via the appropriations process. Largely in reaction to the mass killing at Colorado's Columbine High School, the juvenile-crime authorization became a captive in a fight over gun control. Proposals to regulate gun shows, the source of some weapons used in the massacre, were introduced as amendments to the youth-crime bill and a stalemate ensued.

All the congressional snafus produced another of the bizarre disconnects between ideology and practicality that have long plagued the government's anticrime fight. Republicans, including many in leadership positions after the GOP House takeover in 1994, typically disdain Washington's overregulation of state and local policy. But that principle often is abandoned when it comes to crime-fighting. Then, it seems, detailed directions, or at least incentives, from Capitol Hill are fine.

As various juvenile-crime bills wended their way through Congress in the mid-1990s, opposing factions ended up fighting the bills for their own reasons and leaving few in the center to advocate useful improvements in the law. For example, when some liberals proposed harsher measures against lawbreakers who used guns, National Rifle Association (NRA) backers who wanted the feds to loosen their strictures on gun use withdrew as sponsors of the juvenile-crime bill in the Senate. At the same time, liberals held press conferences and urged supporters to write newspaper op-ed articles and letters to key lawmakers calling the legislation's provisions to ease federal requirements on states a throwback to earlier decades when youthful suspects were routinely jailed with dangerous adults.

This produced a stalemate, so the issue was handed back to the appropriations committees when it came to deciding how much money OJJDP should receive each year. As often happens in Washington, key lawmakers came up with an awkward compromise. They would deliver more money to fight juvenile crime, but—at least in the late 1990s—about half of it went to localities in the form of a loosely structured "Juvenile Accountability Incentive Block Grant." All a city or county would have to do was say that it had considered, or would consider within a year, "legislation, policies, or practices" on four subjects: trying more violent youths as adults, adopting a progressive scale of escalating sanctions, upgrading juvenile crime records, and encouraging parental supervision. It didn't matter whether any of them were enacted; talk was good enough. And because juvenile crime was a popular issue, the money pot kept getting larger.

By 1999, the agency that Arlen Specter had barely saved from extinction less than two decades earlier had more than $500 million each year to spend. The result pleased neither conservatives, who wanted a stronger get-tough approach, nor liberals, who complained that funds were available only for programs in the justice system—not for pure prevention. It was another in a long series of federal giveaways—some of it would do good, some would be wasted. Overall, it was hard to determine, because an evaluation of the wide-ranging effort was blocked in an intramural Justice Department dispute over who would choose the evaluators.

OJJDP deputy director Wilson expressed hope that much of the new infusion of federal aid would go to "rebuilding the infrastructure of the juvenile-justice system" that was being "overwhelmed" by a surge of arrests. Even though youth crime dropped in the mid-1990s, juvenile courts in 1996 were handling 1.8 million cases each year. The 370,000 violent-crime cases filed each year against juveniles represented a 90 percent increase in a decade. Because the courts had not received proportional budget increases, judges typically spent five or ten minutes on each case, usually setting the defendant free (only 31 percent of juveniles found guilty of aggravated assault and 46 percent of robbery convicts were incarcerated, OJJDP reported).[18] Judges "send them home six, seven, or eight times and wait to see who comes back," said Wilson. When the repeat teen criminal finally is dealt with harshly, it may be too late to do much.

As the money spigot was opened, the juvenile court system didn't get it all. Politicians embraced a variety of supposed youth anticrime panaceas that took off during the 1990s. A leading example was military-style boot camps. Like most criminal-justice reforms, the camps were launched with at least a grain of theory: the idea that what many youths from broken inner-city families lacked was discipline. A typical complaint was that a teen who had no parents with regular jobs might have little idea of what was involved in reporting for work every morning.

So state after state began setting up the camps, typically for offenders to spend several months, often for relatively minor crimes. One attraction was that the facilities could be operated on a shoestring compared with heavily fortified juvenile institutions. The strict regimen of boot camps was supposed to instill discipline, and some of them did have an impact on young criminals immediately after their release. Early anecdotal reports asserted that the rates of rearrest were low—under 10 percent, compared with typical recidivism figures of anywhere from 40 to 70 percent for juvenile delinquents generally.

But the problem was that the positive effects of the boot camps typically wore off after youths returned to their home communities—and the same panoply of problems that had propelled them to boot camp in the first place. More extensive studies that tracked boot camp graduates and compared their records to those of delinquents who had been given other penalties began to find that the repeat-crime rate of both groups was not very different. Many states quietly began to close their camps in the late 1990s. *Governing* magazine, which reports on state and local governments, described the case of an Arizona facility that closed after the repeat-crime rate of its "graduates" reached 70 percent. Dennis Palumbo, an Arizona State University criminologist who reviewed the program, noted that one reason it failed was that inmates could "get more drugs in prison than they can get on the street."[19]

Many of the boot camps remained in operation, but the new buzzword became "aftercare"—programs that helped boot camp alumni with school, employment, and other challenges after they returned home. Not surprisingly, these efforts were more expensive and more prone to failure. And they didn't produce the dramatic television footage of juvenile delinquents' doing pushups and jumping jacks that had helped make boot camps popular in the first place.

A variety of campaigns to attack youth gangs during the 1980s and 1990s also were problematic. While youth crime overall rose and fell periodically, the number of gang members seemed to increase steadily. One widely quoted survey found about 2,000 gangs with 100,000 members operating in 286 places in 1980. By 1998, the estimate was up to 28,700 gangs with 780,200 members in 4,800 places.

Despite the many sensational cases of murder or assault by a single teen, experts agreed that organized gangs were responsible for a large chunk of teen violence. "It appears that most gang violence is related to conflicts with other gangs" and not to drug sales, researcher James C. Howell, a former OJJDP staffer, concluded in a federal report published in 1998.[20] The Justice Department supported a succession of antigang projects, from federal criminal prosecutions to social programs aimed at diverting gang members to other pursuits. The criminal cases were successful in amassing impressive totals of gang members sent to prisons, but many of the other efforts were dubious. Echoing the experience of anticrime campaigns elsewhere, Howell declared that "no program has been demonstrated through rigorous evaluation (of which there has been little) to be effective in preventing or reducing serious and violent youth gang delinquency."

A congressionally mandated study of federal anticrime programs that the University of Maryland issued in 1997 concluded that while some antigang efforts showed promise, others had backfired because unsophisticated campaigns to bear down on gangs had mostly solidified them instead, having the counterproductive result of making the gangs more powerful and destructive.[21]

The term "gang" certainly has a negative connotation, but the lack of any agreed-on definition was a major problem. That led to what Mark Fleisher, a criminologist and anthropologist from Illinois State University, termed the "gang industry."[22] Fleisher, who has researched gang culture on the street level, described the phenomenon this way: "To boost police department budgets, city officials can claim that their city's gang problems are growing more menacing, thus frightening legislators and federal agencies into dishing out tax dollars to hire gang detectives, develop gang task forces, buy gang-intelligence computer hardware and software, procure gang detectives' cruisers, and load up on antigang guns and bullets."

As the money flowed in the late 1990s to programs good and bad, tested and untested, to combat juvenile crime, the federal strategy suffered from the same kind of intellectual schizophrenia as it had in previous decades. The dynamics were a bit different this time. In the Justice Department, the liberal bureaucracy and its supporting interest groups were back in control at OJJDP during the Clinton administration.

The congressional thrust had grown markedly more conservative. In the Senate, Arlen Specter had moved on to other interests, and his place eventually was taken by former Alabama prosecutor Jeff Sessions, who took a more hard-nosed approach. Sessions's counterpart in the House was Florida's Bill McCollum, another conservative lawmaker, whose main rallying cry was to make juvenile criminals more "accountable."

The House's attitude was muddled because of the jurisdiction split that went back to the 1970s. Federal juvenile-crime programs reported not to McCollum's Judiciary Committee crime panel but to the more moderate Education and Workforce Committee, where subcommittee chairman Frank Riggs of California, who left Congress in 1999, was more interested in crime-prevention programs. Liberals were pleased that the hardliners didn't control the agenda, but the lack of clear leadership contributed to Congress's failure to pass a formal authorization for OJJDP for many years.

The Clinton administration itself was divided. While it paid lip service to crime prevention, the White House put its main public emphasis on tough-sounding measures like trying juveniles as adults and superficial remedies like curfews and school uniforms. It was no secret that OJJDP's efforts were subsumed by political concerns. Although Attorney General Reno and Shay Bilchik, her OJJDP director, frequently spoke sympathetically to interest groups of juvenile justice professionals, White House advisers Rahm Emanuel (who resigned in 1998) and Bruce Reed usually prevailed on the president to talk tough. Clinton frequently made youth crime the subject of Saturday radio addresses and other public appearances.

Sometimes Justice Department officials were able to use back-channel contacts to First Lady Hillary Rodham Clinton to bypass Emanuel and Reed and persuade the president to give crime-prevention strategies a boost to complement law-enforcement measures.

Often what prevailed was a gimmick like teen curfews, one of the administration's oft-cited remedies, even though studies showed that they had a minimal impact on crime. Civil libertarians protested that in a dubious attempt to thwart a tiny number of criminals, the vast majority of law-abiding youths were unfairly subject to being arrested for walking or driving at night. That didn't stop Clinton and a large number of politicians of both major political parties from reflexively endorsing curfews at every opportunity.

One barometer of the way juvenile crime policy evolved during the Clinton administration was the so-called Ounce of Prevention Council headed by Vice President Al Gore that was supposed to help coordinate the scores of federal programs that dealt in some way with youth problems. As had been the case since OJJDP was set up in the 1970s, a variety of cabinet departments maintained programs that touched on the youth-crime problem, and overlap and duplication were rife. Republicans were quick to criticize the bureaucratic problems, but they had little interest in supporting the council, in part because they had no reason to help build Gore's credentials as a presidential candidate.

Meanwhile, Peter Edelman, the HHS official who had been something of a lone voice for crime prevention within the administration, was getting nowhere. Edelman, who had helped get the Ounce of Prevention Council incorporated into the wide-ranging anticrime law passed by Congress in 1994, wanted to consolidate the myriad programs dealing with troubled youth that were scattered throughout the federal bureaucracy into one unit that could have a greater impact with combined resources. But he got little support from the White House. (Some Justice Department crime fighters were dubious, too. One career official sniffed that the idea of coordinating governmentwide programs through a small council based in the vice president's office "didn't pass the laugh test.")

By the time youth development expert Karen Pittman was hired as director of the Gore council in February 1994, the prevention programs in the crime bill were under aggressive attack by Republicans as pork. Pittman recalled that the White House immediately backed down under pressure and ordered prevention advocates in the administration not even to speak to members of Congress or their aides to promote their cause. "We could never get a foothold [on Capitol Hill] to offer an alternate strategy," Pittman said.[23]

The bureaucratic part of the council's agenda was not controversial. Its staff had counted about 275 federal programs in a dozen cabinet departments touching on crime prevention—spending categories that could be consolidated for more punch. One shortcoming was that local agencies were befuddled over which among dozens of federal funding sources to try tapping.

Another casualty was the recommendations in a report that Edelman helped to produce in the first year of the Clinton administration, with Philip Heymann, deputy attorney general, and Madeleine Kunin, deputy education secretary, outlining what the federal government could do generally to combat violence. The document, which was commissioned by HHS Secretary Donna Shalala and Attorney General Reno, was deliberately framed to go beyond the somewhat limited subjects of crime and justice and to stress prevention ideas on a broad scale. The report called for tough law enforcement but also national and local prevention policies and an "antiviolence movement."[24]

The Edelman-Heymann-Kunin report included nearly 90 pages of specific violence-fighting ideas. But in the atmosphere of competing get-tough provisions of the federal crime bill, the White House refused to make the contents public after it was delivered in early 1994 because they appeared too liberal and went further in the direction of gun control than the administration then was prepared to go. The subcabinet officials who wrote the report "weren't able to sell it upstream," said Webb Hubbell, who observed the process as associate attorney general.[25] Hubbell explained that White House domestic policy advisers, intent on getting Congress to approve Clinton's plan to add 100,000 police officers, didn't want members of Congress to get the idea that the administration favored "major overhauls of criminal justice that would be soft on crime." The report got wide circulation among bureaucrats and was publicized in *U.S. News & World Report* but was mostly ignored in political circles.

The Ounce of Prevention Council was authorized to receive a paltry $25 million per year in the potentially $30 billion crime law enacted by the Democratic-controlled Congress in 1994. One aide to Vice President Gore recalled his making one call to a Republican House leader that helped keep the crime council off a GOP "recession" list for programs to kill. The result was that the council got a minuscule $1 million, which Gore shifted to a council on urban "empowerment zones" that was of more interest to him.

Director Pittman resigned in August 1995, recognizing that the council "wasn't something Gore would go to bat for again." The unit quietly died in 1997 without a public peep from the vice president. Lamented Edelman: "It never amounted to anything—what I had conceptualized kept shrinking and shrinking." The administration "missed a real opportunity to take leadership" on crime prevention, in the view of Pittman, who argued that supporting the Ounce of Prevention Council would not have endangered the 100,000 cops program. "We didn't have to back away from the whole thing," she argued. Pittman noted that the White House remained silent while Kansas Republican Senator Nancy Kassebaum tried to enact a youth development block grant program that would have complemented the Gore council's effort by giving states and localities a way to pay for prevention projects.

The picture of a Clinton administration mostly passive on crime prevention won some measure of agreement from Paul McNulty, who as chief aide to Florida Representative Bill McCollum was the GOP's main staff strategist in the House on crime policy. Republicans might well have funded some of the council's prevention ideas, especially those on consolidating federal programs, he said. McNulty could recall no push from Gore's office to save the program.[26]

It was a similar story for some of the other prevention remedies that got wide discussion in the 1990s, like finding adult mentors for troubled youths and expanding after-school programs to fill kids' time more constructively during one of the highest teen-crime periods. (About 20 percent of violent crimes by juveniles occur between 2 and 6 P.M.) Because most of the $500 million-plus Congress allocated to OJJDP was confined to justice system purposes, only $12 million was allocated for a mentoring program—a tiny sum for such a national project. Experts noted that mentoring usually would help only if long-term relationships were established between troubled teens and their mentors. Some committed volunteers succeeded, but in general, superficial contacts subsidized by a meager program were not likely to accomplish much.

In the uncoordinated federal spending on youth problems, another questionable money pot resulted from a statute called the Safe and Drug-Free Schools and Communities Act, which Congress passed in 1986 to funnel federal aid into crime prevention. This program was administered by the Education Department; like those in other agencies, it seemed to have few restrictions and little oversight.

An extensive review by the *Los Angeles Times* in mid-1998 concluded that much of nearly $6 billion spread out among thousands of school districts was "spent on initiatives that either are ineffective or appear to have little to do with reducing youth violence and substance abuse."[27] The newspaper found federal money going to such items as plastic teeth and toothbrushes, magic shows, fishing trips, and major league baseball tickets to keep kids occupied, as well as various performing acts termed "edutainers."

Misguided educators were not the only ones to blame. Congress ordered that the money be divided among school districts big and small, meaning that some had as little as $53 to spend in a year—not enough for any meaningful activity. Both Congress's General Accounting Office and the Justice Department criticized the program, and retooling was underway in 1999.

Crime prevention didn't suffer a total loss in Washington. When Attorney General Janet Reno was asked in a 1999 interview why federal funding was nowhere near the nearly $7 billion promised in the 1994 crime bill despite her ardent lobbying for it, Reno pointed to charts suggesting that total federal spending for the year had exceeded $6.5 billion. The problem was that most of that money ($4.6 billion) was allocated to the longstanding Head Start program for preschool youngsters. Reno's own Justice Department could claim only about $140 million, most of it in small grants under a program known as Title V for its location in the U.S. juvenile justice law.

Reno could point to one notable victory, helping convince Alaska Republican Ted Stevens, chairman of the Senate Appropriations Committee, to back several hundred million dollars for a federal effort to encourage parenting education.

Instead of significant allocations for crime prevention, politicians kept returning in the late 1990s to the highly visible issue of adult trials for youthful suspects. Although teen arrest rates declined in the late 1990s, the population of teenagers was due to rise again in the early twenty-first century, and some drug-abuse indicators, including a stubbornly constant rate of cocaine use by young people, suggested that the juvenile-crime lull might be temporary.

Candidates and bureaucrats had no incentive to be pessimistic while times were good—at least in terms of measurable crime rates. And there were a few notable success stories, some of which are discussed in Chapter 11. It was logical to conclude that at least some programs supported by the federal government played a part in juvenile crime's decline.

But another plausible argument was that many members of a new teenage generation were recognizing—and rejecting—the powerfully destructive effect of the lethal violence prevalent in their communities. Under this theory, youths were shunning the bloody strife typified by the drug trade, and politicians' bluster had little to do with the decline in juvenile-crime rates. Richard Curtis of New York's John Jay College of Criminal Justice called it the "little brother syndrome," the idea that the latest generation was repulsed by the activities of the crime-prone among their older siblings.[28]

The plain truth was that there was no proof that any government measure taken against juvenile lawbreaking, or a combination of them, was responsible for the good news of the 1990s about the decline of youth violence. By not ensuring that the programs they funded were properly evaluated, politicians left themselves vulnerable to criticism if crime rates increase again.

The most foreboding indicator is a worrisome level of narcotics abuse among teenagers that shows no sign of disappearing despite a longtime focus on arrests, prosecutions, drug seizures, and lectures to users. The nation's hit-and-miss efforts to bring down the alarming persistence of drug-related violence typifies the shallowness of an anticrime policymaking process dominated by partisan politics.

Chapter 6

DRUGS: IS THE WAR WINNABLE?

W HEN the twenty-first century dawned, it seemed that the United States
had been embroiled in a campaign against drug abuse as long as anyone
could remember. In fact, it was only in the last three decades of the twentieth
century that drug control became a major preoccupation of the federal
government.

It wasn't that narcotics was a new problem. A cocaine plague at the turn of
the twentieth century was the target of a grassroots opposition movement, not
a "war" directed from Washington. Congress did attempt to regulate opiates
and cocaine through physicians via the 1914 Harrison Act. But law enforcement—viewed as a tax matter—ended up in the Treasury Department. When
Treasury was given the task of enforcing the prohibition laws, drug and liquor
cases ended up in the department's Prohibition Unit. The narcotics agents were
"embarrassed by their association" with the unpopular prohibition enforcers,
said Yale historian David Musto.[1] After prohibition faded, narcotics rated its
own federal agency—the Federal Bureau of Narcotics, which remained in Treasury until 1968 and was headed for most of that time by Harry Anslinger, a less
well known contemporary of the FBI's J. Edgar Hoover.

What amounted to a ban on marijuana was enacted in 1930, but Congress's
early antidrug statutes did not create the corps of federal "narcs" that became
familiar in later years; rather, they imposed taxes on the manufacture and import

of narcotics. Thus the center of enforcement activity stayed in the Treasury Department, which generally has little to do with street crime. The separation of drug cases from the main federal anticrime apparatus—the Justice Department—set the stage for a longstanding bureaucratic splintering of Washington's antidrug forces. (States enacted their own drug regulations, but because narcotics are processed, shipped, and sold worldwide, it became conventional wisdom that the feds should wield the main enforcement authority.)

Defining narcotics as a federal responsibility would make it a prominent national issue when Congress debated crime policy in the 1980s, but there was no huge controversy in earlier decades. Drugs simply were not a compelling problem in post–World War II America.

The relative absence of drugs from the political agenda was reflected in the 1967 Johnson crime commission report, which devoted only a short chapter to narcotics problems. The basic conclusion was that law enforcement deserved more resources and treatment needed more research—a common theme expressed by politicians for the rest of the twentieth century. It was not until the Nixon administration came into office vowing to deal more strongly with the crime wave of the 1960s that the federal "war on drugs" became truly high profile.

Nixon set the tone for his tough-sounding policies with a campaign speech at Disneyland in 1968 warning that the drug problem was "decimating a generation of Americans."[2] His administration moved on several fronts, concentrating primarily on the most prominent illegal drug of the era: heroin. Nixon mounted drives against smuggling from source countries like Turkey and Mexico and launched several domestic enforcement initiatives, many of them focused on the city of Washington. As chronicled by Dan Baum in Smoke and Mirrors, a history of America's antidrug wars, the capital became—at least in the 1970s— a "place to field test new weapons and tactics," including laws allowing "preventive detention" of drug-crime suspects and "no knock" raids by agents.[3]

Nixon's antidrug efforts both abroad and at home reached a peak that brought welcome news to the administration in the election year of 1972. The agency now named the Bureau of Narcotics and Dangerous Drugs reported a shortage of heroin in eastern cities that usually relied on smuggling from Europe, and serious crime reports in the nation increased only 1 percent in the first half of the year after having risen steadily during Nixon's first three years in office. Journalist Michael Massing asked Nixon adviser Egil Krogh whether the slowing of the crime rate's growth could be fairly attributed to the administration's actions against drugs. Krogh replied, "Was it a success from a political perspective? ... Heck, yes, it was a slam-dunk great success."[4] Nixon handily defeated George McGovern to win a second term.

Another Nixon initiative against drugs that had more long-lasting impact was a new unit called ODALE (Office of Drug Abuse Law Enforcement) that promised something largely missing from the fragmented government effort: a coordinated federal-state-local attack on major drug traffickers. The Justice Department set up units in several major metropolitan areas in which agents from different levels of government would pool their resources so that they could more easily transcend city, county, and state lines.

ODALE boasted of many successes, and its director—a former customs commissioner named Myles Ambrose—functioned in 1972 somewhat the way the "drug czar" would in later years, at least by giving tough-sounding public speeches.

But ODALE had some major problems, too. One day in 1973, Jerry Murphy, the U.S. prosecutor heading the ODALE regional force based in St. Louis, promised the reporter covering his office for the daily *Post-Dispatch* newspaper a good story the next day. What happened that night did turn out to be startling news, but not the kind Murphy anticipated or wanted. His ODALE forces, dressed shabbily to look like narcotics dealers, burst into the homes of two innocent families in Collinsville, an Illinois suburb of St. Louis, in search of drug stashes. The agents terrorized them and ransacked their possessions but found no narcotics. Only later did ODALE discover that it had invaded the wrong premises.

Of course, ODALE agents were not the only ones who ever had a problem of mistaken identity, but the Illinois raids by the supposedly elite federal unit provoked a furor in Washington, led by criticism from respected Illinois Senator Charles Percy. The episode helped persuade Congress later that year to combine the Bureau of Narcotics and Dangerous Drugs with ODALE, along with drug-related functions of the Treasury Department's Customs Service, to form a new agency—the Drug Enforcement Administration (DEA). Policymakers hoped that this new and bigger bureaucracy would enforce the antidrug laws effectively without blatantly violating Americans' civil liberties.

With drug-agent abuses seemingly under control, the late 1970s presidency of Jimmy Carter was marked by a retreat from the harshness of the tough-on-drugs era symbolized by New York Governor Nelson Rockefeller's long prison terms for drug abusers and Nixon's war on heroin. (The Nixon administration also backed drug treatment programs, but the effort got little attention amid the president's fall from office.)

Carter, the former governor of Georgia, chose as his chief adviser on narcotics an Atlanta psychiatrist named Peter Bourne, who had run a clinic in San Francisco's Haight-Ashbury district and thus became, in the words of narcotics-policy analyst Dan Baum, "the closest thing Atlanta had to a drug expert." Bourne, who clearly came from the treatment side of the drug debate, backed Carter's endorsement of decriminalizing marijuana possession.

With the help of some backroom lobbying from the National Organization for the Reform of Marijuana Laws (NORML), the president called, during the summer of 1977, for the end of federal penalties for possessing small amounts of pot. In the days before much of the public was aware of rapidly rising drug use by teens, the suggestion was not shocking. A panel appointed by Nixon had made a similar recommendation in 1972, and several states adopted it.

The Carter years—which turned out to be a one-term Democratic reign in the White House surrounded by 20 years of Republican rule—were relatively scandal free compared with the Watergate years. But higher ethical standards did not equal a crackdown on narcotics from Washington. Instead, pressure came from the grass roots. An organization called PRIDE (Parents' Resource Institute for Drug Education), founded by a couple from academia whose teen-age daughter and her friends had become hooked on pot, had sprung up in Atlanta to work against decriminalization. The number of young addicts was beginning to creep up alarmingly. More than 10 percent of high school seniors admitted using marijuana daily in 1978, a figure difficult for policymakers to ignore.

Another reason that the movement for marijuana decriminalization sputtered was personal. Peter Bourne, who as Carter's principal drug adviser lay the groundwork for the more liberal policy, embarrassed the administration by attending a party sponsored by NORML at which cocaine was used, even if there was no proof Bourne himself snorted.

This misstep alone probably would not have prevented Bourne from playing a significant role in changing the direction of federal antidrug policy had it not been for another one of those episodes that inadvertently had a large impact on Washington's war on crime. One of Bourne's aides asked him to write a sedative prescription for her, using a phony name to conceal her identity. Bourne, who as a licensed physician was entitled to issue prescriptions, did as he was asked. But the woman used the form in a suburban Virginia pharmacy that coincidentally was being checked by a state inspector, who detected the violation. It was a minor offense in the scheme of life, but the fact that the man in charge of the federal government's drug policy had committed it was enough to touch off a firestorm inside the Beltway. Bourne was quickly forced to resign.

As it happened, none of Bourne's successors as drug policy director had a public-health background. As enumerated by Baum, Bourne was followed in turn by "a social worker, a chemist, a pediatrician, a prosecutor, a philosophy professor, a politician, and a policeman" (and later, in 1996, by a military officer). Each of these men put his own stamp on the office, but none of them after Bourne pursued primarily a health approach. The dizzying variety of occupations said a lot about why federal antidrug policy has been so erratic: amazingly, none of the men who came after Bourne had worked as a full-time professional in the drug abuse field.

The Carter administration left office having made little impact on the street-crime problem, but a new stress on law enforcement arrived with the presidency of Ronald Reagan in 1981. Reagan painted Carter as soft on drugs. It would be a stretch to hold the White House responsible, but surveys issued in later years showed that drug abuse reached a national high in the late 1970s—about 25 million Americans at the end of the decade used drugs at least once a month.[5] The public pressure to take action was building.

In the years before the Office of National Drug Control Policy (the drug czar) became the focal point for antinarcotics pronouncements, policy in Washington most often leaned toward law enforcement. So it was natural that the Reagan White House first took on a major bureaucratic challenge in that area.

The DEA—the Nixon-era combination of several antidrug agencies—had been viewed as a poor second cousin to the FBI, which portrayed itself as the premier federal law enforcement agency. Agents of the two bureaucracies, both nominally part of the Justice Department, often went off in their own directions with little coordination. For the most part, FBI agents were glad to slough off to DEA the messy drug probes that had little in common with the FBI's white-collar crime and counterintelligence cases. But in a government whose prosecution force already was divided among more than 90 presidentially appointed

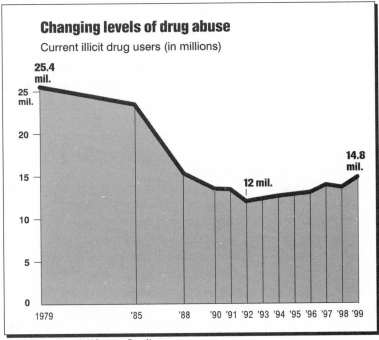

Source: National Household Survey on Drug Abuse

U.S. attorneys, this fragmentation of forces contributed to an uneven enforcement effort. The FBI and DEA each had its own strengths. The question was how to maximize them without promoting even more competition.

An obvious option was a merger, but insiders worried that the cultures of the two agencies—the FBI's buttoned-down routine and DEA's more swashbuckling approach—were so different that their integration would fail. Eventually, the notion of a superficial merger emerged: the DEA chief would report to the FBI director in the Justice Department's chain of command, but the two bureaucracies would remain mostly separate.

At the top, this formulation seemed to work. That was largely because a succession of FBI executives was named to head DEA—men who felt comfortable reporting to their former agency. The DEA directors generally enjoyed good relations with William Webster, who headed the FBI from 1978 to 1987. But the chain of command was far from airtight. Webster recalled that Rudolph Giuliani, who as the number three Justice Department official in the early Reagan years had the job of overseeing law enforcement, frequently went directly to the DEA with orders and queries, bypassing the FBI in the structure that his own administration had put in place. "Giuliani was in the chain of command, but he ignored it and played hell with it," said Webster, who added that Giuliani's aggressiveness was not necessarily harmful because Webster himself had his hands full just trying to manage the FBI.[6] (Giuliani was little known outside of law enforcement circles at the time but later was named U.S. attorney in Manhattan and became a national voice in crime policy when he promoted aggressive policing after being elected mayor of New York City in 1993.)

As they grappled with a disjointed federal anticrime bureaucracy, Reagan-era antidrug officials were beset with the same dilemmas over enforcement versus treatment priorities that loomed over most drug-policy debates of the era. At least rhetorically, most policymakers claimed to support a balanced approach. This meant that the government simultaneously would attempt supply reduction—work to eradicate drugs in source nations and stop them from penetrating U.S. borders—and demand reduction—getting drug users to stop. The latter included combinations of lectures, treatment, cutting off government benefits to users, and seizing the property of drug defendants immediately after arrest.

The balanced approach sounds attractive in theory because it attacks the drug problem from two directions. But it begs the question of the most effective use of government resources—federal, state, and local. Logically, federal authorities can best take command of two broad areas: enforcement at the international and interstate levels, and "bully pulpit" preaching, like First Lady Nancy Reagan's "just say no" campaign of the mid-1980s and the more sophisticated broadcast advertising that was initiated by the White House drug czar starting in 1998, with hundreds of millions of dollars supplied by Congress.

Overall, tough law enforcement usually won out because it was easier to put into motion, quantify, and explain to the public. As the 1980s wore on, "more resources were allocated to supply reduction and taken away from demand reduction, which wasn't so sexy," said New Jersey Democrat William Hughes, who headed the House crime subcommittee during the decade. "Making a bust of two tons of marijuana was newsworthy; reducing recidivism with treatment programs was a long, slow, tedious, difficult process that was not very newsworthy."[7]

The Reagan administration and gung-ho members of Congress in both major parties were enthusiastic about the law enforcement emphasis in the early 1980s when the data showed alarming drug-abuse trends among youth. Some important executive branch insiders were skeptical about putting so many resources into trying to stop drugs at the border. But in the years after the Vietnam War when the United States faced a relative dearth of foreign crises, the idea of getting the military more involved in antidrug enforcement gained strength among those who believed that the Pentagon needed new missions.

Assigning more antidrug tasks to the military had a budget impact that disturbed some enforcers. Webster, the moderate Missouri Republican who was installed as FBI director by Democrat Jimmy Carter and stayed in the Reagan administration, was surprised when he got a $500,000 bill for the first Pentagon AWACS aircraft that flew across southern U.S. borders to look for drug dealers. While the costly reconnaisance no doubt did some good, after reflecting on the usefulness of such measures, Webster concluded that "interdiction was the most expensive and least effective component" of the federal war on drugs. "When we blocked the normal gateways, drugs started pouring into the farmlands of southern Texas," Webster said. "It's hard to stop that."

Webster's misgivings aside, federal priorities remained fairly stable in the 1980s. By fiscal 1987, for example, the total federal antidrug budget hovered under $6 billion, just about equally split among domestic law enforcement, international interdiction, and demand reduction. (Just 11 years later, the federal bureaucracy had shrunk overall, but the antidrug spending total had jumped to nearly $20 billion.)

Advocates of prevention and treatment long have maintained that the tilt toward enforcement has been shortsighted. Certainly, treatment got little consistent support after a promising start in the Nixon administration, as Michael Massing described in *The Fix*. It is possible that a more responsible effort by the Carter administration might have encouraged a shift of federal resources addressing the drug treatment part of the "demand side," but what actually happened—driven by periodic crises and public demands for instant answers— was an emphasis on the two traditional federal priorities, law enforcement and preaching against drugs.

Carlton Turner, a Mississippi marijuana expert installed as Reagan's White House drug adviser before the days of a czar, typified this attitude by disdaining a larger federal role in supporting treatment for inner-city addicts and instead favoring speeches by First Lady Nancy Reagan about marijuana's dangers.

Her catch phrase "just say no," a line from an antidrug film produced by the Advertising Council with federal funds, got little notice until she used it in a speech at an Oakland school in mid-1984. In the next few years, more than 10,000 "Just Say No" clubs aimed at kids between 7 and 14 years old sprouted nationwide. Although it was difficult to link the effort to specific changes in drug abuse, participants were enthusiastic. A review by the inspector general of the Department of Health and Human Services in 1988 said that although many experts called Just Say No simplistic, they credited its simplicity with increasing young people's awareness of narcotics' dangers.

There seemed no doubt that narcotics abuse was becoming more serious, based on annual surveys of high school students, but it was difficult for the public to appreciate the nuances of the drug trade. That was because federal agencies and other experts routinely churned out dubious data on drug use—often exaggerating the problem by issuing "mythical numbers," in the phrase of policy analyst Max Singer, who disputed estimates of crimes committed by New York City heroin addicts in 1971.

The theme was picked up in 1984 by Peter Reuter of the RAND Corporation, who criticized official estimates of the addict population and of the total income from illegal drug sales—the latter produced by an interagency panel called the National Narcotics Intelligence Consumer Committee (often dubbed the "NICK" report). Officials and politicians periodically made alarming pronouncements about narcotics trafficking—warnings that may have had little practical meaning for the average citizen.

Statistics aside, the most telling example of herky-jerky national policymaking on drugs in the 1980s stemmed from the cocaine epidemic that hit during the middle of the decade and remained a flashpoint of controversy for the rest of the century. Instead of a rational discussion of the relative merits of enforcement, treatment, and prevention, the debate focused almost entirely on a racially divisive controversy over the length of prison sentences.

Cocaine reemerged as a public concern after a rise in "freebasing," a method for creating a form of the drug using ether, which carries the potential for igniting if the cocaine is smoked before the ether evaporates. The danger was highlighted in 1980 when popular comedian Richard Pryor was severely burned while freebasing.

Before the cocaine scourge hit hard, the Reagan administration had signaled a determination to take high-visibility actions against drugs. In 1982, the president unveiled what adviser Edwin Meese called "the first comprehensive national strategy for dealing with the drug problem." The plan promised to go beyond traditional law enforcement and include more attention to international initiatives, prevention, education, treatment, and research.

As the cocaine threat was becoming more prominent, Vice President George Bush was tapped to lead a task force that aimed to stem the drug trade dominant in South Florida. Coast Guard patrols were stepped up, and Bush staged a series of photo opportunities to publicize a string of big seizures. Insiders complained that the campaign was as much show as substance. It wasn't that the federal agents weren't trying; rather, it seemed a hopeless task to try plugging holes in the porous border region. No sooner was one big seizure announced than the smugglers found another way to get their contraband into the country.

The flurry of government activity undoubtedly contributed to a drop in some categories of drug abuse in the early 1980s, particularly casual use by the middle class. But enforcement actions seemed to have limited impact in many inner-city neighborhoods, where drug-fueled homicides and other crimes soared in the middle of the decade.

The most serious violence accompanied the spread of crack, a form of cocaine produced by dissolving powder cocaine in sodium bicarbonate and water, boiling the solution, and extracting the resulting solid substance. "Crack simply was 'poor man's freebase,' " said criminologist Jeffrey Fagan of Columbia University, who noted that it was an ingenious product, easy to make on a stovetop from a small, inexpensive amount of cocaine powder.[8]

Crack cocaine became much more prominent in city neighborhoods than the traditional powder form because it could produce a quicker "high," in about a minute compared to anywhere from four minutes to an hour for powder, depending on how it was consumed. Just as significant, it could be purchased at reasonable prices, typically between $5 and $20 for single doses known as "rocks." In the meaninglessness of life in many urban areas, users saw crack as "an oasis with palm trees sticking out of the ground," said Stephen Vicchio of the College of Notre Dame of Maryland, who studied the phenomenon.

Relatively few Americans actually were using crack cocaine. Many estimates put the figure at several hundred thousand hard-core users, most commonly young, urban, unemployed blacks. By the mid-1980s, domination of the crack trade in most urban areas was beginning to come from gangs, some homegrown like those known as the Crips and the Bloods—which were organized in Los Angeles and later spread throughout the country—and others originating in Jamaica, Haiti, and the Dominican Republic.

The spread of crack largely resulted from what amounted to a marketing plan by various drug rings, but it took law enforcers several years to realize what they were up against. This ignorance was documented by Gordon Witkin of *U.S. News & World Report* in a 1991 cover story, "The Men Who Created

Crack."[9] Even though crack had hit the Los Angeles area by 1984, for example, the feds were preoccupied with security arrangements for that summer's Olympic Games and paid little heed to the growing menace. In 1986, Witkin found, agents couldn't decipher street lingo and didn't know whether crack was the same thing as the "rock" that drug users were talking about in California.

By the election season of 1986, crack trafficking had already produced some of the violence that would so alarm law enforcement officials, politicians, and the public. In one widely noted episode, 3 people were killed and 13 wounded in a shootout during the summer of 1985 between two "posses" at a Jamaican event in New Jersey. Veteran drug researcher Paul Goldstein of the New York think tank Narcotic and Drug Research Inc. said that the strife surrounding crack was marked by territorial disputes between rival dealers, robberies of dealers, "and the usually violent retaliation by the dealers or their bosses, elimination of informers . . . punishment for selling adulterated or phony drugs [or] for failing to pay one's debts."[10]

Despite wide concern about crack-related crime, most of the problem stemmed from drug-related business transactions. Only a very small number of violent crimes—3 of 118 crack-related homicides in one study—were committed by people high on drugs. In fact, the exact relationship between drugs and crime has been much debated over the years, with few reliable findings. As a result, criminal justice policy—from arrests to prison sentences—has been notably imprecise when it comes to distinguishing among casual users, addicts, traffickers, kingpins, "mules" who merely transport contraband, and other players in the world of illegal drugs. Often, mid-level dealers who supplied violence-committing addicts escaped significant penalties by cooperating with agents to finger low-level smugglers.

In the case of crack cocaine, what politicians knew in the mid-1980s was that it sounded scary. Lacking detailed information, those who parroted the conventional wisdom that typically dominated anticrime policymaking avoided the issue of exactly how much more dangerous crack was than powder. Officials simply declared the incontrovertible fact that crack was "associated" with violence. Florida politicians, whose constituencies were the hardest hit at the beginning, were among the first to sound the alarm.

The panic hit an early peak in the months before the 1986 congressional election. In Washington, the Democrats—with their bitter experience of having been outmaneuvered in the 1984 crime bill debate still fresh in their minds—were determined to be ahead of the curve. Florida Senator Lawton Chiles was named to head a task force on what the federal government might do, and New Jersey's William Hughes took the lead on the House side of the Capitol.

As often happens in anticrime policymaking, the debate was inflamed by a single dramatic and, in this case, local event. On June 17, 1986, University of

Maryland basketball star Len Bias was chosen by the Boston Celtics as the second selection in the National Basketball Association's college draft. At a party the next night in a Maryland suburb of Washington, D.C., Bias died of a drug overdose. The exact cause of death was not known immediately, but a deputy Maryland medical examiner speculated that Bias had been freebasing crack, and most of the major media duly reported the surmise.

Even though a teammate of Bias testified a year later that the partygoers actually were snorting powder cocaine, the initial reports were enough to send the antidrug warriors in Congress into overdrive to deal with the supposed new menace. (By one count, Bias was linked to crack in 74 segments on national network news programs in July 1986 alone.) Hughes had coincidentally scheduled a meeting of his crime subcommittee on the day that Bias's death was announced, and aides recalled an "ashen-faced" Representative Dan Lungren walking in to announce the news. The episode had occurred so close to the Capitol that every lawmaker had heard of it, and the Celtics connection guaranteed that House Speaker Thomas (Tip) O'Neill of Boston would be deluged with calls from constituents. It seemed clear that lawmakers would have to do something about the crack crisis.

O'Neill returned from the July 4 recess and called on all House committees with any official role in antidrug policy to propose legislation by mid-August. Reagan and Bush ordered an administration version prepared, and the top two elected officials even submitted to urine tests for drugs to demonstrate their sincerity. In a notably understated review of the legislating rush that ensued, the U.S. Sentencing Commission—which had to deal with the aftermath of congressional action toughening sentences for drug abuse for more than a decade—later reported that "Apparently because of the heightened concern, Congress dispensed with much of the typical deliberative legislative process, including committee hearings."[11]

The question was what Congress could do to demonstrate immediate concern, preferably without spending much money. The recent pattern in such circumstances had been to increase the maximum penalty, a strategy followed since the Rockefeller drug laws were enacted by New York legislators during the heroin epidemic of the early 1970s. Columbia criminologist Jeffrey Fagan noted that New York "set the stage in nearly every state for legislation . . . for new presumptive sentencing laws for drug crimes."[12] Now it was Washington's turn to set the pace. Law enforcement wasn't ignored, but federal agents didn't receive any emergency help, either. By coincidence, DEA officials had scheduled an internal briefing in New York City to discuss the crack problem on the same day as Bias's death. One result was a request from alarmed DEA chief John Lawn for $44 million to pay for 200 agents who would concentrate on crack. The White House quietly rejected that idea, even though more immediate enforcement might have done more good than the higher prison sentences that became the focus of public debate.

As the drug agents were fretting behind the scenes, members of Congress and their advisers tossed around ideas for showing the public that they were acting on the crack problem. It began as an exchange of arbitrary numbers, and it soon evolved into a bidding war. The basic concept was simple: crack was more associated with violence than powder, it appeared, so those who sold it deserved a higher penalty. Legislators decided on two tiers of mandatory minimum prison terms for first-time dealers—five and ten years, depending on whether a trafficker was classified as "major" or "serious."

When policymakers revisited the issue during the 1990s, the debate swirled around the ratio between the penalties for crack and for powder, as if those who had written the law in 1986 had carefully studied the difference between the two forms of the drug. But those involved in the evolution of the policy said it didn't happen that way.

Rather, lawmakers and their aides were "pulling numbers out of the air" based on their fragmentary knowledge about how crack was being marketed, said Eric Sterling, a staff member who helped draft the legislation for New Jersey's Hughes.[13] One of the first proposals came from the Reagan administration, which in a bill introduced by Senate Majority Leader Bob Dole suggested what amounted to providing a mandatory minimum penalty for crack dealing that was 20 times higher than the sanction for selling the same amount of powder.

But that differential wouldn't be enough for the Democrats. Sterling conferred with DEA officials on the technicalities and wrote a proposal that would effectively raise the ratio to 50 to 1. "There was nothing scientific about it," recalled Hayden Gregory, Hughes's chief Judiciary aide.[14] The scene at the panel's markup to write the bill's details was described this way by another congressional staff member: "They were filling in the numbers. Hughes leaned over to Eric [Sterling] and asked, 'What number do we put in here?' Eric got a number from DEA, and none of us on the outside were in any position to say otherwise." The bill moved from the Hughes subcommittee to the full Judiciary Committee in a day, superhuman speed in congressional practice, and was rushed through the House.

As often happens in crime debates, the Senate decided to trump the House. Florida's Chiles had met with dozens of sheriffs from his state, who told him of the damage that crack had wrought in their counties. In a series of frenzied closed-door meetings, senators decided to double the differential to the 100 to 1 that eventually made it into the law books. (What the ratio actually meant was that convictions involving 5 kilograms of powder cocaine and 50 grams of crack would produce the same ten-year minimum term.)

In later years, commentators typically characterized the battle as one between conservative, white, hardline Republicans and liberal minority Democrats. But the divisions are rarely that clear, and that is not the way the great drug debate of 1986 evolved. In proclaiming their fervor to attack crack, members of Congress did not talk in terms of 100-to-1 ratios (or any other number) that compared crack penalties to those for powder cocaine offenses, and there was no apparent consideration of what later became clear: that the harshest penalties would be imposed on minorities, who dominated crack sales and use. "Crack was so new and there were no data, so it wasn't debated in racial terms," said a staff member of the Congressional Black Caucus, many of whose members supported the tough-on-crack legislation.

This view was echoed by California's Lungren, who was taken aback that the Democrats had increased criminal penalties even more than the traditionally hardline Republicans had in mind. Democrats said the crack epidemic "was killing the black community," so the GOP went along with the harsh terms, Lungren recalled. "It was not aimed at black defendants. Democrats said, 'We've got to do something to save the black community.'"[15]

It eventually became clear that the outcome would be what New Jersey's Hughes compared to "a good poker game—I'll see you and I'll raise you 20." After seeing a silly amendment pass demanding that Washington stop all narcotics trafficking from Mexico by air within 90 days, Hughes knew that the toughest-sounding penalty would be enacted, whether or not it made any sense. "The benchmark we used was often not based on sound reasoning," Hughes said years later. Even liberal Democrats who normally opposed what they considered draconian sentencing schemes voted for the 100-to-1 crack-to-powder ratio, muttering privately to the crime subcommittee chairman, "Bill, I can't go back to my district and explain a vote against that amendment." Hughes despaired that carefully considered proposals would unravel on the House floor via amendments, "no matter how stupid."

The stiff mandatory minimum penalties were adopted by a Congress seemingly oblivious to its own history on the subject. Scott Wallace, a Senate aide at the time who later tracked the issue as a staff member for the National Legal Aid and Defender Association, noted that Congress had "enacted mandatory minimums in the 1950s and repealed them in 1970 for the same reasons critics cite now: they tie judges' hands."[16] One strong voice for repeal was George H. W. Bush, then a congressman from Texas. But things changed when Bush became vice president in a tough-on-crime administration: he was one of the most vocal cheerleaders for tough sentences during the 1980s.

The 1986 penalties also threatened to conflict with the very sentencing procedure that Congress had put in motion two years earlier: the guidelines then being drafted by a presidentially appointed commission that would give judges a range of possible penalties for each offense. Senator Joseph Biden of Delaware, who as Judiciary Committee chairman backed mandatory minimums at the time, said in a 1997 interview that "I was wrong."[17] The issue should have been left to the Sentencing Commission, he said. Biden blamed the extended popularity of mandatory minimums in Congress on Republicans' "political necessity to get back into the game" of trying to appear tougher than the Democrats.

A Biden adviser was blunter: "It was ironic: we created the Sentencing Commission so that politicians wouldn't be pressured to come up with tougher penalties." But in the rush to do something about crack cocaine, said the staffer, "the commission was pretty much ignored." Senator Edward Kennedy of Massachusetts, who had urged fellow liberals to approve the sentencing guidelines, opposed mandatory minimums in drug cases but essentially was ignored in the furor to get tough. "In dealing with crime, there are simple, easy answers—and they're wrong," Kennedy said in an interview in the late 1990s. "Mandatory minimums undermined one of the most important aspects of the sentencing code: understandable, predictable, certain, and truthful sentences."[18]

Supreme Court Justice Stephen Breyer, a former Kennedy aide who was a key Sentencing Commission member in the late 1980s, said in a 1998 critique that mandatory minimum sentences in drug cases were thwarting the drive for a "rational, coherent set of punishments." One problem was that major drug traffickers could get a break if they helped authorities; minor figures rarely could provide vital evidence. So some small fry were getting the same tough minimum sentences as major traffickers who had informed on others and had their prison terms reduced under the sentencing guidelines. Breyer complained that similar penalties were being imposed on "offenders who are very different, perhaps like a drug lord and a mule."[19] (Try as he might, Kennedy could not get his colleagues to repeal the mandatory minimums, even when he signed up such stalwart conservatives as Strom Thurmond and Orrin Hatch to support the cause.)

While Congress legislated frantically, the crack trade seemed to continue unabated. It shouldn't have been surprising that the dealers were not deterred by the fairly remote possibility of being sent to prison. Peter Reuter and Rob MacCoun of the RAND Corporation, in a study of drug transactions in Washington, D.C., concluded that the imprisonment risk per transaction was 1 per 4,500.[20] If caught, the traffickers would have spent about one third of their crime careers behind bars, the researchers found. But the risk was hardly high enough to dissuade many urban young men from taking up a lucrative occupation, especially when the economy offered few alternatives anywhere near as attractive.

It was too early in 1988 to know whether the 1986 mandatory sentence law on crack had done much good, but Congress upped the ante in that presidential election year by imposing a minimum five-year penalty for mere possession of crack. This move, too, originated in Florida. It was proposed by Representative

Clay Shaw, a former prosecutor and mayor in Ft. Lauderdale, who said that the drug was "eating the core out of the inner city."[21] As Congress rushed to beef up the antidrug statutes it had put on the books only two years earlier, no holds were barred. House members put together a 400-page plan, but the Senate topped that with 600 pages. "Amending sessions on drug bills regularly turned into free-for-alls, in which members tried to outdo each other with the toughest proposals," said Eva Bertram and three co-authors in *Drug War Politics*, a book that reviewed the partisanship over drug policy.[22]

The jockeying went well beyond drugs. "As soon as the Justice Department heard there was going to be a bill" in 1986, recalled a Senate aide who worked on drafting it, "the FBI and other agencies came in with their own packages to piggyback on it. They figured that if everyone else was getting funding, they should, too."

By 1988, the broad positions of the two major parties on drugs seemed barely distinguishable. The GOP did stress the nation's moral decline as a cause of the problem, and the Democrats gave more attention to preventive education.

But party leaders were determined to shore up presidential candidate Michael Dukakis's anticrime credentials. "We wanted drugs to be a big campaign issue in 1988," said Robert Weiner, then an aide to Charles Rangel, the veteran New York City congressman who chaired a special House committee on narcotics.[23] Rangel embraced Nancy Reagan's "just say no" slogan as well as Jesse Jackson's "up with hope, down with dope."

The Democratic strategy proved notably unsuccessful with Dukakis, who was outmaneuvered by Bush on other crime issues, particularly the governor's fur-loughs for Willie Horton and other convicts. Still, the long-term effect was to lock Democratic leaders into rigid positions on crime and drugs. "They inter-nalized the lesson never again to appear soft," said political scientist Bertram.

Before the election, Democrats did succeed in establishing the drug czar office that Senator Biden and others had sought for nearly a decade. The narcotics issue had not been so politically prominent when Reagan had vetoed the idea earlier in the decade. Newly elected President George Bush approved it now, but he seemed to signal that the office would not function as a heavy-duty policymaking unit when he named as the first czar not a narcotics expert but rather William Bennett, who had served as education secretary and was known for his laments about the decline of morality in America. Despite his lack of expertise, Bennett got high marks for effectively using the office's bully pulpit to preach about drugs' dangers. In fact, many who have followed the office's evolution say that Bennett was the most effective drug policy director until Bill Clinton named General Barry McCaffrey, who also was inexperienced in nar-cotics issues but was a forceful public speaker.

Bush's first year in office marked another turning point in the drug war, at least rhetorically. Although casual drug abuse was steady or declining, according to various government surveys, the new administration decided that this was the domestic-policy issue to emphasize. The White House put out the word that Bush would give a nationwide speech on the subject the evening after Labor Day 1989. Polls indicated that public concern about narcotics was growing as the subject got more political prominence.

To capture viewers' attention, Bush focused on a crack arrest in Lafayette Park, across from the White House. The president displayed a plastic package marked "evidence" that had been seized in a "sting" involving a 19-year-old dealer who had been lured to the site by undercover agents, supposedly against the orders of White House aides who had merely wanted to borrow some cocaine so that television viewers could see what it looked like. As recounted by Yale Law Professor Stephen Duke in *America's Longest War*, the teen "needed travel directions from his sham 'customers' to enable him to find the White House," which allowed Bush to "suggest that drugs were being dealt virtually on [his] steps . . . and thus that the country was in grave peril."[24] Bush later defended the ruse.

The emphasis stayed on law enforcement during the Bush years in the White House. Now, nearly two decades after the Nixon-era experiments with forms of drug treatment, Bennett insisted that treatment programs had not been proved sufficiently effective to justify pouring large amounts of federal resources into them.

Conservative Republicans like Bennett weren't the only skeptics. Iowa Representative Neal Smith, powerful chairman of the House committee that controlled Justice Department funding, recalled asking colleague Charles Rangel to name the best treatment program; Smith's aides found later that the agency Rangel cited was successful in keeping only 17 percent of participants off drugs for a year. If that was the best that government-aided treated efforts could do, Smith lamented, "there's not enough money in the treasury to solve the drug problem."[25]

Drug czar Bennett lasted only two years, quitting after the 1990 midterm elections. Bush eventually tapped former Florida Governor Bob Martinez for the job. But he proved an uninspiring choice, and his reign was noted, at least publicly, for a series of controversies over internal personnel and spending issues. The essential story on the drug-abuse front during the period remained roughly the same: casual use was down but hard-core inner-city cocaine problems remained serious.

After Bill Clinton won the White House, he named Lee Brown, a respected former police chief in Atlanta, Houston, and New York City, as drug czar. But the White House was under heavy congressional pressure to cut its own staff. Because the drug policy office was a relatively large unit within the Executive

Office of the President, Clinton aides recognized it as an easy target and slashed its payroll from more than 100 to fewer than 20. Clinton tried to have it both ways, proclaiming that Brown had been given cabinet-level status. Still, it was hard to take seriously the idea that an official with only a few dozen aides could effectively coordinate the antidrug activities of cabinet departments that had hundreds of thousands of employees.

The cutback eventually was acknowledged as a serious political miscalculation. Although the drug czar's office had had only a brief history and had never amounted to a powerful force in shaping federal policy, the Clinton White House took a powerful symbolic hit during the 1994 election year over the staff reduction. Republicans pounded on the idea that the cut showed that Clinton cared little about drugs (never mind that many Republicans had shown little enthusiasm for the drug czar idea in the first place). With some studies suggesting that drug abuse by teens in several categories was beginning to rise again, it seemed that the GOP might have a potent issue to use against Clinton in his 1996 reelection drive.

Protecting his flank, Clinton promised to restore the office to its former strength. The president wasn't helped by the fact that drug czar Brown, although he was clearly knowledgeable about narcotics issues, was so soft spoken in Washington's brash political culture that he was perceived as being shy. Brown may have had the right idea of what segment of drug abuse to attack most aggressively: the problems of hard-core inner-city addicts. But that would not necessarily have much resonance with middle-class voters, who presumably were more interested in what affected them most directly: teenage marijuana use. Rahm Emanuel, a senior White House political operative who by then was masterminding strategy on crime and drugs, helped steer Brown and his office back to the pot issue. The drug czar "may have read the tea leaves wrong" by trying to focus on increased funding for treating hard-core addicts, admitted one aide. At the end of 1995, Brown decided to return to his recent hometown of Houston, where two years later he would be elected mayor.

On the eve of a presidential election year, it was time for a drug czar who would appear more forceful. Clinton made the smart political move of naming General Barry McCaffrey to the job. McCaffrey knew far less about narcotics than did Brown, but the Persian Gulf War hero was virtually impervious to Republican criticism, even though he had appeared before the conservative Heritage Foundation a few weeks before his nomination and questioned whether the longstanding war against drugs was having much impact on the streets of America. (McCaffrey favored the military's involvement in interdiction, but he criticized exercises involving "ships' doing figure eights at 4 A.M." in the Caribbean.) Still, McCaffrey's unassailable record of success in the armed forces reduced the GOP to accusing the president of having dithered on drug policy during his first three years and then of making mostly a symbolic move in an election year by bringing in McCaffrey. Still, the early cutback in the drug czar's staff remained an issue as late as 2000, when George W. Bush cited it as supposed evidence of the Clinton-Gore administration's weakness.

The back-and-forth over the drug czar's office made good fodder inside the Washington Beltway, but it was the dispute over cocaine penalties that repeatedly came to the fore in the public debate on antidrug policy. By the mid-1990s, it had become evident that the difference between the sanctions for crack and powder sales were particularly arbitrary and were especially harsh on minorities. In a study of 1993 federal court cases, the U.S. Sentencing Commission found that 88.3 percent of those convicted of crack cocaine trafficking were black. By contrast, 58 percent of those found guilty of possessing powder cocaine were white. And many blacks who happened to be implicated in crack cases did not have otherwise serious criminal records; the study found that 44 percent of crack offenders had minor rap sheets or none at all. At the end of a 200-page analysis, however, the commission ducked the issue of what to do by condemning the 100-to-1 crack-to-powder penalty ratio but making no recommendation to Congress on what the proper penalty should be.[26]

Essentially, the three branches of government were passing the crack-penalty question back and forth like a hot potato. Congress took it up again during consideration of the 1994 crime bill. After an inconclusive debate, lawmakers ended up sending the question back to the Sentencing Commission. There, members voted 4 to 3 on May 1, 1995, in favor of equalizing crack and powder penalties—a conclusion initially endorsed by Attorney General Janet Reno.

But that begged the question of exactly how the sanctions should be adjusted. Hardliners contended that the powder numbers simply should be raised to the levels of crack; liberals argued the reverse. Clay Shaw, the Florida Republican who had sponsored the tough crack-possession penalty in 1988, now agreed that the issue "deserves a second look." But he deplored the fact that his critics were "pulling out the race card" when many of crack's victims were minorities themselves. Congress could not break the impasse very easily either. It seemed that hardly any legislator ever wanted to be associated with lowering a crime penalty. So instead of resolving the dispute, lawmakers and Clinton agreed on a bill that simply overrode the commission's "equality" finding and sent the issue back for yet another study—all of this nearly a decade after the 100-to-1 ratio law had been enacted.

So once again, the policy battle over crack returned to the divided sentencing panel. Forced to abandon what had proved to be its politically unwise stance of calling for equal powder and crack sentences, the Sentencing Commission this time tried to split the difference, urging in April 1997 that the 500-gram amount that was triggering a five-year term for powder be cut to something between

125 and 375 grams, and that the trigger for the same crack sentence be increased to between 25 and 75 grams. Those numbers sounded more reasonable than a 100-to-1 ratio, but the commission's executive director, John Kramer, admitted later that the proposal was "fairly uninformed by research."[27]

The commissioners advised Congress and the Clinton administration that in making a final decision, they should rely "on more than simply drug quantity," focus on serious traffickers, and coordinate enforcement better with state and local governments. One commissioner, Vice Chairman Michael Gelacak—a nominee of Delaware Senator Joseph Biden—went further. Gelacak issued a concurring opinion that questioned Congress's seeming obsession with adjusting drug penalties. "We cannot punish our way out of this problem," he said. "We need to look at other solutions and stop making false promises."[28]

The debate soon returned to its usual posturing. Attorney General Reno and drug czar McCaffrey said the Clinton administration now had decided on favoring a 10-to-1 penalty ratio between the two forms of cocaine, lowering the crack threshhold and increasing the powder number. Michigan Senator Spencer Abraham, who had taken the lead role for Senate Republicans on the issue, said that any decrease in crack sentences "sends the wrong signal to young people."

Soon another year had gone by, and the nation entered its 12th year under a highly arbitrary scheme for punishing those who sold and misused two major forms of cocaine. Asked about the issue as Congress began its 1999 sessions, Abraham reflected the prevailing view of Republicans who controlled federal policy on drugs when he declared, "There aren't going to be lighter sentences; there's going to be tougher sentences." In a late 1999 interview, Reno agreed that the crack-versus-powder issue was a good example of irrational policymaking, but she downgraded its significance because the crack problem was "dying out."[29]

Whatever the merits of the cocaine sentencing debate, was overall government policy to attack the drug effective? It was hard to say with much certainty. When the Justice Department convened a conference in late 1997 to take stock, Superintendent David Mitchell of the Maryland State Police gave a typically frustrated view from law enforcement: "It seems that the more success we have [in seizing drugs], the less progress we make." Drug czar McCaffrey reported that the number of people who had used crack during the previous month had been stuck at about 400,000 since 1988, although that figure came from a survey of households that was hardly definitive. Measurements of weekly users, the usual proxy for the "hard-core" label, were more difficult to make accurately. Habitual cocaine use had either increased slightly, decreased steadily, or stayed about the same, depending on what source one believed. The most conservative official estimate put weekly coke users overall at more than 500,000, enough to keep a multi-billion-dollar sales industry going.

A separate city-by-city report that examined drug tests taken by arrestees concluded that cocaine use had declined at least 10 percent in major cities like Philadelphia, Washington, and Los Angeles. But the problem had moved to second-tier cities like Atlanta, Denver, Indianapolis, Phoenix, and St. Louis, where federal researchers reported that "the crack epidemic raged on as strong as ever." (A summer 1998 update from McCaffrey said that the market for crack "seems to have stabilized," that "heroin's popularity continues to grow," and that "marijuana also is thriving," hardly a very promsing picture.)

Despite the ups and downs of cocaine use, in general terms, the nation's drug problem has been stable since the mid-1980s, concluded veteran analyst Peter Reuter of the University of Maryland. The fact that cocaine and heroin prices have not increased, despite the tougher enforcement measures and penalties put in place during the last 15 years of the twentieth century, is a "major analytic and policy puzzle," he said.[30] Nor have those two drugs, or marijuana for that matter, become significantly less available, Reuter said. Of course, this does not mean that any particular government antidrug program has been ineffective; it's always possible that drug abuse would have been worse had it not been for official efforts. But when it comes to drugs, as with many of the other major fronts in America's war on crime, credible explanations of whether enforcement, treatment, or prevention are accomplishing much are sadly lacking.

No one claims a silver bullet solution that would end the allure of narcotics, but perhaps the most promising approach that has been largely ignored is intensive treatment for drug users already in the justice system. Although two thirds or more of the 5 million or so persons behind bars or on probation have a drug or alcohol problem, opportunities for them to take part in rehabilitation programs are remarkably rare. Corrections experts agree that as few as one in ten of those prisoners who might benefit from treatment are able to get it (compared with roughly half of the addicted population as a whole).

In the few places where intensive treatment has been tried and studied, advocates point to successes. A Delaware program that concentrated on crack users, for example, found that half of those who took part in treatment during a combination of prison time and "work release" supervision remained drug free during an 18-month follow-up. Only 16 percent of those who received no treatment stayed off drugs.[31] No one argued that the convicts who kept away from drugs would do so forever, but the better record compiled by treatment participants seemed worth trying elsewhere. The Clinton administration moved in 1998 to encourage such efforts by making federal prison-building aid to states contingent on their periodic testing of inmates for drug use. But more testing would not guarantee the availability of treatment slots.

Successful drug treatment programs in the justice system can save money in the long run by holding down the number of convicts who must be incarcerated repeatedly. But it has been an uphill battle to obtain budget allocations. It's still much easier for law enforcers to win higher appropriations by citing higher numbers of arrests and drug seizures, statistics that "give politicians more ammunition than expanding the number of treatment beds," observed James Inciardi, a University of Delaware criminologist who specializes in narcotics issues.

One promising way to divert drug offenders into treatment but to keep them on a short judicial leash was "drug courts" that were set up in hundreds of locations in the 1990s to concentrate narcotics cases in one place. Instead of mixing drug violations among the 13-plus million criminal cases filed each year nationwide, the idea was that specialized judges could better sort out and track defendants who were more amenable to treatment. The judges also would become familiar with the pluses and minuses of different treatment programs. The first such tribunal was set up in Miami in 1989. Attorney General Reno—who had served as Miami's chief prosecutor—touted the idea after she came to Washington, helping to ensure that drug courts received at least modest federal help each year even when other programs that stressed prevention or treatment got little or nothing.

Like many other antidrug efforts, drug courts got decidedly mixed reviews in their early years. Miami reported a 33 percent drop in rearrests for those who had "graduated" from its drug court, compared with other offenders. And a federal survey of repeat-crime rates by drug court graduates in a variety of cities reported figures of 2 to 20 percent, far lower than addicts' usual recidivism rate.

A detailed analysis commissioned by the Justice Department of a pretrial drug court program in Washington, D.C., showed that the concept was far from perfect. Only 41 percent of eligible suspects during a 17-month period took part in treatment for which they were eligible, and only 19 percent graduated. The average time to complete the program was 11 months, rather than the half year that had been anticipated. Most significantly, rearrest rates did not differ markedly between those who took part and those who didn't.[32]

Even if drug courts were hardly ending the narcotics plague, they seemed a reasonable investment of tax dollars. As of 2000, at least 500 courts had been set up with the aid of less than 100 million federal dollars. In some places, officials contended that for defendants who stayed clean after court-supervised treatment, the public saved money that would have been spent on justice-system costs for those who were arrested time and time again.

By the late 1990s, drug prevention and treatment were getting more support in the federal budget, but they still accounted for only about one third of Washington's nearly $20 billion annual drug control allocation—a total that had grown from less than $2 billion when Ronald Reagan declared his war on drugs back in 1982. In mid-1999, drug czar McCaffrey insisted that funding levels for prevention and treatment were "moving in the right direction." If legislators would debate the issues seriously, he said, "we'll start getting rational behavior out of Congress . . . and in another two, three, or five years, we'll probably have the momentum going that we need."

That cautious prediction seemed optimistic given the partisan zigzag course of federal antidrug policy. The reigning political consensus on drug control remained that government's first priority was to take harsh measures against both traffickers and users. Beyond that, key officeholders from both major parties believed that the public would support other efforts only after all the stern actions were tried. "There is a lot of support for treatment," said Democratic political consultant Robert Shrum. "But it must be additive to being tough on crime."

As the crack-versus-powder cocaine battle illustrated, it appeared that the two parties were destined to remain in virtual lockstep on antidrug policy for some years to come. With a hardline Democrat in the White House and Republicans controlling both houses of Congress, analyst Eva Bertram observed that near the twentieth century's end, "the punitive assumptions of the drug war paradigm and the expanded drug war bureaucracy remained entrenched."

What this meant in practice was that each side launched initiatives expanding on its preferred approach, and the two parties fought over long-term goals. In late 1998, congressional Republicans—arguing that Clinton's executive branch had dropped the ball on stopping drug imports at the U.S. border—forced the White House to accept a $2.6 billion plan to beef up military and intelligence operations in Latin America.

For its part, the Clinton administration started a series of dramatic paid television advertisements costing nearly $200 million a year aimed at teenagers, whose abuse of some drugs was rising again, according to several measures in the late 1990s. Although TV ads had been tried off and on for many years, most had been "public service announcements" that aired at odd hours. The new ads looked appealing, with warnings delivered by teens themselves rather than adult authority figures.

Detailed evaluations of this extensive public relations test would not be known for several years, but drug czar McCaffrey said a preliminary survey credited the ads with a "significant" decrease from 43 to 38 percent of teens reporting that they had ever tried marijuana. Roughly half of the youths surveyed had seen some of the major ads, and as many as 69 percent of the teens agreed that "TV ads make them stay away from drugs," McCaffrey said.[33] Teen drug use was declining, as measured by a federal survey of drug use issued in late summer 2000 that asked who had used illegal drugs in the previous month. Yet the study found that nearly 19 percent of people ages 18 to 25 reported recent drug abuse, a rising rate and one about twice as high as that of the 12 to 17 age group.

Faced with this mixed picture, Democratic and Republican leaders warred over long-range projections over who could do better. For the first time, the drug czar issued a ten-year plan. McCaffrey's version aimed at reducing illegal drug use and availability 50 percent by the year 2007.

Before he left Congress in 1999, Republican House Speaker Newt Gingrich upped the ante by calling the Clinton plan a "timetable for defeat" and pushing for an expanded interdiction plan that lawmakers later approved. The GOP argued that drug use could be brought down much faster than Clinton maintained; the Republican defense buildup, for example, promised to reduce the illegal drug flow by 80 percent in three years.

The estimates may have sounded good in sound bites, but there was no solid way to judge whether either of the new plans would be any better than the old ones. Reno, who before she became attorney general had observed the drug flow closely in Miami, said that before the mid-1980s, only about 15 percent of the drugs coming into the southeastern United States had been stopped. The figure increased to 25 percent after Vice President Bush's task force arrived. An unusually candid federal official told a state grand jury reviewing the interdiction efforts that "to have any impact on drugs in America, you would have to interdict 75 percent of the stuff, and that would be economically prohibitive."

At the turn of the twenty-first century, American antidrug policy still was hooked on a strategy that devoted significant resources to the difficult task of interdiction and kept treatment and prevention on an erratic course. While antidrug warriors squabbled over differing priorities, the most potent threat to public safety lay in the intersection of drug trafficking and firearms—another epidemic seemingly out of control in many pockets of America.

Chapter 7

GUNS DON'T KILL?

Guns stir more emotion, sloganeering, and misinformation than any other single aspect of the war on crime. Mention guns and violence to the National Rifle Association (NRA) and its nearly 4 million members and expect to hear some variation of the rallying cry "Guns Don't Kill, People Do." The NRA argues fervently that the focus should be on people who misuse guns, not on the weapons themselves.

The 1 million adherents of the NRA's main adversary, Handgun Control, Inc., respond with versions of former director Pete Shields's book title, 'Guns Don't Die—People Do.'[1] The antigun group stresses the undeniable connection between the wide availability of guns in the United States and the fact that the nation has one of the world's highest rates of lethal violence.

Each of the opposing camp's slogans embodies some truth, but they also illustrate the simplistic notions that have dominated the debate over gun control for decades—controversies that are most heated in Washington because federal statutes dominates gun-law enforcement and regulation.

The plain fact is that many gun controls, whatever their political impact, have only a marginal effect on firearms violence. Like other anticrime policymaking, the regulation of guns has been episodic. Laws and their enforcement have depended as much on public reaction to an extreme event—usually a mass killing or assassination—as on any careful study. The usual pattern is for politicians to enact a gun-control law in response to a tragedy and declare victory, even if the measure probably will have minimal impact.

Between legislative tussles, the two sides in the gun-control wars talk past each other and confound most of the public. The NRA is fond of asserting that 20,000 gun laws and regulations are in place at the federal, state, and local levels and concluding that any worthwhile measures among them have not been enforced enough. Many gun-control advocates agree on the enforcement point, but they say that all the laws and rules fall far short of what is needed: bans or at least stringent limitations on the manufacture and sale of weapons that cannot safely be used for hunting or self-defense.

In a nation with a long heritage of firearms use for hunting, self-defense, and military combat, it should not be surprising that the stock of guns in circulation has climbed steadily over the years. In the 1990s, the best estimates were that more than 235 million firearms were spread out over nearly half of American households.[2] But the vast majority were owned for sports or defensive purposes, and only 1 or 2 percent might ever be used in a crime. Just as the police have found it difficult to bear down on the small number of people who commit most crimes, so have gun-control advocates in trying to keep that tiny number of firearms out of criminal hands.

Government regulation was provoked by unusual crimes almost from the start. A wave of gangland killings and bank robberies in the prohibition era and the early 1930s, for example, led to strict federal curbs on machine guns, but that was the only major national legislation in place for many years. Absent a prominent crime problem, much of the pressure for regulation came from the business sector. In the early 1960s, U.S. gun manufacturers pressed for restrictions on imported firearms, but the industry made little headway.

The most dramatic firearms crime in modern times was the assassination of President John F. Kennedy on November 22, 1963. As shocking as it was, it took two assassinations five years later to produce a major gun-control law. Lee Harvey Oswald purchased the Italian rifle he allegedly used to shoot Kennedy by mail for $21.45 from a Chicago sporting goods company, but that kind of transaction had long been legal. A few critics had sought restrictions on such sales even before the assassination, but they had not stirred much interest. Connecticut Senator Thomas Dodd introduced legislation to regulate the interstate sale of firearms, but it stalled in committee. Then civil rights leader Martin Luther King, Jr., and presidential candidate Robert F. Kennedy were gunned down within two months in the spring of 1968. The assassinations focused national attention on how easy it was for criminals to obtain firearms.

As is typical of controversial legislation, timing was everything. The omnibus 1968 crime law, already speeding toward passage in the spring of that presidential election year, was quickly amended after the shooting of King in April to ban the interstate sale and shipment of handguns, mostly by mail order. The measure also prohibited importation of cheap handguns, which some backers may have intended to keep from minorities whom they blamed for urban riots. The bill passed Congress in early June, the day after Senator Kennedy was shot to death in a Los Angeles hotel kitchen. The crime law's gun provisions, along with the earlier machine gun restrictions, stood for many years as the main federal limitations on the firearms trade.

The King and Kennedy murders helped set a pattern that was to repeat itself over and over. Legislators and bureaucrats based laws largely on the public's emotional reaction to tragic cases and on lobbying by interest groups to build on the sense of crisis. Only later, once agents tried to enforce the measures and their actions were challenged in court, were policymakers forced to consider whether what they had done made sense. Sometimes it did, but more often the results were unproved.

Gun-control campaigners would argue that more laws or regulations were needed to plug holes in the original versions. That scenario seemingly lent credence to the oft-expressed NRA charge that the "antigunners" were embarked on a conspiracy to ban guns, step by step. The opposing arguments typically were expressed in hyperbolic terms, with little discussion of how laws were enforced in the real world. "The great gun debate was largely an emotional one, without any hard facts on either side," said Richard Velde, who watched the laws evolve as a congressional aide in the 1960s and later as head of the federal Law Enforcement Assistance Administration.[3]

An early example of the game-playing that surrounds gun-control debates involved Connecticut's Dodd—a liberal Democrat—and Nebraska's Roman Hruska—a conservative Republican. To publicize the problem of firearms by mail, Dodd tried to attract news photographers by filling tables in the hearing room with guns that could be ordered with few questions asked. Hruska wanted a Nebraska game commissioner to testify that most purchases actually were made by hunters. But Dodd, who headed the subcommittee and controlled its agenda and budget, refused to pay the Nebraskan's travel expenses and scheduled him as the day's final witness. Dodd did not find time to call the Nebraska commissioner to the witness table on the first two days of hearings, requiring him to make a third trip to deliver his message. The shabby treatment of his witness infuriated Hruska, encouraging him to fight harder against Dodd, which helped tone down the final language of the 1968 Gun Control Act.

The Johnson-era statute remained the main federal gun law for many years while the violence toll, including millions of gun crimes, climbed steadily. Demands by some anticrime advocates for more gun controls met a solid wall of opposition, led by the NRA. Founded in 1871, the NRA represents the interests of sportsmen and offers training to millions of gun users, including many law enforcement officers.

Such services were the backbone of NRA operations, but the group became known in the political world for its unwavering opposition to gun controls through a nationwide grassroots network. An alert from NRA's headquarters in downtown Washington, D.C., would produce an avalanche of letters, telegrams, and phone calls to Congress and the White House. (The group, whose location in a city with some of the nation's strictest gun controls was considered an anomaly, later moved to suburban Virginia, a region much more hostile to controls.) At election time, the NRA's views would be transmitted to its members, whose inclination to decide on the single issue of a candidate's position on gun control could make a crucial difference in a race's outcome. As discussed in Chapter 10, campaign disputes over gun control were a major factor in Republicans' seizing the U.S. House of Representatives in 1994 for the first time since the 1950s.

After Ronald Reagan's inauguration as president in 1981, the NRA was aligned solidly with leaders of the executive branch, most Republicans in Congress, and many moderate Democrats as well, plus scores of rank-and-file law enforcement officers around the nation. Members of this unofficial coalition differed on some details, but they generally agreed with the NRA that America's crime problem was primarily due not to a proliferation of guns but rather to a lax criminal-justice system. The NRA's alliance with the police was so strong that "it was not unusual for a new cop to be given a badge, a gun, and an NRA application," said David Doi, a one-time liaison with law enforcement for Handgun Control, Inc. "Most officers were trained by NRA-certified instructors; there was a long history and tradition of the NRA and cops being best friends."[4]

This coziness, at least at the top of many organizations representing law enforcement, was to change radically during the 1980s and 1990s. Hardly anyone predicted that by the time Congress passed a wide-ranging anticrime law in 1994, not only would many key law enforcement leaders have broken with the NRA in favor of gun control, but so would two stalwart NRA supporters, Ronald Reagan and his vice president, George Bush.

Before Republicans became the congressional majority in 1995, two prominent federal gun control laws had become law during a single session of Congress: the 1993 Brady Act, which instituted a national waiting period of up to five days to allow for background checks on handgun purchasers, and the 1994 anticrime law's ban on certain assault-style weapons that had been blamed for some spectacular crimes.

The turnaround was all the more extraordinary because the pro-gun lobby had reached a modern-day congressional high-water mark in 1986. Not satisfied with easily beating down just about all gun-control proposals, the NRA and its allies succeeded that year in passing a law that watered down its main target: the 1968 Gun Control Act. The NRA's chief whipping boys were the enforcers of the law, the agents of the Treasury Department's Bureau of Alcohol, Tobacco, and Firearms (ATF), whom the NRA accused of abusing innocent gun owners in a series of highly publicized incidents.

The campaign that finally succeeded against the Gun Control Act was born in a little-remembered Missouri congressional campaign. Harold Volkmer, a Democratic state legislator from northeast Missouri, watched a young Republican lawyer from the city of Mexico, Missouri, named Christopher Bond (later a Missouri governor and U.S. senator) nearly oust Representative William Hungate in 1968, using Hungate's vote for that year's gun-control measure as a main campaign theme.

When Volkmer succeeded fellow Democrat Hungate in 1977, he was determined to change the law. Knowing that constituents in his largely rural district would back him, he wanted to repeal the statute's ban on the interstate sale of firearms and to limit federal investigations of gun dealers. Volkmer said he was "sick and tired" of federal agents' seizing guns over what he considered minor violations of the 1968 law, so he hired a Missouri prosecutor to help him compile a case against ATF.[5] The NRA saw Volkmer as a godsend to one of its longtime goals. Volkmer introduced the first version of his bill in 1979. Besides resuming interstate gun sales, the measure was designed to make monitoring and prosecution of firearms dealers much more difficult by raising the required standard of proof.

Volkmer got nowhere with the liberals who controlled the House Judiciary Committee, starting with Chairman Peter Rodino of New Jersey, who would not even schedule a hearing. But the Missourian persisted in spreading the word about his mission, and a parallel campaign was launched in the Senate by Idaho Republican James McClure. The result was the McClure-Volkmer bill, which went through a series of drafts in the early 1980s on both sides of the Capitol. The outlook seemed promising on the Senate side in 1984, when liberal Edward Kennedy of Massachusetts, a leading gun-control advocate, agreed to support some of the measure's basic provisions if McClure and Volkmer would retain the ban on interstate sales of handguns, which did not affect much hunting. With Kennedy's endorsement helping to blunt liberal opposition, the Senate approved the bill in 1985.

Still, most Washingtonians who followed crime issues assumed that the McClure-Volkmer bill would die a slow death in the liberal-controlled House Judiciary Committee, which had killed conservative anticrime proposals for years—with the notable exception of the 1984 omnibus crime law. The McClure-Volkmer gutting of the 1968 gun statute probably would have failed had a key opponent not made a major tactical error. Judiciary Chairman Rodino, confident of his ability to squelch any legislation favorable to the gun lobby, declared McClure-Volkmer "dead on arrival."

That insulting assertion made junior legislator Volkmer all the more determined to get his way. Because it now was certain that Rodino would keep McClure-Volkmer bottled up in his committee, Volkmer decided to use an unusual procedure called a "discharge petition" to move the bill. If a majority of House members—218—endorsed it, the measure would bypass Rodino and go to the House floor for debate. The discharge process almost never succeeds, because it is virtually impossible to get a majority of the House to buck the institution's leadership and committee structure.

But the gun lobby and the tireless Missourian would not be stopped. While the liberals who controlled anticrime policymaking in the House paid little attention, Volkmer had almost reached his goal by early 1986. He succeeded on March 12, when Maryland Democrat Roy Dyson signed up. Suddenly, the bill that the liberals detested was guaranteed a vote. (The irony, Volkmer said years later, was that he might well have failed if Rodino had withheld his nasty threat, held hearings, and arranged for his liberal-dominated panel to spend years hacking away at the bill.)

McClure-Volkmer passed the House after an acrimonious debate in early April 1986. The only major chink from the NRA viewpoint was an amendment added during the last moments of floor debate on the bill. New Jersey's William Hughes, the liberals' point man on crime legislation, managed to secure a vote on a provision that banned the manufacture and sale of new machine guns. The amendment was included only as a result of some parliamentary maneuvering. "He didn't play square," charged an angry Volkmer, who complained that Hughes raised the issue with only a few minutes left in the allotted debate period, leaving no time for opponents to make their case. An outraged NRA targeted the measure for repeal in later congressional sessions—a reversal it never was able to pull off. (By some accounts, the NRA was unable to find a single sponsor for the repeal—a rare NRA setback in those years.)

The machine-gun provision did not have much of an impact; there was not exactly a big market in the heavily regulated weapons. But the symbolism was powerful for both sides in the gun debate. Fluke or not, Congress had banned a particular type of firearm—the kind of nose-under-the-camel's-tent argument that the NRA long had been warning its members could be the beginning of the end of wide access to firearms in America. McClure-Volkmer (officially, the Firearm Owners Protection Act) included plenty of other provisions that the gun lobby could be happy about, but it turned out that the NRA's high riding was soon to wane.

The turnaround had started with the issue of "cop-killer bullets" well before

McClure-Volkmer came to a head. In 1981, Representative Mario Biaggi, a New York City cop-turned-congressman, learned of a brand of ammunition that could penetrate the soft body armor sometimes referred to as "bulletproof vests." In fact, the so-called KTW bullets (named for the initials of their creators) had been largely abandoned as standard equipment by police forces. But Biaggi moved ahead anyway with legislation to ban the product. When he started searching for political backing, what he didn't anticipate was a split between the NRA and its historic allies, leaders of law enforcement groups.

The NRA dusted off its traditional argument that it wasn't firearms and ammunition that caused unwarranted deaths and injuries but rather lax punishment of the people who wielded them. "A gun doesn't hop off the table and make you into its first victim," said Tanya Metaksa, a longtime NRA leader who served as its chief lobbyist in the 1990s. "There has to be a criminal behind it."[6] That stance underscored staunch NRA opposition to proposed curbs on even the most deadly forms of guns and ammunition on the ground that allowing any one limitation to be enacted could open the floodgates for a series of bans and, eventually, a disarming of the nation. Law enforcement leaders had usually gone along with that argument, but not when it came to the KTW ammunition. When the NRA refused to endorse what became known as the "cop killer bullet ban," many police leaders asked, "What's the matter? That's a no-brainer," recalled Handgun Control's Doi.

The NRA did not support cop killers, but it believed that the Biaggi measure was drafted far too broadly. The bill, which attempted to ban anything that could penetrate a protective vest, could have barred ammunition commonly used in hunting. ATF was part of the Treasury Department, which took legislative positions on firearms issues. NRA lobbyist James Baker met with John Walker, the Treasury official overseeing ATF, and quickly realized that the department was not up to speed on the nuances.

Baker promptly scribbled down a draft revision that would base the ban on the metallic composition of bullets instead of the extent to which they could pierce vests and handed it to Walker. The Treasury Department and NRA backers in Congress agreed to the change, but the Democrats who controlled the House did not want to approve an NRA-initiated measure. "When it was apparent that our definition was going to pass," said Wayne LaPierre, then the NRA's chief lobbyist, House Speaker Thomas (Tip) O'Neill "pulled the bill from the floor and blamed the NRA. The truth is that he didn't want our better definition to pass so that we could use it in the [1984] election."[7]

After many twists and turns, the ammunition law eventually was enacted in 1986, long after it would have much effect because manufacturing of the product had virtually ended. But the damage to the NRA-police relationship had been done. Despite the behind-the-scenes back-and-forth, gun-control advocates successfully portrayed the NRA as favoring cop killers. That stance, combined with the NRA campaign for the McClure-Volkmer law that weakened firearms regulations, led many police leaders to the realization that the NRA might not have their interests at heart after all. Three of the earliest NRA foes were known by insiders as the "three B's"—Richard Boyd, Neal Behan, and Anthony Bouza. Boyd headed the Fraternal Order of Police (FOP), one of the nation's largest law enforcement unions, in the early 1980s. Behan and Bouza, former New York City officers, had gone on to head police forces in Baltimore County, Maryland, and Minneapolis, respectively.

Boyd steered the FOP into opposing McClure-Volkmer, while Behan and Bouza helped round up prominent chiefs to support the gun-control cause—officials like Lee Brown, who headed police forces in Atlanta, Houston, and later New York City; William Kolender of San Diego; and Joseph Casey of Nashville, later the president of the International Association of Chiefs of Police, the largest organization of police executives. A prize catch was Los Angeles Police Chief Daryl Gates, initially no backer of gun control. Gates became a supporter when his officers began appearing on the list of assault weapon victims. Gates "almost to a fault supported his men," said Handgun Control's Doi.

As it evolved in the 1980s, the police debate with the NRA was more a matter of name-calling and tactics than one of substance. Urban police chiefs believed that moderate gun controls might help bring about at least modest reductions in the crime totals, but the NRA could not brook any dissent from its opposition to any and all gun controls. When a local police chief departed from an NRA position, the group was not hesitant to start purchasing media advertisements against the chief or even trying to oust him.

On the state level, seeds for the acrimonious NRA-police split were planted in California during a battle over Proposition 15, a 1982 ballot initiative that would have banned all future sales of handguns in the state. Groups taking part in the embryonic gun-control movement had debated internally whether such a far-reaching approach would be wise, but they eventually decided to go ahead. Advocates of Proposition 15 built an early lead in public-opinion surveys, but the NRA soon started running full-page newspaper ads featuring county sheriffs and rank-and-file police officers who opposed the measure. The well-funded NRA campaign was a smashing success, and voters soundly defeated Proposition 15.

The election had repercussions far beyond California. Much of the news media had portrayed the vote as the decisive modern-day referendum on guns, and the NRA was the clear winner. "It almost destroyed the gun control movement," said Josh Sugarmann of the Violence Policy Center, a Washington-based think tank that advocates stronger enforcement of gun regulations. "The press built it up as the big battle, we got smeared, and the press walked away [from reporting on gun control] for three years, saying the issue had been settled."[8]

After the Proposition 15 defeat—and with the debates over the McClure-Volkmer bill and cop-killer bullets causing an uproar in law enforcement circles—it became apparent to some police leaders that they would be more successful if they presented a united front. Traditionally, the NRA had strongly overmatched the nearly nonexistent lobbying force of the police. Even when a police official did voice an opinion, it had no effect on election day because most law enforcers stayed out of partisan politics. Similarly, lawmakers did not perceive a long-term interest by police leaders in legislation. A former police chief told *Congressional Quarterly* that he had been advised by members of Congress that the typical view in the Capitol was that "the police will forget what we do here" on gun legislation "but the NRA will never forget."[9]

To help change the balance in the lobbying equation, several police chiefs and the organizations they led joined in 1985 to form a group called the Law Enforcement Steering Committee (LESC) to represent police interests, including support for what they considered reasonable gun controls. The Police Foundation, a Washington-based think tank that had been started by the Ford Foundation and others in the 1970s to promote innovative policing programs, hosted the early meetings and provided staff. Handgun Control Inc. took part in some of the early meetings, but the organization deliberately stayed in the background and let the police leaders take the spotlight.

One of the first major items on the LESC agenda was the by-then losing battle against McClure-Volkmer. Although police officers in uniform appeared at the Capitol to oppose the bill before the House approved it in 1986—a precursor to the phalanxes of men in blue who would provide backdrops in the next several presidential campaigns and crime-bill debates—their mere appearance was ineffective against the intense behind-the-scenes lobbying campaign by the NRA and its supporters. Legislators knew that come election time, it would be NRA members and not police officers who would influence more votes.

Although the police chiefs and the NRA disagreed over the basic issue of whether gun controls would cut crime, the intensely personal split between leaders of the two sides was not inevitable, given their common interest in issues like training police officers. The clash might have been avoided—and the politics of crime policy in the 1980s and beyond could have changed markedly—if leaders of the two sides had not alienated each other. One leading member of the LESC was the Washington-based Police Executive Research Forum (PERF), whose first president was Sheriff John Duffy of San Diego County. "He used to sit down regularly with the NRA and try to knock some sense into them—and ask whether they understood they were alienating law enforcement," said

Handgun Control's David Doi. "He thought he had a couple of deals cut, but the NRA always backed out."

An extreme example of the full-scale war waged by the NRA in the media involved Joseph McNamara, long-time police chief of San Jose, California. Mc-Namara was one of the first law enforcement leaders to support moderate gun control and to criticize the NRA publicly. For his efforts, McNamara got a threat of an NRA lawsuit and an NRA advertisement in national news publications accusing him (incorrectly, he said) of having supported the legalization of drugs.

The NRA also attacked Nashville Police Chief Joseph Casey, who in the mid-1980s headed the International Association of Chiefs of Police (IACP), the nation's most prominent law-enforcement organization. That prompted an IACP counterattack advising its members not to be "intimidated by political extortionists" like the NRA. The NRA helped block two of the three B's—Richard Boyd and Anthony Bouza—from getting new jobs in other jurisdictions, and it distributed bumper stickers urging the chief executive of Baltimore County to "dump [Police Chief Neil] Behan."

In late 1986, Jerald Vaughn, then IACP executive director, met with top NRA executive Warren Cassidy and thought he had persuaded the gun group to stop personal attacks on police chiefs. But nothing changed. As reported by author Osha Gray Davidson, two weeks after the meeting, the NRA again went after San Jose's McNamara. Vaughn protested, but Cassidy responded that "we believe McNamara represents a threat to our people."[10] The war would continue, as lawmakers worried about offending one side or the other. "There is not a single law enforcement leader who has taken a stand for gun control who hasn't taken some flak," said Doi.

The NRA insisted that many rank-and-file officers supported its causes, and that certainly was true as far as attacks on the criminal-justice system were concerned. But the gun-control forces did make inroads in police ranks, particularly with the FOP, which included hundreds of thousands of line officers. Dewey Stokes, an Ohio Republican who was FOP president in the 1980s, supported gun control and even became a political backer of liberal Ohio Senator Howard Metzenbaum, one of the Senate's leading gun-control advocates. Mary Louise Westmoreland Cohen, who worked for Handgun Control and Metzenbaum at different times in the 1980s, said it was clear from the NRA's unsuccessful attempts to depose Stokes as head of FOP that rank-and-file officers supported their leader's stand. "They were not just doing what Dewey Stokes told them to do," Cohen said.[11]

In later years, some NRA leaders admitted that they had hurt their cause by alienating law enforcement leaders in the 1980s. "The NRA did a very lousy public relations job with the police and the general public," said Wayne LaPierre, longtime NRA executive. Even if "it could not have been handled worse from a PR standpoint," LaPierre insisted that when it came to substantive legislative positions, "we did the right thing for our gun owner constituency and our police constituency." Still, the rift was so deep that the IACP never again allowed the NRA to set up displays at the police chiefs' annual conventions.

The outcome of the armor-piercing ammunition battle was an extreme example of the gap between rhetoric and reality that has characterized the American gun-control debate for many years. When Congress in 1986 approved what essentially was the NRA version of the bullet bill, gun-control forces succeeded in leaving the public impression that the NRA somehow favored cop-killer bullets. (The ammunition already had disappeared from the market.) The NRA was put on the defensive and the debate had no real effect on crime, but the police leaders' break with the NRA helped set the stage for more gun-control victories in later years.

A similar public relations war was fought over plastic weapons that supposedly were being devised to thwart metal detectors. Two years later, after another pitched battle between police leaders and the NRA, Congress required firearms to contain specified amounts of metal. Yet there was little evidence that any purely plastic gun was being designed.

These skirmishes were precursors to gun control brouhahas in the 1990s that would feature a scenario unimaginable in earlier decades: the NRA going down to defeat at the hands of law enforcement working with Handgun Control, Inc. The gun-control organization was founded in the early 1970s and was headed, starting in 1976, by Pete Shields, a former Dupont executive, whose son was shot to death in a San Francisco series of murders called the "Zebra killings." Gun control was not a prominent national issue in the 1970s, but Handgun Control forces were galvanized by the 1981 assassination attempt on President Ronald Reagan outside a Washington hotel, a shooting that left his press secretary, James S. Brady, seriously wounded.

John Hinckley, the 25-year-old Coloradan arrested for the crime, had gone to Dallas to purchase the .22-caliber revolver used in the shooting, part of a small arsenal he had assembled in an apparent quest to kill a president in order to impress actress Jodie Foster. Handgun Control used the episode to press for a waiting period on handgun purchases. One reason for the wait was to prevent "impulse" killings by people without firearms who suddenly decided to buy one and attack someone. But the main purpose was to make sure that law enforcement officials had time to check whether prospective gun purchasers were prohibited from buying a gun, most commonly because of a felony record.

Ironically, the waiting period that Handgun Control helped get Congress to enact a dozen years later—named the Brady Act in honor of James Brady and his wife, Sarah—would not by itself have prevented Hinckley from acquiring guns because he had no criminal record. Still, Hinckley later told psychiatrists that the threat of a background check would have dissuaded him. (It was widely and incorrectly reported that the law required a background check. Most police agencies did them, but sheriffs who opposed the statute as an unwarranted federal mandate without any provision for localities to pay the costs won a 1997 Supreme Court ruling that Congress could not constitutionally force them to conduct such checks.)

After the 1981 Reagan shooting, which the president survived without serious permanent injury, the Bradys were targeted early by gun-control forces looking for backers. In an authorized biography of James Brady, journalist Mollie Dickenson reported that Republican Peter Hannaford asked Sarah Brady in 1982 to join the campaign for California's Proposition 15 that would have banned handguns.[12] With law enforcers moving toward favoring gun control, as the daughter of an FBI agent she was inclined to help. But she pulled back after friends reminded her that Reagan, a Californian, opposed most gun controls.

Gun-control backers kept up their efforts to get the Bradys involved. By 1985, Sarah Brady had agreed to join the lobbying against the McClure-Volkmer bill. Dickenson said that Brady checked with Donald Regan, Reagan's chief of staff, to make sure the White House would not be offended. Regan was understanding, mentioning that his wife felt the same way about guns.

Sarah Brady soon became a very visible figure, speaking around the country and appearing on many television programs in support of gun control. Her image, alongside that of her paralyzed husband, was an appealing one, especially to the national news media that generally favored gun controls in editorials and almost always went for "man bites dog" stories like the conversion of Sarah Brady. Describing herself as a conservative Republican, she declared that "we as Americans have too cavalier an attitude about handguns and the problems they cause." The spirited debate over whether gun controls should be weakened further after McClure-Volkmer encouraged the Bradys to pursue the long-running drive to enact the law that eventually bore their name.

In another instance of a backfire from the bitter campaign, Sarah Brady told author Osha Gray Davidson that she called the NRA shortly after McClure-Volkmer was enacted and told someone who answered the phone her plan "to make it my lifetime mission to see that you are destroyed." She and her husband quickly became the best-known advocates of gun control—and the target of NRA fund-raising letters.

Fresh from the McClure-Volkmer defeat, Handgun Control decided to focus on the legislative priority of the waiting period and background check for handgun purchases. The 1968 Gun Control Act barred firearm ownership by felons, but enforcement was sporadic at best. A convict who visited a gun dealer could simply lie on the form asking about a criminal history, and no one would be the wiser. The Brady bill, introduced in 1987, seemed to have no chance in the face of stiff opposition from the NRA, which argued that it would unduly delay gun purchases by law-abiding people while most criminals continued to arm themselves via the black market. Ronald Reagan, a stalwart NRA backer, briefly endorsed a waiting period, but a spokesman quickly withdrew the statement, explaining that the president favored it only if it was enacted by states. (At Sarah Brady's behest, Reagan finally did endorse the federal bill in 1991, long after he left office.)

Having been decisively defeated in the McClure-Volkmer debate, the new coalition of police and gun-control advocates took a while to develop its lobbying potential. Before the House resoundingly rejected the Brady measure for the first time in 1988, Handgun Control's Doi could find enough police in only three cities to stage rallies for the cause. But as they had coalesced to help ban cop-killer ammunition in the mid-1980s, police leaders were able to persuade their troops that waiting periods would be a reasonable step. By 1990, officers appeared at press conferences in three dozen cities to support Brady—not an easy transition for many of them. Noting that officers typically oppose gun curbs and the news media with equal fervor, Doi faced the major challenge of "asking them to appear in front of television cameras to support gun control—two things they hated." Unlike the case of the later campaign against "assault weapons," there was little proof that the absence of waiting periods was putting officers' lives in jeopardy. Now, however, many law enforcement leaders were not heeding the NRA's strident objections.

The fact that police leaders were openly supporting Brady made a crucial difference to some legislators. "Police going public gave politicians cover," said Doi. "They were no longer going against 'Joe NRA' but coming out in favor of local law enforcement." Private lobbying also helped. Doi recalled one Brady bill vote in which an Ohio congressman's help would be pivotal. Doi asked the Cincinnati police chief to call the legislator, which he did, changing the member's vote from no to yes.

The Brady bill made notable progress for the first time in 1990, when the House Judiciary Committee approved a seven-day wait, as it was initially proposed. Then, both houses passed Brady as part of a larger crime bill in 1991. The House vote was dramatic, with 193 members—only 25 short of a majority—casting ballots for an alternative plan that would have rejected the waiting period in favor of an "instant" record check—a proposition always preferred by the NRA to avoid inconveniencing lawful purchasers.

Under instant check, gun dealers would be able to determine quickly via computer whether a prospective buyer had a criminal record. But many Americans wrongly assumed that the FBI's National Crime Information Center included every criminal record nationwide. The reality was that records were spread among a notoriously incomplete patchwork of state and local systems.

The disposition of arrests frequently was not provided, and common names could easily be confused. Opponents of the instant check system maintained that many dangerous gun buyers would easily slip through the net; it was not clear that they would be detected under a waiting period of several days, either.

Even after the Brady bill made it into the broader 1991 anticrime bill, it was not enacted in that congressional session because Senate Republicans in 1992 objected to what they regarded as inadequate provisions to streamline habeas corpus court appeals by death row inmates.

Brady's prospects changed dramatically in 1993, when Bill Clinton moved into the White House. Although he was a moderate or hardliner on many other anticrime issues, including support of capital punishment, Clinton backed gun controls, traditionally a liberal stance. And he had managed to get most major police organizations to endorse his candidacy, largely because of his plan to have the federal government finance 100,000 more local police officers.

The first question for gun-control strategists was whether to include Brady in the omnibus anticrime law that was gathering strength in Congress. Some proponents, noting that the tactic had worked in the previous congressional session (even if the final bill failed for other reasons), saw that approach as a way to increase their chances of success by picking up votes from gun-control foes who supported other provisions in a wide-ranging bill.

Others took the opposite tack and portrayed gun control as a potentially fatal diversion to the main crime bill. They argued that the NRA would attempt to make the entire measure a litmus test on firearms issues and would assemble opposition not only from core NRA supporters but also from legislators who opposed any other clause.

The first competing versions of the omnibus anticrime legislation introduced in the fall of 1993 embodied this dilemma—House Judiciary Chairman Jack Brooks included Brady but his Senate counterpart, Joseph Biden, omitted it. In a decision that proved critical to Brady's passage, Brooks determined that the omnibus approach was too cumbersome for his ideologically divided committee and that the massive crime bill should be split into several smaller pieces. Brooks didn't favor Brady; he hoped the NRA would find some way to kill it. Separation of Brady from the omnibus bill "was an accident of history," said Robert Walker, then Handgun Control's legislative director. "We just happened to be the beneficiary."[13]

Not only did Handgun Control want its prize piece of legislation enacted without getting tied up in an endless debate on a wide-ranging crime bill, passage as a separate measure "would signify to legislators and the public that the gun lobby had suffered a major defeat, and the door would be open to further defeats," Walker said. The House Judiciary Committee, still in relatively liberal Democratic hands, approved the measure by a 23 to 12 vote.

That set in motion an intense effort to pass the most highly publicized federal gun control law in a quarter century. The NRA, realizing that some kind of waiting period might be inevitable given Clinton's support, quickly resumed the strategy of demanding instant record checks. It would take hundreds of millions of dollars and a decade or more to shore up state files, but the Democrats promised to help provide aid even as they favored Brady's required waiting period.

The House debate took place in November soon after the 1993 off-year elections, in which a candidate for governor of Virginia was defeated after advocating gun control—a result the NRA didn't hesitate to point out. Still, the House voted 238 to 189 to approve Brady. In the Senate, Biden had succeeded in keeping Brady out of the omnibus crime bill. Now the question was whether backers would overcome a filibuster that threatened to bury the Brady bill.

Because one senator could block legislation with endless talk, controversial measures like Brady needed 60 votes to invoke "cloture," shutting off debate. Republican leader Bob Dole—leading the opposition as an NRA ally—announced that two cloture votes would be held. By Handgun Control's account, Dole pleaded with fellow Republicans to let the debate continue so that he could negotiate changes that would make the measure somewhat more palatable to the NRA. But Brady supporters, led by Ohio's Howard Metzenbaum, rejected the main Dole demand—that an instant check system be mandated immediately and preempt state and local waiting periods already in effect.

The first cloture vote, in the late afternoon of November 19, failed by 2 to reach the 60 required to stop the filibuster. Dole promised to keep negotiating, although no serious talks actually occurred, and a second vote late that Friday evening produced an identical result. With a Thanksgiving recess looming and their legislation stalled, Brady backers decided on a risky strategy. Metzenbaum and Sarah Brady held a midnight news conference to accuse Republicans of killing the measure, which was popular in public-opinion surveys. The message was aimed particularly at moderate Republicans, who had expressed faith that Dole would come up with a compromise they could support.

The tactic could have hardened GOP opposition to the bill, but things evolved the way Handgun Control hoped. The organization's lobbyist, Walker, went to his office Saturday waiting for the phone to ring. Eventually, it did—a call from the office of Dole's fellow Kansan, Nancy Kassebaum, asking how the negotiations might proceed. Walker delivered a blunt message: Dole had killed the Brady bill; there was little left to negotiate. In a day of back-and-forth, Handgun Control said it would be willing to support only one amendment—a five-year "sunset" provision the House had approved, meaning that the Brady Act would expire late in 1998.

As the weekend wore on, the moderate Republicans—whom Dole needed to keep the filibuster going against the bill—forced their leader to agree to a measure similar to the one he had opposed earlier in the filibuster fight. Anxious to adjourn for Thanksgiving, the Senate approved the bill on a voice vote. A Senate-House conference committee produced a final version that established waiting periods of up to five days to check buyers' records and authorized $200 million annually to help states update their criminal records. The conferees also approved the sunset clause on the questionable assumption that the waiting period would be unnecessary by 1998 because the mass of criminal records would be updated and fully computerized by then.

The House quickly passed the bill, but Dole and Biden squabbled over details. (Handgun Control's Walker credited Biden with a "masterful job of negotiating" that thwarted Dole.) As senators began to leave Washington for Thanksgiving, Dole relented after winning the promise of a vote early in 1994 on allowing the waiting period to expire as soon as two years later. Dole never pressed for the change.

Why did Dole cave in? Pure politics, in Handgun Control's view. Said Walker: "In some polls, 95 percent of Americans supported the bill. Sarah Brady was saying that Dole killed it, not a smart idea for a man who wants to run for president," which Dole did in 1996.

When the law went on the books on February 28, 1994, the waiting period was in effect nationwide. Among 22 million background checks through 1999, 536,000 potential handgun purchases were stopped, more than two thirds of them by indicted or convicted felons. During the same period, the number of deaths by gunfire also dropped, prompting the law's advocates to claim success.

But violence declined generally during the mid-1990s for a long list of reasons. Handgun Control argued that the large number of attemped transactions that were stopped must have deterred at least some criminals. By the year 2000, there was no definitive research establishing that the Brady Act was a major contributor.

The NRA insisted that many of the rejections actually were administrative foul-ups, involving primarily scores of citizens with clean records who were confused with criminals, presumably because of similar names. NRA leaders harped on the fact that only a handful of people had been criminally prosecuted for making a false statement to obtain a firearm, suggesting that the Brady law was not being taken seriously. The Treasury Department, which oversaw gun-law enforcement, responded that state and local authorities had stepped up prosecutions at a rate that more than offset the dip in federal cases. Still, Justice Department officials admitted that only a few hundred federal criminal cases had been filed.

Firearms law enforcers outlined a typical scenario: Someone would enter a gun store and express interest in a particular weapon. The clerk would ask whether the purchaser had a criminal record and get an ambiguous response. That was understandable in a justice system that gives defendants opportunities to expunge their criminal records in minor cases. Gun buyers might not know, or would claim not to understand, the difference between a felony—a bar to a firearms purchase—and a misdemeanor. The clerk would offer to call a law enforcement agency and make a preliminary record check. When the answer was that the purchaser might be ineligible, he or she would beat a hasty retreat without actually filling out a federal form required before the transaction could be attempted. That would deny prosecutors an opportunity to file charges, because the customer had not signed a statement declaring a clean record. Even when a customer submitted a form, it was difficult to prove in court that a false statement was made deliberately.

The back-and-forth over the lack of prosecutions under the Brady law was largely a phony one, with the NRA charging that the statute was a paper tiger, and both the Clinton administration and Handgun Control responding that merely stopping purchases was a victory.

Typical of the crime policy debate, the limited available data often were distorted. In defending the soon-to-expire Brady law in mid-June 1998, for example, Clinton adviser Rahm Emanuel said on "Meet the Press" that "based on police research, 20 percent of the guns purchased that are used in murder are purchased within the week of the murder." That would suggest that a five-day waiting period would stop many homicides. In fact, the 20 percent figure applied to crime guns that agents traced to their source, only a small fraction of those used in murders. It was possible that the guns cited by Emanuel had mostly been acquired on the black market by drug gang members, not from dealers who would do Brady law checks.

Emanuel called for an extension of the five-day wait beyond its scheduled expiration, but there was no significant backing in the Republican-dominated Congress for such a move. A version of the instant check plan that the NRA had sought for many years went into effect in November 1998.

Perhaps the biggest unanswered question was how many ineligible buyers avoided the Brady law by stealing guns or obtaining them through the black market or other means. Research was inconclusive. A survey of imprisoned felons reported in 1986 that only 16 percent acquired their weapons through dealers. The Treasury Department reported in early 1999 that as many as half of the guns used in crimes were purchased through federally licensed dealers.[14]

The Brady law expired with many criminal record systems far from complete, though most were in better shape with the help of several hundred million federal dollars in the 1990s. And the instant check procedure that replaced Brady included all gun purchases, not just handguns. Federal officials believed that gun buyers should pay the $15 or so necessary for each record check, but the NRA protested the new "gun tax" and Congress blocked it.

The Brady Act no doubt prevented some blatantly illegal gun acquisitions by criminals. But more than a decade of hoopla surrounding its enactment did not prove that it put a serious dent in America's handgun crime problem. As criminologist Lawrence Sherman of the University of Pennsylvania explained, "most gun crime is committed by people who are 'legally safe.' " Sherman noted that two thirds of federal firearms violators have no prior convictions on their record—the main cause of Brady Act denials to purchase handguns.

One of the first academic studies of the law said evidence was lacking that Brady helped reduce the nation's homicide rate. Public policy researchers Philip Cook of Duke University and Jens Ludwig of Georgetown University reached that conclusion in mid-2000 after comparing the states that adopted the background checks in 1994 with those that had already been checking purchasers' records.[15]

Roughly the same conclusion could be drawn about the other major new federal gun control enacted in the 1990s, the ban on assault-style weapons, whose passage as part of the omnibus anticrime law of 1994 is discussed in Chapter 10.

A study by criminologist Gary Kleck of Florida State University concluded in 1997 that assault weapons accounted for fewer than 2 percent of the guns used in crime and that the number of police officers killed with such weapons in any one year never exceeded nine, according to FBI records through 1993.[16] Advocates of the ban countered that even if the number of victims was small, assault weapons were involved in about one tenth of police officer killings and that street officers were seeing them more frequently in criminal hands.

The main problem was that by banning several specific gun models, the law did not prevent sales of "copycat" weapons that operated in the same lethal manner, allowing shooters to fire up to 100 rounds rapidly. In a devastating series published in August 1997, the *Los Angeles Times* concluded that thousands of assault weapons still were being sold "because of gaping holes in the [federal and state] laws—the result of industry guile, spotty oversight, and political neglect."[17]

Among a long list of problems pinpointed by the newspaper was that the laws were only prospective—meaning that guns in circulation before the statutes became effective could still be traded and manufactured—and could easily be transported to restrictive states from those with looser laws. Relating a Nevada dealer's description of how easily a reporter could buy an assault weapon called the Poly Tec AK-47 and take it to California, where it could not be legally purchased, the *Times* quoted the dealer as saying, "The only kind of hunting this is good for is the two-legged variety . . . humans."

The ability of buyers to avoid the 1994 banned weapons by acquiring "mechanically equivalent" models means, Florida State's Kleck said, that it is doubtful that the statute will achieve any long-term reduction in the stock of assault weapons. The clear lesson, Kleck declared: "Never place restrictions on a subcategory of weapons without also placing restrictions at least as stringent on more deadly, easily substituted alternative weapons."

Despite the deficiencies in both the Brady and assault weapon laws as anticrime measures, most political analysts classified them as major NRA losses— which they were, in the context of the annual scorecards of interest groups' success records in Congress.

The gun lobby and its allies were much more successful on the state and local levels. Long a champion of the deterrent value of carrying firearms in self-defense, the NRA campaigned for liberalizing "right-to-carry" laws, which make it easy for those without records of serious crimes and involuntary mental treatment to get permits for carrying concealed weapons. Several Southern and Western states had maintained such policies for many years, but Florida in 1987 became the first in a series of 21 more states to ease their concealed-carry laws, bringing the total to 32.

The concealed-carry laws provoked a sharp debate among policymakers and researchers. Critics predicted that the statutes would encourage more shootouts between criminals and citizens trying to defend themselves. University of Maryland criminologists checked cities in Florida and elsewhere after right-to-carry laws were passed and found that gun homicides had increased.

Yet in the provocatively titled *More Guns, Less Crime*, economist John Lott of the University of Chicago asserted in a detailed study published in 1998 that states that liberalized their gun-carrying laws had experienced significantly lower crime rates and no increase in accidental deaths. Lott argued that criminals were deterred much more than most criminologists had theorized by the prospect of confrontations with armed victims.[18]

It was an intriguing theory, but Lott faced the same handicap encountered by other crime analysts: the difficulty of sorting out varying causes of crime reductions. Critics were quick to point out that policies and conditions unrelated to rules on concealed firearms probably played a role. Jens Ludwig of the Northwestern University/University of Chicago Joint Poverty Center declared that Lott "cannot adequately control for the fact that states with right-to-carry laws and those without are different with respect to poverty, gangs, drugs, and police practices." Florida State's Kleck agreed that "the declines in crime coinciding with relaxation of carry laws were largely attributable to other factors" than those cited by Lott.[19]

After decades of squabbles over gun control, America continued to be awash in guns, and there was no proof that thousands of gun laws and regulations were doing much to curb violence. To those who followed crime trends closely, it seemed that better enforcement of existing laws was more promising than new battles over new controls.

That issue, too, became embroiled in politics. The NRA was successful in pushing for expansion of a program begun by the U.S. attorney in Richmond, Virginia, called "Operation Exile" (for the notion of exiling gun criminals to federal prison). After a surge of gun murders—122 in 1997 in the state capital city of 200,000—federal prosecutors decided to bring virtually every gun-law violation into federal court, where tougher sentences could be imposed than in the state courts where similar cases had been handled. Ads on city buses, on billboards, and in broadcast and print media warned that "an illegal gun gets you five years in federal prison." As of mid-March 1999, 215 convicts had been sentenced to terms averaging more than four years in prison, and the Richmond homicide total dropped 33 percent in a year, to its lowest level since 1987.

When even prominent Democrats like Philadelphia Mayor Ed Rendell praised the Exile approach, the NRA decided to make it top priority. Pennsylvania Senator Arlen Specter won an appropriation to try the idea in his state, and the NRA shifted the resources of its CrimeStrike division, which had been set up to promote tough anticrime measures in states, to focus almost exclusively on promoting Exile.

The Clinton Justice Department, long at odds with the NRA on most gun-control issues, resisted putting Exile into effect nationwide, saying, "it would be a mistake . . . to mandate the use of any particular formula across the country." But the administration finally decided it would be better to tout Exile than to fight it. In March 1999, Bill Clinton endorsed Exile in a national radio address. Trying to seize the high ground in the debate over enforcement, his Justice Department pointed out that the NRA had backed Exile a year after federal prosecutors had started it. Clinton then asked Congress for more money to hire gun-law enforcers.

Still, Democratic Party leaders were determined to keep up the fight for gun controls, relying on opinion surveys showing that a solid majority of Americans favored more restrictions. But many of those polls were maddeningly general, reporting support for unspecified kinds of limitations. In recent years, firm majorities of 80 percent have favored registering handguns, but the number drops precipitously when the question involves bans; fewer than 40 percent would ban handguns, and anywhere betwen 48 and 57 percent in different surveys would prohibit possession of any assault-style weapons, hardly enough to support sweeping legislation beyond the 1994 ban on manufacturing certain models.[20]

Backing for stronger restrictions spiked briefly after the Columbine High School massacre in April 1999, but a survey commissioned by the Associated Press several months later showed public ambivalence. The percentage of Americans favoring stricter gun controls fell from 63 percent in the days after the school shooting to 56 percent by summer's end. And 49 percent said that "better enforcement of existing gun laws" was more likely to decrease gun violence than were new laws, favored by 43 percent.[21]

Convinced that most voters favored at least some additional controls, the Clinton White House sought tougher regulations on gun shows and flea markets. Critics said many guns were bought at such sites that ended up in criminal hands, in part through dealers eager to sidestep the federally required instant record checks. But the debate was mired in a dispute over the maximum period for a buyer's background check—24 or 72 hours. Gun-control advocates insisted that the longer period was needed to ensure that problematic cases could be checked; the NRA said it threatened the existence of gun shows, typically held over a weekend.

Any law that might emerge would affect only a small proportion of illegal gun transactions. Reformers said it wasn't only a matter of numbers, noting that at least one weapon used in the mass killing at Columbine High School had been acquired at a gun show.

Trigger locks on handguns were another measure with more bark than bite. Both major party presidential candidates in 2000 favored them, but legislation that would require the locks to be provided with each purchase was stalled in Congress. With Republicans controlling the White House and both houses of Congress in 2001, the odds were very low for any significant new federal gun control legislation. In any case, critics doubted that trigger locks could be effective on a wide scale. Owner use was voluntary, and many of the devices could be disabled easily.

Gun-control advocates pursued another strategy in the early twenty-first century: helping government agencies and private individuals file lawsuits seeking damages against gun manufacturers for injuries caused by firearms, in the same way that tort litigation had attacked the tobacco industry for causing health problems. Plaintiffs won some early rounds, but because many injuries caused by firearms were intended, especially those in self-defense, the gun lawsuits faced tougher odds than the did the tobacco cases. Still, the high cost of litigation might pressure defendants to settle, as manufacturing giant Smith & Wesson did in 2000.

With significant gun legislation stymied in Congress, states might prove a more likely source of change. Massachusetts and Maryland, for example, took actions in 2000 that policymakers hoped would reduce gun misuse by treating firearms as consumer products.

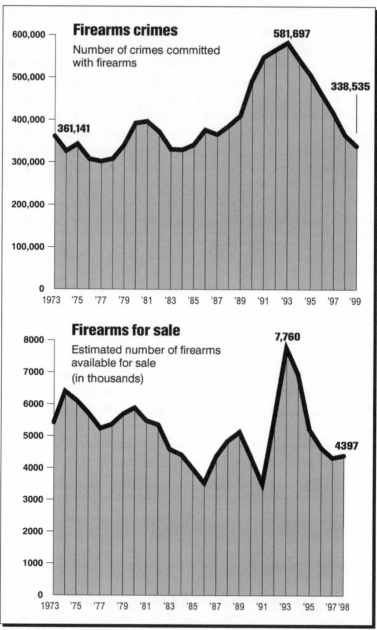

Firearms crimes

Number of crimes committed
with firearms

581,697

361,141

338,535

600,000

500,000

400,000

300,000

200,000

100,000

0

1973 '75   '77   '79   '81   '83   '85   '87   '89   '91   '93   '95   '97 '99

Firearms for sale

Estimated number of firearms
available for sale
(in thousands)

7,760

4397

8000

7000

6000

5000

4000

3000

2000

1000

0

1973 '75   '77   '79   '81   '83   '85   '87   '89   '91   '93   '95   '97 '98

Source for crimes committed: Federal Bureau of Investigation
Sources for firearms availability: U.S. Bureau of Alcohol, Tobacco, and Firearms, U.S. Census Bureau

In the end, gun control at the turn of the century was as much a lightning rod for political contributions and other spending by interest groups as it was a crime-control issue. In the 2000 campaigns alone, the NRA spent at least $20 million supporting candidates and on "infomercials" advocating its viewpoints on television. Gun-control groups would spend far fewer millions of their own.

The gun-control battle was fought most fiercely at the national level because of the crucial federal role in enforcement of gun laws and regulation of firearms. At the same time, Washington's role in a much more fundamental aspect of crime-fighting—local policing—escalated in the 1990s. It lacked the emotionalism of the struggle over gun control, but the rapid growth of federally inspired community policing would come at a high price to taxpayers.

Chapter 8

A COP ON EVERY CORNER?

CALL the police! That cry from crime victims and witnesses reflects the tra-ditional view of patrol officers as the front line against lawbreaking in America. The oft-romanticized notion had local beat officers walking the neighborhood, knowing its secrets, and standing ready to pounce when trouble erupted. Demands for modern technology and better service led to the era of the two-officer patrol car, which cruised around waiting for the next call to the 911 emergency number.

In the twentieth century's last decade, American law enforcement embarked on a remarkable transformation from responding to 911 calls back to walking the beat. Street crime has dropped during the same period, but it is not clear whether a shift in enforcement techniques or other factors are responsible. Most likely, the new policing is a politically inspired, well-intentioned reform with clear benefits but far less impact than its sponsors claim.

Like many other anticrime campaigns, the 1990s drive toward what is known as "community policing" was not an idea that originated in Washington, D.C. But the White House and Congress engineered the nation's most dramatic in-crease in local police manpower. It was a controversial exercise that spent many billions of tax dollars for officers in big cities and small towns, whether or not they were needed.

The debatable more-cops-equals-less-crime theory was a turnabout from the initial police response to the wave of crime and urban unrest that grew during the 1960s. The Johnson crime commission, trying to sort through what was known about how best to manage the nation's then 420,000 police employees, found that important tactical decisions like whether to conduct foot or motor patrols were made "on the basis of guesswork or logic rather than on facts."[1] The panel concluded that "large numbers of visible policemen" were desirable to deter crime but that an officer on every corner would be excessive: "Few Americans would tolerate living under police scrutiny that intense." Portraying America's police forces as being in a state of disarray, the commission highlighted the fragmentation of police duties, poor relations with minorities, and low standards for hiring and training new officers. Hardly any police agencies, for example, required a college education.

The lack of training was especially obvious when many cities were hit by riots in the late 1960s. Officers resorted to brutal responses; many knew of no good alternative. Simultaneously, crime rates continued to rise, and citizens demanded a faster police response. Any idea that officers should be strolling around neighborhoods visiting business owners and residents was discarded in many places in favor of the greater use of patrol cars responding to emergency calls. The most emulated model was the Los Angeles-based "just the facts, ma'am" style exemplified by Jack Webb on the popular *Dragnet* television program.

As crime kept increasing despite what police believed were their much-improved efforts, some chiefs came to believe that they had set themselves up for a fall. It had been easy to take credit for successes when the crime rate had remained steady during the 1950s. But the rise in lawlessness, they now rationalized, had as little to do with their efforts as had the lower levels of the previous decade. "The police did not create and cannot resolve the social conditions that stimulate crime," declared the Johnson crime commission. "They did not start and cannot stop the convulsive social changes that are taking place in America."

This conclusion reflected what now seemed to be a basic fact of policing. Officers were not really omniscient observers of neighborhood problems. Rather, they were stuck with the limited view from their patrol cars. As law enforcement scholar Herman Goldstein of the University of Wisconsin put it, "The police always lagged behind in their capacity to meet the needs of a rapidly changing society."[2]

So the typical police chief's philosophy of the 1960s and 1970s evolved into a belief that his officers could not combat crime alone. It was the other parts of the justice system, of goverment, and of society as a whole that held the key. Some police executives reacted with more than defensive rhetoric to complaints that their forces had overreached. They sent word that officers should essentially lay low and avoid any trouble. In effect, police told politicians and the citizenry that they would do less.

Even if many men and women in blue were becoming less aggressive once they were out on the street, at least they were better trained, partly because of the Johnson crime commission's emphasis on the issue. One of the Law Enforcement Assistance Administration's (LEAA's) most acknowledged successes was the Law Enforcement Education Program (LEEP), which helped pay to educate more than 300,000 officers at about 1,000 colleges and universities during the 1970s. Teaching cops had been a virtually invisible public function. J. Price Foster, a criminologist and educator who headed the LEEP program, said he spent much of his tenure "in an uphill fight to have LEEP become accepted as a first-class citizen in higher education."[3] The theory was that officers with college degrees conducted better investigations and generally treated the public with more respect. "Cops with an educated background are typically less authoritarian," Foster explained.

While it was improving new officers' people skills, LEEP helped create a fast-growing segment of academia by backing the establishment of criminal justice training departments in universities nationwide. Some of LEAA's top officials were dubious about LEEP's drain on the agency's budget—it spent more than $300 million on grants and loans during the decade, a big chunk of the crime-fighting allotment. Still, graduates sung LEEP's praises, and it was well respected in Congress.

Eventually, LEEP was done in not by any well-considered critique but rather by one of the many flukes that have marked the American war on crime. In 1979, the CBS-TV newsmagazine "60 Minutes" broadcast a segment about dentists who had failed to repay their government loans. In response, the Carter administration decided to consolidate educational loan programs that were scattered throughout the bureaucracy into the new Department of Education. The decision might have seemed logical, but it ignored the fact that some of the loan units, like the Justice Department's LEEP, were operating effectively within their original parent agencies.

When Education Department officials arrived to discuss their takeover of the program with Foster, they announced their goal: to reduce the governmentwide loan default rate to 20 percent. An annoyed Foster responded, "Then you'll have to increase LEEP's by 15 percent because it's only 5 percent now." The visitors were surprised, but the news of LEEP's good record didn't stop its transfer to Education, where the program faded when it became just one of many federal loan programs and received no special emphasis. Foster believes that LEEP would have survived had it not been for "60 Minutes" and general lack of interest from the Carter administration.

The 1970s was a time of confusion and rapid change for American law enforcers in ways beyond their levels of education. Most police departments had been relying on vehicle patrols as their main enforcement technique. But a few researchers experimented with changes, some of them featuring a return to the basics. Robert Trojanowicz, a Michigan State University criminologist, obtained money from the Mott Foundation to set up an experiment with foot patrols in Flint, Michigan. Another criminologist, George Kelling, working with the Police Foundation—a Washington-based think tank funded by the Ford Foundation—conducted a landmark study of police patrols in Kansas City that sharply questioned the effectiveness of officers in police cars responding to citizen calls.[4]

That and other new research produced some rather startling conclusions. Summarizing studies of the 1970s, criminologists John Eck and William Spelman concluded that "most serious crimes were unaffected by the standard police actions designed to control them" and that "the public did not notice reductions in patrol, reduced speed responding to nonemergencies, or lack of follow-up investigations."[5] In other words, the police were ineffective, and the public was not clearly aware of what officers did.

True believers in the concept of vehicle patrol said of the research results that the "tactical guts had been ripped out of the model," recalled criminologist Kelling. For police leaders and reformers, Kelling said, the last half of the 1970s and early 1980s were "a very discouraging time—nothing seemed to work—we were all grasping."[6]

The criticism that the reactive model of policing was not working led to the invention of a "problem-oriented" approach developed by Wisconsin's Herman Goldstein and others. It had become obvious, said Goldstein, that "the police were going to have to cultivate an entirely different type of relationship with the citizens they served."

Instead of merely reacting to offense reports as they came in, the new concept was that officers would analyze the major crime patterns in their territories and then aggressively work with citizens on ways to prevent crimes. Not only would this reduce the underlying problems, the theory went, but citizen fear of crime—which often exceeded the actual level of lawbreaking—would also be reduced as residents perceived that action was being taken.

Various forms of problem-oriented policing were instituted in the early 1980s, typically not in the biggest cities but in medium-sized communities where chiefs had the will and the means to make fairly quick and profound changes in their departments. Among them were Goldstein's own Madison, Wisconsin, under Chief David Couper, as well as places like Fresno, California; Newport News, Virginia; St. Petersburg, Florida; Charlotte, North Carolina; and Seattle and Portland, Oregon.

An important advance for the new policing thrust came from a seemingly unlikely source, a nine-page article in the March 1982 issue of *The Atlantic Monthly* titled "Broken Windows." James Q. Wilson, who had written penetrating analyses of crime policy as a Harvard political scientist, joined by criminologist Kelling, by then also a researcher at Harvard, outlined what was then a provocative thesis: that an important key to crime control was attacking the first signs of public disorder.[7]

In *The Atlantic Monthly* 13 years earlier, Wilson had traced the evolution of American police work from "order maintenance" to investigating individual crimes. Kelling had observed the transition on the ground in places like Newark and the notorious Robert Taylor Homes housing project in Chicago. "Above all," concluded the two experts in 1982, "we must return to our long-abandoned view that the police ought to protect communities as well as individuals."

The article was not one of academic theory but rather one that "gave legitimacy and voice to unarticulated citizen demands," said Kelling, who said that many Bostonians who worked with him on anticrime projects the summer after the article was published were so enthusiastic about it that they handed copies to him—not realizing he was the co-author. (Kelling credited Wilson for the "broken windows" metaphor.)

"Broken Windows" has long been cited as a bible by urban crime fighters. But like many solid anticrime concepts, it often is misinterpreted, either deliberately or mistakenly. Wilson and Kelling essentially echoed the problem-oriented policing theory's call for law enforcers to work with community members in planning well-thought-out initiatives. Instead, some police officials interpreted it as merely an excuse for them to become more aggressive. Chicago authorities, for example, cited the article to justify police sweeps against street-crime suspects, arresting everyone in sight in certain dangerous areas. "This was exactly what we were not talking about," Kelling said. "The toughest sell was to combat the tendency of most police departments to think of 'order maintenance' in terms of sweeps: officers stopping everything that moved."

While the policing strategists debated, one activist pushed the idea of beefing up urban police forces, but not with just any warm bodies in blue uniforms. Adam Walinsky, a brash New York lawyer who had campaigned for Robert Kennedy in the 1960s, was a long-time critic of big-city law enforcement. Seizing on the success of the Kennedy administration's Peace Corps and its enthusiastic college volunteers, Walinsky wrote a 17-page "Proposal For a Fundamental Restructuring of the Police." Later nicknamed the "Police Corps," Walinsky's idea was to provide a steady stream of highly educated officers through a constantly renewing group of college graduates whose education would be subsidized by the government.

As Walinsky analyzed the problem, by 1970, officers were being "drawn from an increasingly narrow base" among the less educated elements of the population. "People tend to assume that a man is a patrolman essentially because he cannot do better elsewhere," Walinsky declared. Providing qualified applicants with $12,000 scholarships and giving them deferments from the military draft that was summoning many young American men to tours of duty in Vietnam would help transform the police from "among the most alienated people in American society," he argued.[8]

The Police Foundation, headed in the mid-1970s by former LEAA Director Charles Rogovin, took a dim view. Foundation official Thomas McBride told Walinsky that the think tank was turning down his request for start-up funds, citing unspecified concerns with "local factors (political, community, police leadership, civil service, etc.) which would permit and support substantial changes." Walinsky interpreted the snub as an acceptance of the status quo as local leaders defined it. After Jimmy Carter won the White House in 1976, Walinsky tried out his proposal with a Carter domestic policy aide but got nowhere.

By the 1980s, as head of a panel called the New York State Investigations Commission, Walinsky had observed large-scale police layoffs in New York City and elsewhere as part of a round of budget cutting. He also noticed that police executives, rather than fighting back hard, had adopted the "don't blame me" response, essentially arguing that crime was caused by poverty, discrimination, poor housing, and other urban ills. "The police deliberately made themselves not responsible," Walinsky believed.

While Walinsky fretted, he happened to receive a federally sponsored research report dated February 26, 1982, titled "Governmental Responses to Rising Crime." He read the document, written by Northwestern University political scientists Herbert Jacob and Robert Lineberry, with amazement.[9] It essentially outlined, with facts and figures, the unformed theories he had been pondering for many years. There seemed to be an inverse relationship between crime and the number of police. "The number of police officers for each reported violent crime fell from 3.32 in 1948 to 0.5 in 1978" read the lead sentence of a Justice Department press release on the report. In a study that took three and a half years and covered all cities with populations over 50,000—396 in all—the analysts found that in a time period when crime had increased fourfold, public resources to fight crime had only doubled. "Police per capita rose by approximately 50 percent during the [30-year] period while crime increased some 400 percent," Justice Department crime research chief James Underwood said. Walinsky read the report and "understood immediately what had been going on," he recalled years later. "I thought, 'this is nuts, we have to change it.'"

The report was hardly scientific proof of the police-crime relationship, but it was enough for Walinsky to go back to refining his idea for the equivalent of a Reserve Officers Training Corps system for recruiting new police officers. He shipped off a new version to the Police Foundation in Washington, but the response was that an infusion of college students into police ranks would be so strongly opposed by police unions—which would view it as a ploy to take away permanent police jobs—that it was not even worth studying.

Many others would have given up at that point, but not Walinsky. He was so convinced that his idea was worthwhile that he assembled a group of associates, including urban scholar Jonathan Rubenstein, former FBI official Neil Welch, and New York prosecutor Lawrence Kurlander, to draft a detailed plan which he published in a small booklet. Walinsky talked up his idea to editors and writers at the *New York Times* and other major news outlets. He got positive signals from the Police Executive Research Forum, another law enforcement think tank in which several progressive police chiefs were active. The Washington-based forum had planned a meeting in Atlanta, so Walinsky flew down to met with chiefs like Lee Brown (later New York City police commissioner and federal drug czar), Charleston, South Carolina's Reuben Greenberg, and San Jose's Joseph McNamara.

The Walinsky concept met with approval from elitists, but some blacks came to believe that it was somehow aimed at keeping minorities out of law enforcement. Walinsky strongly disputed that notion, eventually winning over the largest group of black chiefs, the National Organization of Black Law Enforcement Executives.

The campaign for the Police Corps endured a long series of political ups and downs. Walinsky backed an opponent of Mario Cuomo for New York governor. When Cuomo emerged victorious, the Police Corps was in disfavor. Meanwhile, crime in the early 1980s was in one of its periodic downward trajectories. Many experts argued that the crime rate essentially was being driven by demography and that violence was bound to fall, regardless of what law enforcement did. Walinsky argued the point with Cuomo, who told him that he could put Police Corps members "in purple jump suits and say that would reduce crime . . . and crime WOULD go down, not because I put them in purple jump suits but because of population." (Serious crime fell until the mid-1980s, when it defied demography and started rising again, in part because of crack cocaine's spread.)

Making little headway in New York, Walinsky took his case to Rudolph Giuliani, the number three official in the Justice Department, who was, de facto, the top national law enforcement policymaker because his superiors, Attorney General William French Smith and Deputy Edward Schmults, had backgrounds in civil law. Giuliani sent his fellow New Yorker to James (Chips) Stewart, the former Oakland police officer who headed the Justice Department's research unit, the National Institute of Justice. Stewart commissioned a study of the Police Corps's feasibility. Walinsky asserted that the report backed his idea, but Stewart refused to release it after reviewers told him it was methodologically flawed.

The indefatigable Walinsky, his pet project stalled again, began plotting strategy for the 1988 presidential campaign. He approached Kathleen Kennedy Townsend, a daughter of Robert Kennedy, who was aiding the likely Democratic candidate, Michael Dukakis, the governor of Massachusetts. Walinsky got word that Dukakis would not support the Police Corps "in your lifetime" because of the anticipated opposition of police unions.

At that point, Walinsky decided that his prospects might be better in the Republican camp. He got in touch with Rob Quartel, a policy aide for George Bush's campaign. Quartel was enthusiastic, especially when Walinsky told him that Dukakis had avoided the Police Corps. Quartel and Walinsky tossed around the numbers. They agreed that 100,000 would be a reasonable goal—a number later adopted by Bill Clinton. (Walinsky called the 100,000, which would amount to roughly a 20 percent increase in the number of police officers nationwide, "nothing but a round number." When he first saw the Northwestern academics' analysis in 1982, his impulse had been to seek a doubling of police strength.)

But Quartel found a potential roadblock as he began to seek endorsements higher in the Bush campaign chain. The problem was Daryl Gates, then Los Angeles police chief and "Bush's favorite cop," in the view of insiders. Gates had lobbied fellow chiefs to oppose the Police Corps when it came up for an endorsement vote in various law enforcement organizations, and it seemed that he might lead similar opposition within the Bush camp. But Quartel persuaded Gates to relent, and the way was clear for Bush to back the idea.

As the campaign got seriously underway, Walinsky was optimistic that Bush would jump in where Dukakis had feared to tread. But he heard from Bush pollster Robert Teeter, who reported that the vice president would campaign for 100,000 cops only if he needed a boost in the polls. By late October 1988, Bush was riding so high that there seemingly was no need to make new and potentially controversial proposals. Bush missed the chance to grab an idea that would prove a big winner for Bill Clinton four years later.

Walinsky started pressuring the new president's domestic policy aides. But budget limitations loomed as an insurmountable obstacle. Bush's budget chief, Richard Darman, opposed the Police Corps idea as a "new entitlement." A Bush adviser reported to Walinsky that "we're not going anywhere" and advised him to head for Capitol Hill.

So Walinsky made a bipartisan pitch in Congress, scaling down the target number to 80,000 because it sounded like less of a big leap. In mid-1989, a coalition of Senate liberals and moderates that included Massachusetts's Edward Kennedy, New Jersey's Bill Bradley, New Hampshire's Warren Rudman, Pennsylvania's Arlen Specter, and Tennessee's Jim Sasser introduced a bill to start the Police Corps.

Walinsky had a more difficult time finding sponsors in the House. Democrats didn't want to be alone in bucking organized labor on the issue, so they stood by while Walinsky tried to round up some Republicans. His big breakthrough was winning support from conservative activist Paul Weyrich, whom he had wooed at a lunch set up by a mutual friend Walinsky had met through Yale Law School alumni circles. Walinsky ended up speaking at a lunch to the likes of prominent House Republicans Newt Gingrich of Georgia and Bob Dornan of California, who came on board. Walinsky then was able to get liberals like Barney Frank of Massachusetts to join the cause.

By most standards, the feat of getting ideological opposites like Gingrich and Frank to agree with him should have made Walinsky a winner. But he violated some niceties of congressional politics. By amassing support from all points on the political spectrum, he alienated some of those he needed most, like House crime subcommittee chairman William Hughes. The New Jerseyan advised him to dump prickly supporters like Specter and Dornan, who could offend as many people as they attracted.

On November 2, 1989, Hughes convened a hearing on a Dornan-Frank bill to establish the Police Corps. Dornan told how the plan would increase the nation's police forces by 100,000 over four years—remarkably similar to the idea that Bill Clinton would advance three years later. Dornan conceded that people like his friend Daryl Gates, the Los Angeles police chief, opposed the corps on the ground that it would produce cops with an "elitist attitude."[10]

The Police Corps was opposed at the Hughes hearing by Robert Scully, president of the National Association of Police Organizations, one of the nation's largest umbrella groups of police unions. Scully called criticism of law enforcement by Walinsky, who had testified directly before he did, a "direct slap in the face." A former Detroit union leader, Scully told the panel that police officers should be hired and regulated through the collective bargaining process.

Hughes was skeptical, too. He told the hearing that the Police Corps would cost federal taxpayers $1.7 billion per year and questioned whether that would be "the best way to spend that much money in the war on crime." (The figure sounded high in 1989, but by the time the $30 billion anticrime authorization was enacted five years later it, seemed paltry.)

It wasn't the money itself that worried those who looked closely at the Police Corps. It was the fact that the appropriation might not deliver high-quality police work for very long. "It was a very attractive concept—it made people feel good," explained a House Judiciary Committee staff member. "But when you start looking at it, it doesn't do what it purports to do—the price tag is overwhelming."

Hughes proposed a more modest version of the Police Corps but got nowhere. Key senators like Kennedy and Specter got Walinsky's project incorporated in the Senate version of the omnibus crime bill of 1990. Walinsky said House Judiciary Chairman Jack Brooks promised to "take care of it" in the

House. But the Police Corps was nowhere to be found when the bill arrived at a conference committee.

Walinsky sufficed with small victories. Senators Robert Byrd of West Virginia and Tennessee's James Sasser had a Police Corps experiment authorized for West Virginia and Washington, D.C., but it never got off the ground. Walinsky decided to approach the centrist Democratic Leadership Council (DLC), which was seeking practical, middle-ground solutions to major policy problems. He was advised to see one of the group's leaders, Arkansas Governor Bill Clinton.

By then traveling to Washington from his New York home to spend several days each week pressing his cause, Walinsky learned when the DLC was holding its next leadership meeting and buttonholed Clinton in a hallway. The governor expressed interest, and Walinsky sent him background materials. In 1989, Clinton backed the Police Corps.

Two years later, Walinsky got a "frantic call" from Clinton's office. A state senator had heard about the Police Corps from a local police group and planned a bill to start it. The governor wanted to get out in front. Walinsky briefed Clinton aides, and Clinton got a modest version adopted in Arkansas. The first 15 scholarships were awarded in June 1992, while Clinton campaigned for the White House.

Walinsky was still having difficulties on Capitol Hill. He picked up support from leading senators like Bob Dole and George Mitchell but again ran into a roadblock in the House's Jack Brooks. The Texan once had said that he supported the Police Corps. Now, the powerful Judiciary Committee chairman killed the idea by lobbying panel members privately. Brooks may have been reflecting opposition from police unions. After the deed was done, he excoriated Walinsky in a public committee meeting for bothering his panel with the "dumbest thing I ever heard."

Once again, Walinsky refused to stop, recruiting a coalition that included Democratic leaders like Richard Gephardt of Missouri and Dave McCurdy of Oklahoma, joined by conservatives assembled by California's Dornan, to approve the Police Corps on the House floor over Brooks's objection. But the project ended up in the wide-ranging 1992 crime bill, which was derailed by disputes over the death penalty and other issues and became the only major federal election-year anticrime legislation between 1984 and 1996 to fail.

Others in Washington began to pick up on the idea of helping localities hire police officers. Justice Department research chief Stewart had discussed community policing with Harvard anticrime experts in the mid-1980s, and his agency awarded modest grants for experiments. In the 1992 crime bill's early stages, New York Representative Charles Schumer, who was making a name for himself on the House crime subcommittee, proposed his own version of "cops on the beat" legislation to promote what was evolving into the notion of community policing. Schumer's initial plan would have paid for equipment purchases but not officer hiring.

While Congress dithered, law enforcement leaders in a few places tried out their own concepts of community policing. In one of the most extensive tests. Police Chief Darrel Stephens of Newport News, Va., won a $1.2 million federal grant in the mid-1980s to develop a form of problem-oriented policing, the model theorized by Wisconsin Professor Herman Goldstein that based deployment of officers on careful analysis of crime trends. The project got an enthusiastic review in *U.S. News & World Report*, which in 1986 highlighted its successes in dealing with domestic violence and "public order" offenses like prostitution and rowdy behavior.[11] Justice Department research chief Stewart declared that problem-oriented policing "could be one of the biggest advances in policing cities since Sir Robert Peel put men in blue uniforms on the streets of London 157 years ago."

A few other places picked up on the trend. West Coast centers like San Diego, Portland, and Seattle were among the early advocates. In New York City—which sometimes served as a bellwether for crime trends good and bad—Police Commissioner Benjamin Ward created community policing units in a few neighborhoods. The New York subway system imported criminologist George Kelling of "Broken Windows" fame from Boston to test his order maintenance theory in the crime-ridden transportation system starting in 1988, working with a transit security chief named William Bratton.

The well-planned crackdown worked so well that Bratton was given a chance to put it into action citywide as the city's police commissioner. Bratton and many who analyzed his efforts to make police precinct commanders accountable for crime rates in their areas concluded that it had at least something to do with New York City's sharp decrease in violent crime during the 1990s. To be sure, it wasn't clear that the Bratton initiative could be labeled community policing. The element of increasing the responsibility of local commanders and measuring it through a statistical system known as Compstat may have played a larger part in cutting crime than merely putting more officers on the street.

Bratton's direct role was curtailed when he resigned in a spectacular falling out with Rudolph Giuliani, who had moved from his Justice Department career to win an against-the-odds two terms as a Republican mayor in largely Democratic New York City. Giuliani and Bratton butted heads over primacy in claiming credit for the city's crime-rate decline.

While various cities retooled their police forces, at least in minor ways, a few got some attention from Washington. LEAA had officially died in the early 1980s, but the Justice Department had managed to maintain a surprisingly high total of state and local anticrime aid funds—$780 million a year at the time the Bush administration left office in 1992, much of it concentrating on antidrug projects through the Byrne Program, named for a fallen New York City officer.

Research chief Stewart's ideas had won the enthusiastic backing of Attorney General Edwin Meese, who had become a police buff during his days in California government. But the emphasis shifted after President Bush replaced Meese with former Pennsylvania Governor Richard Thornburgh.

By the time Thornburgh brought in Notre Dame law professor Jimmy Gurule to oversee Justice Department grant programs in 1990, policing was getting less attention. Gurule found that his agency was spending a minuscule $10 million on community policing. Gurule quickly became enamored of the subject but was distressed about how his bureaucracy was handling it. "I kept hearing success stories about significant crime decreases in participating [police] precincts," Gurule said. "I asked, 'What have we got for our money—what bang for our buck?' But the staff couldn't answer my questions because the programs hadn't been evaluated."[12]

Gurule discovered a pattern that had plagued LEAA in earlier years—"cozy relationships between government staffers and grantees" in which both sides assumed that grant recipients had an entitlement to federal funding and that "it's never going to end." Such arrangements didn't exactly encourage tough evaluations.

Years later, Gurule admitted what Adam Walinsky had realized in 1988: that George Bush was too slow in picking up on what became a political winner for Bill Clinton in 1992. Craig Uchida, a Justice Department careerist who worked on community policing programs from 1988 to 1997, said, "I don't think [the Republicans] cared. They viewed community policing as part of a liberal, soft-on-crime-agenda. It didn't resonate well for them."[13]

Indeed, on July 28, 1992, the Bush administration issued a 60-page manifesto titled "Combating Violent Crime: 24 recommendations to strengthen criminal justice."[14] The somewhat unusual number evolved, according to a Justice Department insider, when Attorney General William Barr eliminated what would have been the 25th item—community policing—on the ground that "it sounds too much like social work."

Meanwhile, Walinsky pressed ahead for his national Police Corps plan. Things looked promising on the Democratic presidential campaign trail in 1992, at least at the outset. With the endorsement of leading candidate Bill Clinton seemingly in the bag, Walinsky was thrilled when the Arkansan cited the Police Corps in a campaign stop before the New Hampshire primary. When the National District Attorneys Association asked Clinton and Bush to talk about their law enforcement ideas, Clinton's first proposal—as published in the group's newsletter in 1992—was the Police Corps. The candidate used language borrowed from Walinsky's standard pitch. Clinton later mentioned community-based policing, with no allusion to 100,000 cops.

Despite his seeming reliance on Walinsky's formulation, Clinton's interest in expanding police forces went beyond the Police Corps, insisted Bruce Reed, the president's chief domestic policy adviser starting in his campaign days. As Clinton traveled the country in the months before he formally became a candidate in 1991, he spoke about the latest trends in policing with prominent chiefs like Charleston's Reuben Greenberg and New York City's Lee Brown (later Clinton's drug czar). Reed and colleague John Kroger, who had worked for beat-cop advocate Charles Schumer in the House, pressed Clinton to give a speech on his crime-fighting views, but the governor never got around to it in 1991.

By 1992, Reed was exchanging ideas with Ronald Klain, a top Senate Judiciary aide to Joseph Biden, who had pushed unsuccessfully for a provision in that year's federal anticrime bill that might have paid for 50,000 more officers. That seemed like a significant but not extravagant total during a period of moderate Republican control of the White House. (Clinton advisers estimated that the number of officers nationwide had risen by 50,000 between 1988 and 1991 even without a special federal program.)

That wouldn't be the final word from the two young Democratic strategists. The Reed-Klain relationship was more than professional: Reed's wife had attended law school with Klain, who was godfather to the Reeds' daughter. As the campaign season back-and-forth between Reed and Klain progressed during the spring of 1992, the goal for the policing program would change arbitrarily and dramatically. Klain said Biden could reintroduce the 50,000 cops provision during a Clinton presidency. Reed asked how many police officers already were at work around the country. When Klain said the national total was about 500,000, Reed remarked that a 10 percent increase didn't appear impressive enough. How about a 20 percent jump, or 100,000? the Clinton aide asked. It sounded fine to Klain. "We all agreed that [100,000] sounded like a good increase," Reed said. "We wanted a significant enough increase that it wouldn't look like a modest program." Reed said he and Kroger came up with the figure independently, but the round number was the same one that Walinsky and Republican operative Quartel had proposed in 1988.[15]

Reed and Kroger sent Clinton a memo suggesting the major anticrime ideas he should stress in his presidential campaign, including the addition of 100,000 police officers. The next task was getting the candidate to commit himself in a speech. The two aides expanded the never-delivered draft they had written the previous winter. As it happened, the first two best opportunities to plug the idea would come in Houston, where Mayor Bob Lanier had made a name for himself by paying his officers large sums of overtime money to deal with a crime crisis.

In an appearance before a U.S. Conference of Mayors convention in Houston on June 21, Clinton used a combination of the Walinsky plan and 100,000 cops. He told the mayors that the first phase would be a "domestic Peace Corps" along the lines of Walinsky's suggestion. Later, 100,000 officers would be added, Clinton said. But that was just a warm-up for Clinton's next big anticrime salvo in George Bush's home town. In vanquishing Michael Dukakis four years earlier, Bush often had trumpeted his law enforcement support by appearing on stage with uniformed police officers. Clinton was not going to let Bush win that battle in 1992. His advance team made sure that the governor was surrounded by men and women in blue on July 23, when he planned the full address on crime that his policy advisers long had awaited.

But just as a long series of local officials and organizations were being introduced on the steps of City Hall, Reed glanced at fellow Clinton aide Bruce Lindsey and said, "looks like it's going to storm." As Clinton went to the podium, the heavens opened. But even as the ink smeared on his notes, Clinton gamely told the audience "if you stay, I will . . . I'm willing to get wet to turn this country around."

After giving his usual plug for gun control ("take the AK-47s and the Uzis off the streets in America"), Clinton lambasted Bush for using the crime issue to win the White House in 1988 and then trying to cut the budget for state and local anticrime aid by $100 million. Then he presented a blend of Walinsky's Police Corps and the new 100,000 cops goal. First, members of a downsized military would be retrained as police officers. Then college students would be supported if they went into police or other service work. Although Clinton did not lay out exactly how the 100,000 total was to be met, he told his audience he would "never forget . . . the fact that you all stayed when it rained." And so the Clinton cops plan was launched in waterlogged Houston.

The National Association of Police Organizations (NAPO) represented 135,000 officers around the country. The group had endorsed Ronald Reagan both times he ran for the White House but took no position in the Bush-Dukakis race. This time, things were different. Members of NAPO's local unit had heard Clinton's proposal in Houston and liked it. After all, 100,000 more cops could mean many more NAPO members. After assessing Clinton's and Bush's strengths and weaknesses, the national NAPO board endorsed Clinton for president less than a month later.

In the meantime, Clinton had unveiled the 100,000 police idea to the Democratic National Convention. Before that showcase speech, the governor had separately called for reducing the federal workforce by 100,000. Reed suggested linking the two ideas by having the police paid for by the money saved by trimming the federal bureaucracy—an idea that later was expanded and incorporated in the 1994 crime law. As he had done in the Houston appearances,

Clinton related his police plan to his proposed national service program, listing law enforcement as one of four jobs that volunteers might perform.

It was not until October 17 that Clinton made a detailed speech on his anticrime ideas. It was scheduled for the Radisson Hotel in the Detroit suburb of Romulus. He was joined by various law enforcers, including state attorneys general, local district attorneys, and NAPO leader Scully, whom he singled out for mention. After making a pitch for the Brady bill's handgun-purchase waiting period and a ban on assault-style weapons, Clinton declared, "We ought to have 100,000 more police officers on the street," and proceeded to recite one of Adam Walinsky's favorite sound bites: "Thirty years ago there were three police officers in this country for every serious crime. Today there are three serious crimes for every police officer." Even though no one had proved such a proposition scientifically, the solution seemed obvious: more police, less crime.

As usual, the candidate was a bit vague on how the plan might be put into effect. He endorsed the pending crime bill in Congress, which he said included "funds for people at the local level," and repeated his praise for the idea of converting those who were leaving the downscaled armed forces to become local police officers. And there was another boost for expanding the concept of the "national police corps." Clinton used a similar formulation in *Putting People First*, his campaign manifesto that was published in book form.[16] The first anticrime plank was "fight crime by putting 100,000 new police officers on the streets; create a National Police Corps and offer veterans and active military personnel a chance to become law enforcement officers."

After Clinton won the election and his aides began to talk about details of the revised crime bill that would be proposed in Congress, they used the same description. However, the advisers also knew about what one called the "tremendous skepticism" among Washington elites about whether the Arkansan could actually put his New Democrat ideas on social issues into practice. Among other things, one transition memo warned, critics would examine Clinton's proposals in detail, making sure that a "hidden agenda, particularly a liberal Trojan horse, does not lurk inside."

It was during this period that 100,000 community police officers became the Clinton buzzword and the Police Corps was little discussed publicly. A disappointed Walinsky suspected that the president-elect had bowed to opposition from the police unions. He noted that Scully of NAPO once had endorsed the Police Corps but changed his stance after he was criticized by some of his group's other leaders. Scully did tell Clinton campaign aides during the summer of 1992 that NAPO "wanted nothing to do with the Police Corps," but he denied that his organization made Clinton's deemphasizing of Walinsky's idea a quid pro quo for NAPO's backing of the Democratic candidate.[17] Scully called Walinsky "well meaning" and praised his lobbying "like a Diehard battery—24 hours a day, 7 days a week." But Scully said most police leaders concluded that they could not depend on a force dominated by college students. "If the shooting starts," Scully declared, "we don't want them to go the other way."

The real reason for NAPO's endorsement of Clinton, Scully said, was accumulated frustration over what he termed the Bush administration's "intransigence" on issues of interest to law enforcement. A majority of NAPO's card-carrying members were Republicans, by Scully's estimate, so it was no surprise that one board member made a motion during the group's 1992 annual convention to support Bush's reelection. Scully and other members immediately countered the proposal, pointing out that Bush had vetoed legislation backed by NAPO and that the White House had been quick to order federal prosecution of the Los Angeles police officers accused of beating motorist Rodney King after the cops were acquitted by a state jury. Those factors, plus Clinton's support of gun control, were enough to persuade a majority of NAPO's board to endorse the Clinton-Gore ticket.

Whatever role the Police Corps may have played in the endorsement decision, Clinton's advisers had heard the union message. Meanwhile, Adam Walinsky, having lost support where it could have been decisive—the White House—pressed ahead in Congress and managed to get a modest Police Corps provision included in the big 1994 crime law. But the funding disappeared in a late-night negotiation when Republican budget watcher John Kasich of Ohio objected. The Corps again had won congressional endorsement, but with no guaranteed dollar figure attached. While Clinton's 100,000 cops plan took the spotlight with a definite allocation in the anticrime trust fund, Walinsky had to suffice with small victories.

As the White House won approval for what could amount to nearly $9 billion for police hiring nationwide, the Police Corps eked out a meager $10 million budget in 1996 for experiments in 17 places. The largest recipient was Maryland, where the program was supported by Kathleen Kennedy Townsend, the early Walinsky backer who had gone on to become the state's lieutenant governor. One of the big problems in developing the Corps was that it had only a skeleton federal staff to administer it, compared to the huge COPS (Community Oriented Policing Services) program. Walinsky himself frequently called staff members operating the program in various states with advice, sometimes making it seem that he was in charge even though he lacked a formal role.

It was too early to assess the results, but the Police Corps appeared to be living up to its critics' charge that it was expensive. As of mid-2000, about $54 million in federal funds had been spent on nearly 700 cadets, with a projected cost of $110,000 per officer. It seemed that most of the initial recruits would have entered police work regardless of the program, said Antony Pate, who was conducting the formal evaluation.[18]

What derailed the Police Corps in the Clinton presidency? Clinton advisers knew their leader had endorsed it and so were predisposed to favor it. But they recognized the union opposition and the fact that the Police Corps was too indirect a way to increase the size of the nation's permanent police force. An internal memo circulated in Clinton's domestic policy unit after the 1992 election disputed Walinsky's basic analysis. The biggest problem in American policing at that point, maintained Clinton aides, was not a lack of trained candidates for police jobs but a shortage of funds to pay salaries. The advisers pointed out that despite the seemingly wide support on Capitol Hill for the Police Corps, key members of Congress responsible for appropriations would dislike the setup because it resembled an entitlement for students. "We must be careful not to speak too glowingly of the new college-educated cops," warned the policy aides.

One presidential adviser recalled surveying police chiefs around the country soon after Clinton took office and finding few interested in the Police Corps—a conclusion that bolstered the White House's decision to downplay the idea. At the same time, a group of career Justice Department experts convened by Attorney General Reno quickly advised that the Police Corps "made no sense," in the words of one key participant.

Despite the coolness in the field, the Clinton camp didn't bury the Police Corps. About six weeks before he took office, when the president-elect's policy aides took a first crack at estimating where the 100,000 new cops would come from, nearly half of them were attributed to the Police Corps, another 35,000 to members of the downsized military, and another 20,000 or so in aid to states and localities to rehire cops who had been laid off in budget cutbacks.

Clinton's anticrime stance may have been a significant factor in his victory at the polls, but the economy outranked crime. As the new president's budget gurus grappled with the spending issues that would define the early months of his term, domestic policy aide Reed was disappointed to find that the budget advisers had shortchanged the police plan. He worried that if Clinton was seen as backing off from any of the major themes that marked his campaign, he would be written off as just another politician who had made empty promises.

In a memo to Clinton and Vice President-elect Al Gore just before Christmas 1992, Reed urged the leaders to follow through on their "five signature ideas" in the domestic policy area—national service, reinvention of government, welfare reform, youth apprenticeship programs, and 100,000 cops—via proposed legislation and executive orders before inauguration day to "signal your willingness to put your mark on issues that too many Democrats have ducked in the past."

Now installed in the White House after January 20, Reed found the economic team questioning whether the expensive 100,000 cops program really could be financed after all. So Reed and Jose Cerda, a former congressional aide who handled law enforcement issues both in the presidential campaign and now in the domestic policy office, went "hat in hand" to the various power centers in the new administration. "The White House was not the most organized place in 1993," Reed said, "so we had to lobby every possible decision maker—and loop back to make sure they didn't change their minds." Reed and Cerda found themselves conducting what they viewed as "crime tutorials," explaining to Clinton advisers why they should support the 100,000 police plan. Sometimes they found themselves resorting to a public relations justification as much as a substantive one: "It was a signature issue for the president," they would say. "It will be extremely embarrassing to him if we don't do it."

The key to immediate funding of any big new program at the start of the administration was to win inclusion in a $30 billion stimulus package of government spending that the White House advocated. Reed and Cerda argued that police hiring would be a popular, tangible component. At a key decision-making point, Reed paged economic adviser Gene Sperling, who returned his call from the Oval Office. Reed made a pitch for a rather modest $200 million police-hiring pot, which Sperling immediately checked with Clinton and got a presidential endorsement. The amount later was reduced to about $150 million, which Reed and Cerda welcomed as a chance to test the idea on a scale vastly smaller than 100,000 (the $150 million would pay for 2,005 officers under what Congress called the Police Hiring Supplement).

Few White House aides outside of Reed and Cerda's circles expressed much interest in law enforcement early in 1993, when the economy and health care topped the Clinton agenda. But that year was to be a watershed in one important category that influences anticrime policy: sensational killings. The first was the murder of basketball star Michael Jordan's father in North Carolina in June. It hardly was representative of any trend; if anything, the national murder total was headed down. Still, after the Jordan case hit the front pages day after day, internal White House strategy meetings on domestic policy suddenly became much better attended. The time-tested scenario was about to repeat itself with a vengeance: it would take a spate of high-profile murders to focus policymakers' attention. "Crime just exploded" as an issue, Reed recalled.

Beefing up police forces suddenly gained currency as the quick fix to combat crime in 1993, but the details were very much up for grabs. With Clinton's campaign promise clashing with budget realities, the consensus of key Democrats in Congress and the administration was to seek $3.4 billion in the omnibus crime legislation. That would pay for 50,000 officers as a "down payment" for the 100,000 to fulfill Clinton's vow. Adam Walinsky's influence continued to be felt on Capitol Hill, with Senators Joseph Biden, Edward Kennedy, and others pressing for the Police Corps to be a stronger part of the new program, while the White House tried to deemphasize it.

The Corps continued as part of Clinton's overall plan, but after surveying the arguments on competing ideas, advisers Reed and Cerda told Clinton in late April 1993 that "we do not believe the Police Corps is a cost-effective means for increasing police force levels." By May, they had reallocated the 100,000 to attribute half to general hiring under the crime bill. The rest were divided among five other programs, the largest being 20,000 from Clinton's national service plan, which superficially resembled the Police Corps because it would involve hiring young people as cops.

While the important players negotiated over money to be included in the big crime bill they hoped would make it to the floors of both houses of Congress by the end of 1993, there were differences over the relatively modest sums being included in the more immediate stimulus package. Biden and Jack Brooks, the Judiciary Committee chairmen from the two houses, had agreed that $100 million was a good round number to get the police-hiring program started. But Biden envisioned the total as an annual one, while Brooks believed that it would be spread over four years. "We just put in $100 million and let them see it their own way," Reed said.

White House aides were perturbed that a significant doubter of the 100,000 cops idea was Clinton's own attorney general, Janet Reno, who would be the point person lobbying for it in Congress and whose department would run the program. The tall Floridian had entered the administration as Clinton's third choice, outside Clinton's Arkansas circle. Reno, resistant to inheriting a Clinton promise, was "leery of the politics of the campaign driving her criminal-justice policy," said Webb Hubbell, the Clinton crony and Arkansas lawyer who ran the Justice Department until Reno was confirmed in March 1993.[19]

That spring, the administration convened about a dozen Justice Department career officials to start filling in the details of the cops proposal. One of them was Uchida, the National Institute of Justice researcher who had followed the issue since 1988. "We were skeptical," he said. "We were asking where they pulled the [100,000] number from, how would we get enough money, whether anyone really wanted the plan." Another member characterized the group's attitude as one of "huge resistance" and "hostility," explaining that "we didn't want to be a part of something that didn't make sense." Among other things, the careerists were dubious about the initial White House idea of getting some of the new cops through the Americorps volunteer program.

Such questions found a receptive audience in Reno, who had been a politically popular prosecutor in her home of Dade County, Florida, and had lots of experience on the receiving end of federal anticrime grants. She was critical of Washington's record of overpromising. Domestic policy adviser Reed found Reno "extraordinarily skeptical" about promising to pay for 100,000 cops. At that point, it was not clear where the money would come from; at worst, it might have to be taken from traditional Justice Department responsibilities like investigating and prosecuting cases. The attorney general was "afraid that it was going to consume her other priorities," Reed said. "She was worried that we would put out some big number and that it would turn out that the money wasn't there."

As the summer of 1993 wore on, pressure was building on Clinton from Democratic anticrime leaders in Congress like Biden and New York Representative Charles Schumer to announce the White House's version of the crime bill that the Democrats had been drafting. On July 29, Reno wrote a memo to the President agreeing that "we need police on the steeet" but declaring that "we do not have enough money" for 100,000. She said the Justice Department would finance what, in the context of the big budget numbers being tossed around, was a ridiculously small "community police corps" at a cost of $5 million each year for five years. Over the next few days, White House aides advised the president to ignore Reno and push ahead on his pledge for 100,000 cops.

On August 10, 1993, the night before the White House planned the formal announcement of its stance on the new omnibus crime bill—highlighted by the police-hiring plan—Reed arranged a conference call with Reno and Clinton media adviser David Gergen to talk through the notion once more. But that provided insufficient to get a final answer from the attorney general.

The next day, just before Clinton and Gore were to make the announcement from the Oval Office, Reno again expressed fears that the money wouldn't be available to pay for the massive program. As Reed tried to assure Reno that the funds were now contained in what were known as the "baseline" spending assumptions of the Office of Management and Budget, a nervous Gore asked if he should scratch a promised number of additional police officers from his introduction.

Reno finally gave her assent and the ceremony went according to plan, but not before White House adviser Bruce Reed informed Adam Walinsky that his treasured Police Corps would not be a key part of the 100,000 cops plan in Clinton's crime bill. Reed described Walinsky as angry but resigned to his fate.

Reno had some justification for her fears. Said Cerda: "We were asking for an extraordinary amount of money and a huge new federal responsibility."[20] Some of the Democrats in Congress who controlled the appropriations process "thought we were crazy," Cerda said. The White House crime fighters kept finding themselves trying to overcome internal "skepticism on whether the crime issue mattered." The doubts extended to Capitol Hill, where crime had not made it high on the agendas of many leaders by the summer of 1993. At one point, Clinton advised House Speaker Thomas Foley and Majority Leader Richard Gephardt that, based on his travels around the country to promote his platform, they should get more serious about crime. "The issue is on everyone's minds—it's going to explode," Reed recalled Clinton's telling the leaders.

While Reed tried to keep crime atop Clinton's own domestic priority list, Cerda and other White House staffers worked on some of the plan's crucial details, which were not specified in the announcement of the crime bill. One issue was what kind of officers Washington would be financing. Clinton had referred repeatedly to community policing, but that remained a slippery concept. It sounded fine to put more officers out on the street, but what, exactly, would they do?

The White House got some important advice from an unexpected source. A New York City police officer named Rana Sampson had gone on to Harvard Law School and then worked at the Police Executive Research Forum (PERF) think tank in Washington. PERF's executive director was Darrel Stephens, who had helped develop problem-oriented policing back in the 1980s as police chief in Newport News, Virginia. Sampson had won a position as a White House Fellow, and just at the right time, she found herself in a key place to provide advice on the emerging community-policing program.

Reflecting the view of many law enforcement leaders, Sampson urged that the new officers be deployed not merely as a public-relations gesture but in the problem-solving model of Wisconsin's Herman Goldstein: working with citizens and performing crime analyses that would focus on the most significant community problems. In a memo to Reno in the summer of 1993, Sampson explained that the modern vision of community policing was not, as some commentators had tried to explain it, just returning to the days of police officers' walking beats. Nor was it a series of gimmicks like bike patrols or block watches, she said. Rather, the idea amounted to an overhaul of the way officers dealt with other public agencies, community groups, and private citizens—a "transformation in the way we deliver services." By some accounts, the Sampson memo marked a crucial turning point in convincing a reluctant Reno to support 100,000 cops wholeheartedly.

Sampson was essentially educating political appointees and aides on the nuances of how policing techniques had changed in the previous decade. The ideas Sampson explained were well known within the Justice Department's grant-making agencies, which had tried to accomplish more or less the same goal in the half dozen or more demonstration projects going back to the Bush administration under Jimmy Gurule, who oversaw local anticrime aid at the Justice Department.

But Justice bureaucrats who had monitored the issue advised the White House to go slow, pointing out that at first, many police departments that obtained federal funds to set up community-policing projects tended to marginalize them. They were not fundamentally changing their way of doing business. Sampson urged her colleagues to consult with police leaders around the nation who were sophisticated in community-policing concepts, including San Diego's Jerry Sanders, New York's William Bratton, and Chicago's Matt Rodriguez.

The White House found enthusiasm for its ideas in the field—probably because of the promise of money from Washington—but some careerists at the Justice Department remained skeptical, essentially for the reasons their boss, Reno, had suggested: that the promised money might not be appropriated and that devoting too much of a limited budget to one model might stifle other innovative ideas.

After all the internal debate, what became the COPS program proved to be one of the least controversial initiatives in the 1994 crime bill, whose tortuous route to passage is described in Chapter 10. Most members of Congress realized that adding local police officers during a time of public concern about crime could only be a political winner. Perhaps most surprisingly, when Senate leaders agreed on the idea of a "trust fund" to pay for the crime bill over five years, the amount dedicated to hiring police officers more than doubled in an instant, to $8.9 billion, in order to cover Clinton's original 100,000 proposal.

Still, the numbers were being pulled out of the air. Some police leaders found themselves in the uncomfortable position of questioning a program that clearly would benefit their constituencies. Stephens, the former Newport News police chief who had come to Washington as director of PERF, asked in public appearances whether police chiefs would be able to sustain public expectations that would come with the influx. "If we need more police officers, how many do we need?" Stephens said. "Is 100,000 too many? Too little?"

An administration insider with experience in police work reported "broad-based concern among progressive groups that 100,000 cops was an unfortunate campaign promise." The main worry, said the aide, was that the program would end up being "more concerned with fattening personnel rosters than in shaping the strategy of police departments."

But skepticism was drowned out by politicians, who saw the program as a godsend for strapped local budgets (not to mention their own reelection prospects). Stephens moved to St. Petersburg, Florida, where he was police chief and later city administrator, before returning to policing as chief in Charlotte, North Carolina. In St. Petersburg, Stephens urged that city officials shun the COPS program and its funding restrictions (localities were required to put up 25 percent of the officers' costs), but the mayor applied anyway.

Unlike the atmosphere surrounding the first big federal crime bill in 1968, hardly anyone raised the specter of a national police force in the debate in Congress and law enforcement circles while the details of Clinton's plan were being decided. The feared FBI Director J. Edgar Hoover had died in 1972, and his successors exhibited little desire to function as some sort of federal police chief. Instead, the main debate was over whether the federal aid could become a form of permanent entitlement, as some members of Congress had feared about the Police Corps.

The Clinton administration and congressional Democrats decided that the new officers would be funded for a maximum of three years and that cities must pledge to retain the positions after federal aid expired. Instead of being given a pure handout, "mayors and governors should be forced to make a decision" on funding, said Delaware's Biden, a prime sponsor of the program.[21]

Another glitch arose in Congress in the summer of 1994 over how much of the COPS money could go to technology or to hiring police employees who would take over an existing cop's job, freeing that officer to go out on the street. New York City favored that approach, and New York Representative Schumer, who headed the crime subcommittee, wanted one fourth of COPS funds reserved for such redeployment. The White House was opposed. One aide quipped that "25,000 secretaries doesn't have the same ring as 100,000 cops."

Judiciary Chairman Brooks, reflecting Houston's reliance on overtime, wanted to allow some money to be used for that purpose, which one 100,000 cops supporter said might pervert the program into one with "a lot of cops making $100,000." A Justice Department official expressed the fear that "we'd be creating a slush fund for overtime." Eventually, the White House permitted no more than 20 percent of the first year's COPS funds to be used for redeployment or overtime.

But would the cops go where the crime was? Experts long had urged that limited justice-system resources be focused on the places where violence was worst—often called the "hot spots" theory. But that would have meant pouring a huge percentage of officers into big cities—a politically unsalable idea when nearly every member of Congress wanted some cops for his or her districts. Supporting dispersal of the new officers nationwide was "the only way to break the logjam," said Clinton aide Reed. So half of the new cops were reserved for jurisdictions with populations under 150,000. The concession considerably weakened the punch of the program by setting aside officers for places that might not need them at the expense of the most crime-ridden cities.

The virtually unanimous popularity of the police plan helped the controversial crime bill through the final shoals of partisan attacks in the seemingly endless congressional session of summer 1994. When the law finally was signed in September, the administration was determined to get the money out fast. The 1994 midterm elections were fast approaching, and the Democrats wanted to demonstrate that their big crime law would not turn out to be yet another empty promise from Washington. Even though the statute technically was just an authorization to spend, the Democrats who still held the reins of the congressional appropriations process made sure that hard cash would be available when the new fiscal year started on October 1, a little more than two weeks after the signing ceremony.

Normally, federal anticrime funds would be doled out by the bureaucrats at 633 Indiana Avenue, who had done the job ever since the LEAA days of the 1970s. But the caution they had expressed to Clinton political operatives had convinced the administration's higher-ups to keep the multi-billion-dollar program out of the grant-giving Office of Justice Programs. "They were viewed as incompetent, not being able to handle that kind of money," said one Clinton adviser.

The projected budget for COPS was almost as large as the entire existing federal anticrime-grant program. "It would have been like putting an elephant on the back of a flea," said a Justice Department policymaker. So the administration took the extraordinary step of installing the new COPS office in the main Justice Department, under the control of the number three official, a political appointee from Chicago named John Schmidt, who had taken Webb Hubbell's job.

The struggle over who would run the new program wasn't easy to resolve. Jack Nadol, a Justice Department veteran who was acting head of the Bureau of Justice Assistance (BJA), which usually oversaw anticrime grants, argued unsuccessfully that his employees should get the administrative power, as the "shock troops" who would get the money out as fast as the political appointees wanted. Nadol believed that Clinton's aides had unfairly tagged his unit as an unresponsive bureaucracy.[22] But Uchida, the career Justice official who had helped plan the COPS program, angered colleagues by supporting the new office to run it, saying that "the bureaucratic nature of the whole process would have made it a major project to get the money out the door."

Members of Congress wanted the money out instantly, with an election looming. Some Capitol staffers called Nadol, who noted that there applications for cops totaling $300 million were still on file from localities that could not be funded under the 1993 economic stimulus legislation that included a "police hiring supplement." Congress immediately put $200 million in an appropriations bill for the new fiscal year. (Nadol said he was unfairly accused of making an end run around Clinton's political advisers; the opposite was true, he said: "If it hadn't been for the career people, the COPS office would never have got off the ground.")

Everyone wanted the money disbursed as fast as possible. Biden, a veteran of federal anticrime grants, remembered the LEAA era, when some police departments hired consultants to help them through the federal application maze. So Biden met with Attorney General Reno soon after the law cleared Congress and supported a startling idea: limit to one page the application form that cities had to fill out to share in the federal dollars. Ronald Klain, who had moved from Biden's staff to the Justice Department and was overseeing the crime law's implementation, quickly agreed.

Justice got the message during the same week from Jerry Abramson, Louisville mayor and head of the U.S. Conference of Mayors, which had lobbied hard for the COPS program. It fell to another Reno aide, Kent Markus, to get the application down to size. That required many meetings and maneuvers to get around requirements of federal law and the Office of Management and Budget.

The tiny form may have been a bit less amazing than its proponents made it out to be. Nadol, the careerist, insisted later that all the editing made little difference because to get their funds, the cities that used the 1-page application still had to fill out a 15-page supplement seeking more details. Justice also took the unusual step of advising cities in advance how many new cops they were likely to get so that they could start the hiring routine while Washington processed the paperwork.

The Clinton administration lost no time in getting COPS underway. On the 12th day of the new fiscal year, the White House handed out more than $200 million to communities in all 50 states and Puerto Rico, including 332 police departments, 46 sheriffs' offices, and 6 Indian tribes. One staffer reported that to find 5,000 officers to fund in such a short time, the Justice Department combined more than 2,000 previously employed in other programs with nearly 3,000 that had been rejected under a stopgap 1993 funding law.[23]

That was followed by a relentless series of upbeat press releases about the COPS program, chronicling every several hundred additions to the total. The Justice Department proved adept at creating acronyms for variations on the theme, setting up categories like COPS AHEAD (Accelerated Hiring Education and Deployment) and COPS FAST (Funding Accelerated for Smaller Towns). One Texas sheriff who had a question marveled that no one in Washington had returned his phone call so quickly since Texan Sam Rayburn was House speaker.

All the while, Janet Reno met frequently with those running the program. "She would cross-examine us to make sure there were no mistakes, no political intrusiveness," said Uchida, who moved from Justice's research unit to the COPS office.

The quick action to get the Treasury checks out helped fend off what could have become an abrupt halt to the Democrats' most prominent national anticrime thrust since LEAA. Part of the "Contract With America" that House Republicans had proclaimed before they unexpectedly won control in the November 1994 elections was a plank to convert the 100,000 cops into block grants that would allow localities more leeway in spending and, not coincidentally, take from Clinton the credit of setting the program's direction.

By mid-February 1995, the House had approved the overhaul. But Clinton vowed to veto the change. His aides protested that the GOP scheme posed the danger of revisiting the flaws in the old LEAA program, which allowed states leeway in spending federal anticrime funds. (The Clinton advisers conveniently ignored the point that LEAA was created by a Democratic administration and overseen for its first decade by a Democratic-controlled Congress.)

In a compromise, the COPS program was continued, but Republicans were able to add a "Local Law Enforcement Block Grants" program that set aside a little more than $500 million each year that states and localities could use not only for police hiring but also for overtime, equipment purchases, school security, and other anticrime needs. That allowed both sides to claim victory. The Democrats preserved their essential program, while Republicans could boast of a version they said was easier for local officials to use.

Although local police chiefs were enthusiastic about the idea of an infusion of federal funds, the Clinton administration struck out trying to find a prominent law enforcer to head their prize program. The top candidate was Tom Potter, a respected retired chief from Portland, Ore. Potter had accepted the job and made plans to move to Washington when the news broke that his daughter had admitted to being a lesbian and Potter supported the rights of gay police officers. That was apparently a no-no even in a presidency that enjoyed wide backing from gays. Potter was dumped.

Another well-known chief, St. Louis's Clarence Harmon (later elected mayor), turned down the job. So the White House was left with Joseph Brann, a mostly unknown chief from the medium-sized California city of Hayward, who had been slated to be Potter's deputy. (A much bigger catch for Clinton would have been New York Police Commissioner William Bratton, whom the administration could not persuade to take a high-profile job.)

Meanwhile, it was unlikely that the net result of COPS would be a permanent addition of 100,000 officers to the nation's police forces. During the 1996 election campaign, Attorney General Reno was forced to admit that only about 17,000 cops actually had hit the streets. That was mostly a result of a natural lag in the funding and training process; often, fewer than 10 percent of applicants made it past the first round of screening, and a police academy's courses typically took six to eight months. The reasonable explanation didn't stop Republicans from taking potshots, accusing Clinton of a gross overpromise.

A more serious concern was that cities would not keep their new officers after the federal funding's three-year cycle or would seek extensions, thus putting Washington in the position of helping to finance local officers indefinitely. Most cities insisted that they would continue to pay for the officers after the federal grants dried up, but some cities faltered and others asked for extensions.

Some experts were dubious about the long-term impact of the COPS program on crime. An infusion of highly trained officers into hot spots might make a notable dent in lawbreaking there, but the political imperative was to spread 100,000 officers nationwide into cities and townships big and small, whether or not they really needed them.

One of the most devastating assessments came from Wisconsin's Herman Goldstein, the academic father of problem-oriented policing. Clinton's big round number "makes people feel good, but it's a cockeyed notion that when spread over the country, it can have a major impact," Goldstein said. "It's a symbolic gesture with relatively little practical use." Goldstein complained, too, that Washington's dictating the terms of its grants provided a "disincentive for communities to take the initiative." Some Washington insiders grumbled that Goldstein was piqued that his brand of problem-oriented policing was not required for cities to get federal aid.

When the final analysis is completed on the COPS program, two of the key questions will be how much it really promoted smart community policing and how many officers actually were put on the street. In its first few years, it seemed that those running COPS would accept just about any reasonable definition of what was eligible for funding. Milwaukee, for example, used the federal funds to embrace the kind of aggressive policing against "quality of life" violations practiced in New York City. Whether or not the tactics were successful, they did not necessarily incorporate the careful analysis of crime patterns and laying plans to combat them by the cop on the beat that many saw as the core of community policing.

John Hart, a deputy director of the COPS program who resigned in 1999, admitted that most cities were declared eligible for federal aid if they could establish that they planned to use it for "community needs," even if many of the strategies involved did not fit the traditional definition of community policing.[24] Applications asking only for heavy-handed tactics like SWAT teams would be rejected.

Former Justice Department official Uchida agreed that virtually all applications were approved; for the most part, the only ones turned down were submitted by sheriffs' offices judged not equipped to pursue even general community policing concepts. "The federal government shouldn't be in the business of picking and choosing," said John Schmidt, who oversaw COPS as associate attorney general before returning to a Chicago law practice.[25] Schmidt also believed that it would have been "micromanaging" for the Justice Department to insist on a strict definition of community policing.

For an evaluation of COPS, researchers from the Urban Institute identified 47 elements of community policing, including police partnerships in the community, problem-solving programs, crime prevention tactics, and organizational change. Police departments already were using an average of 22 elements before COPS and added about 10 during the program's early years, reported lead researcher Jeffrey Roth. But cities not receiving federal funds implemented community policing techniques at nearly the same rate.[26]

As for numbers, on paper the COPS program funded its 100,000 goal during 1999, but only 39,000 to 55,400 of them were additional officers expected to remain on the job in 2003, said the federal evaluation. Most of the rest were counted as community cops because they had been "redeployed," a perfectly legal but somewhat misleading accounting procedure that allowed cities to spend their federal funds on equipment and other management changes that ostensibly freed up the time of officers for community policing.

The redeployment option was largely the work of Representative Schumer, who intended to help his hometown New York City police force. New York had expanded its ranks before the 1994 crime law and now needed technical support. Even though Schumer got his way, officials like Uchida insisted that the COPS office scrutinize the redeployment requests carefully. For example, much of New York City's huge request for $93 million in one year was sharply trimmed.

Cities were supposed to use their money from Washington only for net additions to their police forces. But a strict accounting would take years, so no one really knew what the true total would be. The Urban Institute predicted that the net addition of officers by 2003 would range from 62,700 to 83,900. Many experts projected that when all was said and done, the actual increase among America's police forces from the COPS program would be far closer to 50,000 than 100,000. "We'll be lucky to have 40,000 to 50,000 extra police on the street," conceded Uchida, who argued that even such a 10 percent infusion would be a "resounding success."

The failure to put 100,000 extra officers on the street was cited in two 1999 reports by the Justice Department's own inspector general, who noted the discrepancy with Clinton's promises in 1992 and 1993 to accomplish the goal by the year 2000. The inspector general said that most departments getting federal money had no system to track the redeployment process and that nearly half were using federal money to replace local allocations, not to supplement them. (COPS officials responded that the report had covered only 1 percent of grantees that had been identified as problematic recipients.[27])

Ironically, a net addition of 50,000 would equal the figure that some Clinton aides had proposed during the president's first campaign and early years in office. And this was fine with some of the administration's internal skeptics. "I'm perfectly happy if we don't get to 100,000," said one official, who stressed that the most important goal should be to concentrate any additional officers where they were most needed.

After the COPS program had been in operation for a few years, some city leaders began expressing the fear that after their three-year burst of federal aid expired, they would be unable to obtain local funding for many of the new police positions beyond the one-year federal retention period.

Other areas still wanted federally funded positions. Despite the questions about numbers that had dogged COPS, it enjoyed popular resonance, as mayors constantly touted it. Jeff Griffin, a Republican business executive who had won two terms as mayor of Reno, Nevada, was a typical example. Griffin, who in 2000 chaired the U.S. Conference of Mayors commitee that dealt with crime issues, supported extension of the COPS program beyond its initial six years. Differing with some of his GOP colleagues in Congress who would just as soon have buried Clinton's program, Griffin backed expanding COPS to fund police technology and help other members of the justice system like probation offices, whom he described as "creaking" under increased caseloads. (Reno had won federal aid for eight new officers, which Griffin said helped shuffle personnel so that an antigang unit could be created.[28])

Perhaps as significant as the persistent support from local officials, Clinton was in such political hot water over the Monica Lewinsky affair that the day his Senate impeachment trial started in January 1999, the embattled president made his way across the Potomac River to the Alexandria, Va., police department and announced that he would seek $6.4 billion to extend COPS by as many as 50,000 officers.

If the timing was intended to divert attention from the first presidential impeachment trial in 130 years, it did not work. The call for a major expansion of what had been the Democrats' signature anticrime program nearly six years earlier caused hardly a ripple in the news media.

Still, the administration's rhetoric flowed generously. When COPS director Brann appeared before a House committee in March 1999 to seek his annual appropriation, he credited the program for much of the nation's crime-rate decline and attributed to experts he did not name the conclusion that "more police on the street means less crime." Unfortunately, the research to back up that statement was far from definitive. One 1996 study of 56 big cities and 49 states concluded that increasing police numbers might reduce lawbreaking, but reviewer Lawrence Sherman, then of the University of Maryland, said that "what the causal mechanism for that effect may be or how it may be enhanced . . . is not clear."[29]

In the summer of 1999, Brann quietly left office. His administrative power had been largely handed over to John Hart, a longtime Clinton political operative, who himself departed soon after Brann to return to his primary field of expertise, health care administration. The program then was put into the hands of Thomas Frazier, a respected police executive who had been targeted for replacement as Baltimore's police commissioner by the city's incoming mayor, who ran on a platform that criticized Frazier for embracing a form of community policing that was not aggressive enough against street crime.

The sixth and final year of initial COPS funding under the 1994 crime law was an exercise extraordinary even for Washington in misleading appropriations for crime fighting. Overall, it worked out well for the White House, which requested $1.275 billion and received $913 million after Clinton vetoed the legislation as insufficient. The reality was far different. The total included $318 million held over from the previous year, and only $209 million of that was allotted for hiring new officers under the COPS concept. Some $220 million of the remainder was designated for hiring—mostly for school resource officers and enforcement on Indian lands. Most of the rest went for technology, including bulletproof vests. Still, Robert Scully of NAPO, an enthusiastic supporter of COPS, expressed confidence that Congress would continue it in some form past Clinton's presidency to "keep the American public happy."

The political focus on officer numbers made it seem as if COPS was mainly an employment program, but the redeployment provision meant that much federal money was being spent on equipment, just as in the 1970s LEAA days. Many police departments were able to buy computers, laptops for patrol cars, and even fax machines.

Federal support for local police was so popular that it would almost certainly continue in some form under the presidency of George W. Bush. The new president would inherit a COPS program budgeted at least at $600 million annually. "There's too much political advantage," former COPS official Uchida told U.S. News & World Report. "No one in their right mind would say, 'Let's cut the COPS office.' Whether it's been effective or not doesn't matter." It seemed most likely that Bush would ask Congress to downgrade and revamp the COPS program. The Republicans were expected to shift the focus on hiring to one on block grants that localities that could use for police technology and other law enforcement functions.

COPS did not create a national police force of the kind that J. Edgar Hoover's critics had feared, but the influence of the Justice Department and Congress was deeply felt in the operations of police departments all over the nation. It would not be clear until well into the twenty-first century whether American taxpayers were getting their money's worth.

The Clinton administration surely had spread the gospel of community policing nationwide, helping to cement a trend that had been long advocated by reformers of American policing but had never taken hold in most police forces, largely owing to a lack of consistent funding. "COPS jumped into a fast-running river and threw more water into it," concluded William Geller, a Chicago police consultant who followed the program closely.[30]

Even if COPS wasted federal resources on places that didn't need them, it also modernized some hidebound police forces. But it was not certain whether communities large and small could continue to depend on the White House and Congress for crucial law enforcement support or whether advances in policing would return to their former haphazard ways.

As dramatic as the growth of the nation's police forces was, the expansion of the prison and jail populations dwarfed it in numerical terms. A get-tough sentencing orgy by federal and state legislators, who acted with the same absence of careful deliberation that had marked the surge in police hiring, packed correctional institutions nationwide.

Chapter 9

THREE STRIKES: BASEBALL
TO CRIME

SINCE the 1960s, presidents and congressional leaders have tried to sell voters on the idea that Washington, D.C., is the fount of wisdom on how to stamp out violent crime. A long series of commissions, federal aid programs, and conferences has been premised on the view that the feds are first and best when it comes to making Americans safe. The news media reinforce the notion by faithfully reporting the anticrime pronouncements of presidents, attorneys general, and congressional leaders.

In 1994, Americans watching the State of the Union Address heard this stern warning from President Bill Clinton: "Those who commit repeated violent crimes must be told: Commit a third violent crime and you'll be put away for good." It may have sounded like a new idea to most viewers, but many on the West Coast realized that this was another example of a national political leader's adopting an idea from the states.

Rhetoric aside, the nation's capital usually is one of the the last places to originate innovative anticrime ideas. In the case of "three strikes and you're out," one of the fastest-moving fads of the 1990s, Clinton's pronouncement was emblematic of a national movement to tinker with sentencing laws that probably did some good, but often at the expense of rationality and fairness.

The three strikes saga began in the largest city of the "other Washington"— Seattle. John Carlson, the son of a police officer, had grown up hearing his father's gripes about the gaping holes in the criminal justice system. In a typical case, Dad would arrest a man for robbery. If the suspect was convicted after seemingly endless challenges to the evidence and delays in court, he might spend a few years in prison. Then he'd be caught again and again, always winning release far before the end of the term the judge had given him. Eventually, he might commit some horrible crime that finally would convince a court to impose a long sentence. By then, too much damage had been done.

After graduating from the University of Washington in 1981 and working briefly for the Census Bureau, Carlson dabbled in politics and decided to try his hand at being a conservative activist. By 1986, he had landed a commentator's spot on local television, delivering his prescriptions on government spending, regulatory reform, education, and, of course, crime. In the fall of 1988, Carlson pondered how he could convince viewers of his idea that "the main reason we have a crime problem is that too many criminals don't fear the law." What he needed, Carlson decided, was a "short, snappy, and to the point" slogan to encapsulate the idea. Experimenting over the course of a day, he eventually settled on a baseball metaphor, "three strikes, you're out."[1]

Under the Carlson scheme, anyone who had been convicted and penalized for two serious crimes would have the book thrown at him if it happened a third time: life behind bars—no probation, no parole. Carlson announced his plan October 16, 1988, in his regular stint on KIRO, the CBS television affiliate in Seattle. It was a flop. Hardly anyone reacted to the catchy slogan, and Carlson moved on to other issues.

But the parade of shocking crimes continued. One of the most horrifying occurred the year after Carlson's TV appearance, when a woman named Diana Ballasiotes was abducted and stabbed to death by a convicted rapist who had been released from prison. Grieving associates started a group called Friends of Diana to seek harsher penalties for sex crimes. Diana's mother, Ida, vowed to run for the state legislature. In time, Carlson and Ballasiotes discovered their mutual interest in getting tough on criminals and joined forces to push for three strikes.

It was slow going at first. Washington State had approved a new criminal-sentencing scheme in 1981. It went into effect three years later, stiffening penalties for many violent crimes. By 1992, when Carlson and Ballasiotes were plotting to advance the three strikes idea, key state legislators had no reason to believe that their longstanding set of sentencing guidelines for judges (which preceded the mid-1980s federal version) needed an overhaul. The state's prison population was growing steadily. But critics like Carlson and Ballasiotes pointed out that many convicts also were being placed in community-based programs that could put them in a good position to escape and commit new atrocities.

With legislative action to fine-tune the state's criminal penalties nowhere in sight, Carlson and fellow conservative David LaCourse decided to try bypassing lawmakers and mounting a petition campaign to put three strikes on a statewide ballot. They needed nearly 200,000 signatures, a daunting task in a sprawling state of 4 million people. They sought support from groups like the Washington Council on Crime and Delinquency, an umbrella organization that represented much of the criminal-justice establishment. Not surprisingly, a panel of prosecutors, defense lawyers, prison experts, and interested private citizens was cool to an idea that would constrict its members' authority. "It was a nice slogan, but it sounded like a 'habitual offender' law we already had," recalled Larry Fehr, the group's director.[2] The council told Carlson and LaCourse that it wouldn't bother to take a stand unless the proposal actually made it on the ballot. One again, three strikes had struck out.

Criminals continued their vicious ways, and Carlson, LaCourse, and Ballasiotes pressed on. By early 1993, enough high-profile crimes by repeat offenders had taken place that they were able to persuade some leading politicians, including liberal Governor Mike Lowry, to endorse three strikes. But the plan foundered in a sea of bickering among politicians over conflicting ideas on reforming Washington State's punishment practices. Carlson and his backers were determined to launch another petition drive, one they estimated would take a $125,000 war chest to succeed.

Unlike the previous year, when their ragtag team had failed miserably, this time around, the activists—who now called themselves Washington Citizens for Justice—found a powerful and wealthy ally: the National Rifle Association. The NRA had been successfully warding off gun-control measures in Congress, state legislatures, and city councils for many years, but the battles were getting tougher. The NRA could make a plausible case that gun control was an ineffective anticrime tool. But that argument was losing appeal as more Americans, particularly police officers, were falling victim to firearms violence. Antigun forces were winning unexpected victories, partly by depicting the NRA as a narrow-minded organization interested only in the negative goal of defeating gun-control proposals. NRA leaders, recognizing the advantage of taking an aggressive anticrime stance, started a national drive called CrimeStrike to campaign for tougher prison sentences and to protest unwarranted parole releases.

Washington State's Carlson and his three strikes idea was one of the first beneficiaries of CrimeStrike. The NRA gave the group $55,000 and used its extensive mailing list, blanketing 360,000 homes with "urgent" appeals that produced more than half of the signatures Carlson needed. It was clear by the July 2 deadline for ballot submissions that three strikes, officially Proposition 593, would go before the voters in November.

Justice system professionals like prosecutors and prison wardens viewed three strikes with disdain. They figured that it would stop few criminals, who rarely fear that they will be caught, and that it would cost the taxpayers plenty to house, feed, and provide medical care for the few who did receive lifetime terms. They also knew that the law would not be enforced uniformly. In some cases, prosecutors would get around what they regarded as unjust penalties simply by not filing a third felony charge if that would mean life in prison for a suspect they decided did not deserve one. In other cases where three-time-loser charges would be filed even for relatively minor crimes, Washington State residents would end up paying the tab of $25,000 or more each year for housing inmates in their last 20 or 30 years of life, long after most of them would be committing crimes if they had been released. Typically, violent crime is an occupation of men under 35.

By the fall of 1993, when the campaign for three strikes was in full swing, the opponents had organized into an informal coalition of civil libertarians, religious leaders, and criminal defense lawyers. The critics included the crime and delinquency council that had given Carlson the brushoff the previous year.

But it was too late to stop three strikes. Carlson had tapped into a rich vein of public anger over repeat criminals. He and the NRA hardly needed to stage much of a campaign, although he did distribute the requisite pamphlets and bumper stickers, and flew in prominent backers like former federal drug czar William Bennett to campaign for the proposition. Carlson's "timing was perfect," said the crime council's Fehr. "The public believed that the crime problem was running rampant, and elected officials would not dare speak out against the idea."

State prison system director Chase Riveland could hardly contain himself. He knew that after the turn of the twenty-first century, his agency would be forced to care for what could amount to hundreds of elderly inmates serving three strikes sentences. As a senior executive branch official, Riveland generally stayed away from controversial public issues, but he eventually said, "Our official position is that we are neither for nor against that stupid initiative." Still, an overwhelming 77 percent of voters ignored warning signs from the establishment figures and approved three strikes in November.

The repercussions were wide. In a development that stunned Carlson, a sensational crime down the coast in California provided added impetus for an idea that had fallen flat five years earlier.

In early December 1993, police found the body of 12-year-old Polly Klaas, who had been abducted nearly two months earlier from a slumber party in her bedroom in the central California town of Petaluma. Polly had been strangled and her corpse left in the woods. A few days earlier, police had arrested 39-year-old Richard Allen Davis, a career criminal who had spent most of his adult life in prison. Davis had served five years for kidnapping a woman at a public transit station and attempting to sexually assault her. Three years after his release, he was back behind bars for a 16-year term for kidnapping yet another woman.

Yet Davis had been set free several weeks before Polly Klaas was seized. He had served only half of his stated sentence, released for good behavior under California's determinate sentencing system, which specified release dates and curbed wardens' discretion to extend custody. On parole at the time of the Klaas crime, Davis was not taken into custody when he was stopped for drunk driving while authorities were investigating the kidnapping. He was finally picked up after a convenience store clerk spotted him doing a double-take after seeing a poster of Klaas.

Public outrage was intense about the justice system's seeming failures. Davis was the perfect candidate for the kind of three strikes law that was being advocated in Washington State.

Although Polly Klaas would become the tragic poster girl for three strikes, that wasn't her family's idea. Marc Klaas, Polly's father, was approached at her memorial service by a state senator, Mike Thompson, with an idea that he said "would prevent what happened to Polly from happening again."[3] It wasn't three strikes, but rather a bill that would give police officers instant access to suspects' criminal history data from squad car computers. Klaas spoke to his family and decided that he had a "90-day window of opportunity" to help enact a crime-control reform like Thompson's "before Polly would be forgotten, I would be forgotten, and we would move on to the next crime du jour, which turned out to be the O. J. Simpson case."

While Klaas was working with Thompson, another grieving California father was ready to seize on the Klaas case to push the cause of three strikes. In late June 1992, 18-year-old Kimber Reynolds was leaving a restaurant in Fresno when two men on a motorcycle demanded her purse. She resisted, and one of the men shot her in the head with a .357 magnum, killing her. The murderer, who had been in and out of custody on drug, robbery, and auto theft charges, died later in a shootout with police. Mike Reynolds, a wedding photographer who had no experience in the political arena, wanted to use his daughter's death as the prime example in a campaign to toughen California's penalties for chronic offenders. But as shocking as the murder of Kimber Reynolds was, it had not captured enough public support to prod the state's legislators into action.

The snatching of a 12-year-old from her home was one horrible degree worse than the shooting of a college student near a restaurant. Reynolds didn't hesitate to take advantage of the new outrage. With the case of Polly Klaas fresh in citizens' minds and the Washington State initiative getting more attention as a "solution" to repeat criminality, Reynolds and other crime-victim advocates blitzed the radio talk show circuit in San Francisco, Los Angeles, and other population centers. Suddenly, politicians could not embrace three strikes fast enough. The idea that had drawn mostly yawns when John Carlson had taken it to the airwaves in 1988 became the newest crime-control fad.

Now one grieving father was drawn into another's crusade. Marc Klaas, who initially had not been very interested in three strikes, was approached by Reynolds. "I was very distraught," Klaas recalled later. When Reynolds and his allies said "this would have prevented the crime against your child, I said 'that sounds good to me.'" Klaas promptly endorsed it without much thought.

Even before the Klaas incident, it was becoming evident that three strikes and other tough-on-convicts measures would become fodder for candidates of both major political parties in 1993. It wasn't a national election year, but as often happens because of a quirky off-year campaign schedule, the governor's races in New Jersey and Virginia captured the political and media spotlight. Crime was a major issue in Virginia, a moderate to conservative state that had elected Democratic governors in the previous three contests. In 1993, a relatively unknown Republican named George Allen, making his first race for statewide office, trounced an incumbent state attorney general by stumping for an end to parole and a stiffening of prison terms for repeat violators. (He was later able to help get versions of both enacted during his term.)

Allen's victory was noticed in the U.S. Senate, which the same week as the Virginia election happened to be debating what eventually became the huge anticrime law of 1994. The fact that a Republican like Allen would campaign on an anticrime platform was not surprising. What was astounding in late 1993 and early 1994 was the rapid spread of the three strikes idea among Democrats, whose anticrime policies had traditionally emphasized attempting to rehabilitate lawbreakers and spending money on social programs they believed would steer youths away from trouble—the supposedly "soft-on-crime" approach.

Three strikes was backed by Kathleen Brown, the leading Democratic candidate for California governor in 1994 and the political heiress of the family that had built a Democratic Party dynasty in the state (father Edmund and brother Jerry both had served as governor). Another supporter was Mario Cuomo, the New York State governor who was the embodiment of modern-day liberalism. Cuomo's enthusiastic endorsement of the idea was based on the premise that it would apply only to a few cases. Mirroring an argument of gun-control advocates that even restrictions that have a small impact are acceptable, Cuomo supported three strikes if it might prevent "only one rape, one murder, one assault."

The Democrats' surprising shift toward harshness went far beyond three strikes. Both Brown and Cuomo said that despite their personal opposition to capital punishment, they would carry out executions if the public approved. They were trying to have it both ways, but their new stance recognized that they could not survive politically against vast public approval for the ultimate penalty. (Nonetheless, both Democrats lost.)

In California, Marc Klaas was having second thoughts. He had endorsed three strikes in a moment of anguish. Now he and his family concluded that Reynolds's plan was too broad. In some ways, it made little sense. It was fine to treat repeat criminals harshly, but the possibility that just about any felony could count as the third offense meant that a three-time bicycle thief could get a prison term five times as long as that of a first-time murderer. Klaas and his allies drafted what they considered a more focused version and withdrew their support of the Reynolds draft. But it was too late to pull back. Three strikes "was gaining the momentum of a freight train running downhill—it was a done deal," Klaas said. "Many politicians jumped on three strikes whether they believed in it or not."

Three strikes passion would not come to a head in California until well into 1994, but the high-profile spate of crimes nationwide—plus the decisive Washington State referendum results in November 1993—was building pressure on Bill Clinton. The president's health-care reforms were tottering in Congress, but the Senate in November had approved a major anticrime bill that included the White House plan to add 100,000 community patrol officers. It was beginning to appear that crime would be an issue more promising than health care for the Democrats in election year 1994.

The shift of emphasis made particular sense for Clinton. As a centrist "New Democrat," he had broken with traditional liberalism and endorsed capital punishment—pointedly interrupting his 1992 presidential campaign to give his official blessing to an execution in Arkansas. But the new president also had called for a balanced anticrime policy that included treatment for drug abusers, and he generally had avoided simplistic notions like three strikes. The White House was notably mum about the idea in the fall of 1993.

Then the anticrime bandwagon of the mid-1990s was encouraged in a grisly way by another sensational crime. On December 7, 1993, a man boarded a Long Island Rail Road commuter train near New York City and opened fire with an assault-style gun, killing 6 passengers and wounding 19. As bad as it was, the episode was not much more serious than some shooting sprees that had received little attention in inner cities. But the fact that the victims this time were defenseless upper-middle-class commuters provided another stunning example of unprovoked violence that seemed to cry out for action. Unlike the killer of Polly Klaas, however, this time the perpetrator apparently was not a career criminal but rather a mentally disturbed immigrant named Colin Ferguson.

The cumulative effect of the 1993 spate of high-profile crimes was having an impact on public opinion. Even though official counts showed later that violent crime declined in 1993, the news media reflected public worries (and inflamed them, critics charged). The number of crime stories on the three biggest television networks' nightly news programs doubled during the year. Weekly magazines that track public concerns stepped up their coverage. *Business Week* ran a cover story on the economics of crime in December 1993. *Newsweek* followed with a cover story on crime in its first issue of 1994, *U.S. News & World Report* did the same the next week, and *Time* magazine weighed in exactly three weeks later.

As the date for the State of the Union Address approached in late January 1994, it became clear to Clinton's advisers that simple or not, three strikes was an idea whose time had come. When Clinton mounted the podium in the House chamber on January 25 to announce his plans for the year, three strikes, along with health care and welfare reform, got the loudest bursts of applause.

All the cheers on Capitol Hill for three strikes masked the fact that it would apply to only a tiny number of federal cases. Only serious violent offenses would be counted, and the detailed definitions excluded drug cases and crimes that did not threaten human life. In an insiders' account of anticrime policymaking in the early years of the Clinton administration, Democratic strategists Harry Chernoff, Christopher Kelly, and John Kroger said that the president's endorsement of three strikes "proved an embarrassment" later, when six Clinton advisers promptly opposed the idea.[4]

When a House subcommittee held a hearing in March on the Clinton administration's proposal, Justice Department official Jo Ann Harris was somewhat defensive, declaring that the plan "does not sweep so broadly" as to include undeserving defendants. For example, a conviction would not count as a strike if a suspect could prove he did not use a gun or another dangerous weapon and did not cause death or serious bodily injury. The Justice Department estimated at the time that no more than 200 cases each year would be filed. The actual number of three strikes convictions was far lower—only 35 in the law's first two years. The department could not provide a total of cases filed through 2000.

The important advance from the viewpoint of the White House and Congress was that federal prosecutors had more power to put a few persistent offenders behind bars for life. In reality, it was another episode in the predominant pattern of modern crime-fighting in America: an idea from the grass roots that would do little about lawbreaking overall but nevertheless had captured the fancy of the nation's political leadership.

The lightning-quick spread of three strikes was especially notable because the essential idea of enhanced punishment for repeat criminals wasn't exactly novel. Before John Carlson's catchy slogan was popularized, most states already had enacted laws that provided escalating penalties for convictions after the first. A survey in 1991 found that all but about a dozen states had enacted what amounted to two-strikes or three-strikes laws, including California, New York, and others that later were thrust into the national spotlight in the debate over three strikes. In essence, three strikes was a glitzy label for practices that many states had tried for years.

Three strikes's triumph was the symbolic culmination of a late-twentieth-century turnaround in the way American criminals were penalized. In the nation's early decades, the English tradition of sending serious offenders to far-away penal colonies had been replaced by the establishment of local penitentiaries, where convicts were sent for fixed terms.

By the early twentieth century, a new theory had taken hold: that many criminals could be "rehabilitated." This notion relied in large part on "indeterminate" sentences, wide ranges of possible prison terms. Under those laws, convicts would receive sentences that may have sounded high to them, their victims, and the public—perhaps 15 to 25 years, or 25 years to life for violent crimes.

But years (or sometimes only a few months) later, usually out of the public eye, judges or corrections officials could exercise their discretion and set a shorter time a convict actually would spend behind bars. It usually was much less than the term originally announced, a reduced figure supposedly justified by convicts' exemplary records while in custody and their potential for going straight.

Those in charge of these malleable systems of punishment argued that officials in corrections agencies who had observed a convict closely and were most familiar with his background and behavior were in the best position to decide his fate. Prison and parole officials knew that predicting future criminality was no science and that they would make mistakes, but they believed they could judge correctly in the vast majority of cases.

As an important side benefit, officials could use the indeterminate penalty system as a way to control crowding in penal institutions. When the cells became stuffed, the congestion could be eased by quietly freeing inmates within a year of release by slashing a few months from their sentences. Because the inmates would be gaining their freedom soon anyway, the reasoning went, it wouldn't hurt much to advance the date if doing so might avert tense conditions and even violence behind the walls.

As comforting as the indeterminate sentencing system was to those who ran it, critics—many of them crime victims and leaders of organizations advocating their cause like NRA's CrimeStrike—charged that it had become terribly flawed. One of their main propositions was subjective and highly debatable but powerful nevertheless. Penalties had become too lax, the hardliners contended, because the typical criminals of the latter twentieth century simply were more violent than their counterparts in earlier decades.

That was difficult to prove, but another potent argument was that public confidence in the justice system suffered when harsh-sounding sentences were imposed and convicts then were routinely released after serving only about a third of their stated time. A survey taken since 1980 by the National Opinion Research Center showed consistently that 70 percent or more of Americans believed that their local judges were not severe enough on lawbreakers.[5] The results reflected public frustration over repeat criminals. Survey respondents probably were influenced by cases reported by the news media, which typically report on chronic lawbreakers, not convicts who did their time and then stayed out of trouble.

With one "bad news" tale after another, it's not surprising that critics believed the corrections establishment of judges, wardens, and parole officers erred too often on the side of the convict. It wasn't that hard-bitten officials were closet liberals. Often they were highly skeptical of criminals' vows to go straight. But many inmates did find religion, sometimes literally. After studying their criminal records, authorities might be swayed by solemn assurances that inmates would live law-abiding lives outside prison walls. Rarely hearing from the victim or the victim's family, wardens or parole boards might order releases, at the same time making cells available for newly sentenced defendants, who often were backlogged in county jails.

In fact, the movement into and out of state prisons in America seemed to support the "revolving door" image so popular among critics. Even after a binge of tough-sentencing laws in the 1990s, in 1996—a year when the state prison population was a little over 1 million—more than 500,000 convicts were admitted and about 450,000 inmates were released.

Not surprisingly, many convicts committed new crimes after leaving custody. Since crime rates started to rise steadily in the 1960s, it seemed that the public became less and less tolerant of the justice system's apparent miscalculations. Just as significant was a growing realization among experts that the longstanding idea that convicts could be rehabilitated was largely unproved, if not misguided. New York State launched a landmark study in the late 1960s. Governor Nelson Rockefeller named a Special Committee on Criminal Offenders, which asked sociologist Robert Martinson to examine the evidence. In 1970, Martinson concluded that with a few exceptions, "the rehabilitative efforts that have been reported so far have had no appreciable effect on recidivism."[6]

The Martinson report was not initially released to the public. Its pessimistic conclusion did not begin to sink in widely until he wrote a summary in the journal The Public Interest in 1974 under the title "What Works? Questions and Answers about Prison Reform." Martinson's strong doubts soon resulted in his findings being dubbed the "nothing works" report, a label that stuck for decades.

In some respects, Martinson's conclusions merely confirmed what politicians and their constituents already believed. In policy terms, it provided ammunition to overhaul the laws on criminal sentencing in some states. The most popular idea was to mandate minimum prison sentences for specified offenses in order to prevent judges and wardens from setting convicts free after they had served only a few weeks or months. More broadly, the new sentencing structures aimed to make the norm "determinate" sentencing that narrowed the discretion of judges and corrections officials.

New York State took the mandatory minimum route in 1973 when it enacted tough antidrug laws, setting penalties that ranged from required minimums of 1, 6, or 15 years to life behind bars, depending on the offense level. What Nelson Rockefeller called "the nation's toughest drug law" was "so harsh that even prosecutors and the police were aghast" and tried to soften its bite, to little avail, said legal historian Lawrence Friedman.[7]

The Rockfeller laws curbed parole releases, which were becoming a more common target of critics. It wasn't the notion of parole officers' keeping tabs on convicts after their release that bothered most detractors, but rather the idea that a prisoner would be released "early" on parole. Of course, any date before the end of a stated term could be declared early, even if such a release was standard practice for all inmates. Some states in the 1970s began restricting or eliminating parole, and others turned to the sentencing guidelines idea— pioneered by Minnesota and later incorporated into the federal justice system— that dictated to judges the mininum and maximum penalties, depending on the seriousness of an offense and the extent of the defendant's record.

It seemed that the average amount of time that inmates were serving was on the increase, but data were so imperfect that in the 1970s, no one knew for sure. One problem with the new schemes to make sentences more definitive was that they could lead to criminals' release just as arbitrary as under the former in-determinate system. In essence, politicians were substituting their imperfect judgments on proper sentences for the sometimes flawed conclusions of justice-system employees.

The sensational 1993 case of Polly Klaas may have resulted from a prominent example of lawmakers' good intentions gone wrong. The California legislature had enacted a prescribed sentence for rape, but it did not take into account the dangerousness of a career convict like Klaas's killer, Richard Davis. Even if authorities had reason to argue that Davis should not be set free, they were powerless to keep him in custody under the determinate sentencing law that had eliminated their discretion. (Marc Klaas, Polly's father, later got to know Bill Baker, a conservative California legislator who sponsored the law that allowed Davis to be freed. "He apologized for putting my daughter's killer on the street," Klaas said, generously suggesting that "it apparently was not a well-researched piece of legislation.") In fact, many convicts ended up serving less time under determinate sentences than they would have under the previous indeterminate system—a result that might or might not have been appropriate, depending on the circumstances. It certainly was not what most conservative reformers had expected.

Some advocates of three strikes who complained about the early release of criminals conveniently ignored the fact that the determinate-term "solution" extolled by anticrime hardliners had failed in Davis's case and undoubtedly in many others. The plain fact was that no arbitrary sentence length could guarantee that a convict would never strike again unless he was kept in custody forever. But most politicians ignored that fact, pretending that effective reform was just a matter of racheting up sentencing totals.

As they focused their fire on what they viewed as lenient penalties being meted out by judges and parole boards, conservative critics began to draw a bead on the misleading numbers that long had been used to characterize prison terms. Justice-system professionals believed it was useful to threaten convicts with long maximum penalties that could be shortened if they behaved, with devices like "good time" awarded periodically to prisoners who avoided infractions.

Everyone in the know realized that criminals typically would serve about one third of the stated time they got in court. A 25-year term, for example, meant a little more than 8 years behind bars for anything close to a model prisoner. Everyone knew except the general public, which probably assumed that a 15-year sentence meant 15 years in prison. As the movement to aid crime victims grew in the 1970s and 1980s, victim advocates became more strident in calling attention to the discrepancies.

The supposedly short average prison terms was a particular focus of criticism. A leading example was a widely publicized estimate that murderers served an average of only seven years in prison. That may have been true once, but it vastly understated reality in the latter twentieth century, argued criminologists James Lynch of The American University and William Sabol of the Urban Institute in Washington, D.C. In a 1998 study,[8] they noted that it was based on an analysis of convict releases from prison before the mid-1990s. Because the data did not account for harsher sentencing laws of recent years, many convicts serving longer terms were far from being set free. Lynch and Sabol estimated that the actual time served by the typical modern murderer was between 12 and 17 years. Of course, many relatives of victims would judge even that range far too low.

As legislators in various states grappled in the late 1970s and early 1980s with ways to standardize punishment levels, the damage done by releasing criminals after short prison terms was on the agenda of the Conservative Opportunity

Society of Republican rebels in Congress. After Reagan took the White House, junior GOP members like Georgia's Newt Gingrich and California's Dan Lungren recognized that as a minority within a minority, their best chance of attracting attention might lie in coming up with pithy slogans. "We had to capture the language—the terms of the debate," said Lungren, who was one of the group's leaders on the crime issue. "So we sat down and thought about the words we used to explain what we were doing."[9] On prison terms, he said, "to explain that people were being sentenced to time that they never served, we thought long and hard [and adopted] the phrase 'truth in sentencing.'" To conservative reformers, the idea was that convicts should serve the time that judges gave them, with no early parole releases.

The federal no-parole policy was enacted as part of the sentencing guideline scheme in Congress's wide-ranging 1984 anticrime law, but it took another decade for legislators to pressure states on truth in sentencing. Even then, it came in a notably discounted form. The 1994 crime law, in authorizing billions of dollars to help states build prisons, gave funding priority to those that had passed truth-in-sentencing laws. But the whole truth wouldn't be necessary: requiring convicts to serve 85 percent of their stated sentences would be good enough for a state to win money from Washington. (The arbitrary 85 percent figure was drawn from the 1984 federal anticrime law that defined as 15 percent the maximum amount of "good time" that inmates could earn through good behavior to be eligible for release.)

On top of the mandatory minimum prison terms that had become popular from coast to coast since the 1980s, truth in sentencing spread rapidly after the 1994 federal law was passed. Only 5 states had adopted the 85 percent standard in 1993; six years later, the total had reached 27, plus 13 that had adopted some form of truth in sentencing that did not include the 85 percent rule.

One state that refused to go along with the truth-in-sentencing binge was Texas. It wasn't that Texas was lax on crime; to the contrary, it was known as one of the toughest states. Rather, Texans wanted to do things their own way, starting in the 1980s. "We are the only state without prison overcrowding," boasted Tony Fabelo, executive director of the state's Criminal Justice Policy Council. "We are ahead of the game . . . [in building prisons] . . . we have never been liberal in Texas."[10]

Indeed, in an astounding burst of construction, Texas increased prison-bed capacity from 41,166 in 1989 to a projected 150,285 by mid-2000.[11] In the years before the prison-construction boom began, county jails suffered from what Fabelo called a "gigantic backlog" of convicts awaiting a state prison cell. So Texas created an unusual system of state-run jails that included a 5,500-bed drug treatment network. The state had the highest incarceration rate in the nation in 1995 (exceeded later by Louisiana). But Texas also ranked high in crime rates, although its 15th place nationally in 1995 was down from 3rd in 1989.

With crime policy so prominent in 1994, it wasn't surprising that it was a major issue in the bitterly fought Texas gubernatorial campaign. Incumbent Democrat Ann Richards bragged that she had slashed from 79 to 29 percent the requests for parole approved. Republican George W. Bush, who beat Richards partly on the crime issue, tried to go Richards one better by promising to "deny parole totally for the most heinous offenses." Indeed, the parole rate dropped to 14 percent by 1997, but the trend was started by Richards.

Bush also pledged to be tougher on juvenile crime, and a law expanding penalties for teen offenses was enacted during his governorship. Bush allies argued that the governor had devoted considerable effort to developing a balanced prevention-and-punishment policy on juvenile crime, including "tough love academies" for delinquents who had not compiled lengthy and violent records. It seemed that Bush had taken more opportunities than Vice President Gore, his opponent for the presidency, to immerse himself in youth-policy issues.

Still, Ann Richards did most of the heavy lifting in the 1990s on Texas's anticrime policy, and Bush had no unique claim on the crime issue. "Richards built our [prison] capacity; Bush is continuing to build on the tough-on-crime mentality of the state legislature," said Bill Kelly of the Center for Criminal Justice Research at the University of Texas.[12]

Congress dangled the prospect of billions of dollars in prison-building aid to states in 1994, but it was doubtful that Washington was the driving force behind longer prison terms, because the trend was well underway before the 1994 law passed. The impact was further muddled in 1996 when, out of the public eye, key members of Congress managed to change important details in the prison-aid law in ways that benefited them. It had become clear that the requirements imposed to obtain money from Washington were unfavorable to states represented by lawmakers who controlled the Justice Department's purse strings.

So they rewrote the rules to make them compatible with existing state sentencing systems. The result was that more money could flow to states like Utah, home of Senate Judiciary Committee Chairman Orrin Hatch, and New Hampshire, represented by Judd Gregg, chairman of the Senate appropriations panel for the Justice Department. The losers were states like California and Texas that did not happen to have members of Congress on the relevant committees. (In early 1999, after the prison-aid law had been on the books for a little more than four years, the Clinton administration abruptly proposed to end it. But the Republican-dominated Congress kept it going anyway in reduced form.)

In a way, the truth-in-sentencing movement was the culmination of an unprecedented boom in incarceration in the last quarter of the twentieth century. In 1975, fewer than 250,000 people were housed in American prisons on any given day. By 1998, that total was up to 1.2 million. Adding those in local jails on any given day, the population behind bars exceeded 2 million by the year 2000. The rate of growth was slowing a bit as the century ended, but the totals seemed destined to keep rising even as the crime rate fell.

Tougher sentencing had spread relentlessly and almost universally, except when a state prison system reached capacity and early releases became necessary as a safety valve. In fact, truth in sentencing often was honored in the breach. Even some states that abolished parole, implying to citizens that convicts would not be set free before the end of their stated terms, retained "sneaky, back-door mechanisms" to release inmates quietly when institutions became overcrowded, said Pamala Griset, a Florida criminologist who studied sentencing practices. The release rules have gone by various euphemisms, like "controlled release" and "good time," shorthand for giving prisoners time off for good behavior.[13]

North Carolina instituted a truth-in-sentencing system that many experts hailed as more realistic than those in many other states. That was because it was tied to the state's actual prison capacity. Unlike typical sentencing "reforms" that almost always increased penalties, North Carolina actually lowered some

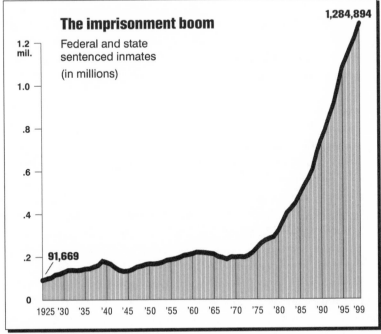

The imprisonment boom

Federal and state sentenced inmates (in millions)

1,284,894

91,669

Source: U.S Justice Department

so that others could be increased without overfilling institutions. Making any sanctions less severe was virtually unheard of elsewhere during the get-tough 1980s and 1990s.

For the most part, reform of state criminal sentencing laws was a convoluted process little understood by many legislators, not to mention the public. In most places, it took several years to draw up and implement an overhaul of sentencing, a winding path that made the rapid march of "three strikes, you're out" extraordinary by comparison. The momentum generated by the Washington State referendum of 1993 helped prompt at least 24 states and the federal government to enact three-strikes laws, many of them variations on long-existing statutes, by the end of 1995.[14]

To hear the inflated rhetoric of its backers, three strikes might have been expected to wipe out violent crime. Indeed, Lungren, who moved from Congress to become attorney general of California (losing the race for governor in 1998), argued that three strikes was responsible for much of his state's decline in violence in the late 1990s. Bill Jones, the prime sponsor of the law as a state legislator and later California's secretary of state, was more specific, claiming credit for preventing 1 million crimes and saving $21.7 billion (based on estimates of crimes' financial impact).

The private Justice Policy Institute took issue with Jones. Examining cases and statistics from the state's 12 largest counties through 1997, the organization asserted that crime went down by about the same rate whether or not a county aggressively invoked the three-strikes law. Other analysts said it was difficult to single out the impact of three strikes because of a 1998 law called "10–20-life" that imposed additional penalties of 10 years, 20 years, or life in prison on gun-toting criminals, a measure that may have affected crime totals as much as did three strikes.

The reality was that the laws did not have the wide impact their advocates had claimed. A central reason was the limited resources of the criminal-justice system that put the statutes into practice. Even before the rash of three-strikes laws, criminal courts in most urban centers were clogged. Now defendants who were faced with potential life prison terms had little incentive to plead guilty, the way that the vast majority of criminal cases in the United States end. Admitting guilt on a three-strikes offense would simply send them to prison, no questions asked. Why not roll the dice and hope for an acquittal at trial or that an overburdened prosecutor's office would reduce the charges?

Savvy defense attorneys knew there was no way that most three-strikes cases could go to trial. The voters who had been so enthusiastic about voting yes when three strikes appeared on the ballot did not, by and large, give their elected representatives a green light to spend significantly more tax money on judges, prosecutors, defense attorneys, courthouses, and, in many cases, prisons.

The best early evidence on the effect of three strikes emanated from Washington State and California, the two states that led the way in passage. Details of the statutes differed in several key respects. To be eligible for a life-without-parole sentence in Washington, a criminal had to commit specified types of serious felonies. California convicts needed to follow a different course to qualify: their second conviction for particular felonies (like robbery and rape) doubled the prison time, and any further felony required a "life" term—although release was possible after 25 years.

California's much broader law had a distinct impact on the criminal-justice process in many areas of the state. As defendants predictably were reluctant to plead guilty to any charge that could put them away for life, three-strikes cases in Los Angeles remained pending 41 percent longer than other cases and were three times more likely to go to trial than other felonies, a 1997 federal study reported. Los Angeles County attributed increased costs of $200 million or more to processing cases under the three-strikes law in its first several years.

The initial estimates of the laws' effect on the prison systems of both states seem to have been overstated. Washington State had expected 40 to 75 three-strikes convicts each year, but only 121 were sentenced in the law's first four years. Even so, critics insisted that the law had gone too far. "It casts too broad a net," said Stephanie Adraktas, a public defender in Seattle, who cited "small time robber after small time robber" who will likely die in prison because he was convicted of three "garden-variety robberies" in which no one was injured.[15]

Adraktas cited the anomaly that a suspect charged with a low-level robbery served an average of three months in prison on the first offense but life on the third. After the law had been in effect for more than five years, she insisted that it had had "zero deterrent effect" because many of those charged under it were desperate drug addicts who had no appreciation of the statute's workings.

David LaCourse, one of the three-strikes drafters, insisted that most of those imprisoned under the law had records more serious than three minor robberies, and records of the state's sentencing commission seemed to bear him out. If a few defendants were sent away for life despite relatively meager records, "I don't care," LaCourse said, "The burden is on the defendant to show why he or she no longer is dangerous."[16] Sitting behind a desk name plate reading "Dave Lock 'em Up LaCourse," he said it was fine if a future governor wanted to grant clemency to an elderly three-strikes convict deemed no longer a threat. That way, an elected official and not an unknown parole official would be accountable, he said.

The public was not persuaded that three strikes was unfairly enforced. The law was so popular that the Carlson-LaCourse team led a successful initiative campaign in 1994 called Hard Time for Armed Crime that required adding 12 months to a prison sentence for using a gun in most felonies.

California had projected a huge increase in the prison population—nearly 100,000 between 1995 and mid-2001—but the state lowered the figure by nearly 40,000 after far fewer two- and three-strike convicts arrived than the state had anticipated. Still, California expected a shortage of 70,000 prison beds by 2006.

Despite the widely varying estimates, there was no doubt that the three-strikes law was being used extensively. It figured in 40,000 California convictions over its first four years, the vast majority of them in two-strikes cases. There was considerable variation around the state, with few cases filed in San Francisco and half of the cases in Los Angeles County alone. The discrepancies were due somewhat to sheer differences in population and crime rates, but southern California prosecutors tended to be more hard-nosed in bringing cases.

What was actually happening in courthouses around the state was documented by the *Los Angeles Times* and other news reports from prosecutors and defense attorneys. Most of the truly violent repeat criminals were drawing heavy prison time, just as would have happened to most of them before the three-strikes law was passed. In the vast number of other cases, discretion was moving from the corrections part of the justice system, including the wardens and parole officers who used to decide when many prisoners were released, to prosecutors, who had the power to decide what charges should be filed. Of course, this was a traditional prerogative of prosecutors, but it made a crucial difference when, depending on how seriously a prosecutor decided to treat a case, a defendant could end up serving ten years or life in prison.

Prosecutors were exercising their wide discretion in different ways. Those in southern California typically filed more three-strikes charges and usually prevailed, albeit at the cost of delaying cases caught in the crush. Many prosecutors in the generally more liberal northern California area filed lesser charges in cases they believed did not deserve long sentences, thus avoiding the mandatory penalties of the two- and three-strike sections of the law. So even though three strikes did end up treating many defendants more harshly, it was hardly uniform.

As might have been expected from the way the law was drafted, courts became tied up in knots trying to interpret crucial distinctions. Consider Russell Benson, who was convicted of stealing a carton of cigarettes from a discount store. Benson had two convictions on his record for knifing a neighbor 15 years earlier. If the earlier episode were counted as one strike, he could get a maximum sentence of six years. If it counted as two strikes, the sentence would be 25 years to life.

On May 14, 1998, the California Supreme Court upheld the longer term by a 4 to 3 vote. The majority said the language of the three-strikes law was clear and should be taken literally. Dissenters warned that the decision would have unintended consequences. They predicted that in future cases, trial judges would look more carefully at separate charges arising from the same incident and would toss out marginal counts. Then, if the one remaining charge was overturned by an appeals court, the suspect would be free altogether, "exactly what should not happen," said one judge. The defense lawyer in the case told the *Los Angeles Times*: "I don't think voters had a clue that this is what they were getting when they enacted this."[17]

Because the California three-strikes law for the most part merely transferred power from the corrections establishment to prosecutors and continued to include a large variety of crimes among permissible strikes, its impact on violent crime is debatable. David Schichor and Dale Sechrest, criminologists at California State University who analyzed the law's impact by 1996, concluded that it was not reaching many violent offenders because of variations in its implementation. As for those who had been successfully prosecuted, the criminologists forecast more violence in prisons as California's budget became more strained by higher spending on correctional institutions.[18]

Citing data showing that half of third strikers were convicted of a nonviolent crime, Joe Klaas, Polly's grandfather, concluded in 1999 that the law had failed to "target the hard-core offenders it set out to reach and has diverted critical funds from crime prevention and education." Klaas supported legislation that would have required a study of three strikes' costs and benefits, but Governor Gray Davis vetoed it.

Newly enacted strikes laws of different varieties were rarely invoked in their first several years on the books in other states, except for Georgia, found a survey by the private Campaign for an Effective Crime Policy in late 1998. In Georgia, nearly 2,000 persons had been sentenced under laws covering "seven deadly sins" that provide for minimum sentences of ten years without parole for the first strike and life without parole for the second strike. Florida and Nevada had convicted more than 100 criminals under three-strikes laws, but 15 other states had 6 or fewer convictions. The anticrime-advocacy campaign questioned whether three strikes "is reducing public safety rather than enhancing it." The group cited "the burdens placed on crowded jails and . . . increased prison costs [that] divert funds from education and social programs that may be more effective in preventing crime in the long run."[19]

Indeed, opponents of mandatory minimum sentences contended that in state after state, putting convicts behind bars for longer periods than they arguably deserved ended up diverting funds from allocations for educational institutions. A 1998 analysis by the Washington-based Justice Policy Institute and the Correctional Association of New York found, for example, that New York State prison spending had grown by $761 million in the previous decade, while state budgets for colleges had dropped by $615 million.[20] The critics noted that it cost $30,000 each year to house an inmate in the state prison system, enough to pay for the education of nine students in the state university system.

As beguiling as the trade-off argument was, states couldn't just exchange inmates for college students. The broader question was whether the public was getting its money's worth out of harsher punishment practices. It was difficult to prove, in large part because changes in criminal-justice procedures usually turned out to be less dramatic than the politicians who advocated them proclaimed.

In the case of three strikes and other mandatory sentencing laws, the justice system seemed to be making adjustments so that the time most convicts would spend behind bars might not vary much in the end. Sometimes appearances of harshness were directly contradicted by reality. It was an article of faith in the 1980s and 1990s, for example, that sentences were getting longer. That presumption was based on state legislatures' enactment of laws by the dozens that established minimum sentences for drug defendants and others.

The U.S. Justice Department tried to sort out all the state sentencing changes and found, in a 1999 report, that the average length of sentences imposed on new convicts actually decreased from 72 months in 1990 to 68 months in 1996.[21]

Because truth in sentencing was only 85 percent truthful and had not been enacted universally, those convicted of violent crimes served relatively little time even in the 1990s. The average term that inmates spent behind bars for murder, rape, robbery, and aggravated assault did increase, but only from 43 months in 1993 to 49 months—a little over four years—in 1997. Overall, taking "good time" reductions and early release policies into account, the Justice Department concluded that the average new state inmate in 1996 would be expected to serve 42 months compared with 40 months in 1990—only a small victory for the advocates of longer terms. The reality was that "growing numbers of people are spending a little more time" in prison, said Allen Beck of the U.S. Bureau of Justice Statistics.[22]

Although the average time incarcerated exceeds three years, many terms are short enough that 40 percent of inmates will gain release within a year, Beck said. The door continued revolving.

If many of the sentence-enhancement laws around the nation were less tough than some of their proponents made them out to be, what was keeping the imprisonment total rising in the late 1990s? The answer lay in a combination of undramatic but important changes in the justice process that together made a difference.

Even if the time served by prisoners rose by only a few months per inmate, when it was multiplied by hundreds of thousands of convicts, that small increase caused a big rise in the daily population behind bars. The justice system was harsher, too, on probationers and parolees who were picked up on new charges or simply failed drug tests. Such convicts accounted for nearly half of the new admissions each year in some prison systems; nationally, parole violators comprised 34.5 percent of state prison admissions in 1997, up from 23.4 percent in 1985. The high failure rate gave ammunition to critics who maintained that parole and other forms of supervised release from prison were terribly flawed. Of course, it also indicated that parole supervision was becoming stricter.

Critics boasted of eliminating parole, but what actually happened depended on crucial definitions. In most cases, what states did was to prevent bureaucrats from releasing inmates before their stated terms ended. Many prisoners still ended up under community supervision after they were set free—just a bit later than would have happened in previous years.

In 1998, legislators in Kentucky, New York, and Wisconsin voted to abolish parole. But the laws were not so simple as they sounded. New York allowed "post-release supervision," for example, and Wisconsin provided that offenders had to serve the complete sentence plus supervision after prison at least as long as 25 percent of the time served in prison. Parole survived, but under a different name.

Representing parole officers, Mario Paparozzi, president of the American Probation and Parole Association, said that no-parole schemes sounded tough but eliminated the opportunity for "citizen-oriented" boards to review convicts' cases. Paparozzi argued that parole review hearings provided a chance for crime victims to have their say, which they normally do not in the plea bargains that end most cases.

The most troublesome offense category fueling the 1990s prison-population increase was drugs. One third of parole violators were drug offenders. Unlike many other kinds of convicts, their freedom could be conditioned easily on the result of a urine test for drugs. Congress and the Clinton administration helped institutionalize the practice by making state eligibility for federal prison-building aid contingent on conducting drug testing throughout the justice system.

Twenty-one percent of state prison inmates in 1998 were there for drug crimes compared with only 6.5 percent in 1979. And that didn't include many other violent offenders—who accounted for about half of inmates overall—whose crimes were drug-related. Drug offenders were the single largest category of prison admissions in 1996, exceeding those who committed both violent and property crimes.

Many justice reformers argued that too many were incarcerated on the basis of minor drug crimes, but it was impossible to say, based on the data alone, how many inmates deserved to be in some other kind of corrections program or released altogether.

A common criticism was that many inmates were behind bars for "simple" drug possession of tiny amounts. Four ounces of cocaine sounds tiny, but Katherine Lapp, criminal justice adviser to New York Governor George Pataki, pointed out that "four ounces is enough to get several high schools high."[23]

Criminals had a tougher time at the front end of the system, too. Better investigative and prosecutorial techniques, on top of changes in the law that favored the state in disputes over how evidence was gathered, contributed to higher conviction and imprisonment rates. Since 1980, the odds that an arrest will lead to a prison term—still fairly low overall—have increased for many kinds of crime. For robbers, the figure rose from about 25 to 28 percent between 1980 and 1996; for burglars, it went from about 11 percent to 17 percent. The increase was far sharper for drug defendants. Only 19 out of 1,000 arrestees in 1980 ended up in prison; by 1996, the figure was up to 77—still not very high but enough to swell the prison rolls in an era when the annual drug arrest total had risen to 1.3 million.[24]

The prosecution numbers were startlingly low to any American who believed that an arrest was tantamount to imprisonment. Only for the crime of murder does a majority of arrestees go to a state prison (61 percent in 1996). Still, the rising totals are having an impact. Dissecting the incarceration boom, Alfred Blumstein of Carnegie Mellon University and Allen Beck of the U.S. Bureau of Justice Statistics concluded that the higher incarceration rate of arrestees accounted for more than 40 percent of the national inmate increase since 1980.[25]

Such fine-tuned analyses did not provide dramatic rhetoric for the political arena. Instead, candidates tended to focus simply on results—longer prison terms and lower crime rates—rather than how a defendant arrived behind bars. Advocates of longer terms argued that there was a cause-and-effect relationship with the crime-rate decrease. Convicts could not rob and kill private citizens from their cells, of course, and anecdotal evidence suggested that word of the more draconian sentences being imposed, especially for narcotics offenses, was filtering out to the street and was having some deterrent effect.

Opponents of relying on incarceration as a primary weapon in the fight against crime contended that the undeniable trends toward larger prison systems and lower rates of street crime were largely developing independently. Criminologist Blumstein pointed out, for example, that while it was fashionable in the 1990s for conservatives to cite the simultaneous drop in reported crime and rise in imprisonment, in the late 1980s the trend was different: correctional populations were growing, but violent crime was also on the rise.

In many categories of offenses, particularly drug sales, those who went to prison were quickly replaced by a younger generation of traffickers. It seemed clear that the higher level of incarcerating drug offenders could not be correlated very strongly with any lower rate of narcotics violations.

Critics pointed out, too, that a close examination of crime-rate declines state by state did not show a strong correlation between places with three-strikes laws or other particularly harsh sentencing systems and lower crime rates. In fact, some of the states with the sharpest decreases in lawbreaking had not turned notably hard on criminals. "Crime rates began to drop in California before passage of 'three strikes' and have dropped as much or more in some states without a three strikes law," said law professor Walter Dickey of the University of Wisconsin, who compiled the Campaign for an Effective Crime Policy's 1998 report on the three-strikes phenomenon.[26] A 1996 analysis for the U.S. Justice Department on sentencing overhauls over recent years declared that "states should not be lulled into the belief that [sentencing] reform can solve the crime problem or even necessarily reduce state crime rates."[27]

One reason it was difficult to prove a broad crime-imprisonment link was that state incarceration rates varied dramatically, far more than did their crime rates. Southern states tended to use prison much more—Texas and Louisiana locked up about 700 per 100,000 citizens, for example—while some midwestern and northeastern states were at the other end of the scale: comparable figures for North Dakota, Minnesota, Maine, and Vermont ranged between 112 and 140 per 100,000 population in 1997. On a state level, crime and imprisonment totals generally did not track very closely.[28]

Studies on the complex causation question were sparse, but an extensive report on violence in America by the National Research Council—an arm of the National Academy of Sciences—concluded in 1993 that a tripling of the average time served for violent crimes between 1975 and 1989 may have prevented about 10 to 15 percent of crimes that otherwise would have been committed.[29] New calculations by William Spelman of the University of Texas found that "the prison buildup was responsible for about one-fourth of the crime drop" of the 1990s.[30]

That's a fairly large number, but not one that would necessarily justify the way billions of dollars were being allocated to prison building and operations. States spent $4 to $5 billion on construction for most years in the 1990s, said the American Correctional Association. Budgets for annual operations neared $33 billion in 1999, according to the Criminal Justice Institute, a private research organization.[31]

As was true of much anticrime policy, because no one could prove or disprove a link between prison populations and the crime rate, most federal and state policymakers were reluctant to pull back from their punitive course. A good example was New York State's Rockfeller drug laws. The statutes were softened a bit in the late 1970s, but many provisions survived through various ups and downs in rates of drug abuse.

By the late 1990s, critics had amassed evidence of what they said was disproportionate use of the laws against mid- or low-level drug traffickers. A bipartisan group charged that the statutes' persistence had "handcuffed our judges, filled our prisons to dangerously overcrowded conditions, and denied sufficient drug treatment alternatives to nonviolent addicted offenders who need help."

Governor George Pataki, who had been elected as a Republican anticrime hardliner, proposed shortly after taking office in 1995 that the laws be reviewed again so that drug defendants who were nonviolent might not be subject to sentences ranging from 15 years to life. Daniel Feldman, a Brooklyn Democrat who had made similar proposals for years as a member of the state assembly to little avail, said Pataki's change of heart "should hit New York's consciousness with the force of Nixon's opening to China."[32]

Six years after Pataki spoke, the state legislature had not acted, reflecting some of the convoluted politics of image versus reality that tend to infuse debates on sentencing policy. Some lawmakers welcomed the prison-building boom as profitable for the economies of their districts; penitentiaries were a primary source of new employment in some rural areas. Others relied on increasing revenues to pay for bricks and mortar. Feldman credited Pataki with acting as a true fiscal conservative but faulted Republicans in the legislature for "saying 'lock up criminals but don't raise taxes.' "

Katherine Lapp, Pataki's criminal justice adviser, said that the state had alleviated the most severe problem the laws had brought on by selectively releasing nonviolent drug offenders earlier and by creating treatment programs for first offenders that would allow them to plead guilty to lesser offenses and avoid the Rockefeller laws' tough bite.

While admitting that a few convicts probably deserved early release via clemency, Lapp contended that the actual number of unduly harsh sentences was far lower than critics had contended. Although a series of anecdotes implied otherwise, only 50 inmates among the state's 70,000 were behind bars only for possessing drugs and had no previous convictions on their records, Lapp said.

So mandatory minimum prison terms lived on in New York State, just as they did in the huge federal criminal justice system. The tough federal rules for drug cases were assailed by liberals, criminal defense lawyers, and some judges almost from their inception. The critics got some unlikely support from a Washington, D.C., woman named Julie Stewart, who was working at the libertarian Cato Institute in 1990 when her brother, Jeff, was arrested for marijuana possession. "I remember thinking, 'Oh, how stupid, but it's only marijuana," she said.[33] Stewart had not focused on the fact that in Congress's orgy of racheting up drug penalties during the 1980s, the offense could bring her brother a five-year mandatory prison term—a penalty she viewed as far too harsh for a first offense.

A novice in criminal-sentencing issues, Stewart began calling everyone she could think of to learn how the marijuana law had been passed and what could be done to prevent its use against nonviolent first offenders. When she learned that there was no organized lobby against such measures, Stewart founded Families Against Mandatory Minimums (FAMM) in mid-1991. Naively, she believed that she could help lead a drive to soften the law and then return to her former professional pursuits after only a few years.

But there was little sentiment in the Bush administration and key congressional offices to revisit drug sentencing. It was not until the Clinton administration took office in 1993 that the issue would get high-level consideration. The National Association of Criminal Defense Lawyers held a "fly-in" each year for members to visit Washington and lobby their representatives in Congress. The defenders had not received a very welcome audience in the previous 12 years of Republican White House occupancy.

It was a different story when Clinton's attorney general, Janet Reno, appeared at the group's reception in March 1993. It was one of her first public appearances in the capital, and "the room was electrified," Stewart said. "If the president had walked in, he would not have received so welcome a reception. People hoped she would use her experience and knowledge to persuade the president to adopt a reasonable policy."

Reno was no Ramsey Clark–type liberal on crime, but the former Miami prosecutor had a reputation for thoughtful anticrime policy based on a realistic view of the justice system and not ideology.

In May 1993, Reno called publicly for a review of mandatory minimum sentences in federal drug cases, assigning her deputy, Philip Heymann, to prepare a report. The action attracted attention in a city where criminal penalties had gone in only one direction—up—for many years. After Reno indicated a willingness to question high drug penalties, critics of the law like Julie Stewart were ready to cite cases like that of 19-year-old Keith Edwards of Connecticut, who had received a 10-year term for possessing 50 grams of crack cocaine. The judge, a Republican former prosecutor, said Congress had forced him "to send a young man like you to jail for ten years for a crime that doesn't deserve more than three or four."

Heymann eventually found that nonviolent drug offenders made up about one fifth of the federal inmate population, more than 16,000 inmates at the time. But he stopped short of concluding that mandatory sentences for those convicts were a bad idea. Heymann believed that the study would be released in the fall of 1993, while the omnibus crime bill was pending in Congress. But the White House ordered it held up, fearing that it would be seen as the Clinton administration's opposing mandatory minimum sentences. Finally, a few weeks after Heymann resigned, the report was issued with no fanfare in early February late on a Friday afternoon—typically the burial ground in the capital for news that officials would prefer get little attention. The U.S. Sentencing Commission, which Congress had created in 1984 to oversee federal criminal sentences, later explored the issue and repeated its opposition to mandatory minimum terms, with little effect.

With the omnibus crime bill looming, it seemed a propitious time for at least a modest reform. Two liberal senators, Paul Simon of Illinois and Edward Kennedy of Massachusetts, enlisted conservative Strom Thurmond of South Carolina to join in a move to create a "safety valve" to excuse first-time nonviolent offenders from the mandatory minimums. Simon heard from a federal judge he knew who said he was thinking of resigning over having to sentence a young, black defendant to more than ten years in prison for a drug crime for which "a white kid from the suburbs would be in the Betty Ford Clinic."[34]

The senators hoped the measure could be passed with little public notice, but they had no such luck in the highly charged atmosphere of 1994. Senate Judiciary Committee Chairman Orrin Hatch of Utah—supported by a last-minute push from a new organization of line-level federal prosecutors—blew the whistle and stopped the bill. A Simon aide charged that Hatch, who had expressed concern about unduly harsh sentences, had privately called the proposal "the right thing to do, but he couldn't do it for political reasons."

An 11th-hour pitched battle between conservatives and liberals over the issue in the tense negotiations in August 1994 to iron out final details produced a compromise that the "safety valve" would apply to future cases only. Even though that left perhaps thousands already in custody with no remedy, sentencing-reform advocates viewed the provision as a success. Most of those eligible for the safety valve, about 4,700 in 1998, were able to invoke it to avoid serving mandatory minimums, often shaving a year or so off of a five-year sentence.

The only notable recent rollback of mandatory minimum sentences occurred in Michigan, where legislators in 1998 repealed a 20-year-old law that required a life-without-parole sentence for possessing at least 650 grams of heroin or cocaine (the so-called 650 lifer law). Like the case with many federal defendants, the statute pulled in many first-time offenders. The new law changed the penalty to a term of 20 years to life and allowed parole for the 169 prisoners serving terms under the statute. The repeal was spearheaded by Julie Stewart's Families Against Mandatory Minimums group. Far from accomplishing her goal in the early 1990s, by 1999 Stewart was publishing a periodic 32-page newsletter on the organization's various battles.

Tough criminal-sentencing laws have remained on the books in large part because those who opposed them have failed to win wide public support for a credible alternative—especially when it comes to serious offenders. The argument that spending billions of public dollars each year on prisons was taking money from education, public works, and other worthwhile causes had some resonance. But the point lost force in the late 1990s, when many states were showing budget surpluses. If anything, they had even more resources to spend on prison construction.

Advocates also pressed the case for targeted rehabilitation programs outside of prison walls, which they contended were much cheaper and much more effective in preventing recidivism. While there was anecdotal evidence supporting the cost-effectiveness of such "intermediate sanctions" in some places, it was far from conclusive. Part of the reason was something of a catch-22: nonprison programs could not be proved worthwhile unless they were tried on a large scale. Otherwise, critics would say that the success stories were mostly self-selected cases of the few convicts who could turn their lives around. But the more criminals were involved in programs outside of prison walls, the higher the chance that one or more would commit a horrible crime while under public supervision—thus endangering the experiment.

That was the essential story of the most prominent such case in the modern era: the Massachusetts furlough program of Willie Horton fame. In the fall of 1988, President George Bush used furloughs successfully to win reelection in his campaign against Massachusetts Governor Michael Dukakis. In 1974, William Horton was one of three men implicated in the killing of a gas-station attendant. Even though he was sentenced to a life prison term with no chance of parole, Horton won the chance to spend short stints of up to two days out of prison—a practice supported by corrections officials as a control mechanism that would give inmates an incentive to behave well.

After a series of uneventful furloughs, Horton disappeared during a 48-hour release in 1986. As journalist David C. Anderson wrote in a book reviewing the case and its consequences, "in hindsight, it suddenly seemed clear to everyone that Horton was no good and never should have been granted furloughs."[35] Horton made his way to Maryland, where he was convicted of breaking into the home of a young couple, tying up the man and raping his wife. Back in Massachusetts, the *Eagle-Tribune* newspaper in the town of Lawrence, where Horton's original crime had occurred, made a major issue of the case. Eventually, with his presidential campaign looming, Dukakis was forced to suspend furloughs for prisoners serving life terms.

The state legislature formally ended the program in 1988, with Dukakis's support, but the damage had been done for the man who soon would be the Democratic presidential candidate. Earlier in the same month that Dukakis signed the bill banning furloughs for lifers, Al Gore, then a U.S. senator from Tennessee and one of his rivals for the Democratic nomination, demanded to know why Dukakis had allowed such furloughs in the first place. Dukakis avoided an answer, but the issue soon was picked up by George Bush's presidential campaign—helped by a major story about the case in the *Reader's Digest* titled "Getting Away With Murder."

Political ad producer Roger Ailes came up with a television spot depicting the Horton case as one in a series of revolving-door inmate releases under the Dukakis regime. Then an independent organization supporting Bush issued an ad showing Horton's mug shot, describing his crimes, and declaring, "Weekend prison passes. Dukakis on crime." Using the unflattering photo of the black Horton was widely criticized as racist, but the Bush campaign eventually distanced itself from the spot.

Crime emerged as a major issue in the presidential campaign, although furloughs and the Horton ads were overshadowed by Dukakis's performance in a debate with Bush. When moderator Bernard Shaw asked the governor whether he would favor the death penalty for someone who raped and murdered his wife, Dukakis said no, blandly suggesting that there were "better and more effective ways to deal with violent crime."

As an intellectual matter, the answer made some sense. Surely, executions were not the proper response to most violent crimes. But it utterly failed to capture the emotions that the crime issue stirred in the electorate or to show much empathy with crime victims and their relatives.

Whatever the merits of Bush and Dukakis as crime fighters, the furlough issue did not get a fair airing in 1988. Furlough programs did have flaws, and some states moved to correct them amid the publicity over the Horton case. Still, one unmistakable result of the 1988 presidential campaign was that "furlough" became a dirty word in American politics. The number of furloughs granted to state inmates exceeded 230,000 in 1990, but by 1996 it had dropped to about 156,000, according to the trade journal *Corrections Compendium*, which blamed the decrease on "ripples from the Horton shock wave."[36] At least four major states—Colorado, Georgia, Illinois, and Missouri—ended furloughs altogether, even though the success rate reported by states was 98 percent; after omitting technical rules violations, less than one half of 1 percent of furloughs resulted in a new crime. Apparently, the journal concluded, many jurisdictions decided that "one such crime is too many."

Regardless of the outcome of debates over furloughs and parole, the plain fact was that the vast majority of Americans imprisoned for street crimes will gain their release eventually. Many will have passed their crime-prone years; others will return to their old ways. In 1999, the Justice Department estimated that roughly 500,000 convicts were being released from custody every year, almost one fourth of them with no supervision, including "some of the baddest of the bad actors," said Assistant Attorney General Laurie Robinson.

Attorney General Janet Reno, who had become a fan of judges assigned to handle special categories of criminal cases while advocating "drug courts," proposed that states create new entities known as "reentry courts" to help guide the newly freed criminals back to productive lives. The idea had promise, even if it was essentially a reinvention of parole agencies that had compiled a checkered record over the years.

Despite the spread of three strikes and other sentence enhancements, by the turn of the twenty-first century, the unprecedented growth of prisons in America was beginning to slow down. The 1999 increase in prison population was 3.4 percent, less than the average annual figure of 6.5 percent between 1990 and 1999. Several states, most prominently New York, actually reported decreases in their inmate populations for the first time in years. The liberals who long had campaigned for limiting prison expansion were joined in March 1999 by a prominent conservative, John DiIulio of the University of Pennsylvania, who called for a "zero prison growth" policy, citing research suggesting that "the nation has 'maxed out' on the public-safety value of incarceration."[37]

DiIulio's view, echoed by many other experts who followed the justice system closely, was that the eventual verdict on the American penalty system would be rendered not on the basis of gimmicks like sentencing guidelines and three strikes but rather, as DiIulio put it, on "how the system works at the margin." The question is not whether a three-time offender gets a 40- or 50-year term, but how the first-time serious offender is treated. It's a decision, when multiplied by millions of defendants, that will affect prison populations markedly over the years.

With the costs of incarceration mounting, there was some evidence as the twentieth century ended that criminal-justice policymakers were seriously rethinking the mandatory-sentencing practices that were packing prisons with elderly and nonviolent felons along with the truly violent. In 1999, the conservative Heritage Foundation and the liberal National Center on Institutions and Alternatives explored the possibility of drafting a model plan for putting older prisoners who were past their crime-committing ages in low-security facilities or releasing them entirely. Truth-in-sentencing advocates were likely to oppose such plans, however.

In a recent survey for the U.S. Justice Department of the turmoil in American policies on punishment since the mid-1970s, law professor Michael Tonry of the University of Cambridge concluded that "sentencing and corrections policies are fractured or fracturing." As happened with the three-strikes movement, "what look like monolithic tough-on-crime policies in many jurisdictions are being undermined from within by new, individualized programs and approaches."[38]

Yet any quick turnaround of policies that had taken many decades to evolve seemed unlikely. With public treasuries relatively flush and evidence that the imprisonment boom, even if somewhat overdone, had played a part in declining crime rates, the forces that had built the United States into the world's imprisonment leader were likely to keep that policy entrenched for a long time to come.

When a crime and punishment issue periodically bursts onto the political scene, it usually becomes a battle between hardliners and their opponents, often derided as the "anti-incarceration lobby."

The result is a cycle. Get-tough measures go too far, then "alternative sanctions" supplant them for lesser offenders, until too many misdeeds by probationers and parolees fuel a new cry to lock them up and throw away the key.

One such outburst hit a modern-day peak in 1994, when the national politics of crime embroiled Washington in its most cataclysmic battle in a generation over which party had the best formula to fight violence.

Chapter 10

CAPITOL CRIME
EXTRAVAGANZA

IN four decades of horrific crimes across America since the modern-day crime wave began in the early 1960s, it seemed that 1993 and 1994 were two of the worst. On August 3, 1993, the father of basketball superstar Michael Jordan was found murdered in an automobile in North Carolina; on October 1, 1993, 12-year-old Polly Klaas was snatched from her bedroom in Petaluma, California, and was found murdered two months later. A few days after Klaas's body was discovered in December, six Long Island Rall Road commuters were surprised on their way home and wantonly gunned down in a rail car. A dozen foreign tourists were killed in a string of Florida incidents. Then, in mid-1994, former football star O. J. Simpson was charged with the bloody fatal stabbings of his ex-wife and a friend.

These spectacular cases, plus the usual scores of local atrocities that filled television screens and front pages of newspapers, pushed crime above the economy as public worry number one. They sent the same message to every politician in the land: it was time to take action. The eventual result was Washington's costliest anticrime program ever, one that came to fruition long after the crime rate was headed sharply down.

By sheer coincidence, four days after the arrest of O. J. Simpson and his attempt to flee in a mesmerizing nationally televised police pursuit, key members of Congress gathered in an attempt to resolve a five-year-long wrangle over launching a new federal war against crime. As the sun blazed in the capital on that afternoon of Tuesday, June 16, 1994, they began heading for the cool comfort of the modern Hart Senate Office Building. In the middle of a second-floor room the size of a basketball court sat a rectangular arrangement of tables covered with red cloth. An aide carefully set tumblers of ice water at places reserved for the 20 lawmakers with the most power to shape federal crime policy—9 from the Senate and 11 from the House.

The meeting of what is known as a "conference committee" marked the opening shot in what would be a tortuous two-month-long struggle between the two houses of Congress to produce the most far-reaching and controversial federal anticrime law in American history. It would help end decades of Democratic control of the House of Representatives, and would ensure a big Washington influence on state and local anticrime policy into the next century. Along the way, a fairly ambitious plan to help states and cities hire police officers and build prisons had ballooned into a $30 billion "Christmas tree" bill that promised money for all sorts of causes.

Some 1,100 pages of verbiage that emerged from bills passed by the House and Senate, which this elite group was supposed to reconcile, promised to do everything from help states prosecute wife batterers to threaten execution of anyone who dared murder a federal poultry inspector. Now this panel was starting to hammer out the details of what Bill Clinton and just about every candidate on the 1994 ballot hoped to trumpet as proof that they were tough anticrime warriors.

The bitter back-and-forth that started that warm June day did not involve the landmark subject that the Clinton White House had envisioned would symbolize the president's first two years in office. That honor was reserved, initally, for an overhaul of the nation's health care system. But the health plan had foundered in a sea of bickering among special interest groups and inept White House efforts. There would be no consensus on that subject even in a Congress that the Democrats still controlled.

So as the summer of 1994 and the midterm elections approached, it seemed that taking credit for a better way to fight crime would be the Democrats' best chance to declare a major domestic policy accomplishment. And the only way that could happen was to start with some kind of agreement in the conference committee that was meeting in the Hart Building. It was already fairly late in an election year congressional session for wide-ranging and controversial legislation to be resolved. Lawmakers typically adjourned for vacation in early August and returned for only a month of legislating before a final frenzied month of campaigning.

A conference committee plays a simple, straightforward role—at least according to the civics textbooks. Members of both houses are appointed to settle disagreements between two versions of legislation, often splitting the difference or discarding provisions that are unacceptable to one side or the other. But in the reality of Washington, conference committees often do not proceed according to political science theory.

Typically, one or both bills that go to conference include provisions that sound politically appealing but that thoughtful members know would be unwise or infeasible to implement. The ostensible proponents vote for their pet causes to make key constituents or interest groups happy, on the assumption that in some back room of the Capitol, the conference committee will cast the dubious language aside.

Some conference panels violate the textbook rules and invalidate legislation approved by both houses. Others have been known to invent new provisions that neither house passed, sometimes in middle-of-the-night sessions far from the revealing cameras of C-SPAN. The power of conference committees is legendary. Missing a crucial session can be fatal politically because the version of a bill that emerges from the conference committee usually is the final one. Senior Republican senators still complain about the day that they were unexpectedly summoned from a Washington Redskins football game—one of the premier events on fall Sunday afternoons in the capital—to a crime-bill conference committee whose presiding Democrats probably were hoping that their adversaries had remained at RFK Stadium.

The key policymakers made it their business to be present at the conference committee meeting on June 16, 1994. As lobbyists lined up for seats and Clinton aides huddled on the sidelines, panel members began to file in. There was Joseph Biden, the tall Delawarean then in his eighth year of the often exasperating role of chairing the fractious Senate Judiciary Committee. The 51-year-old Biden, a senator since the age of 29, had become a household name three years earlier when he presided over the sensational hearings on sex harassment charges against Supeme Court nominee Clarence Thomas. Unbeknown to most Americans who identified him with Supreme Court nomination hearings and with a short-lived presidential campaign in 1988, however, Biden had devoted his prime legislative efforts to the very issue that brought him to the Hart Building that day: forging a consensus on crime policy.

Biden's counterpart in the House was feisty Texan Jack Brooks, chairman of the House Judiciary Committee. A grizzled veteran of more than four decades in Congress, the 73-year-old conservative Democrat had amassed considerable power, largely out of the public eye. The cigar-chomping Brooks ran the committee with an iron hand, playing his strategy close to the vest on a wide range of crime, antitrust, and other legal issues. Brooks wouldn't mention it in public this day, but in the back rooms of the Capitol, he was advocating the cause of gun owners, preparing to fight this year against a popular ban on assault-type weapons.

Biden and Brooks were joined by other colorful Capitol habitues. There was Orrin Hatch, conservative Utah lawyer and the Senate GOP's point man on the crime bill. And Edward Kennedy, the Massachusetts icon who once had headed the Senate Judiciary panel but had concentrated in recent years on labor and health matters. One center of attention with his bright green striped tie was Charles Schumer, an indefatigable Brooklynite—liberal on most social issues but tough on crime—who headed the House subcommittee that had written most of the pending crime bill. (Schumer, who had joined with Biden to move the Democratic Party toward the center on crime issues, would win a Senate seat four years later.) Liberal Democrats like California's Don Edwards, New Jersey's William Hughes, and Michigan's John Conyers prepared to favor social spending and defendants' rights. (Edwards and Hughes, who were retiring from Congress, would be making their last stand on crime legislation.) Conservative Republicans like Florida's Bill McCollum and Wisconsin's James Sensenbrenner devoted their energies to issues like building prisons and expanding the death penalty.

Biden banged the gavel at 3:05 P.M. and promptly nominated Brooks as conference chair. Because "American citizens fear for their safety every waking moment," the gruff Texan declared, Congress should pass a "balanced package" that combined "hard-nosed punishment with forward-looking prevention." When it was Biden's turn, the senator held up a fat spiral notebook containing the 1,100 pages of proposals that had been approved by one house or the other and estimated that everyone in the room agreed on all but "40, 50, or 60 pages." For several years, he said, Congress "has found it easier to criticize crime bills than to pass one. Whether the cry was 'too tough' or 'not tough enough,' or 'too little money' or 'not enough,' we focused on our differences and failed to get what we agreed on done. This year, we must again choose between politics and getting results."

But the hopeful words of the Judiciary chairmen were promptly countered by partisan carping that set the stage for a struggle that would take all summer and, unforeseen by most in the room that day, would play a large part in giving the Republicans control of the House. Instead of using the day for actual legislating, the leaders of the two parties' anticrime forces set their rhetorical markers. Republican Sensenbrenner, a onetime lawyer in Cedarburg, Wisconsin, argued that the mostly Democratic proposals on the table embodied a familiar— and objectionable—theme: unrealistic pledges to throw tax dollars at a complex social problem. "Congress has a history of overpromising, making good headlines but coming up way short," he complained.

That was a warmup for the acerbic Hatch, who had made an 18-year Senate career out of jousting with liberals over everything from labor policy to Supreme Court nominees. A Mormon bishop who took a hard line against lawbreaking, Hatch wasted no time mocking Democratic plans to spend several billion dollars on job training and recreation for youth in the name of crime prevention. Even though he had backed many of the proposals when they had come to the Senate floor the previous November, Hatch now argued that the real problem was that "our nation's criminal justice sytem lacks credibility." Congress should spend more on building prison cells and less on "1960s-style Great Society social spending boondoggles," he declared.

Hatch displayed a chart of violence and imprisonment rates over three decades. Zigzagging lines on a graph purported to show that after prison populations increased, national crime totals tended to fall, or at least rise at a slower rate. The Utahn argued that Congress must provide huge sums for new prisons "immediately, rather than simply promising that the money will be forthcoming after the 1996 election."

Liberal Kennedy, one of Hatch's most frequent debating foes over the years, ridiculed the Republican's visual aid as "the most incredible chart I've ever seen." Kennedy said the convoluted calculations on crime and punishment reminded him of a story about a hospital patient whose temperature rose one day from 100 to 104 degrees and the next day from 104 to 106. "They said he must be getting better because he is getting sicker slower," joked the jowly Democratic patriarch.

So proceeded what soon would turn into the Great Crime Debate of 1994. The legislation was far more than a routine bill. Seeds had been planted in 1988, when Congress had passed its fourth consecutive biennial election-year omnibus anticrime law. Although George Bush then made crime a "wedge" issue in thrashing Michael Dukakis for the presidency, virtually nothing was accomplished legislatively on the subject during the next four years. The main sticking point had been habeas corpus reform, the long-running wrangle over the civil appeals filed by convicts—most prominently those on death row—challenging their convictions. Hardliners and civil libertarians seemingly came close but never could forge an agreement during the Bush years. The ever-present threat of a Senate filibuster kept other crime proposals bottled up, even those that would enjoy much popular appeal in later years, like adding community police officers.

Determined to seize on Bush's unexpected weakness on the crime-policy front, Clinton made a hard-nosed attack a centerpiece of his "New Democrat" campaign for the White House in 1992. One of his main goals was to pass a version of the crime bill that Bush had failed to get through. Although Clinton's support for more police officers and capital punishment was clear, the other details almost seemed not to matter. "The Democratic approach can be summarized in a few brief words: more police, fewer guns," said Harry Chernoff, Christopher Kelly, and John Kroger, three Democratic anticrime strategists who traced the 1994 law's evolution in the *Harvard Journal of Legislation*.[1]

When the former Arkansas governor actually took office, he and his advisers decided that health care should get top billing. The Clinton entourage seemed to be following a tenet of its presidential campaign: limit the public "message" to one subject at a time. Frustrated advocates of action on crime grumbled that the strategy might have been a reasonable one for a candidate competing fiercely for print and broadcast media attention, but once in the White House, Clinton should have been more aggressive. "A president has such an ability to be in the news that he can talk about five different issues and be heard on them," said a top Democratic congressional staffer working on crime legislation. "That took a long time to sink in."

Clinton had been urged by chief domestic policy aide Bruce Reed and Democratic Leadership Council director Al From to make crime a top issue of his first 100 days in office, but the president rejected the advice. Calling this a "tremendous strategic error," strategists Chernoff, Kelly, and Kroger concluded that Clinton at that point "felt that crime was not sufficiently urgent and would not be a priority that would define his presidency."

A more practical stumbling block for the administration was that the Justice Department, the cabinet agency that normally would be out front advocating anticrime legislation, was headed by two officials, Attorney General Janet Reno and her deputy, Philip Heymann, who had other problems and priorities. When Reno took office in March 1993, the Branch Davidian crisis in Waco, Texas, was well underway. The new attorney general would spend much of her public time in her first few months on the job dealing with the aftermath of the federal decision to storm the compound, provoking the deadly fire that engulfed the cult.

Democrats in Congress who were among the leaders on the crime issue—principally Delaware's Biden and New York's Schumer—were anxious to get going in 1993, finally seeing their chance to put a firm Democratic stamp on crime policy. Biden hoped the new bill would prove the culmination of his appeals to the Democratic caucus in the late 1980s. As the Delawarean saw it, "the Republicans always would take the least important but most controversial aspect of crime control—like the death penalty or the *Miranda* ruling—and beat us about the head with it." Biden told colleagues that even if the Republicans won those points, "it wouldn't have the impact of adding 5,000 cops." "If you do it my way," he said, "it will be the last time that Republicans will be able to run at Democrats for being soft on crime."[2] Senate Majority Leader George Mitchell of Maine gave Biden the go-ahead to develop a comprehensive proposal.

In the House, Judiciary Committee Chairman Brooks initially was reluctant to plunge in. "He would say, 'I don't care if there is a crime bill or not; there are plenty of crime laws on the books already,' " reported an aide to another committee Democrat. "He was deathly afraid—as it turned out he was right to be—of having to grapple with the gun-control issue."

It was a different story with Schumer, who had taken the helm of the crime subcommittee when Bill Hughes of New Jersey had assumed the chairmanship of another panel. Schumer, who saw himself as something of a New Democrat like Clinton, believed that the crime issue was a way to position himself in a run for higher office (which served him well in his 1998 victory over Republican Senator Alfonse D'Amato). Schumer's staff met every Wednesday evening for months on end in 1993 talking about how they could get the White House off the dime.

Finally, Clinton held a hastily arranged White House photo opportunity in August 1993 to affirm that he did, indeed, want to move ahead on the crime issue. But he did not actually file a piece of legislation. In fact, one of the myths that evolved was that Congress was considering the "Clinton crime bill." In truth, Clinton never did draft a full anticrime plan but rather sent delegates to take part in congressional drafting and negotiating sessions.

Although he had campaigned for a vaguely defined crime bill—often citing the 1992 Bush administration's version that was stalled in Congress—insiders reported that Clinton at first seemed willing to accept just about anything Congress gave him—as long as it included police-hiring and gun-control provisions. White House strategists advised the Justice Department that "we weren't going to propose anything" beyond 100,000 cops, Heymann said.[3] Peter Edelman, a law professor from Georgetown University who worked on crime issues for Clinton at the Health and Human Services Department until he resigned in protest against the president's welfare reform plan, believed that the president was "willing to take the political lowest common denominator so that he could say he was indeed a New Democrat" and "sign something called a crime bill."[4] One key Justice Department strategist termed the Clinton move not to submit his own bill a "horrible decision" that essentially abandoned significant leverage that the new administration would have been able to exert over the legislative process.

In some ways, the Justice Department was out of sync with the White House on both philosophical and substantive grounds. Heymann, a Harvard law professor who had headed the department's criminal division during the Carter administration, took a traditional view that the federal government should have only a limited role in local law enforcement. Both he and Webb Hubbell, the former Arkansas official who served in the department's number three job and was its main link to the White House, were ill-informed about detailed provisions that had been drafted on Capitol Hill in the previous few years. "It was amateur hour," reported one staff member who observed the process. "They were operating without the history of the fights that had occurred before." Even though women's rights advocates had spent years negotiating fine points of legislation they wanted, for example, the staffer recalled that "Hubbell would say, 'Phil, what about this violence against women stuff?' "

Biden did ask the administration to work on the habeas corpus issue of convict appeals that had snagged the 1992 crime bill, but when the White House submitted no legislative drafts on other subjects, Biden and his counterparts in the House filed similar wide-ranging anticrime bills in each house on September 23, 1993. (Habeas corpus reform ended up becoming a major issue in the 1993–94 legislative battle and was not enacted until two years later.)

As had happened with the big crime legislation in the 1980s, the Senate took the lead in assembling a catchall bill. Under normal congressional procedures, such a wide-ranging measure would be carefully considered first by the appropriate committee—in this case, the Judiciary panel headed by Biden. But when it comes to crime legislation, Congress ignores many of its normal practices. Lawmakers—especially in the Senate—assume that so many members will be able to attach their own proposals via floor amendments that sending the bill to committee first may be a waste of time. The typical scenario was outlined by a veteran congressional staffer: "In the Senate, everyone votes for everything— 'I'm for your amendment, you're for my amendment'—knowing that it's going to be sorted out later on by people who know what they're talking about."

That is how the big crime bill of 1993–94 began, even though it provided a rare opportunity for Democrats to coalesce around the issue. In modern times, it was only at 16-year intervals that Democrats had both controlled Congress and freshly installed a president: 1961 with John Kennedy, 1977 with Jimmy Carter, and now 1993 with Bill Clinton. But by the fall of 1993, they had little to show for their dominance in Washington. With health care reform flagging, passing a crime bill would be a major achievement. So Senate Majority Leader Mitchell and Biden scheduled floor debate for early November 1993, bypassing the Judiciary Committee. In Mitchell's defense, it wasn't the first time the Senate had taken up many of the bill's provisions. Biden drew much of the bill from the Bush-era legislation that had failed, and he highlighted the first installment of the Clinton cops plan and a Violence Against Women Act that would fund a variety of services for female victims. The price tag was only $3 to $4 billion, no blockbuster by 1990s standards.

Even a crime bill that was modest compared with some big-spending defense measures was no sure thing. As senators began marching to the floor to tout their pet provisions when the floor debate began in early November, Biden and Mitchell became increasingly worried about how the package would be financed.

Having observed the fate of anticrime legislation over more than two decades, Biden was critical of the typical pattern: Congress would overpromise and then would not deliver when it came time to vote on actual appropriations.

A few weeks before the debate, John Hilley, who was Mitchell's chief of staff and had worked for the Budget Committee, came up with an idea. The Clinton administration had been advocating a huge cut in the federal bureaucracy: 272,000 jobs over the next five years. Why not take the money that would be saved, more than $20 billion by most estimates, and allocate it to a "trust fund" that would be devoted to the anticrime program? Hilley broached the idea to Mitchell and then to Biden.

The Democratic leaders were enthusiastic, but they immediately recognized a huge obstacle. With the notable exception of Social Security, trust funds were disdained by congressional appropriators because they cordoned off money for one purpose and thus prevented shifting allocations each year among differing priorities. The guardian of this process in the Senate was crusty Robert Byrd of West Virginia, the former majority leader who now headed the Appropriations Committee and was a stickler for procedure. "We had to convince Byrd—this involved real money," Hilley recalled.[5] For several weeks, Mitchell, Biden, and their aides closely held the trust fund idea while they plotted ways to persuade Byrd of its worth. The key senators began talking to Byrd, with no immediate success; the negotiating continued even after the crime bill debate began on the Senate floor.

Finally, Byrd became convinced that the trust fund would prove a political winner for the Democrats. His party could proclaim that it had solved the problem of funding anticrime aid, and the trust fund would forestall fights later over whether the billions of dollars Congress had authorized would better be spent on something else. That's what Biden most wanted to avoid: election-year anticrime promises being abandoned later, when crime was not a high-profile public issue. Once Byrd gave the okay, the trust fund idea raced through the other key players in the crime debate within an hour.

Biden identified an important Republican to convince, Phil Gramm of Texas. The conservative Gramm, who was also an important Senate budget watcher, had long been campaigning for tougher prison terms. But building new prisons would cost money, too, and Biden had feared a bitter battle over the merits of Gramm's prisons versus Clinton's police officers. With the trust fund, both sides could win. Biden, standing in front of Byrd's Senate desk, called Gramm over and sold him on the trust fund idea, although Biden had to go along with some new minimum mandatory prison sentences Gramm was supporting in order to win the Texan's vote. Seemingly within moments, a fairly modest crime bill had turned into a behemoth that would end up exceeding $30 billion before the debating was over nearly a year later.

The crime bill's money issues were getting top billing, but gun control also was looming. The Brady bill's waiting period for handgun purchases was being debated as a separate measure, while restrictions on assault-style weapons—a major public issue since the Stockton, Calif., schoolyard AK-47 shooting in 1989—remained an issue for the omnibus crime bill.

Assault weapons might have been discarded by congressional leaders as one of those politically insoluble questions had it not been for an accident of timing: another in America's series of tragic gun massacres, the murder of eight people in an office building at 101 California Street in San Francisco. The episode on July 1, 1993, galvanized gun-control organizations and Senator Dianne Feinstein, whose national political career could be traced to her own experience with gun violence: her rise to San Francisco mayor in 1978 after Mayor George Moscone and City Supervisor Harvey Milk were assassinated.

On August 3, the Senate Judiciary Committee held a hearing on assault weapons, highlighted by testimony from Stephen Sposato, whose wife, Jody, was one of those gunned down at 101 California Street by a man wielding an assault-style gun known as a Tec 9. Accompanied by his infant daughter, Sposato told senators, "My life is completely shattered. . . . The sight of our 10-month-old daughter placing dirt on her mother's grave is a sight and pain I pray no other person must experience." Robert Walker of Handgun Control Inc. said the "extraordinarily powerful testimony . . . riveted the entire, packed room . . . and it was a high point in public anxiety."[6]

More than emotion was involved. Just as Peter Rodino had insulted Harold Volkmer in the House a decade earlier, something of the reverse chemistry occurred this time. Senator Larry Craig of Idaho, a staunch National Rifle Association (NRA) supporter, had lectured Feinstein on the floor that she knew little about guns. Feinstein retorted that "I am quite familar with firearms. I became mayor as a product of assassination." Feinstein noted that she had to arm herself and receive firearms training after she was threatened in the wake of the killings—a powerful rebuttal that stunned Craig.

Democrats Howard Metzenbaum of Ohio and Dennis DeConcini of Arizona had tried for several years to ban assault weapons, whether by name or general description, a chancy exercise that never commanded a filibuster-proof Senate majority under heavy NRA opposition.

Now it was Feinstein's turn, and the determined Californian decided to take on the opposition's most potent argument: the fear that a ban on a so-called assault weapon would inadvertently deny hunters their firearm of choice. She went from senator to senator assembling a list of every conceivable hunting weapon, more than 650 in all that the bill would declare legal, leaving 19 banned guns. An attempt to table a crime bill provision that Feinstein was using as a vehicle for her plan failed by a dramatic 51-to-49 vote. The decisive vote was cast by Colorado's Ben Nighthorse Campbell, who as a House member had opposed an assault-weapon ban.

Eight days later, after a Veterans Day recess, the Senate approved the ban, 56 to 43. Though historic in the annals of gun-control legislation, the assault-weapon vote got relatively little attention amid the more presssing controversy over the Brady bill and the evolving multi-billion-dollar authorization for anticrime programs. But Feinstein's success was little short of amazing, considering that Metzenbaum's attempts at similar bans in the early 1990s had attracted fewer than 30 favorable votes. The NRA grudgingly credited Feinstein with turning the tide. "She shepherded her coterie of victims, parading them around so they could talk about how to get rid of these 'nasty, nasty' guns," complained NRA lobbyist Tanya Metaksa. "Then she went through a 'shooter's bible' [a standard reference on firearms] and said, 'bad, good, bad, good, bad,' based on looks and nothing else."[7] Feinstein insisted that her choices were made on a logical basis.

Suddenly, an anticrime bill that could have amounted to much more rhetoric than actual help from Washington was beginning to look like more than just words. Cops, prisons, violence against women, crime prevention—it all could be funded. The Democrats and the Republicans both could claim credit, even if many members of both parties remained nervous about the politics of the assault-weapon ban. The GOP's Orrin Hatch joked to Biden that the bill should be renamed the Biden-Hatch bill. In general, Republicans decided that they had better go with the flow rather than dump on the Democrats. Within a week, the Senate had passed a huge crime bill, with a price tag that had ballooned to $22 billion in a week, thanks to the planned cuts in the federal workforce. The combined approach of law enforcement (Clinton's 100,000 community police officers), prison-building grants to states, and potentially billions of dollars for crime prevention projects seemingly was on its way to passage.

By the time Congress quit for the Christmas holidays, the pressure was building for major political moves against crime. The passage of "three strikes and you're out" in Washington State, combined with the unusual spate of prominent street crimes that were committed in the fall of 1993, had crime policymakers focusing on Clinton's State of the Union Address in January 1994 and its expected endorsement of the crime bill—with the possible addition of three strikes. (Clinton did endorse three strikes, but the Justice Department apparently had no forewarning of the president's plans and later softened its support for the concept.)

As had happened a year earlier, the small band within the administration who were anxious for the president to make an important mark on crime issues hoped that Clinton would take the opportunity to press for an immediate conference committee vote on the crime bill and thus achieve an early 1994

230	CRIME & POLITICS

legislative triumph. But once again, he declined. White House Press Secretary Dee Dee Myers said, "It is up to Congress to work out all the details."

Now the focus would be on the House, where Judiciary Chairman Brooks waited for the Clinton administration to indicate what it liked and disliked about the Senate version. One threshhold issue was the perennial one of capital punishment that had carried over from the Bush presidency. Because a Democratic president also favored executions, congressional liberals would have a difficult time stopping the Senate proposal to add death penalties for more federal crimes. So the Congressional Black Caucus and other liberals began pushing for a "Racial Justice Act" that would allow statistics on racial disparities in the death penalty to be introduced in trials—another issue that threatened to tie up the crime bill.

The delay allowed time for more debate over controversial provisions on which the Clinton administration might go either way, like another spate of mandatory minimum prison sentences, as well as a proposal for federal authorities to build regional prisons that would accommodate inmate overflows from states.

As the weeks passed and it became clear that there would be no quick resolution, some Republicans began to have second thoughts about the idea that spending lots of federal money from a trust fund would allow everyone to claim victory. If the Senate bill were enacted, they began to realize, Biden's vision would largely be validated. Even if the measure did include many ideas that the Republicans had been pushing for years, the Democrats would get the credit for just about everything, because they controlled the White House and Congress. The longstanding public view that the Republicans were better than the Democrats at fighting crime might shift.

Now it dawned on Republicans that they had more to gain by taking a hardline view. Veteran GOP Judiciary Committee member Sensenbrenner told colleagues that "we can defeat this bill and craft a real crime bill that will give the crime issue back to the Republicans for the upcoming election." Democratic strategists Chernoff, Kelly, and Kroger's interpretation was that the GOP could "humiliate the president once again with a devastating legislative failure and . . . prevent the actual benefits of the legislation from being realized" during Clinton's first term.

Republican pollster Frank Luntz affirmed the GOP fears. If the Senate bill were to be enacted, the Democrats might reap an unwarranted political victory, he reported, because the public actually favored tougher measures. In fact, public opinion on crime was notoriously malleable, depending on how the questions were asked. But it was fairly easy for Luntz to argue that the Democrats' professed balance between prevention and punishment that was embodied in the Senate bill should not win the day.[8]

Luntz and allies in Congress argued that the legislation should be tilted toward harsher treatment of prisoners and away from supposedly soft-on-crime prevention programs. (Separately, House Speaker Newt Gingrich, probably relying on the same surveys, called for a "fundamental overhaul of the prison system," including a 48-hour work week for inmates.) In a memo during the summer of 1994, Luntz said voters "are far more concerned that convicted criminals remain behind bars than teenagers in inner cities learn to ballroom dance and slam dunk from the foul line in the pale moonlight." The last point was an allusion to the midnight basketball programs that liberals touted as a way to keep teens out of trouble.

Of course, the crime bill did not really present a choice of ballroom dancing or hard prison time. But by portraying it that way, the Republicans could continually press for more punitive measures and threaten to abandon the measure if it remained too weak and supposedly laden with pork-barrel spending.

As the 1994 legislative session moved into high gear, Biden was surprised when Hatch told him that despite all the Republican enthusiasm back in November when the Senate had voted, the GOP now had decided that the bill was not tough enough. Senate Republicans "were falling off like leaves," Biden recalled. The erosion was particularly distressing to Biden because the GOP now planned to assail prevention programs as pork, even though moderate Republicans like New Mexico's Pete Domenici and Missouri's John Danforth had pleaded for much of the spending on prevention.

While the assault from the right built momentum, something of a mirror-image opposition from the left was being started by liberals on the House side of the Capitol. Spearheaded by Congressional Black Caucus member Craig Washington of Texas, the liberals decided that Biden's crime bill included too few measures that might prevent crime. So the House members crafted their own version of a crime bill that would feature prevention, in many cases including projects that would give the GOP an easier target to attack. (Even liberal Clinton aide Edelman, who sympathized with the liberals' goals, later called much of their proposal "badly designed and ill-conceived.")

Despite all the rumblings, the White House and Senate Democrats were optimistic that the crime bill could go into the law books by Memorial Day 1994, a scenario that proved wildly inaccurate. The House would not go along with such a speedy schedule, proceeding slowly on a series of limited bills. Judiciary Chairman Jack Brooks, eager to avoid the gun issue, had split the omnibus crime bill into several smaller proposals so that firearms amendments could not be added under House rules.

The separate measures finally won floor approval on April 21, with the understanding that the assault-weapon ban would be considered by itself a few weeks later. Because House Democratic leaders like Speaker Thomas Foley and

Majority Whip David Bonior opposed the assault-weapon provision, they refused to order the party's apparatus to "whip" the vote—in House parlance,
leaning on party members to commit their support. Instead, it fell to New York's
Schumer—who had emerged as the leading gun-control advocate—to organize
his own group of backers.

It wasn't only NRA allies who were balking. California's Don Edwards, for
example, was a liberal who might have been expected to campaign for gun
control. Indeed, Schumer invited Edwards to join his "whip" campaign. Edwards
attended the first organizational meeting, but he declined to continue. The Californian believed that the ban would do more harm to Democrats in the 1994
elections than it would help in the fight against crime. "We lost people all over
the South and Midwest because of issues like that," Edwards said later.[9] But he
voted for the Schumer assault-weapon bill and refused to argue with the New
Yorker over his strategy, even after Judiciary Chairman Brooks summoned Edwards to his office and said "You've got to call Schumer off."

Schumer persisted, assisted by California's Dianne Feinstein, who in an action
unusual for a senator, lobbied key House members. An important turning point
was winning the support of Illinois Republican Henry Hyde, who had opposed
a ban in 1991 but voted for it in the Judiciary Committee after becoming convinced that assault weapons had no legitimate "utility." Still, for a Congress that
had enacted only a few major gun-control measures in several decades, it was
hardly a solid bet that the House would approve the assault-weapon bill.

Advocates had the advantage of about 10 days between the April 26 committee action and the scheduled May 5 floor vote to step up the pressure. While
the NRA waged its usual spirited grassroots campaign of opposition, gun-
control supporters mounted one of their biggest-ever drives of their own in the
districts of wavering House members. They identified police officers, mayors,
city council members, teachers, doctors, and any other respectable citizens they
could find to call or write their representatives. Just as significant may have been
the White House's decision to put on a full-cabinet press, having every department head speak out for the measure in early May. Even Agriculture Secretary
Mike Espy, whom the NRA had touted as a supporter when he was a Mississippi
congressman, joined the chorus. Clinton domestic-policy adviser Bruce Reed
knew that including assault weapons would make passage of the bill more
treacherous, but he heard the president order his team "to go to the mat on
this one."

One of the last whip counts showed opponents winning by ten votes, but
that only energized the advocates. Undecided members needed political cover,
so some of their aides asked Handgun Control how former presidents Ronald
Reagan and Gerald Ford stood. Handgun Control's Walker called the ex-

presidents' offices and quickly got their support. (Strangely, Reagan had not personally lobbied the previous fall for the Brady bill, even though it got its momentum from the episode in which he and his aide had been shot.) Reagan and Ford wrote letters of support for the assault-weapon ban, and each made calls to several House members, which Walker said were responsible for switching four or five votes. As in previous gun-control battles, law enforcement support was key. Police union members made calls from the offices of supportive House members, sometimes getting undecided lawmakers to agree to a "yes" vote in exchange or a promise of a reelection endorsement that might feature gun-control advocates James and Sarah Brady. Insiders credit the police groups with delivering about 15 crucial last-minute votes.

As decision day loomed, it seemed too close to call. Some pessimistic supporters thought it might be just as well if the measure lost. As one staffer put it, "it would be a perfect bloody shirt" for Democrats to wave at Republicans in that fall's elections. NRA lobbyist Metaksa, for her part, became convinced that the administration would prevail by offering "casinos, bridges," and other executive branch promises of pork-barrel projects to obtain a favorable vote on assault weapons. The big question, she believed, was how narrow a victory advocates could eke out in order to minimize the number of House members who would face NRA opposition in November.

The answer was the narrowest possible margin. Last-minute vote switches often obscure members' true intentions, but this decision left little wiggle room. Indiana Democrat Andrew Jacobs, Jr., supplied what may have been the deciding vote for the measure, making the total 216 to 214. Jacobs said he actually opposed the gun ban but favored a provision that limited the size of ammunition clips.

Many black members supported the assault-weapon ban unenthusiastically, because they anticipated opposing the crime bill as an antiminority piece of legislation overall, with all of its death-penalty provisions. Schumer made the case that "gun control is a way to say 'Let's do something about crime without beating up on African-Americans,' " said one of his aides.

To those who believed that the bill would prevail because it included something for everyone, all of the pieces for a potential grand compromise seemed in place. But Judiciary Chair Brooks and other insiders knew that keeping the gun issue on the table would make final passage precarious. The fact that it had taken until May to vote on assault weapons meant that the entire bill had no chance of enactment by Memorial Day. It was now the spring of an election year, and congressional leaders were starting to set interim deadlines for legislation according to the start of holiday recesses. Bills that don't make it through the process by Memorial Day are next targeted for July 4. If the legislation doesn't emerge by Independence Day, congressional leaders start talking about the summer recess, usually in early August. The only other window usually is the month of September, when anything remotely controversial can easily be stopped by a filibuster and sometimes merely by the threat of one.

As Judiciary Committee members gave their speeches during the June 16 conference committee session, passage by July 4 looked impossible. The two hours of rhetoric that flowed in the Hart Building that afternoon bore little resemblance to what was happening behind the scenes. In closed-door meetings, issues barely mentioned in public had produced a stalemate that threatened to derail the crime bill and to dim the chances that the Democratic Party could reclaim an issue that for years had been attracting middle-class voters to the GOP.

One was gun control. The assault-weapon ban had been approved on both sides of the Capitol, albeit just barely in the House—votes that the civics text-books suggest should have made the provision a sure thing. But that was not stopping Brooks and others backed by the powerful NRA, who were maneu-vering to kill or emasculate the provision. It wouldn't have been the first time that a measure approved by each House had disappeared in order to preserve a major bill.

The other vital issue was race. After each house had added more than 60 new federal death penalties, with Clinton's backing, the Congressional Black Caucus and other liberals balked. They persuaded a bare majority of the House to include their "racial justice" provision that would give defendants a way to challenge execution orders they believed were being meted out disproportion-ately to minorities.

Republicans and prosecutors around the country protested that although "ra-cial justice" sounded progressive, it actually would enable suspects to tie capital cases in knots, thwarting huge majorities of Americans who favored imposing the ultimate penalty. Senate Republicans vowed to filibuster the crime bill to death if the conferees approved racial justice. But the Black Caucus and its allies threatened to sabotage the bill in the House if racial justice was dropped by the conference committee. Each side argued, with some justification, that the pro-vision could bring down the entire bill.

The Clinton administration tried to sidestep the potentially disastrous debate. To persuade Black Caucus members that it was trying, the White House had Attorney General Reno and California's Don Edwards try to talk some potential "swing" senators into supporting the racial justice concept, but they failed mis-erably. Edwards reported that South Carolina Democrat Ernest Hollings, for example, "laughed in my face," convincing Edwards that the issue was "too hot politically." Concluded Biden: "We don't have the votes for anything that has 'racial justice' in it."

Two weeks after the conferees had gathered around the red tables in the Hart

Building, the Democrats' optimistic speeches were distant memories. With the Democrats in disarray, the Republicans seized the moment before the July 4 recess and called a press conference. Hatch and other GOP leaders produced a new, supposedly improved anticrime plan. As the cameras rolled, they denounced the Democrats for once again failing to act on the nation's number one problem.

The White House and its Democratic allies on the Hill knew that only by presenting something approaching a united front could they hope to overcome the combined impact of ideological conservatives and fervent liberals that had been blocking anticrime legislation for years. It seemingly came down to an option of dropping either the assault-weapon ban or the racial justice provision. Bill Clinton favored keeping the weapon clause, as did majorities in public-opinion surveys. The alternative of eliminating it, which the White House insists was never really on the table, would immediately pick up the votes of some conservative NRA supporters for the overall bill but lose the support of liberal gun controllers.

Racial justice seemed a safer bet to abandon. Most Americans didn't understand the concept in detail, and it was only the Congressional Black Caucus and a few of its stalwart backers—not more than about 50 votes in the 435-member House—that might be lost. Besides, the White House would ask those members to support a multi-billion-dollar package of prevention programs like "midnight basketball" leagues for their urban districts that would keep troubled youths occupied and, supporters hoped, away from crime.

When lawmakers returned from the July 4 recess, Clinton administration aides put their strategy in motion. To show their sympathy for racial justice, they kept trying to convince wavering senators to pledge opposition to conservative senators who planned to filibuster against the proposal. But that effort came up short. Now it seemed that many Black Caucus members would tepidly back the emerging consensus: prevention money but no racial justice provision.

The spending provisions inserted in the House to attract Black Caucus support—which had ballooned the crime bill's authorized total to more than $30 billion over five years—almost proved disastrous at the end in the public relations arena. Perhaps the most vulnerable to criticism was a $1.6 billion Local Partnership Act championed by John Conyers, a veteran lawmaker from Detroit and senior Democrat after Brooks on the Judiciary Committee. Critics described the provision as a huge federal giveaway to cities, most of them under the control of Democratic mayors.

Although the crime bill's money for social programs might have aided many worthwhile efforts (it's impossible to say for sure, because the Republican-dominated Congress that took office in 1995 funded little of it), critics naturally focused on debatable ones like midnight basketball and classes in dance, arts, and crafts. In a classic sound bite delivered on the "Today" program in mid-August 1994, House Minority Whip Newt Gingrich said, "When people dial 911, they want a policeman . . . they don't want a social worker." In a guide for 1994 congressional candidates, the NRA declared that "it is somewhat absurd to suggest that the answer to neighborhood crime is a program which encourages youngsters to remain on the streets for most of the night."[10] (Of course, no one asserted that midnight basketball was "the" answer to crime or that it promoted the idea of teenagers cruising the streets in the wee hours.)

As the summer of 1994 wore on, the Democrats were girding to defend social programs as part of a balanced package that included roughly equal amounts for cops, prisons, and prevention. But time was running short. Clinton was still holding out hope for his top legislative priority: health care reform. Now crime had moved ahead of health care on the cramped congressional agenda. If Congress did not act on crime before its month-long August recess, there would be no chance for health care in the one remaining month of deliberations before the legislators quit for the final preelection campaign push.

With the compromise seemingly falling into place, Brooks announced that the conference committee would gather again on July 27—about six weeks after its initial meeting. This time, the group assembled on Brooks's home turf, the House Judiciary Committee hearing room in the Rayburn Building. Before the members convened, Biden, Brooks, and other key Democrats had worked up a plan to split the difference on dozens of items that divided the two houses. Unknown to many members, however, the two powerful chairmen had inserted a few favored provisions that had not made it through the legislative process so far—another no-no under the how-a-bill-becomes-a-law process.

Most egregiously, Brooks had included a $10 million authorization for his alma mater, Lamar University, to start a special program for training officers at several south Texas prisons. In the context of a $30 billion bill, the money was insignificant, but in terms of symbolism, it reeked of pork-barrel spending.

The conference proceeded for nearly three days nonstop, and the Democratic strategy looked viable as the weary members wrapped up their work on Friday morning, July 29. Racial justice was dead, the assault-weapon ban was alive (despite opposition from Brooks), and the Republicans lost a series of party-line votes on proposals to toughen the sentencing provisions and to slash prevention funds. As the August recess loomed, it looked as if a crime bill might squeak though Congress after six years of stalemate.

Still, there were backstage concerns that the assault-weapon ban could be vulnerable. House Speaker Thomas Foley, who represented rural areas of Washington State, was a longtime NRA sympathizer. One afternoon, he invited New York's Schumer in for a chat that Schumer expected would include a demand that the New Yorker relent and drop his prize provision in the name of party unity, pressure that Schumer was determined to resist. The session turned out to be a low-key one, however, with Foley reminding Schumer about the power of the NRA and urging him to negotiate with conservative Democrats who sided with the gun lobby. Knowing that the assault-weapon ban could prove key to the overall bill's fate, Schumer aides talked endlessly about what they would advise if the Democratic leadership—or the White House—decided to cave in on the issue.

Despite the conference committee's agreement, the fight for passage on the floor was far from over. Negotiators had to agree on the language of dozens of compromises made during the exhausting conference and, most importantly, line up the 218 votes necessary to make sure that the monstrous bill actually got through. Two major obstacles loomed. Many Black Caucus members and other liberals continued to oppose the bill as too punitive. More significantly, Republicans had coalesced on an opposition strategy. Seizing on Brooks's Lamar University money, on top of the billions of dollars for unproved prevention programs, the GOP unleashed a sustained attack on pork in the bill.

The NRA, which wanted most of all to kill the measure's assault-weapon ban, decided to launch a televised ad campaign in mid-August of five 30-second spots introduced by actor Charlton Heston (who would be elected NRA president in 1998) proclaiming that what "What President Clinton's not telling you about the crime bill . . . should be a crime." Among other things, the ads asserted inaccurately that the bill prohibited teaching "thou shall not kill," a provision that supposedly prevented invoking the Ten Commandments in crime-prevention projects.

Entering what was supposed to be the last week before the summer recess, the Democrats were forced to make a crucial decision: vote without absolute assurance of success or delay again, angering anxious members and endangering health care. They decided to go for broke, hoping that undecided members could be swayed by last-minute pressure from the president and the Democratic leadership, as had happened several times on other legislation during Clinton's first year.

Essentially, the bill's sponsors had three places to go for undecided votes—Republicans, liberal Democrats, and Democrats aligned with the NRA. Because the House Democratic leadership rarely appealed directly to Republicans, it tried with the other two categories but failed. Liberals opposed to the death penalty would not abandon that principle and support a bill that might dramatically expand the reach of federal capital punishment. Moderate and conservative Democrats who feared NRA opposition would not budge with the assault-weapon ban still included.

The first step to get the bill to the floor was approval of a rule setting the terms of the debate. Usually, this was a formality. Democratic leaders scheduled the vote on the crime bill rule for late Thursday afternoon, August 11, already late in the month for lawmakers eager for their election-year summer recess. Insiders knew that the vote would be close, but the assumption was that Clinton and House Speaker Foley would pull out a last-minute victory, as they usually had in similar situations. But this time, the "yes" votes on the electronic tally board didn't fall into line. The Democrats of 1994 suffered a stunning defeat, 225 to 210.

The enormity of the vote quickly spread through Washington. It wasn't only that the crime bill was reeling; but it seemed as if the Clinton presidency itself was in jeopardy. His own party could not even get a floor vote scheduled on a major piece of legislation The news media were having a field day. If Clinton could not prevail on a relatively popular crime bill, seemingly every Washington pundit agreed, how could he accomplish anything truly controversial like health care reform?

The panic immediately hit the White House. Senior Clinton advisers gathered in the office of Communications Director Mark Gearan. They knew that the National Association of Police Organizations happened to be holding its annual meeting that week in Minneapolis. Some aides thought it would be a good opportunity for Clinton to stage a public appeal for his endangered bill. The president himself showed up and asked for advice. When someone mentioned the police meeting, Clinton announced, "Let's do it." In a virtually unprecedented exercise in emergency planning, the White House entourage was airborne a few hours later to Minnesota, where Clinton made his impassioned plea and got helpful national media coverage.

Somehow, the bill had to be salvaged. Appeals to Black Caucus members who had voted "no" because of their opposition to the death penalty without the racial justice provision yielded far from enough switches. Still, a few members like Georgia's John Lewis relented and supported Clinton while protesting that they had never voted for capital punishment. In the end, the leadership had no choice but to seek a compromise with the Republicans, a tactic that they almost never employed because the Democrats had held such a decisive majority overall, seemingly forever.

An extraordinary series of private caucuses between key members of both parties was convened to review controversial provisions of the huge bill, one by one. For the Republicans, this was an opportunity unparalleled in modern times to influence a major piece of legislation. Republicans insisted on cutting the billions allotted to prevention, as well as adding tougher provisions like one for lifetime tracking of sexual predators. Brooks kept returning to the idea of jettisoning the assault-weapon ban. Optimists hoped that some agreement could be reached as early as Friday, August 19, a week before the delayed date that Congress had set to start its summer break. But the high-stakes talks went into the night, resuming Saturday morning and stretching throughout the day.

Assault weapons was the single most contentious provision. From Clinton's viewpoint, removing it would be a double-edged sword. The absence of an assault-weapon ban probably would guarantee easy approval for the bill that he now was claiming as his own even though it had largely been written on Capitol Hill. And it would soften or eliminate NRA opposition to many Democratic candidates for touting the ban. At the same time, eliminating the ban would take away an issue that could win November votes for Democrats in many urban areas. Gun-control advocates, led by Schumer and including major police groups, firmly believed that the clause should remain in the bill.

Depending on one's perspective, Clinton was either a stubborn hero or a fool to hold firm. The probability was that only decisive presidential leadership could save such a controversial idea. What the White House apparently did not foresee was that in the view of history, the president's insistence would be a factor in his party's losing control of the House only three months later, a transformation that would significantly curtail his legislative record and cloud the remainder of his presidency.

At various times during the climactic August 19–21 weekend when the final version of the bill was put together, it appeared that the assault-weapon ban might be watered down or eliminated. As had been the case all year, Brooks was the pivotal figure. As chairman of the conference committee, which had to meet eventually and approve the final version of the overall bill, the Texan wielded considerable power. And this was no routine issue for Brooks, who was in trouble politically on various fronts. He had delivered federal money to his district for years, but the tide was turning against long-serving Democrats who were labeled as deliverers of political pork. Allowing an assault-weapon ban to be passed on his watch would bring the power of the NRA down on him as well.

Before the climactic August weekend of negotiating on the crime bill, Brooks had sent word that he would not call a meeting of the all-powerful conference committee until there was a compromise on assault weapons. On Friday evening, August 19, Brooks stormed out of a session with key negotiators and said he would not return until the firearms questions were worked out to his satisfaction. One observer described Brooks holed up in his office "smoking his cigar and saying, 'I'm not reconvening the conference until you give me something on guns,' " presumably a clause that did not ban any weapon immediately.

Some House Democratic leaders wanted to try removing the assault-weapons section from the bill for a separate vote, which probably would have killed it. Another idea, advanced by critics who feared that the ban would be used gradually to expand the list of prohibited weapons, was to insert a provision that the Treasury Department's Bureau of Alcohol, Tobacco, and Firearms must re-view any weapons to be added to the original banned list of 19.

In the end, the main sticking point was the effective date. Brooks and the NRA wanted to ban the 19 categories of assault-style weapons at issue only after six months had passed. Handgun Control responded that there already was a large inventory of the weapons and that a delay would make the bill useless. Presumably, buyers would rush to accumulate weapons before the law went into effect, and "we'd never get rid of the stockpile," said Handgun Control lobbyist Robert Walker. Schumer understood at one point that Brooks and the NRA would accept a compromise on the date and other issues. Schumer aide David Yassky tried to fashion it on a typewriter in the suite of Majority Leader Richard Gephardt (where many of the final talks were taking place), with senior Clinton aide George Stephanopoulos looking on.

Representatives of Handgun Control were unhappy at having to concede anything significant, but Schumer thought he would have to swallow the deal as the price for passage of the crime bill. But then Brooks's camp said the new compromise was inadequate and made several more demands. Schumer didn't know if he was being suckered into retreating further and further or whether it was a misunderstanding in the heat of the moment. In any case, a Schumer adviser said the "notion of compromise with 'NRA Democrats' was alive until the very end." NRA lobbyist Metaksa recalled rejecting various feelers on com-promises that might have reduced the number of banned guns or changed the provision on ammunition magazine capacity. "We would have lost our credi-bility," she said. "How can you tell 200 members of Congress who have been with us through all of this that we're throwing in the towel?"

As for the crime bill overall, some Republicans, thrilled at the prospect that they finally could play a decisive role in important legislation, wanted more. An exasperated Senator Biden, who was observing the give-and-take among the House members, reported to colleagues at one point that Republicans said they had only four items left to negotiate. But the GOP kept coming up with more new demands. As the talks dragged on, "there have been 40," Biden complained. "[Republican leader Newt] Gingrich has never had so much attention."

Feeling their oats, some GOP members decided that their leaders were not being tough enough. Two dozen of them staged a press conference on the Cap-itol lawn early Saturday evening demanding a "back to basics" bill that elimi-nated all the prevention money and added even tougher sentencing measures. The GOP negotiators decided that would go too far, however, and plowed ahead on a plan to trim the prevention money by more than $2 billion and to eliminate some of the programs most vulnerable to being labeled pork, including Brooks's Texas prison program and a line item for midnight basketball, which had en-dured more than its share of ridicule.

Meanwhile, Brooks—seeing no give on the assault-weapon issue after his 24-hour holdout—decided to give in late Saturday night. Although the Democratic leadership—including Foley, Gephardt, and Bonior—"were more than willing to abandon" Schumer's tough stance on assault weapons, said Handgun Control lobbyist Walker, "the president was insistent—there never was any weakness on his part."

At 1 A.M. Sunday, Brooks called the conference committee back to order in the Rayburn Building. Two more hours of wrangling ensued, interrupted by recesses in which GOP members caucused in the hall to discuss the last remaining questions. The Republicans portrayed themselves as accepting Democratic provisions only under duress. Utah's Hatch, who had abandoned his usual coat and tie for a work shirt and blue jeans, declared the Republican conclusion that "the bill is still insufficiently tough on criminals."

But the time for compromising finally ran out. The conferees voted for the scaled-down bill shortly before 3 A.M., and a House vote was set for that very afternoon so that members could start their long-delayed vacations.

After members reconvened on the floor, the first crucial decision was a vote to send the bill back to conference to consider the conservative Republicans' plan to eliminate crime-prevention money. If that approach had prevailed, the ensuing new round of talks might well have killed the crime issue for 1994, as members would have demanded a start to their summer recess. Enough GOP members had faith in their leadership—which was proud of the concessions they had forced on the Democrats—to defeat the alternate plan. At 7:31 P.M. Sunday, August 21, the 218th vote was cast for the rewritten conference report. The crime bill that had been close to dead ten days earlier when the House unexpectedly defeated the rule was still alive.

But that wasn't the end of the battle. Republicans in the Senate, having seen the success of their House counterparts, decided to play the same game and hold out for their own version of new cuts. The anxious Democratic brain trust, led by Biden and Majority Leader Mitchell, worried that the same scenario could play out in the Senate: a new compromise that would have to be sent back to the House, where a similar back-and-forth would ensue and keep the bill tied up forever. By this time, the usual long summer recess had been decimated—and the risk remained that no bill would survive.

Two days after the House acted, the GOP strategy was working. Forty-one Senate Republicans—enough to keep a filibuster going—demanded that the assault-weapon ban be dropped and prevention funding reduced. Republican leader Bob Dole said he and his colleagues had concluded that it was better to let the bill die than to give in on their two major points. North Dakota Democrat Byron Dorgan compared the struggle to "a migraine headache—it goes on and on and on."

In a final concession, Mitchell proposed a vote on cutting $5 billion for crime prevention. When Dole refused, several moderate Republicans bolted and said they would not go along with further stalling. Mitchell's strategy worked, and a dramatic vote on Thursday, August 25, cut off the Republican filibuster threat by a one-vote margin and spelled victory for the crime bill after the longest summer congressional session in memory. Bill Clinton and the Democrats had won the day, if just barely, and the federal government was about to launch its costliest war against crime.

Superficially, the Democrats had achieved their goal: a balanced anticrime bill that included money for the three "P's" of police officers, prisons, and prevention. The authorization totals—meaning the maximum that Congress could appropriate from the trust fund in the next six years—were $13.5 billion for 100,000 cops and other law enforcement needs, $9.8 billion for prisons, and $6.9 billion for prevention.

The sums for prisons and prevention turned out to be meaningless because they were mostly not spent by later Congresses—again proving Biden's lament about politicians overpromising on crime.

The political price had been gigantic. The Republicans could boast accurately that they had forced the Democrats to back down on a score of issues. And the assault-weapon ban had survived, but it proved to be a classic pyrrhic victory for the Democrats. The NRA would redouble its efforts to defeat members in marginal districts that had voted for the gun-control measure.

The NRA succeeded in helping to knock off not only House Judiciary Chairman Brooks but more than a dozen other Democrats, providing what some analysts believed was the margin of victory that allowed Republicans to take over the House for the first time in 40 years and helped it retake the Senate, too.

Bill Clinton and the NRA agreed on very little, but the 1994 congressional election was a rare subject of accord. Republicans took the House by 14 seats, and the NRA argues that its several million dollars in campaign spending had a big influence in 27 GOP victories. The president offered a similar analysis, contending that the Democrats lost 20 seats over the assault-weapon ban. "The NRA is the reason the Republicans control the House," Clinton declared.[11]

Of course, the NRA could be expected to exaggerate its influence, and Clinton may have found it convenient to blame his party's problems on a single demon. Political scientists who studied the campaign said that other issues like congressional votes on the federal budget and the North American Free Trade Agreement, as well as unique factors in each district contest—like the relative experience of the candidates and spending levels—also played major roles.

Even if it is impossible to single out a decisive factor behind the Republican takeover, there is no doubt that the prominent struggle over the 1994 crime law loomed large. White House domestic policy adviser Bruce Reed, who had a big part in the negotiations that led to passage of the bill, conceded that the events of August 1994 "demonstrated that the Democrats weren't really in charge of the House." In Reed's view, "There was a general sense that the Democrats couldn't get the job done," a perception that had as much to do with health care as with crime. The problems the party was experiencing with the two issues simultaneously produced what Reed called "the worst period in any Democrat's life that anyone could remember."[12]

The Republicans weren't satisfied with using the crime law to help take over Congress. In their first week in charge in 1995, they started a campaign to rewrite the crime law they had just helped enact. Picking up where he had left off the previous summer, Hatch—who replaced Biden as Senate Judiciary chairman—declared that the new law had "wasted billions on duplicative social spending programs," allocated too little money for prison building, and "created an unwieldy grant program" to hire 100,000 cops.

The White House was not about to give up on its showcase program, however, and it rallied support among mayors and police chiefs to save COPS. But the Republicans insisted on creating a $500 million "Local Law Enforcement Block Grant" program that would allow localities to spend federal funds on programs other than police hiring.

It seemed that some of the lessons from the 1970s on federal anticrime spending had been lost. Both parties then had agreed to end LEAA, largely on the ground that its scattershot spending approach had yielded little proof of success. Now, a decade and a half after LEAA had closed its doors, Congress not only had re-created it but was spending at a level many times higher than that of LEAA at its height.

LEAA's annual appropriation never reached $1 billion, but the Justice Department's fiscal year 2000 budget request for the LEAA successor Office of Justice Programs was $5.5 billion. And that didn't even count the prison-building program from the 1994 crime law, which the Clinton administration wanted to halt but the Republicans would continue anyway, and the GOP local law enforcement block grant, which the congressional majority party would insist on keeping.

Having little else legislatively to show for his first two years in the White House, Bill Clinton claimed the 1994 crime law for years afterward as one of his greatest accomplishments—even if he had little to do with writing it other than the 100,000 cops plan. In fact, it might have been the most significant law on a single topic during his presidency in terms of the sheer breadth of a single piece of legislation. For congressional Democrats, however, the experience was mostly a political disaster.

Did the law, with its dozens and dozens of provisions, have much impact on crime? The picture was mixed. Crime rates were heading down before much of the money was allocated, and they might start to rise again before the funds are fully committed.

In terms of spending, the single most significant piece of the law was the addition of tens of thousands of police officers. The prison construction section would prove less important. During the law's six years, less than $2 billion of the nearly $9 billion authorization was spent, adding some 32,000 inmate beds. Although that is the equivalent of 60 new 500-bed prisons, it affects only a small percentage of the nation's 2 million inmates, and many states would have spent money on prison construction regardless of the federal law. The Clinton Office of Management and Budget tried to end the program in 1999, but congressional Republicans insisted that it continue, allocating nearly $700 million for fiscal 2001.

The Violence Against Women Act, which provided up to $1.6 billion for items like expanding women's shelters and reinstituting a national hotline on family violence, may have greater impact, considering that the problem got relatively little federal attention in previous years.

One provision that may have given federal regulators more than they bargained for was named for Jacob Wetterling, a Minnesota youth whose family campaigned for reform after he disappeared in an apparent kidnapping. The law required convicted sex offenders to register after their release from custody, and it set requirements on the release of information on the offenders to law enforcement personnel. Congress added to the law twice in 1996. In a reaction to the case of Megan Kanka, a seven-year-old New Jersey girl who was sexually assaulted and murdered in the summer of 1994, Republican Representative Dick Zimmer succeeded in getting Congress to enact Megan's Law, which required that communities be notified of sex offenders in their midst. Later in the year, in another law named for a victim, lawmakers enacted the Pam Lynchner Act, which required the FBI to set up a database that would enable tracking sex offenders. (Lynchner, victim of an attempted sexual assault, founded the Texas-based anticrime group Justice For All before she was killed in the crash of TWA Flight 800.) The law also directs the FBI to create systems of sex offender registration and community notification in states without "minimally sufficient" procedures.

The new statutes, along with similar state laws, spawned a series of court challenges, as well as a new federal bureaucracy to administer aid offered to qualifying states for their own sex offender programs. Civil libertarians protested that the laws tagged offenders for life. There were vigilante cases like that of the New Jersey former convict whose home was raked by gunfire in June 1998; after he was identified as an ex-offender, one shot missed a neighbor by a few feet.

Meanwhile, the regulations to put the laws into effect were so complex that many states received two-year extensions to comply with the Wetterling Act and Megan's Law, until September 12, 1999. It was virtually impossible to establish in the laws' early years whether they had prevented any repeat crimes. Many states rushed in the late 1990s to establish online sex-offender registries, but the sponsor of the Virginia version admitted that it amounted to a "feel-good politically popular approach" that might "give the public a false sense of security." Susan Paisner, a criminologist who analyzed the trend in the *Washington Post*, concluded that the main impact of identifying sex offenders indefinitely might be to drive them further underground and discourage them from seeking further rehabilitation, even after they supposedly had finished with the criminal justice process.[13]

One clear conclusion was that victims of high-profile crimes would be drawn into lending their names to hurriedly drawn "reform" laws. Following the spate of sex offender laws, Congress in 2000 enacted "Aimee's Law," a proposal to give states financial incentives if they cracked down on parole violators who crossed state lines. It was named after Aimee Willard, a Virginia college student who was abducted and killed in 1996 in her native Pennsylvania by a paroled murderer from Nevada. John Stein of the National Organization for Victim Assistance quipped that the phenomenon would end only after "the market in names is saturated."

Among other controversial provisions in the big 1994 federal anticrime law, the disputed additions to the federal death penalty had rarely been used by the late 1990s, and the law's firearms sections had a limited effect. One example of the triumph of public relations over realistic enforcement plans: When Clinton met with his U.S. attorneys from around the nation soon after the law was passed, his aides were casting about for a specific theme that he could highlight. The White House settled on a proclamation that the lawyers should give top priority to cases under provisions that made it a crime to possess firearms on school grounds or to transfer guns to juveniles. Some prosecutors reportedly resented the presidential directive on cases that were not likely to occur very often. Indeed, a minuscule 24 cases were filed nationwide under the clauses in 1997 and 1998 combined.

Because Congress did not insist on a thorough evaluation beginning as soon as the law became effective, the sad fact was that five years after the massive statute had tied Washington politicians in knots and played a big part in putting Congress in Republican hands, no one knew whether the law had a significant impact on street crime or had spawned major spending boondoggles.

Despite Republican proclamations that they had fought off Democratic-inspired bills laden with pork, the GOP-controlled Congress showed the same affinity as its predecessor Democrats for earmarking federal dollars for favored programs.

"Grabbing a Slice of Washington's Pork" declared a front-page headline in *Youth Today*, the newspaper of the American Youth Work Center, a Washington-based policy organization that asked of some of the crime bill's beneficiaries, "How did those guys get a million dollar federal set-aside without even submitting an application?"[14] The organization listed a page of 1998 congressional directives, including $2.3 million for a culinary arts program and other vocational classes for youth in Kansas City, $1.9 million for a regional youth detention facility in Missoula, Mont., and $40 million for the national Boys & Girls Clubs. Among the critics was Arizona Republican Senator John McCain, who complained that many earmarked projects "have not been considered on an appropriate merit-based prioritization basis."

Justice Department insiders complained that congressional earmarks were eating up 90 percent of the "discretionary" money allotted to the Bureau of Justice Assistance (BJA), meaning that the agency was prevented from funding major initiatives and had to be content with a series of small projects. Unlike the LEAA days, when Washington had the power to review state anticrime plans before handing out money, the modern BJA had no such authority. States could dole out the aid more or less as they pleased, with no assurance that they had a well-thought-out spending plan. Nancy Gist, BJA director during the Clinton administration, lamented the "deterioration of criminal justice planning" by the states.

Politically, enactment of the 1994 law probably improved the Democrats' standing in the public mind as a party that knew how to attack the crime problem, even if a survey by ABC News in September 1994 found that 58 percent of respondents believed that the law would not reduce crime. Still, the coincidence of the national crime decline in the years after passage of the law should allow the Democrats to tout their powers as crime fighters.

While impeachment, war in the Balkans, and other issues grabbed the headlines during Clinton's second term, the president kept up a steady stream of anticrime rhetoric and proposals. It was not clear if this emphasis would continue under Clinton's political heirs. Al Gore sought to take over the reins of the community policing program and spoke out on safe issues like more bulletproof vests for officers and techniques of mapping high-crime areas. Crime was lower on Gore's agenda than it was on Clinton's; the vice president emphasized crime items that dealt with technology and urban "livability."

On the Republican side, Dennis Hastert, who assumed the House speakership in 1999, had chaired predecessor Newt Gingrich's antidrug task force and named a similar panel after he was promoted. In the Senate, Judiciary Chairman Hatch assailed Clinton's fiscal 2000 budget plan as weak on crime. It was obvious that the GOP would continue the same lines of attack born in the trenches of the

1994 crime-law battle. Republicans argued that the Democrats were weak on prison building and on fighting drugs. The GOP also faulted Clinton for trying to eliminate block grant programs for both local law enforcement and juvenile justice.

Budget compromises in the late 1990s kept the fragmented anticrime programs going. In a time of fiscal surpluses, there was little impetus to slow down spending for anything that a politician could assert had the potential for attacking crime.

The 1994 crime law's big-spending programs were supposed to end in 2000. But the White House and congressional appropriators kept on spending until it was clear whether President George W. Bush and Congress wanted to make any significant changes in 2001.

Six years after the crime issue had dominated Washington and helped end the Democrats' control of the House of Representatives, it was full speed ahead for a sprawling Justice Department bureaucracy, whose 85-page spending catalogue spanned everything from closed-circuit televising of child abuse victims' testimony to fighting violence against Indian women.

Chapter 11

SMARTER WAYS TO
FIGHT CRIME

As America's crime rate waxes and wanes, it is easy for politicians and police chiefs to claim victories and explain away defeats. When the statistics say lawbreaking is declining, as they did in the late 1990s, anything and everything seems responsible. That includes more patrol officers, expanded prisons, community organizing, bureaucratic overhauls, fancy burglar alarms, midnight basketball, McGruff the Crime Dog, and all sorts of treatment or counseling programs. With mostly anecdotes and little definitive research to judge by, advocates take credit for whatever they do.

When crime rates increased in the 1960s, 1970s, and late 1980s, those who ran government and social programs sidestepped the possibility that they had contributed to the problem. They attributed crime's ravages to demographic and social forces, a troubled economy, excesses of the news and entertainment media, and failures of families, schools, and churches.

Officeholders tend to fixate on data that purport to show whether crime is up or down, avoiding the fact that "crime" is a loosely defined term that is really a mix of phenomena, including incidents, arrests, threats, and accidents, any of which can be reported or not. The *Philadelphia Inquirer* provided a vivid illustration in 1998 when it found that in their zeal to prove that crime was down, the city's police officers often erased reports of violent acts or redefined them as trivial episodes.[1] In national terms, the FBI's Uniform Crime

Reports vastly undercount crime totals by including only reports to police agencies.

The shortcomings go beyond police agencies. Coordination among the levels of officialdom that make up the justice system—from the lowliest police recruit to the county jail warden to the trial court judge to the state attorney general to the Chief Justice of the United States—could stand significant improvement even after the billions of dollars that Washington and lower-level governments have poured into justice-system upgrades since the 1960s.

U.S. Justice Department aid to state and local anticrime programs jumped from less than $1 billion per year in the mid-1970s to more than $5 billion in the late 1990s—a notable rise even when adjusted for inflation. But the impact of all the spending is questionable. "Politically, Washington must pretend that it can do a lot about crime," said James Q. Wilson of the University of California at Los Angeles. "Practically, it can do very little."[2]

For one thing, most criminal-justice agencies are state or local units. Only a minority of crimes are reported to any authority, and far fewer result in an arrest that leads to a sanction in court. For those eventually sentenced to prison, the average time served behind bars remains about ten years for homicide and only a few years for lesser offenses. The system handles so few cases in relation to overall crime rates that the most effective remedies for crime may lie within families and in communities at large, not in taxpayer-financed projects. Joseph Califano, a former Health, Education, and Welfare secretary who later headed

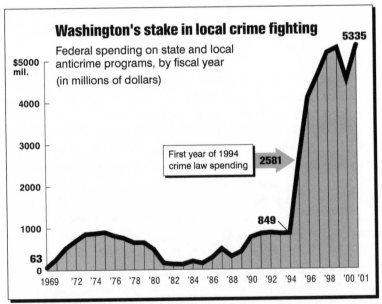

Washington's stake in local crime fighting

Federal spending on state and local anticrime programs, by fiscal year

(in millions of dollars)

First year of 1994 crime law spending   2581

5335

849

$5000 mil.

4000

3000

2000

1000

63

0

1969   '72   '74   '76   '78   '80   '82   '84   '86   '88   '90   '92   '94   '96   '98   '00 '01

Source: U.S. Justice Department

a private national center on substance abuse, argued that more intense parental determination to influence their children would have a greater impact on reducing drug abuse than would larger government programs.

Despite all the systemic flaws, public servants and the private sector entities that work with them have developed plenty of proved techniques and promising ideas, several of which are described here.

Why have some of the potentially most effective measures not been pursued vigorously? Often they become ensnarled in the political maelstrom—either dismissed as being too soft on crime (supposedly not punishing offenders sufficiently) or too harsh on presumably law-abiding citizens (for example, forcing every employee in a workplace to take a drug test or dispersing loiterers).

Others are rejected as too expensive, without a rigorous comparison to the alternatives. A cost-benefit analysis might find that a relatively labor-intensive program for vocational training of offenders in the community is cheaper and better for public safety than is incarcerating them for many years, then releasing them—often to commit new crimes.

One of the few certainties in criminological studies is that there is no single "silver bullet" solution to crime. And neither of the major competing philosophies—get tough or crime prevention—has a monopoly on effective action.

With those caveats, here are some promising ways of dealing with the violence that has wracked America for decades:

1. Cohesive community campaigns. Recognizing that government cannot stop street violence, community-based solutions have been discussed since the war against crime began in earnest in the 1960s. The Johnson crime commission report contended that "controlling crime is the business of every American." A new evaluation of the Chicago neighborhoods study described in Chapter 5 called "attacking public disorder through tough police tactics" a weak strategy compared with promoting "informal efforts among residents" that demonstrates "to participants and observers alike that people in the neighborhood could be relied upon to maintain public order."[3]

Until recently, rhetoric usually prevailed over action. Typically, after a highly publicized crime or a series of them, a group of citizens and merchants meet with local police officers to exchange crime-fighting tips. Citizens mount their own patrol efforts, complete with walkie-talkies and cell phones.

But many of the most extensive campaigns have been waged in the places that least needed them because they had the lowest crime rates. And if the immediate crime problem ebbed, in many cases so did the citizen action. One result of short-lived neighborhood action may have been that a ring of muggers or burglars was displaced to the next block or community, but there was no real long-term crime prevention. If gangs or other lawbreakers remained, many residents took the more drastic action of moving away.

Not only is voluntarism a sporadic activity for most people, but citizen anticrime efforts face the obstacle of erratic and underfunded government aid programs. Even if private citizens could identify likely lawbreakers and crime hot spots, most activists lack enough backup resources from government or the private sector. Part of the problem is legalistic. For an unsanctioned group, amassing enough evidence to win a court case might be impossible. There were many more community police officers as a result of the 1994 federal anticrime law, but they couldn't be on every block 24 hours a day. And even if the police are out in force, the rest of the justice system—judges, probation officers, jailers, and so on—typically are not. Nor do most social service agencies have the wherewithal to provide enough of necessities like health care, drug treatment, and job referrals.

In an extensive review of community-based anticrime programs, criminologists Dennis Rosenbaum, Arthur Lurigio, and Robert Davis pointed out that many citizen efforts have overburdened the justice system with demands for more arrests, prosecutions, and generally "mean-spirited" and "punitive crime control policies." Many citizen-government collaborations had produced good results, the experts found, but such arrangements "can be extremely challenging for everyone involved because of political, bureaucratic, and philosophical differences."[4]

Still, a few areas have developed sophisticated responses to local violence that succeeded in coordinating government, business, and private citizen resources. No one claimed that a single model could work everywhere, but these programs scored successes:

- After a wave of gun violence among teenagers, Boston began to attack the problem from several vantage points simultaneously. Every year between 1988 and 1994, between 5 and 14 youths under age 17 had been shot to death. But instead of merely threatening to try teenagers in adult courts or debating new gun controls, law enforcement authorities in the mid-1990s put together the "Ceasefire Initiative," which studied patterns of both gang activity and firearms sales and focused on those who were selling guns illegally under existing laws.

By 1995, the enforcers had identified 61 gangs with 1,300 members. In "Operation Scrap Iron," aimed at disarming the most dangerous youths, cops and agents then held formal meetings with gang members, warning them of heavy penalties if the violence persisted, a deterrence strategy that largely succeeded. "Coercion works on kids who are most resistant to everything else," said David Kennedy of Harvard's Kennedy School of Government.

The authorities went well beyond tough talk. Many criminals already are involved in the justice process, more on probation than anywhere else. But probation is a weak link in the system, with overworked officers able to check on their probationers only once or twice a week. In Boston, officers were enlisted to crack down on everyone on their supervision list, often riding with investigators in "Operation Night Light" so that they could take immediate action against violators. Besides the traditional community anticrime groups, the religious community in the inner city actively joined the cause. A group of black clergymen called the Ten Point Coalition cajoled and helped problem teens, often one to one.

These measures did not eliminate violent crime, but Boston's plague of youth gun fatalities declined to zero in 1996 and 1997.

- "In 1993, homicide was the leading cause of death of youth in East Bay corridor communities." So concluded a depressing analysis after a series of high-profile killings in several dozen towns east of San Francisco.[5] The report helped establish a government-business-private citizen anticrime coalition that started with the cities of Richmond, Berkeley, and Oakland and eventually took in 27 towns, 18 school districts, 23 law enforcement agencies, and a host of other entities and individuals in an area comprising 1.5 million people.

What made the East Bay Public Safety Corridor Partnership different from most such campaigns was the highly organized, detailed planning that spanned many diverse interests. Spearheaded by Maria Theresa Viramontes, a local resident who had become alarmed about the violence involving teenagers in her area, the campaign consciously stayed away from adopting a consensus view on the causes and cures of crime, but rather embraced a broad approach to combat it, one that included both youth crime prevention and tough law enforcement. The partnership, which got aid from Washington, was notable for winning the endorsements of politicians in the area at all levels.

The campaign may sound matter-of-fact, but such coalitions are difficult to assemble in a region that includes jursidictions of various sizes, from Emeryville's 5,600 residents to Fremont's 187,400. The effort won national recognition after virtually all of its cities experienced a consistent crime downturn starting in 1993, before the trend was established nationwide.

- A district north of Manhattan's Times Square was plagued by serious crimes that usually fell short of violence but damaged the community nevertheless, including prostitution, graffiti, drug addicts on the sidewalks, and subway fare jumpers. Police either ignored such offenses or arrested suspects who were shipped to a court far downtown, where many cases were quietly dropped. Perpetrators found the system so lax that they often moved on to more serious offenses.

Crime-weary New Yorkers seemed resigned to the prevalence of quality-of-life offenses in the early 1990s. They reasoned that the police had to spend their time on violent crimes and that relatively minor street problems were a permanent feature of city life.

A few businesses and community leaders decided not to accept this status quo. They raised money to set up the Midtown Community Court in 1993. The basic idea was to test the long-theorized but rarely tried idea that immediate sanctions, backed up by social services and harsher penalties for failing to comply, would make a dent in crime. Instead of police officers' shuffling paper case files downtown, a local judge could hear cases immediately, armed with computer technology that could pinpoint suspects' criminal records and progress— or lack of it—in a variety of treatment programs or community service assignments. The idea was not to impose draconian penalties but to take some action promptly that would make an impression on chronic offenders.

The early results were positive. Within about three years, Midtown had become one of New York's busiest intake courts, handling 16,000 cases a year and sentencing offenders to community service worth $175,000 in labor costs. The compliance rate was 75 percent, one of the city's highest. Arrests for prostitution fell more than 60 percent and those for illegal vending 24 percent. The highly visible public service sentences, like cleaning graffiti off walls, said court director John Feinblatt, gave local residents and organizations "tangible evidence that the criminal-justice system is accountable to the community."[6] (Like many anticrime ideas, this one was a turnabout on an old theme: New York City closed neighborhood magistrate courts in 1962 in the name of efficiency, but "its cost was remoteness," Feinblatt said.)

Even if the Midtown Court was a success, resources weren't available to replicate it easily. Many neighborhoods lacked the bedrock support of longstanding businesses that would provide needed funds. A similar "community justice center" was set up in a crime-plagued area of Brooklyn called Red Hook, but it took several years to open. Even then, community courts covered only a tiny proportion of New York City. Still, as word of the New York experiments spread, other cities planned their own versions, including Portland, Oregon, Hartford, Baltimore, and Philadelphia.

The courts were only one part of the justice apparatus that lost touch with the community they were supposed to serve. Prosecutors, who make crucial decisions on whether arrests generated by police officers are pursued, typically worked in central downtown offices. They evaluated cases as they came in, but the results may or may not have addressed the problems that local residents judged most important, particularly quality-of-life violations.

Under the same principles that guided the Midtown Community Court, cities like Portland, Oregon, Indianapolis, and Washington, D.C., launched "community prosecution" programs. Instead of sticking to their offices and making decisions strictly based on individual cases, prosecutors met with community groups to discuss crime-fighting priorities, sometimes establishing field offices in troubled areas. The aim was to file cases that helped solve problems rather than just to amass a high conviction rate. Many citizens, seeing the officials move in, pitched in and helped with jobs like neighborhood clean-up work. Instead of merely complaining about the failure of "downtown" to help them, they were willing to help make up for "the limits of the criminal justice system" to solve problems, said Barbara Boland, a Washington, D.C., researcher who studied community prosecution.

Some analysts branded the idea a gimmick and noted that prosecutors, usually chosen in partisan elections, should be sensitive to constituents' needs. But what is important to a ward captain may not be a burning issue to a typical property owner. Few disputed the idea that prosecutors, often the linchpin in keeping the criminal court process going, would benefit by immersion in community problems.

- Residents of many cities knew about drug problems in certain trouble spots that could not always be handled by traditional enforcement techniques. "Crack houses" might be hotbeds of violence but difficult to penetrate because most illegal activity took place indoors. Informants and undercover officers could try to investigate, but that could be labor-intensive and might not nab drug kingpins. In Milwaukee, San Diego, and elsewhere, neighborhood groups and housing authorities collaborated to invoke civil remedies like building code violation charges against landlords who failed to stop drug sales on their properties. Often, judges declared such structures nuisances and closed them down.

"Civil nuisance" remedies were hardly the stuff that topped local television newscasts, which tended to feature hostage crises or auto crashes. But they could keep many traffickers off-balance and make neighborhoods more livable for nearby residents who took action.

Several volumes of detailed suggestions on how to mount local antidrug drives were compiled by the President's Commission on Model State Drug Laws, created by Congress in 1988. But the panel was victimized by an egregious case of bad timing. President Bush appointed its 24 members near the end of his term in 1992, and the group—headed by Indianapolis Mayor Stephen Gold-smith—delivered its recommendations to the administration of Bill Clinton, which had its own priorities and paid little heed to the Bush commission's ideas.

- Another proved weapon that failed to get its deserved share of attention is architectural methods of preventing crime in the places where it is most likely to occur. Known by the cumbersome initials CPTED—crime prevention through environmental design—the technique was described in a 1972 book by New York urban planner Oscar Newman on "defensible space." Despite its logic—and an overlap with the later "broken windows" formulation of James Q. Wilson and George Kelling—Newman's idea didn't take off. That was probably because one of its main ingredients was erecting barriers—whether gates, walls, or traffic hindrances—an idea that made many property owners wary and carried connotations of segregated communities.

It wasn't until the early 1990s that a small Dayton, Ohio, neighborhood called Five Oaks put the idea into practice extensively by erecting more than 50 wrought iron barricades and creating cul-de-sacs that criminals presumably would avoid. Crime dropped sharply, although it was clearly more a matter of stabilizing the area than attacking crime's root causes. In Five Oaks and in other communities like Oak Park, Illinois, Bridgeport, Connecticut, and Charlotte, North Carolina, planners used defensible space principles to identify places where lawbreaking was most likely to occur and plotted ways to clean them up and fortify them—often installing simple but effective barriers.

The Justice Department issued a cautiously optimistic report on the design theory in 1997. Crime had dropped in places where it was implemented, although some of the decline came at the cost of displacing criminal activity to other areas. As with other crime-fighting methods, no one argued that CPTED was the be-all and end-all. But it was hard to understand how it could have been mostly ignored for decades.

2. Targeted drug treatment. To clarify the relationship between drugs and crime, the federal Drug Use Forecasting program (later Arrestee Drug Abuse Monitoring, or ADAM) found that two thirds of those picked up by police officers in 15 major cities tested positive for at least one drug.[7] In Chicago, the figure exceeded 80 percent in 1997.

A Justice Department survey reported in 1999 that an astounding 83 percent of state prison inmates had used drugs in the past; one third of prisoners said they committed the offense that landed them behind bars under the influence of drugs. (Including alcohol, the "under the influence" figure reached 52 percent.[8])

Whether drugs are a cause or a symptom of violence is debated endlessly, but the big mystery is why testing and treatment are not carried out more intensively within the justice system—the place with literally a captive audience. No one claims that tests are always accurate or that treatment is universally effective. But only a small fraction of inmates who might benefit from treatment are able to get it, and testing of the millions on probation and parole has been done sporadically.

Despite the growing number of inmates with drug problems, the percentage getting treatment has dropped sharply, from 24.5 percent of state prisoners in 1991 to only 9.7 percent in 1997. In federal prisons, where 73 percent of inmates had used drugs, the percentage in treatment fell from 15.7 to 9.2 in the same period.[9]

A persistent critic of the inexplicable imbalance in resources, Mark Kleiman of the University of California at Los Angeles, noted that although three fourths of America's convicts are on probation and parole, about 90 percent of public expenditures on corrections programs go to running prisons.[10] As a result, several million people who have admitted engaging in criminal activity—many of them drug users—can freely roam the streets with hardly any restraints.

In the event that a probation officer discovers something amiss, there are two usually ineffective options: telling the convict to straighten up or threatening to take him or her back to court. Kleiman urged an overhaul of probation and parole practices, partly along the lines of the Boston antigang program, in which probation officers have the authority to jail suspects immediately. Many criminals, he argued, would be deterred much more by the threat of immediate sanctions than by the prospect of returning to custody at some indefinite time in the future.

An effort by Bill Clinton to address the problem in 1996 shows the pluses and minuses of mixing politics and criminal justice. Facing tough criticism by Republican presidential candidate Bob Dole on the drug issue, Clinton picked up on Kleiman's ideas and announced in the summer of 1996 that he wanted to encourage drug testing throughout the criminal justice system.

Kleiman estimated that a national testing plan could be implemented for under $4 billion a year, a small percent of government antidrug spending. He calculated that it could reduce cocaine and heroin sales by 40 percent and produce many other benefits, including that "the user-offenders in the program would be healthier, more employable, and less likely to wind up back in prison."

The White House got Congress to enact the concept before its election-season adjournment that year. States that wanted federal aid for prison construction were required to test their inmates. As a result, most states reported by mid-1999 that more than 90 percent of their prisoners were clean. That was believed to be a big improvement, but no one knew for sure because testing was not widespread until recently.

Why weren't most of the millions of convicts on probation—the most common criminal sanction—consistently tested for drugs? Justice Department officials decided they could not require drug monitoring for probationers because they were supervised on a county or city level, whereas the federal aid program was directed at state governments. To critics like Kleiman, that huge gap represented a bureaucratic failure of leadership. Some insiders were more caustic, calling the case a perfect example of soft-headed bureaucrats' undermining a policy agreed on by the president and Congress. Those implementing the law said that trying to reform state practices via federal-aid rules in a complex area like corrections policy is a messy way of policymaking.

Some experiments did proceed. Justice Department researchers backed a program called "Breaking the Cycle" in Birmingham, Alabama, in 1997. The basic idea was to see if the justice system could stop or at least slow the revolving door for drug abusers. Birmingham had worked on the problem on a smaller scale for 25 years under a federal program called "Treatment Alternatives to Street Crime" but was plagued by system overload. The county jail held 1,200 prisoners, well over its capacity of 750; and probation officers had as many as 140 convicts on their lists, far too many to supervise effectively.[11]

With federal support, Breaking the Cycle arrestees got drug tests more quickly to qualify for release on bond, and many were offered treatment faster than they would have been under the old system—usually a few days instead of six months. The number of offenders in treatment more than doubled to nearly 3,000 by May 1998, the average length of treatment was up to 232 days from as few as 120, and more than 70 percent of the defendants were showing up for treatment and appointments with attorneys—a high compliance rate for such programs. A Justice Department report in 2001 said the program had a "substantial impact" on drug use.

Some who observed the project said it suffered from inconsistent sentences issued by judges. Still, the Justice Department was encouraged enough to extend the idea with grants to Jacksonville, Florida, and Tacoma, Washington.

The notion of expanded drug testing was mired in a sharp debate over tactics. Some experts insisted that judges penalize defendants or probationers who failed drug tests even if treatment was not available. Others argued that treatment was a necessary component; the problem was that many programs were so expensive that they couldn't accommodate many referrals, thus rendering the testing ineffective. UCLA's Kleiman maintained that the Breaking the Cycle model fell short and that officials in Connecticut and elsewhere did better with a more stringent approach that penalized those who failed drug tests, whether or not treatment was available.

3. Early prevention. Some youths commit acts of violence with no warning, but in most cases there is some indication of trouble, whether a school discipline problem or a tendency to act out at home or with peers. Of course, every boisterous act does not signal a potential hardened criminal, but criminal-justice and social service agencies typically become involved too late to stop a serious string of youth crimes.

A prime reason is that teachers and administrators in schools, the places where misbehavior patterns normally would be spotted at early ages, have been prone to take one of two actions. Students who commit truly dangerous acts like bringing loaded firearms onto school property often are expelled, which may solve the school's immediate problem but does nothing about the danger. "You then have a kid on the street with a gun," complained Barry Krisberg of the National Council on Crime and Delinquency.[12] Fear of overreaction (or lawsuits) means that in most cases, minor assaults in the classroom are ignored, or kids who act out are given mild discipline.

These tepid responses are not solely due to timid educators. Counseling services may not be available for children who need them, and a principal might not be able to persuade a family to have a child examined for a possible mental illness. Also, civil libertarians complain that some educators take the idea of spotting troublemakers too far by basing disciplinary actions on supposedly generic profiles of misbehaving students.

A few theorists have tried to create frameworks for dealing with troubled youths. Federal juvenile crime officials have endorsed an approach called "Communities That Care," mapped out by social work expert J. David Hawkins at the University of Washington. In essence, the model calls for assembling community leaders who control key resources to form a board that decides on prevention strategies based on a long list of proved risk factors, such as whether a youth comes from an impoverished or broken family, or has a poor academic or social record in school. The program then recommends action that promotes "bonding" between problem teens and responsible adults or peers, whether through individual mentoring or some group activity.

Communities That Care offers officials in a region a detailed structure they can adapt to set up a comprehensive program. Of course, such plans may be costly, particularly if they involve such programs as prenatal care and home counseling visits for people like low-income single parents. But they may pay off in reduced justice-system costs years later, say analyses by the RAND Corporation.

Enthusiasm about Communities That Care in some places does not mean that every such approach will work. One federally supported program provided intensive social services to high risk adolescents in Austin, Texas, Bridgeport, Connecticut; Memphis, Tennessee; Savannah, Georgia, and Seattle, Washington.

But despite mentoring, after-school activities, and other aid, the teens' behavior was little different after two years. "This really took us aback," said Adele Harrell of the Urban Institute in Washington, D.C., who evaluated the program. One problem was that the help from outside experts could go only so far. Problems within many families of the targeted youths were "worse than we imagined," Harrell said. One lesson is that aid to troubled teens often must be intense and longstanding. It isn't enough for a mentor to counsel a youth just once a month.

Early intervention schemes operating in the late 1990s reached only a small number of America's violence-prone young people. Because they were targeted, appropriately, at high-crime areas, they might have failed to stop notably violent episodes in or near suburban and rural schools between 1997 and 1999. A series of shooting sprees by teenagers in Mississippi, Arkansas, Oregon, Colorado, and elsewhere featured the common element that the accused killers had hinted to friends or others that they planned violence.

Even if existing programs probably did head off other potential incidents, warning systems were not in place nationwide to ensure that troubled youths were actually afforded treatment. Belatedly, government officials and private authorities tried to expand programs to deal with the problem, such as the employment of more psychologists in schools.

An ambitious attempt to cull the truly effective youth crime prevention ideas from the long list of experiments began in the late 1990s by a private project called "Blueprints for Violence Prevention." A study of 500 programs found only 10 that could demonstrate scientifically proved results, including a life skills training curriculum in New York State and an intensive big brothers-big sisters mentoring program in Pennsylvania. Unfortunately, the programs that don't work are "the ones you're most likely to see in your community," warned University of Colorado criminologist Delbert Elliott, who helped direct the study.

4. Bolstering the justice system. No one contends that a better justice apparatus will magically solve the crime problem. And despite public concern about crime, taxpayers and their elected representatives have been reluctant to boost dramatically the share of annual budgets devoted to the justice process. In fact, in many places there has been a disconnect between the amount of citizen worrying—as expressed in opinion polls—and the sums spent on basic services that deal with fighting crime and aiding victims. This happens even though since 1982, anywhere from 60 to 75 percent of Americans have told pollsters that they believe more public money should be spent on anticrime programs.

The Justice Department has estimated that government at all levels spends about $112 billion a year on the justice system.[13] That may sound like a lot, but it amounts to only a tiny fraction of the $3 trillion available for all public purposes.

Even if Washington spent anywhere near the $6 billion per year authorized in the 1994 anticrime law, it would represent a national increase of only a few percentage points—and most of that would go to police personnel costs and prison bricks and mortar.

Public agencies cannot eliminate crime, but an efficient justice system can help. It's not just a question of handling caseloads better. Gary LaFree, a sociologist from the University of New Mexico, theorized that gradually increasing trust in government by many minorities lies behind much of the crime-rate decrease of the 1990s.[14]

Here are steps that might have even impact, at each stage of the process:

Police. Officer ranks have increased, but more attention should be given to assuring the quality of services through better training, the highest-technology equipment, and better scrutiny of officer wrongdoing.

It may not be necessary for each officer to earn a college degree, but minimum standards could be raised. Only about half of police departments even require graduation from high school, the Police Executive Research Forum reported in 1998.[15] A city council member in Washington, D.C., opposed requiring the city's recruits to attend college for at least two years, even after the police chief complained that so many officers could not write coherent reports that many cases were being thrown out of court.

Courts. The judicial system is the most overlooked part of the justice process. Many judges recoil from lobbying and then, predictably, get short shrift when budgets are allocated. (Courts and lawyers end up with only about 20 percent of state justice spending.) The 1994 federal anticrime law is a prime example: Congress authorized billions of dollars for police officers and prisons but almost nothing for the important agencies in between: prosecutors, public defenders, and courts. Not surprisingly, several years later, defendants in Baltimore and elsewhere were being released because authorities could not provide them with timely trials.

Even before the federal law was enacted, it took an average of four to five months to process a state criminal case even if the defendant pleaded guilty and six to eight months if the case went to trial. Those intervals are likely to increase as the larger corps of police officers make more arrests. More money isn't the only answer—many prosecutors' offices and courts could operate more efficiently—but the lack of balance in funding key parts of the justice system is striking.

One positive note is a steady improvement in technology that allows many judges who formerly depended on paper-and-pencil records to obtain instant computerized background information on defendants and sentencing options.

As for prosecutors, one major challenge is to broaden their training beyond the legalistic niceties of winning cases to more sophisticated concepts of how to get justice for the community. The Justice Department launched a project on "community safety lawyering" in 1998 by Roger Conner, an attorney-activist who has long advocated more innovative lawyer involvement in public-safety issues. The basic idea is for lawyers to help to solve neighborhood problems through creative uses of legal concepts like sophisticated dispute resolution rather than merely filing criminal charges. But prosecutors' traditional notions of functions have long been ingrained, starting in law school.

Corrections. Two million Americans are behind bars; do most of them belong there? Hardliners like University of Pennsylvania political scientist John DiIulio have stressed that more than 90 percent of state inmates were convicted of violent crimes or are repeat offenders; presumably, most deserve to be in prison (even if many of the repeat offenses are nonviolent). Liberals emphasize that a high percentage of prisoners are first-time convicts with narcotics violations or a nonviolent crime; arguably, they might be just as well off in a less secure facility where they could perform more productive work. (An inmate's most recent court docket entry may mask a violent history.)

The debate over who should be in prison obscures the question of why there are so few meaningful activities for inmates, whether education, work, or drug treatment. Most prisoners are required to perform some tasks, but usually not those likely to help them get decent jobs after release. A major culprit is the lack of public resources, buttressed by some opinion surveys showing that the public believes prisoners deserve few "perks."

The battle over how to provide more rehabilitative jobs for prisoners has been fought mainly out of the public spotlight. Then-U.S. Chief Justice Warren Burger tried to raise the issue's profile in the early 1980s with speeches and conferences under the rubric of "factories within fences," but it never became a prominent subject for policymakers.

The most visible battleground has been Federal Prison Industries, which by 1998 was the 37th largest supplier to the federal bureaucracy, with 20,000 inmates producing more than $500 million each year worth of furniture, textiles, and other products and services, much of which went to government agencies under a law requiring 25 percent of their purchases to come from prisons.

That large and growing pool of business was more than enough to attract the attention of small business owners and organized labor, whose advocates in Congress want to require the federal industry program to compete on an equal basis with the private sector.

As important as it is to keep inmates occupied, the most overlooked area of corrections is supervision of convicts already on the streets. A record 4.1 million were on probation or parole in 1999—twice as many as the number incarcerated. Yet those on the streets typically live unstructured lives, in touch only superficially and occasionally with the officers supposed to be monitoring them.

Reformers have tried to address this population in programs with labels like "intermediate sanctions" and "intensive probation." Among the many forms these plans have taken (often in combination) are boot camps, community service, house arrest (requiring convicts to stay at home during specified hours), financial restitution to victims, and "day reporting centers" (where criminals report to specified locations each day on the way to or from a job, class, or social service).

Despite successes, these options have been severely limited by officials' reluctance to expand them in the face of the virtual certainty that some participants will commit new crimes. Journalist David C. Anderson examined intermediate sanctions in his 1998 book *Sensible Justice*, concluding that when they "are given the resources they need and are allowed to work, the [programs] easily prove their value [by giving] offenders the chance to turn their lives around, to the benefit of everyone."[16]

Political scientist DiIulio cited a decade-long effort in New Jersey to expand well-run alternatives to prison over the reservations of a "hidebound corrections establishment." DiIulio headed a task force that suggested improvements to Governor James Florio, but the proposals were rejected. Later, DiIulio worked with a judge named Daniel Coburn to institute an effective victim-restitution program that has collected tens of millions of dollars. Uncollected fines, said DiIulio, are "a corrosive element of justice—people lose confidence in the system."[17]

Some nonprison punishment programs have operated in the shadows for years but have not been tested with large numbers of convicts. Hundreds of small-scale experiments have been run under a federal program called "Treatment Alternatives to Street Crime" that dates from the LEAA days of the early 1970s. Many projects struggled financially after LEAA closed its doors in the early 1980s; more than 300 survived into the 1990s, but there was no assurance of consistent funding.

Crime victims. Nearly four decades of high victimization rates in the United States have helped to build a strong movement among those who suffered directly and their friends and relatives. Police officers, prosecutors, and judges overall are more sympathetic to victims' plights, but their rights are far from assured despite constitutional amendments and favorable laws in most states. An amendment aimed at making up for the shortcomings of the state provisions has failed in Congress because of the criticism that it would unduly complicate the justice process.

Enhancing victims' rights and compensation might improve public opinion about the justice system. But victims' advocates have had more success when they support harsh and popular-sounding remedies like the 1996 federal curb on habeas corpus appeals by convicts. The appeal system needed reform, but the one advocated by victims of the 1995 Oklahoma City federal building bombing curbed the filing of appeals and did little to improve the quality of defense lawyers for defendants—the most serious problem leading to prolonged court appeals.

A fundamental shortcoming of victim participation in criminal cases has been that they typically become most involved only at the end—at sentencing, when they may be asked to express their feelings to a judge in a highly charged setting that puts the emphasis on vengeance.

Under a "restorative justice" concept being tried in an increasing number of communities, victims are brought in earlier, sometimes confronting defendants directly with requests for restitution or apologies (which some criminals say they find more difficult than going to jail). "Restorative justice places victims at the center of the justice system," said Joseph Lehman, corrections director of Washington State. Some jurisdictions have operated such programs for years. Prosecutors in Polk County, Iowa, obtained victim-offender restitution agreements exceeding more than $1 million between 1992 and 1996 in 2,600 cases from kidnapping to theft. It's an open question whether the concept can be applied to a large proportion of violent crimes.

Some areas allow community boards of citizens to recommend penalties after hearing from the victim and the offender. Although the procedure has been used effectively, it may not be appropriate for cases of severe violence or when guilt is in question.

Domestic violence. The justice system long has treated most crimes in the home less seriously than street crimes. That view has changed somewhat as links between child abuse and spouse beating with other forms of violence have been exposed. "Violence does beget violence," said criminologist Cathy Spatz Widom of the University of Albany, who noted that being victimized or neglected as a child increases one's risk of being arrested later for a violent offense. But prosecuting crimes against children still gets relatively little priority.

Congress did pass the Violence Against Women Act in the 1994 federal crime law, but the subject generally deserves more attention by policymakers. Follow-up legislation, for example, would provide more funding for battered-women's shelters and for a legal-aid network for victims.

Trends and statistics. Lags in government data on crime trends constantly frustrated Attorney General Janet Reno, who found that Justice Department officials often published data several years old, making it impossible to pinpoint current crime and justice problems. And many statistics are not gathered on a large enough scale to provide city-by-city breakdowns. Yet the Bureau of Justice Statistics has limped along with an annual budget of under $30 million, a tiny figure by Washington standards.

In 1999, the National Institute of Justice started an experiment called COMPASS, testing in Seattle whether crime can be measured on an up-to-date basis, neighborhood by neighborhood. But the program got off to a shaky start; Attorney General Reno had to persuade reluctant local officials to cooperate.

Accountability. It's easy to call for spending more government money, but politicians are much fonder of demanding accountability from criminals than from the anticrime agencies that get tax money allocated freely by the lawmakers. Scientific evaluations are not easy, because there are few agreed-on performance measures. Grading justice-system agencies according to the rise and fall of crime rates is inadvisable because of all the factors that influence crime but have nothing to do with government.

Judging police officers by their arrest numbers encourages arrest as the solution to problems where it actually might be counterproductive. Measuring prosecutors and judges by the harshness of their sentences or by conviction rates could be terribly flawed if penalties are unfair or are ineffective in heading off future offenses.

For corrections agencies, the almost reflexive reliance on data on repeat criminality is fraught with flaws. Simple claims that "our recidivism rate is only 15 percent" are dubious. What this usually means is that "we know 15 percent of the people we released were rearrested within the last year in our jurisdiction." But that doesn't account for crimes that occurred elsewhere or for all the offenses that didn't lead to an arrest. Recidivism comparisons should take into account convicts' prior records, how long they were in custody, and what kind of treatment or counseling they may have received.

Not only should evaluation measures be refined, but public agencies should be held to account for their occasional terrible foul-ups. In one such episode that soured the public on justice-system agencies, a Washington, D.C., convict named Leo Wright, serving a prison term of at least 20 years for the murder of a taxi driver, was mistakenly paroled several years early, later robbing a teenage girl and slashing her to death. Three years after the crime, a special investigator in 1999 blamed a police officer and two corrections officials.

Even if such tragic cases are rare, probing them seriously might bolster public opinion of the justice system. (Fewer than one fourth of Americans express a "great deal" or "quite a lot" of confidence in justice agencies—a figure that should give policymakers pause.)

5. **Better media reporting.** Crime is a historic staple of news coverage, and both broadcast and print media are likely to keep giving saturation coverage to sensational episodes, whether it's the arrest of O. J. Simpson or the Columbine High School massacre.

But journalists could do much more to inform the public about criminal justice policy issues. Executive branch officials, legislators, and judges bear the ultimate responsibility for making policy, but they and their constituents might insist on more effective practices if the citizens overall were more knowledgeable.

Serious crime by teenagers, for example, is the most visible component of what criminologist Jeffrey Fagan of Columbia University calls a "thin layer of lethal violence" that in recent decades "has dominated popular and political discourse about crime—it has shaped the outcomes of presidential and statewide elections."[18] Most of this phenomenon must be attributed to the candidates and their advisers, whether pollsters or advertising consultants. But the news media bear some of the blame by seeming to accept uncritically the idea that political sloganeering and hasty legislating about the worst crimes actually would do much to stop crime.

This stems not from a malicious desire of news executives to misinform audiences but rather from a reliance on formulaic methods. In the case of juvenile crime, this has meant an overabundance of reporting on after-the-fact remedies for the worst teen killers, most prominently whether they should be tried as adults. It sometimes seems that anyone who tries to broaden the debate to a subject like crime prevention is labeled a liberal who is not interested in holding wrongdoers accountable.

The media, which love to cover debates between ideological opposites, tend to frame the argument as one between conservative hardliners and soft-on-crime liberals. Those who usually get lost in such squabbles are pragmatists who may have better ways of enforcing existing laws or heading off problems before they start—ideas that have no ideological label.

Most media coverage of crime has been driven by the police blotter—the reports gathered up daily from law enforcement agencies by wire service, newspaper, and broadcast reporters. Many stories would benefit from being reported in a context that may not be known to entry-level police and court beat reporters who regard their jobs as way stations to other assignments. The foibles of American crime reporting were well documented by David J. Krajicek, who noted in his 1998 book *Scooped!* that crime and court news items are so easy to come by that they usually fill about one third of daily newspapers and up to half of local television newscasts.[19]

Even if most crime reports are individually accurate, their overall impression may be to exaggerate the extent and danger of crime in the nation. Public opinion surveys have shown, for example, that many Americans believe that more than half of serious crimes are violent, when the actual figure is about 15 percent, and that juveniles are responsible for a much higher proportion of violence than they actually are.

The drumbeat of news about individual crimes usually obscures serious discussion of smart anticrime practices. And policy tends to be made during times of perceived crisis. Congress passed major antidrug bills in 1986 and 1988 during the cocaine surge that, as bad as it was in some urban neighborhoods, affected only a tiny percentage of Americans directly. The massive 1994 crime law was approved in the midst of all the attention to the unusual spate of sensational cases like Polly Klaas and O. J. Simpson, while crime overall actually was declining—a fact that did not become widely apparent for several more years because of the usual lags in reporting.

Increasing concern over the role of the news media in crime policy prompted the Ford and Edna McConnell Clark foundations to sponsor a conference on the subject in 1996 run by New York's private Vera Institute of Justice and the *Columbia Journalism Review*. Discussion there among journalists and justice practitioners led to the formation in 1997 of a new national organization called Criminal Justice Journalists, which aims to provide news reporters, editors, and producers with more reliable information about crime and justice policy.

At the same time, some news organizations mounted more ambitious efforts to cover crime in ways more meaningful to typical readers and viewers. The *Virginian Pilot*, a daily newspaper in Norfolk, started a weekly page of news about crime and how to fight it sensibly. The *Omaha World-Herald* published a 12-page special report in November 1998 that detailed the ups and downs of crime over nearly a decade in each of the city's neighborhoods.[20] The report took two years to compile because Omaha officials, fearing that the newspaper would stigmatize high-crime areas, refused to provide data. The newspaper sued to get the information, declaring, "we believe people can handle the truth."

Other newspapers, including major dailies in Charlotte, North Carolina, and St. Paul, Minnesota, tried experiments under the label of "public" or "civic" journalism in the 1990s. The details differed, but they included sending staff members into neighborhoods not only to report on crime problems but also to take part in community meetings in order to learn residents' concerns and discuss possible solutions in a more structured way than usually occurred in crisis sessions after a horrible crime. Many traditional journalists were wary about the process or opposed it outright. They said civic journalism could improperly push reporters and editors over the line between observing events and participating in them.

Some broadcast journalists changed their practices. The most widely noted experiment took place at the highest-rated local television news station in Austin, Texas, which issued guidelines on crime coverage that generally required news staffers to establish that a crime had some relevance to the local community before airing a report on it. The policy stirred controversy when the station shunned a report on a fatal brawl in a bar 30 miles away that involved only Mexican visitors and no local residents. Competitors predictably accused the station of censoring the news.

One of the most ambitious studies of media crime coverage, conducted in Orlando, established in 1998 that most news consumers, both print and broadcast, were satisfied with the quantity and quality of crime news. The study by Florida State University criminologist Ted Chiricos and others found that citizens who were the most consistent watchers of local television news and its relentless crime coverage were more fearful of crime and more punitive in their attitudes toward offenders.[21]

Even if much news reporting of crime was far more sophisticated than in the "Front Page" days of the 1930s, it was not realistic to expect major changes quickly in view of the long history of crime's primacy on the airwaves and front pages. David Krajicek traced the American press's tabloid tendencies at least as far back as Benjamin Franklin's older brother, who started a newspaper in 1721 that featured sex and crime. When that tradition was continued by newspapers, magazines, and then television and its proliferation of cable outlets, the options for those interested in following crime expanded rapidly in the Internet age. In late 1998, entrepreneur Marshall Davidson led a group of investors who launched a website called APBnews.com that promised a comprehensive report on crime in both its real-life and entertainment forms, complete with audio from police scanners in selected cities. The ambitious effort attracted more than 1 million online visitors each month, but it suffered financial problems and was sold to a firm called SafetyTips.com in mid-2000.

In many cases, the media were responding to real public curiosity about crime; in others, stories of violence from faraway cities seemingly were broadcast or printed mostly because the film or hard copy existed, rather than because of any considered journalistic judgment that the news was more significant than some local development. Critics charged that many television stations were influenced by consultants who insisted that more crime coverage produced higher ratings and more advertising dollars.

But as much as critics across the ideological spectrum faulted the news media for government's failures to deal effectively with crime, they essentially were blaming the messenger. Even if editorial writers sometimes wrote misguided prescriptions, it was hard to establish that the media were setting a poor agenda for politicians and bureaucrats. And the opinion surveys that went beyond superficialities of Americans' views on crime and punishment showed public opinion to be much more sophisticated than "lock them up and throw away the key."

It's true that more than 70 percent of Americans said repeatedly over the years that courts are not harsh enough on convicts. Yet when Sam Houston State University in Texas asked a representative sample about the most important goal of prison, more than 80 percent chose rehabilitation or crime prevention and deterrence; fewer than 15 percent opted for punishment. "Americans clearly favor sending criminals to prison (and for long terms in the case of serious felony offenders), but simultaneously support the provision of education, training, substance abuse treatment, and work stills programs within prisons," said Timothy Flanagan, who oversaw the survey.

Clear majorities rated as effective such nonprison programs as probation, electronic monitoring, house arrest, and boot camps.[22] "While it is often assumed that popular attitudes are overwhelmingly punitive, more careful and nuanced analyses stress their complex and equivocal natures," said Indiana University criminologist Katherine Beckett.[23]

6. Wise use of private-sector crime-fighting. This book has chronicled public policymaking on crime, but that should not obscure the growing role of the private sector. Given the high level of public concern about crime, businesses have been quick to enter the fray.

The challenge for public officials is to recognize and regulate private resources effectively, both to complement taxpayer-funded projects and to provide services more efficiently.

Private security firms employ 1.5 million people and do $100 billion in annual business, analysts at Hallcrest Systems, Inc., have estimated, dwarfing the public sector.[24] Besides selling basic services like guards, alarm systems, and armored cars, some firms offer everything from tracking devices for foiling auto thieves to kits for fingerprinting children in case of kidnapping. The National Crime Prevention Council of McGruff the Crime Dog fame, the recipient of a longstanding annual federal subsidy, authorizes the marketing of a long product list. Opinion differs on whether all of the profiteering from crime control is merely a response to legitimate public demand or a way for entrepreneurs to capitalize on making many citizens more fearful than they need to be.

Perhaps the most controversial private-sector role has been evolving at the corrections end of the justice system. Private interests have run small rehabilitation-oriented programs for many decades, particularly for teenagers. But starting in the mid-1980s, some began trying to enter prison operations on a major scale. About 70,000 convicts or pretrial prisoners are housed in private lockups, less than 5 percent of the nation's total.

The growth of private prisons was much slower than their advocates had predicted. Analysts questioned how much money they could save while housing inmates under constitutional conditions, and public employee unions resisted, their members' jobs in the balance. The Tennessee-based Corrections Corporation of America, largest of the private prison firms, failed by 1999 to achieve its goal of running that state's entire prison system on contract, and proposals to privatize major facilities in Florida stalled amid questions by state legislators. The deaths of four inmates and a guard in prisons operated by the Wackenhut Corporation in New Mexico caused that state to rethink privatization in 1999.

There were certainly some legitimate grounds for criticism. Missouri canceled a contract to put some inmates in a private detention center in Brazoria County, Tex., after a videotape showed guards kicking inmates on the floor, shooting them with a stun gun, and ordering a dog to attack them. Corrections Corporation of America opened a prison in Youngstown, Ohio, in 1997 with 900 inmates from Washington, D.C. But after various disruptions, escapes, stabbings, and two homicides, federal investigator John Clark reported "pivotal failures in . . . security and operational management" in a 1998 report.[25] The fiasco helped make it unlikely that the firm would win one of the largest private-prison contracts to date, a congressional mandate to put several thousand inmates from the capital into the hands of private operators.

But private firms do not have a monopoly on poor treatment of prisoners, and it was possible that the new companies—most of which had employed former wardens and other experts—could teach government policymakers valuable lessons in how to economize.

A more troublesome question is whether the existence of private companies that are building facilities "on spec" and then offering them for rent to states with overcrowded cells unduly influenced the expansion of prisons. So far, the evidence is not convincing that the private sector is primarily responsible for a "prison-industrial complex."

In California, the state with the single largest prison population, officials did build more lockups in anticipation of the three-strikes law's impact. But that did not come at the urging of industry but rather because of support from the powerful union of state prison guards, which has kept most private facilities out of the state. Still, Corrections Corporation of America in 1999 finished a $100 million 2,300-bed maximum security facility on speculation in the Mojave Desert, hoping that the state or at least some of its counties would pay to send inmates there. The prison guard union helped pass a bill to bar out-of-state convicts from being housed in the institution.

7. Dampen the political rhetoric. Perhaps the single most important, and most difficult to achieve, reform in America's battle against crime would be a transformation of the debate over crime policy from an orgy of emotional but largely hollow and oversimplified talk into rational decisionmaking.

For many years, the contentious questions have been posed mostly in terms of absolutes and labels. Supposedly, hardliners favor capital punishment, long prison terms, and chain gangs; soft-on-crime forces lobby for rehabilitation, alternatives to incarceration, and midnight basketball-style crime prevention. Anyone who wants both risks being labeled as a hopelessly muddled thinker.

Another flaw in the political dialogue is the seeming reliance on legislation as a cure-all. The assumption seems to be that for any problem, a new law is needed. In fact, legislation may be the least effective remedy. Maybe an administrative or personnel change is more warranted.

Recent attempts to pierce the rhetorical stalemate have foundered amid sniping over sponsors' motives. The Sentencing Project, a Washington, D.C.-based private agency that promotes nonprison sentences, helped organize a national Campaign for an Effective Crime Policy to sponsor studies and conferences on practical anticrime initiatives. Although the group has issued reasonably balanced literature, it has been tagged as liberal-oriented and has been unable to attract much interest from conservatives.

Washington's Brookings Institution provided a setting to reach some consensus among federal officials when it sponsored private sessions on justice policy in the 1980s involving leaders of the three branches of government. A series of meetings, arranged by Brookings official Warren Cikins, attracted the attorney general, the chairmen of the House and Senate Judiciary Committees, the Chief Justice of the United States, and other high-level officials discussing justice-system problems candidly.[26] As high-minded as the give-and-take may have been in private, it did not stop the spate of ill-informed legislating in Congress, and the sessions ended in the 1990s.

From the conservative side, John DiIulio mounted a project in 1996, also under Brookings auspices, aimed at reconciling basic ideological differences on crime among academic experts and producing a "bipartisan consensus on crime policies for the next century." The group issued a reasonable ten points of agreement, but its conclusion that crime should cease being a "favorite campaign battering ram of both parties" in national elections went unheeded.[27] The "consensus" panel of prominent crime scholars, which included conservatives like James Q. Wilson of the University of California at Los Angeles and liberals like Ethan Nadelmann of the George Soros–backed Lindesmith Center on drug studies, was not heard from again.

Yet another volume attempting to reach a consensus appeared in 1999, asserting that the aim of criminal-justice policies should not be the impossible elimination of crime but "a minimization of the amount of harm that crime imposes." Some 15 crime experts under the sponsorship of the University of California at Berkeley tried to reconcile disagreements in the crime-policy debate under the title "Minimizing Harm." But the result was "considerable cacophony," said Don Gibbons of Portland State University.[28]

In the meantime, crime took its usual prominent place in 1998 political advertising. Among the year's "dirty dozen" negative ads selected by the political weekly *National Journal*:[29]

- New York U.S. Senator Alfonse D'Amato's blast at opponent Charles Schumer for voting "to allow violent criminals to leave jail before serving their full sentences" and "against tougher penalties for child pornographers." (Never mind that Schumer is one of the toughest anticrime Democrats.)
- Criticism by then Illinois U.S. Senator Carol Moseley-Braun's supporters of her opponent, Peter Fitzgerald, for voting "to let people carry concealed weapons in public. In the mall, on the playground, wherever they choose."
- California U.S. Senator Barbara Boxer's denunciation of opponent Matt Fong as "the gun lobby's favorite candidate . . . because he's against new bans on Saturday night specials and assault weapons."
- Kentucky congressional candidate Ernest Fletcher's featuring a rape victim who criticized his opponent for serving as the defense lawyer for her assailant. The victim said that the challenger was "more concerned with criminals' rights than victims' rights."

Boxer and Fletcher won; D'Amato and Moseley-Braun were ousted.

If violence rates continue to decline, it is possible that the debate will recede. But the emergence of other presidential candidates or a series of high-profile crimes like those in 1993 and 1994 could prompt another push for simplistic solutions. Surveys in 1999 showing public safety remaining at or near the top of public concerns will prove an irresistible target for some candidates.

Despite a greater effort by some news outlets to scrutinize the accuracy of political ads, many anticrime policies cannot be put to an immediate test. The best antidote to crime demagoguery might be a massive, thoughtful dose of even-handed research into what works and what doesn't. It sounds simple, but such studies have not been pursued with much vigor. Thousands of dedicated researchers have conducted competent projects, but they have fallen short overall. "The effectiveness of most crime prevention strategies will remain unknown until the nation invests more in evaluating them," said a report by University of Maryland criminologists to Congress in 1997.[30]

And much research has been politicized, trivialized, or ignored. Some examples:

- Drug Abuse Resistance Education (DARE), the program that brings police officers into the classrooms of about 70 percent of the nation's school districts to lecture about the dangers of drugs, has long been popular. But when experts from North Carolina's Research Triangle Institute dared to question its efficacy, the federal crime research agency refused to publish the institute's report, under a barrage of criticism by DARE officials, who had an obvious vested interest in keeping their program going strong. By mounting political support, DARE lost little strength even after another study said it was actually encouraging some students to try drugs. The disputed program unexpectedly scored points when one of its attackers, Stephen Glass of *The New Republic*, was found to have fabricated sources (even if his material critical of DARE may have been accurate).[31] Justice Department insiders agreed that DARE's value was questionable, but asserted that trying to cut its federal funding would alienate key congressional supporters of worthwhile Justice Department projects. DARE finally agreed in 2001 to revise its curriculum.

• Scientists who have tried to pursue possible links between crime and genetic or physiological factors have been marginalized and even accused of racism. A federal conference on the subject was canceled in the mid-1990s after members of the Congressional Black Caucus objected.

One leading advocate of research into crime's biological bases, C. Ray Jeffery of Florida State University, argued that research on the most serious juvenile offenders is flawed by a concentration on efforts to modify behavior. Even if 95 percent of delinquents can be helped by improving family, school, and community conditions, he said, the "major neurological defects" of the others must be addressed. Yet the subject is largely shunned by researchers who fear being labeled politically incorrect.

In the same vein, some of the nation's most spectacular crimes have been committed by persons with severe mental illnesses. But the subject had relatively little attention from anticrime policymakers until the Justice Department held a major conference in mid-1999 to discuss the problem.

In another controversial thrust, some medical experts and epidemiologists argued in recent years that crime should be viewed as a public health issue as well as a legal one. They said the longstanding practice of analyzing crime mainly on the basis of crime numbers reported to police departments and the Justice Department's victimization survey misses important conclusions that experts trained in tracking diseases could bring to bear on the problem. One popular theory was that a main reason for the reduction of in crime rates in the 1990s was a variety of forces combining to produce a "tipping point," much as occurs in the course of defeating a major contagious ailment.

Critics, most prominently the National Rifle Association, charged that the crime-as-health-policy campaign was a thinly disguised effort to advocate gun control. It's true that some key leaders of the movement were prominent gun-control advocates. But instead of examining the substantive issues carefully, Congress allowed the disagreement to turn into a pitched battle over the budget of the federal Centers for Disease Control, which had served as a focal point for the health approach. Millions of dollars that might have gone to establishing whether the thrust was worthwhile were eliminated.

In one promising effort that did get underway, the National Science Foundation started a major research project on violence based at Carnegie Mellon University and including scholars from other institutions nationwide. Headed by respected researcher Alfred Blumstein, who got his start with the Johnson-era crime commission 30 years earlier, it had the potential of avoiding some of the politicized debates that had engulfed federal cabinet departments over appropriate research boundaries.

- Domestic violence was turned into a political issue by feminists. When criminologist Lawrence Sherman, now of the University of Pennsylvania, published research in the early 1980s that supported arrests in virtually every case of alleged spouse beating, women's-rights advocates cheered.[32] But when Sherman concluded a few years later that he had been wrong and that locking up abusers might be wrongheaded if, for example, they might lose their jobs in the process, he was quickly condemned by feminists who urged police to press ahead with mandatory-arrest programs.

Later, as chairman of the University of Maryland's criminology department, Sherman helped mastermind the 1997 comprehensive critique to Congress of federally supported crime prevention efforts. After meticulously sorting the evidence on hundreds of programs, Sherman and colleagues concluded that "by scientific standards, there are very few programs of proven effectiveness." The researchers explained that this did not mean that most programs were worthless. Rather, there was not enough solid evidence to know. The encyclopedic Maryland volume was largely ignored because of Washington's focus on the Clinton-Lewinsky scandal that emerged shortly after it was issued, but it got some attention in the halls of Congress and the Justice Department.

More research was not just the mantra of self-interested criminologists. Political scientist James Q. Wilson, long regarded a conservative crime policy theorist, called for a campaign to "persuade members of Congress and their constituents that they are doing something about crime by spending money on R&D evaluation." That approach got a boost from Laurie Robinson, the assistant attorney general under Janet Reno responsible for federal spending on state and local anticrime projects. "Data and knowledge should drive crime policy," she argued. "We must be courageous enough to risk failure—trial and error are the essence of the scientific process."

Sherman called for 10 percent of the potential $30 billion in the 1994 federal crime law to be reserved for evaluation, but the 1999 budget for the Justice

Department's research arm, the National Institute of Justice (NIJ), remained a paltry $30 million. A Clinton administration proposal in 2000 that a minuscule 1 percent of anticrime funds be reserved for scientific studies stirred little interest in Congress, where members would rather spend everything on projects that would tangibly benefit their districts than on academic studies. In fact, the House voted in 2000 to reduce the crime-research budget by $2 million.

The declining crime rate of the late 1990s could affect anticrime policymaking in Washington for good or ill. If the issue dropped off the top of the list of Americans' concerns, it is possible that calmer, more reasoned decisionmaking could take place "beneath the radar screen," in the words of the Justice Department's Robinson.

The optimistic view was that lowering the profile of crime policy for a time could provide breathing room to repair the federal anticrime funding apparatus, which was fragmented among six agencies, each headed by an official appointed by the president and confirmed by the Senate. Despite nearly three decades of tinkering, the bureaucracy never was really streamlined.

A scathing internal Justice Department report in 1990 described the Bush-era Office of Justice Programs as "complex, fragmented, and conflict prone."[33] It concluded that the federal anticrime grant program "is more a confederation of semi-autonomous units than a unified and traditional hierarchical organization." The study, by the department's management division, cited "feast or famine" funding cycles, "management paralysis," and generally poor morale.

Nine years later, the agencies' funding had jumped dramatically but the management problems remained. Assistant Attorney General Robinson admitted that the agencies under her bailiwick have "grown like topsy—and it hasn't worked well." She called the structure "incredibly inefficient—we waste huge resources on duplication."

Agency veterans maintained that agencies collectively the size of a Fortune 200 company had improved, but typical of chronic snags were these:

- After a U.S. senator from New Mexico proposed an anticrime project for his state, officials from the various federal aid offices gathered to discuss it. They found that many of them had no idea of the existence of other federal projects in New Mexico monitored from the same Justice Department building.
- Without knowing what the other was doing, two agencies each made grants to different nonprofit groups during the same summer to report on juveniles in adult prisons. Two agencies each awarded money to develop curricula on hate crimes. A Justice Department report to Congress said that the two projects were coordinated only "because the same organization successfully bid on both bureaus' projects!"

- When the National Institute of Justice attempted to do an independent evaluation of a major new block grant program aimed at making juvenile delinquents more accoutable for their crimes, the administrator of the juvenile justice agency, Shay Bilchik, blocked it by insisting on veto power over the choice of evaluators. Bilchik said that the evaluation would proceed and that his agency was best qualified to choose the appropriate social scientists.
- A similar dispute between the COPS program, located in the main Justice Department, and the National Institute of Justice, delayed final results of the formal evaluation of the 100,000 cops hiring program until well into Congress's consideration of whether to extend it past its originally scheduled six years. The Clinton administration could do little more than declare that its showcase program was a success.

Critics cited these examples and others to bolster their case that the fragmented system of presidentially appointed bureau heads ensconced in their own fiefdoms was unworkable.

In 1999, the Clinton Justice Department asked Congress to overhaul the agencies in time for the next presidential term in 2001. As logical as the plan sounded, it was opposed by advocates of agencies on juvenile justice and crime victim aid, who complained that stripping their agencies of power could downgrade their importance. Noting that three fourths of the juvenile justice agencies's budgets would be dispersed elsewhere under the plan, Mark Soler of the private Youth Law Center said that "authority and influence generally depend on control of the purse, and the plan all but empties [the agency's] purse."

So Congress overhauled only the Bureau of Justice Assistance, which makes most of the anticrime grants to states and localities. That outcome was criticized by the bureau's departing director, Nancy Gist, who argued that reorganizing a single agency would not solve the coordination problem.

Paradoxically, declining crime rates could rob the federal government's anticrime programs just as LEAA, which died in the early 1980s, when crime dropped off the priority agendas of key officials in Congress and the executive branch. A decline could shut down promising research and local programs just when they have a chance to reach fruition—and risk a repeat of the cycle that plagued crime-fighting in the United States in the second half of the twentieth century. "That would be shortsighted," said University of Pennsylvania criminologist Lawrence Sherman. "When crime goes up again, we'll wish we had done more."

Americans who want future generations to profit from knowledge that might spare them from another crime plague should hope that the promising ideas that emerged in the latter twentieth century are pursued aggressively in the twenty-first.

NOTES

CHAPTER 1   WHEN NATIONAL POLITICS MET CRIME

1. Thomas E. Cronin, Tania Z. Cronin, and Michael E. Milakovich, *U.S. vs. Crime in the Streets* (Bloomington: Indiana University Press, 1981), p. 18.

2. Gerald Caplan, "Reflections on the Nationalization of Crime, 1964–1968," *Law and the Social Order*, Volume 1973, No. 3 (1973), p. 589.

3. Interview with Ruth. See also Henry S. Ruth, Jr., "To Dust Shall Ye Return," in Symposium: "The Challenge of Crime in a Free Society," *Notre Dame Lawyer*, Volume 43 (1968), pp. 811–834.

4. The President's Commission on Law Enforcement and Administration of Justice, *The Challenge of Crime in a Free Society* (New York: Avon Books, 1968), p. 37.

5. Interview with Vorenberg.

6. Interview with Silver.

7. Interview with Katzenbach.

8. Lloyd E. Ohlin, "Report on the President's Commission on Law Enforcement and Administration of Justice," in M. Komarovsky (ed.), *Sociology and Public Policy: The Case of Presidential Commissions* (New York: Elsevier, 1975), pp. 93–115.

9. Interview with Biderman.

10. Interview with Blumstein.

11. Ramsey Clark, *Crime in America* (New York: Simon & Schuster, 1970), p. 9.

12. Caplan, ibid., p. 610.

13. Interview with Velde.

CHAPTER 2   THE RISE AND FALL OF LEAA

1. Thomas E. Cronin, Tania Z. Cronin and Michael E. Milakovich, *U.S. vs. Crime in the Streets* (Bloomington: Indiana University Press, 1981), p. 31.

2. Interview with Murphy.

3. Departments of State, Justice, and Commerce, the Judiciary, and Related Agencies, Appropriations for 1968, Hearings before a Subcommittee of the Committee on Appropriations, U.S. House of Representatives, February 14, 1967, p. 453.

4. Interview with Skoler.

5. Interview with Velde.

6. Interview with Gregg.

7. Interview with Pomeroy.

8. Interview with Skoler.

9. Richard Harris, *Justice* (New York: Avon Books, 1970), p. 136.

10. Interview with Madden.

11. Interview with Rogovin.

12. Interview with Harris.

13. Interview with Murray.

14. Interview with Leonard.

15. Cronin, Cronin, and Milakovich, ibid., p. 90.

16. Block Grant Programs of the Law Enforcement Assistance Administration, Twelfth Report by the Committee on Government Operations, House of Representatives, May 18, 1972.

17. *Law Enforcement: The Federal Role*, Report of the Twentieth Century Fund Task Force on the Law Enforcement Assistance Administration (New York: McGraw-Hill, 1976), p. 56.

18. Interview with Rogovin.

19. *Understanding Crime: An Evaluation of the National Institute of Law Enforcement and Criminal Justice* (Washington, D.C.: National Academy of Sciences, 1977).

20. Interview with Velde.

21. *A National Strategy to Reduce Crime*, National Advisory Commission on Criminal Justice Standards and Goals (Washington, D.C., 1973).

22. Interview with Santarelli.

23. Interview with Allen.

24. Interview with Feinberg.

25. Interview with Wormeli.

26. Interview with Fiederowicz.

27. Restructuring the Justice Department's Program of Assistance to State and Local Governments for Crime Control and Criminal Justice System Improvement, Report to the Attorney General (Washington, D.C.: Department of Justice Study Group, June 23, 1977).

28. Griffin B. Bell with Ronald J. Ostrow, *Taking Care of the Law* (New York: William Morrow, 1982), pp. 86–89, 152–154.

29. Norval Morris and Gordon Hawkins, *The Honest Politician's Guide to Crime Control* (Chicago: University of Chicago Press, 1970), p. 65.

30. Interview with Smith.

31. Interview with Dogin.

32. Interview with Kennedy.

33. Interview with Michel.

34. Interview with Diegelman.

CHAPTER 3   THE "GET-TOUGH" 1980S

1. Attorney General's Task Force on Violent Crime, Final Report, U.S. Department of Justice, August 17, 1981.

2. Interview with Biden.

3. Interview with Gitenstein.

4. Interview with Sawyer.

5. Interview with Meese.

6. Charles R. Wise, *The Dynamics of Legislation* (San Francisco: Jossey-Bass, 1991), p. 227.

7. Interview with Herrington.

8. Martin L. Forst and Martha-Elin Blomquist, *Missing Children: Rhetoric and Reality* (New York: Lexington Books, 1991), p. 39.

9. Interview with Lungren.

10. Interview with Smith.

11. Interview with Green.

12. Marvin E. Frankel, *Criminal Sentences: Law Without Order* (New York: Hill and Wang, 1973.)

13. Interview with Feinberg.

14. Interview with Parent.

15. Interview with Wilkins.

16. Kate Stith and Jose A. Cabranes, *Fear of Judging, Sentencing Guidelines in the Federal Courts* (Chicago: University of Chicago Press, 1998).

17. *The Federal Sentencing Guidelines: A Report on the Operation of the Guidelines System and Short-Term Impacts on Disparity in Sentencing, Use of Incarceration, and Prosecutorial Discretion and Plea Bargaining* (Washington, D.C.: U.S. Sentencing Commission, December 1991).

18. Mary Pat Flaherty and Joan Biskupic, "Justice by the Numbers," *The Washington Post*, October 6–10, 1996.

CHAPTER 4   MAKING A FEDERAL CASE OF IT

1. H. Scott Wallace, "The Drive to Federalize Is a Road to Ruin," *Criminal Justice* (Washington, D.C.: Section of Criminal Justice, American Bar Association, Fall 1993).

2. "The Federalization of Criminal Law" (Washington, D.C.: Task Force on the Federalization of Criminal Law, American Bar Association, Criminal Justice Section, 1998).

3. Dan Baum, *Smoke and Mirrors: The War on Drugs and the Politics of Failure* (Boston: Little, Brown, 1996) p. 197.

4. Interview with Specter.

5. Naftali Bendavid, "How Much More Can Courts, Prisons Take?," *Legal Times*, June 7, 1993.

6. Franklin E. Zimring and Gordon Hawkins, "Toward a Principled Basis for Federal Criminal Legislation," *Annals of the American Academy of Political and Social Science*, Volume 543, No. 15 (1996), p. 20.

7. Michael R. Rand, *Carjacking* (Washington, D.C.: Bureau of Justice Statistics, U.S. Department of Justice, March 1994).

8. Edwin Meese III and Rhett DeHart, "How Washington Subverts Your Local Sheriff," *Policy Review*, January-Feburary 1996, p. 50.

9. *United States v. Lopez*, 115 S.Ct. 1624 (1995).

10. U.S. Court of Appeals for the Ninth Circuit, *U.S. v. Pappadopoulos*, 93–10577 (1995); U.S. Supreme Court, *U.S. v. Jones*, 99–5739 (2000).

11. Stephen M. Saland, speech at the Brookings Institution, May 13, 1993.

12. Judicial Business, Administrative Office of the U.S. Courts Web site, www.aousc.gov, March 2000.

13. See generally Lord Windlesham, *Politics, Punishment, and Populism* (New York: Oxford University Press, 1998).

14. Louis J. Freeh, remarks to U.S. Conference of Mayors, Washington, D.C., January 26, 1995.

15. Jim McGee and Brian Duffy, *Main Justice* (New York: Simon & Schuster, 1996).

16. Anti-Violent Crime Initiative, The Attorney General's Progress Report to the President (Washington, D.C.: U.S. Department of Justice, September 1996).

17. Philip B. Heymann and Mark H. Moore, "The Federal Role in Dealing with Violent Street Crime: Principles, Questions, and Cautions," *Annals of the American Academy of Political and Social Science*, Volume 543, No. 103 (1996), p. 112.

18. *Law Enforcement in a New Century and a Changing World*, report of the Commission on the Advancement of Federal Law Enforcement (Washington, D.C.: Government Printing Office, February 1, 2000).

19. Philip P. Pan, "FBI to Help Prince George's In Crime 'Blitz'," *The Washington Post*, March 12, 1997.

CHAPTER 5   NOT GETTING THEM YOUNG

1. Thomas E. Cronin, Tania Z. Cronin, and Michael E. Milakovich, *U.S. vs. Crime in the Streets* (Bloomington: Indiana University Press, 1981), pp. 111ff.

2. Interview with Edelman.

3. Interview with Specter.

4. Interview with Mattingly.

5. Interview with Lauer.

6. Rita Kramer, *At a Tender Age* (New York: Henry Holt, 1988), p. 263.

7. Leo Hunter (pseudonym), in Robert Rector and Michael Sanera, eds., "Turning the Iron Triangle Upside Down: Alfred Regnery and Juvenile Justice," in *Steering the Elephant: How Washington Works* (New York: Universe Books, 1987).

8. Interview with Wootton.

9. Interview with Heck.

10. M. Wolfgang, R. M. Figlio, and T. Sellin, *Delinquency in a Birth Cohort* (Chicago: University of Chicago Press, 1972).

11. David M. Kennedy, "Pulling Levers: Chronic Offenders, High-Crime Settings, and a Theory of Prevention," *Valparaiso University Law Review*, Volume 31, No. 2 (Spring 1997), p. 450.

12. Interview with Stewart.

13. Interview with Furman.

14. Interview with Agopian.

15. John J. DiIulio, Jr., "The Coming of the Super-Predators," *The Weekly Standard*, November 27, 1995.

16. Donna M. Bishop, Charles E. Frazier, Lonn Lanza-Kaduce, Lawrence Winner, and Frank Orlando, "The Transfer of Juveniles to Criminal Court: Does It Make a Difference?," *Crime and Delinquency* Vol. 42, No. 2 (April 1996), pp. 171–191.

17. Interview with Shorstein.

18. Howard N. Snyder and Melissa Sickmund, *Juvenile Offenders and Victims: 1999 National Report*, National Center for Juvenile Justice for U.S. Office of Juvenile Justice and Delinquency Prevention, (Washington, D.C.: 1999), pp. 144, 159.

19. Misty Allen, "Boot Camps Fail to Pass Muster," *Governing* (November 1997), pp. 40–41.

20. James C. Howell, *Youth Gangs: An Overview* (Washington, D.C.: U.S. Office of Juvenile Justice and Delinquency Prevention, U.S. Department of Justice, August 1998).

21. Lawrence W. Sherman, Denise C. Gottfredson, Doris L. MacKenzie, John Eck, Peter Reuter, and Shawn D. Bushway, "Preventing Crime: What Works, What Doesn't, What's Promising," report to Congress (Washington, D.C.: U.S. Department of Justice, 1997).

22. Mark S. Fleisher, *Dead End Kids: Gang Girls and the Boys They Know* (Madison: University of Wisconsin Press, 1998), p. 7.

23. Interview with Pittman.

24. Unpublished report to the President and the Domestic Policy Council from the Interdepartmental Working Group on Violence, (1994).

25. Interview with Hubbell.

26. Interview with McNulty.

27. Ralph Frammolino, "Failing Grade for Safe Schools Plan," *Los Angeles Times*, September 6, 1998.

28. James Lardner, "Criminals on Crime; Cons, Ex-Cons, and Street-Savvy Kids Say Violence Got So Bad It Even Scared Them," *U.S. News & World Report*, May 25, 1998, pp. 37–39.

CHAPTER 6   DRUGS: IS THE WAR WINNABLE?

1. See generally David F. Musto, M.D., *The American Disease: Origins of Narcotic Control*, expanded edition (New York: Oxford University Press, 1993).

2. Michael Massing, *The Fix* (New York: Simon & Schuster, 1998), p. 97.

3. Dan Baum, *Smoke and Mirrors: The War on Drugs and the Politics of Failure* (Boston: Little, Brown, 1996), p. 16.

4. Massing, ibid., p. 124.

5. Eva Bertram, Morris Blachman, Kenneth Sharpe, and Peter Andreas, *Drug War Politics: The Price of Denial* (Berkeley: University of California Press, 1996), p. 269.

6. Interview with Webster.

7. Interview with Hughes.

8. Jeffrey Fagan, "Crack in Context: Myths and Realities from America's Latest Drug Epidemic," paper, School of Public Health, Columbia University (1997).

9. Gordon Witkin, "The Men Who Created Crack," *U.S. News & World Report*, August 19, 1991, pp. 44–53.

10. Paul J. Goldstein, "The Drug/Violence Nexus: A Tripartite Conceptual Framework," *Journal of Drug Issues*, Vol. 15 (1985), pp. 493–5060.

11. "Cocaine and Federal Sentencing Policy," (Washington, D.C.: U.S. Sentencing Commission, 1995), p. 117.

12. Fagan, ibid.

13. Interview with Sterling.

14. Interview with Gregory.

15. Interview with Lungren.

16. Interview with Wallace.

17. Interview with Biden.

18. Interview with Kennedy.

19. Stephen Breyer, "Federal Sentencing Guidelines Revisited," speech at the University of Nebraska College of Law (November 18, 1998).

20. Peter Reuter, "Can We Make Prohibition Work Better? An Assessment of American Drug Policy" (Washington, D.C.: National Institute of Justice, Perspectives on Crime and Justice Series, February 11, 1997).

21. Interview with Shaw.

22. Bertram et al., ibid., p. 136.

23. Interview with Weiner.

24. Stephen B. Duke and Albert C. Gross, *America's Longest War* (New York: G. P. Putnam's Sons, 1993), p. xv.

25. Interview with Smith.

26. Ibid.

27. Interview with Kramer.

28. Michael S. Gelacak, "Cocaine and Federal Sentencing Policy, Concurring Opinion" (Washington, D.C.: U.S. Sentencing Commission, April 29, 1997).

29. Interview with Reno.

30. Reuter, ibid.

31. Steven S. Martin, John P. O'Connell, Clifford A. Butzin, Charles Huenke, and James A. Inciardi, "The Impact of a Therapeutic Community Continuum of Treatment for Drug-Involved Offenders on Long-Term Recidivism: A Multivariate Survival Analysis," paper presented at the annual meeting of the American Society of Criminology, November 19, 1997.

32. "Looking at a Decade of Drug Courts" (Washington, D.C.: Drug Courts Program Office, Office of Justice Programs, U.S. Department of Justice, June 1998).

33. "Investing in Our Nation's Youth: National Youth Anti-Drug Media Campaign," Phase II Final Report (Washington, D.C.: Office of National Drug Control Policy, 1999).

CHAPTER 7   GUNS DON'T KILL?

1. Pete Shields, *Guns Don't Die—People Do* (New York: Arbor House, 1981).

2. Gary Kleck, *Targeting Guns: Firearms and Their Control* (New York: Aldine de Gruyter, 1997), p. 64.

3. Interview with Velde.

4. Interview with Doi.

5. Interview with Volkmer.

6. Interview with Metaksa.

7. Interview with LaPierre.

8. Interview with Sugarmann.

9. Nadine Cohodas, "Police Groups, New to Lobbying Scene, Face Off Against NRA in Gun Bill Battle," *Congressional Quarterly Weekly Report* (March 22, 1986).

10. Osha Gray Davidson, *Under Fire: The NRA and the Battle for Gun Control*, (New York: Henry Holt, 1993), pp. 104ff.

11. Interview with Cohen.

12. Mollie Dickenson, *Thumbs Up: The Life and Courageous Comeback of White House Press Secretary Jim Brady* (New York: William Morrow, 1987).

13. Interview with Walker.

14. Fox Butterfield, "Study Exposes Illegal Traffic in New Guns," *New York Times*, February 21, 1999.

15. J. Ludwig and P. J. Cook, "Homicide and Suicide Rates Associated With Implementation of the Brady Handgun Violence Prevention Act," Journal of the American Medical Association, Volume 284, No.5, (August 2, 2000), pp. 585–591.

16. Kleck, ibid.

17. Jeff Brazil and Steve Berry, "Outgunned: The Holes in America's Assault Weapons Laws" *Los Angeles Times*, August 24–27, 1997.

18. John R. Lott, Jr., *More Guns, Less Crime*, (Chicago: University of Chicago Press, 1998).

19. Kleck, ibid., p. 372.

20. Kathleen Maguire and Ann L. Pastore, eds., Sourcebook of Criminal Justice Statistics (Washington, D.C.: U.S. Department of Justice Bureau of Justice Statistics, 1998), p. 141.

21. Will Lester, "Men, Women Differ Widely in Gun-Control Poll," Associated Press, September 1999.

CHAPTER 8   A COP ON EVERY CORNER?

1. The President's Crime Commission on Law Enforcement and Administration of Justice, *The Challenge of Crime in a Free Society*, (New York: Avon Books, 1968), p. 250.

2. Herman Goldstein, *Problem-Oriented Policing* (Philadelphia: Temple University Press, 1990).

3. Interview with Foster.

4. G. L. Kelling, T. Pate, D. Dieckman, and C. E. Brown, *The Kansas City Preventive Patrol Experiment* (Washington, D.C.: Police Foundation, 1974).

5. John Eck and William Spelman, "Who Ya Gonna Call? The Police as Problem-Busters" *Crime and Delinquency*, Vol. 33 (January 1987), pp. 31–52.

6. Interview with Kelling.

7. James Q. Wilson and George L. Kelling, "Broken Windows," *The Atlantic Monthly*, March 1982.

8. Interview with Walinsky.

9. Herbert Jacob and Robert L. Lineberry, "Governmental Responses to Crime" (Northwestern University, Center for Urban Affairs and Policy Research, Washington, D.C.: U.S. Department of Justice, 1982).

10. The Police Corps Act, hearing before the Subcommittee on Crime, Committee on the Judiciary, House of Representatives, 101st Congress, November 2, 1989.

11. "How to Stop Crime the Brainy Way," *U.S. News & World Report*, July 21, 1986, p. 55.

12. Interview with Gurule.

13. Interview with Uchida.

14. "Combating Violent Crime: 24 Recommendations to Strengthen Criminal Justice" (Washington, D.C.: Office of the Attorney General, July 28, 1992).

15. Interview with Reed.

16. Governor Bill Clinton and Senator Al Gore, *Putting People First: How We Can All Change America* (New York: Times Books, 1992).

17. Interview with Scully.

18. Interview with Pate.

19. Interview with Hubbell.

20. Interview with Cerda.

21. Interview with Biden.

22. Interview with Nadol.

23. Jeff Glasser, "The Case of the Missing Cops," *U.S. News & World Report*, July 17, 2000, pp. 22–23.

24. Interview with Hart.

25. Interview with Schmidt.

26. Jeffrey A. Roth et al., "National Evaluation of the "COPS Program—Title 1 of the 1994 Crime Act" (Washington, D.C.: National Institute of Justice, August 2000).

27. Michael R. Bromwich, "Management and Administration of the Community Oriented Policing Services Grant Program" (Washington, D.C.: Inspector General's Office, U.S. Department of Justice, July 1999).

28. Interview with Griffin.

29. Lawrence Sherman, Denise C. Gottfredson, Doris L. Mackenzie, John Eck, Peter Reuter, and Shawn D. Bushway, "Preventing Crime: What Works, What Doesn't, What's Promising," report to Congress (Washington, D.C.: U.S. Department of Justice, 1997).

30. Interview with Geller.

CHAPTER 9   THREE STRIKES: BASEBALL TO CRIME

1. Interview with Carlson.

2. Interview with Fehr.

3. Interview with Klaas.

4. Harry A. Chernoff, Christopher M. Kelly, and John R. Kroger, "The Politics of Crime," *Harvard Journal on Legislation*, Volume 33 (Summer 1996), p. 527.

5. Kathleen Maguire and Ann L. Pastore, eds., Sourcebook of Criminal Justice Statistics, (Washington, D.C.: U.S. Department of Justice, Bureau of Justice Statistics, 1999), p. 129.

6. David J. Krajicek, *Scooped* (New York: Columbia University Press, 1998), pp. 153, 156–159.

7. Lawrence Friedman, *Crime and Punishment in American History* (New York: Basic Books, 1993), p. 411.

8. James P. Lynch and William J. Sabol, "Did Getting Tough on Crime Pay?" (Washington, D.C.: The Urban Institute, 1997).

9. Interview with Lungren.

10. Interview with Fabelo.

11. *The Big Picture in Juvenile and Adult Criminal Justice* (Austin, Tex.: Criminal Justice Policy Council, January 1999).

12. Interview with Kelly.

13. Interview with Griset.

14. John Clark, James Austin, and D. Alan Henry, "Three Strikes and You're Out: A Review of State Legislation," Research in Brief, (Washington, D.C.: National Institute of Justice, U.S. Department of Justice, September 1997).

15. Interview with Adraktas.

16. Interview with LaCourse.

17. Maura Dolan, "State High Court Ruling Toughens 3-Strikes Law, *Los Angeles Times*, May 15, 1998.

18. David Schichor and Dale K. Secrest, *Three Strikes and You're Out: Vengeance as Public Policy* (Thousand Oaks, Calif.: Sage Publications, 1996).

19. Walter J. Dickey and Pam Stiebs Hollenhorst, *"Three Strikes": Five Years Later* (Washington D.C.: Campaign for an Effective Crime Policy, 1998).

20. "New York State: 700 Million Dollars Pumped into Prisons; 600 Million Slashed from Colleges Since 1988" (Washington, D.C. and New York: Justice Policy Institute and Correctional Association of New York, December 1, 1998).

21. U.S. Bureau of Justice Statistics, U.S. Department of Justice.

22. Ibid.

23. Interview with Lapp.

24. Alfred Blumstein and Allen J. Beck, "Factors Contributing to the Growth in U.S. Prison Populations," in *Crime and Justice: A Review of Research on Corrections* (Chicago: University of Chicago Press, 1999).

25. Ibid.

26. Dickey and Stiebs Hollenhorst, ibid.

27. *National Assessment of Structured Sentencing* (Washington, D.C.: U.S. Bureau of Justice Assistance, U.S. Department of Justice, February 1996), p. 115.

28. *Prisoners in 1998*, (Washington, D.C.: U.S. Bureau of Justice Statistics, U.S. Department of Justice, August 1999).

29. Albert J. Reiss, Jr., and Jeffrey A. Roth, *Understanding and Preventing Violence* (Washington, D.C.: National Academy Press, 1993), p. 293.

30. William Spelman, "The Limited Importance of Prison Expansion," in Alfred Blumstein and Joel Wallman, *The Crime Drop in America* (Cambridge: Cambridge University Press, 2000).

31. Camille Graham Camp and George M. Camp, *The Corrections Yearbook 1999* (Middletown, Conn.: Criminal Justice Institute, 2000).

32. Interview with Feldman.

33. Interview with Stewart.

34. Interview with Simon.

35. David C. Anderson, *Crime & the Politics of Hysteria* (New York: Times Books, 1995).

36. "Inmate Furloughs in the Wake of Willie Horton," *Corrections Compendium*, (April 1997), p. 10–12.

37. John J. DiIulio, Jr., "Two Million Prisoners Are Enough," *The Wall Street Journal*, March 12, 1999.

38. Michael Tonry, "Reconsidering Indeterminate and Structured Sentencing" (Washington, D.C.: National Institute of Justice, Papers from the Executive Sessions on Sentencing and Corrections, 1999).

CHAPTER 10   CAPITOL CRIME EXTRAVAGANZA

1. Harry A. Chernoff, Christopher M. Kelly, and John R. Kroger, "The Politics of Crime," *Harvard Journal on Legislation*, Volume 33 (Summer 1996), p. 527.

2. Interview with Biden.

3. Interview with Heymann.

4. Interview with Edelman.

5. Interview with Hilley.

6. Interview with Walker.

7. Interview with Metaksa.

8. John King, "Crunch Time for Health Care and Crime; Consultants Offer Advice Aplenty," Associated Press, August 16, 1994.

9. Interview with Edwards.

10. National Rifle Association, "The Clinton Crime Bill: A Guide for Congressional Candidates" (1994).

11. "A Conversation with President Clinton," *The Plain Dealer (Cleveland)*, January 14, 1995.

12. Interview with Reed.

13. Susan R. Paisner, "Exposed: Online Registries of Sex Offenders May Do More Harm Than Good," *The Washington Post*, February 21, 1999.

14. *Youth Today*, Volume 8, No. 2, (February 1999), p. 1.

CHAPTER 11   SMARTER WAYS TO FIGHT CRIME

1. Mark Fazlollah, Michael Matza, and Craig R. McCoy, "How to Cut City's Crime Rate: Don't Report It," *Philadelphia Inquirer*, November 1, 1998.

2. James Q. Wilson, "What, If Anything, Can the Federal Government Do About Crime?" address to National Institute of Justice, December 10, 1996.

3. Robert J. Sampson and Stephen W. Raudenbush, "Systematic Social Observation of Public Spaces: A New Look at Disorder in Urban Neighborhoods" *American Journal of Sociology*, Volume 105, No.3 (November 1999), pp. 603–651.

4. Dennis P. Rosenbaum, Arthur J. Lurigio, and Robert C. Davis, *The Prevention of Crime: Social and Situational Strategies* (Belmont, Calif.: West/Wadsworth, 1998).

5. Needs Assessment Study, Resource Development Associates, East Bay Public Safety Corridor Partnership (1996).

6. John Feinblatt and Greg Berman, "Responding to the Community: Principles for Planning and Creating a Community Court," U.S. Bureau of Justice Assistance Bulletin (Washington, D.C.: U.S. Department of Justice, 1997).

7. "Arrestee Drug Abuse Monitoring Program (ADAM)," 1998 Annual Report, (Washington, D.C.: National Institute of Justice, U.S. Department of Justice, April 1999).

8. "Substance Abuse and Treatment, State and Federal Prisoners" (Washington, D.C.: U.S. Bureau of Justice Statistics, U.S. Department of Justice, January 5, 1999).

9. Ibid.

10. Interview with Kleiman.

11. Adele Harrell, Foster Cook, and John Carver, "Breaking the Cycle of Drug Abuse in Birmingham," National Institute of Justice *Journal*, (July 1998), pp. 9–13.

12. Interview with Krisberg.

13. "Expenditure and Employment Statistics" (Washington, D.C.: U.S. Bureau of Justice Statistics, U.S. Department of Justice, 1999.

14. Gary LaFree, *Losing Legitimacy: Street Crime and the Decline of Social Institutions in America* (Boulder, Colo.: Westview, 1998).

15. "PERF Collects Survey Data on Police Education and Police Executive Employment," *Subject to Debate*, a newsletter of the Police Executive Research Forum (January-February 1998), p. 1.

16. David C. Anderson, *Sensible Justice: Alternatives to Prison* (New York: The New Press, 1998).

17. Interview with DiIulio.

18. Jeffrey Fagan, "Continuity and Change in American Crime: Lessons from Three Decades," Symposium on the 30th Anniversary of the President's Commission on Law Enforcement and the Administration of Justice, Washington, D.C., 1997.

19. David J. Krajicek, *Scooped!* (New York: Columbia University Press, 1998).

20. Carol Napolitano et. al., "East vs. West: Omaha Crime Isn't That Simple," *Omaha World Herald*, November 8, 1998.

21. Ted Chiricos, presentations to Poynter Institute, St. Petersburg, Fla., October 1998, and Criminal Justice Journalists, Washington, D.C., November 1998: *News Consumption and Perceptions of Crime: An Assessment of Media Content and Public Opinion in Orlando Florida* (Tallahassee, Fla.: The Collins Center for Public Policy; St. Petersburg, Fla.: The Poynter Institute, December 1998).

22. Kathleen Maguire and Ann L. Pastore, eds., Sourcebook of Criminal Justice Statistics (Washington, D.C.: U.S. Department of Justice, Bureau of Justice Statistics, 1998), p. 131.

23. Katherine Beckett, *Making Crime Pay* (New York: Oxford University Press, 1997), p. 107.

24. William C. Cunningham, John J. Strauchs, and Clifford Van Meter, *Private Security Trends, 1970–2000, The Hallcrest Report II* (Boston: Butterworth-Heinemann, 1990).

25. John L. Clark, "Inspection and Review of the Northeast Ohio Correctional Center," report to the Attorney General by the Office of the Corrections Trustee for the District of Columbia, November 25, 1998.

26. Interview with Cikins.

27. John J. DiIulio, Jr. et al., "Crime Policies for the Twenty-First Century: Ten Points of Consensus" (Washington, D.C.: The Brookings Institution, October 24, 1996).

28. Don C. Gibbons, "Review Essay: Crime, Criminologists, and Public Policy," *Crime & Delinquency*, July 1, 1999, pp. 400–413.

29. "The Campaign's Dirty Dozen," *National Journal*, November 14, 1998, pp. 2738–40.

30. Lawrence Sherman, Denise C. Gottfredson, Doris L. MacKenzie, John Eck, Peter Reuter, and Shawn D. Bushway, "Preventing Crime: What Works, What Doesn't, What's Promising," report to Congress (Washington, D.C.: U.S. Department of Justice, 1997).

31. Stephen Glass, "Don't You D.A.R.E: An Anti-Drug Program Strong-Arms Its Critics," *The New Republic*, March 3, 1997, pp. 18–28.

32. Lawrence Sherman, *Policing Domestic Violence* (New York: The Free Press, 1992).

33. A management review of the Office of Justice Programs; (Washington, D.C.: Justice Management Division, U.S. Department of Justice, November 1990).

BIBLIOGRAPHY

Anderson, David C., *Crimes of Justice*. New York: Times Books, 1988.

Anderson, David C., *Crime & the Politics of Hysteria*. New York: Times Books, 1995.

Anderson, David C., *Sensible Justice; Alternatives to Prison*. New York: The New Press, 1998.

Baum, Dan, *Smoke and Mirrors; The War on Drugs and the Politics of Failure*. Boston: Little, Brown, 1996.

Beckett, Katherine, *Making Crime Pay*. New York: Oxford University Press, 1997.

Bell, Griffin B., with Ronald J. Ostrow, *Taking Care of the Law*. New York: William Morrow, 1982.

Bennett, William J., John J. DiIulio, Jr., and John P. Walters, *Body Count*. New York: Simon & Schuster, 1996.

Bertram, Eva, Morris Blachman, Kenneth Sharpe, and Peter Andreas, *Drug War Politics: The Price of Denial*. Berkeley: University of California Press, 1996.

Blumstein, Alfred, and Joel Wallman, eds., *The Crime Drop in America*. New York: Cambridge University Press, 2000.

Burnham, David, *Above the Law*. New York: Scribner, 1996.

Butterfield, Fox, *All God's Children; The Bosket Family and the American Tradition of Violence*. New York: Alfred A. Knopf, 1995.

Camp, Camille Graham, and George M. Camp, *The Corrections Yearbook 1999*. Middletown, Conn.: Criminal Justice Institute, 2000.

Clark, Ramsey, *Crime in America*. New York: Simon & Schuster, 1970.

Clinton, Governor Bill, and Senator Al Gore, *Putting People First: How We Can All Change America*. New York: Times Books, 1992.

Conley, John A. *The 1967 President's Crime Commission Report: Its Impact 25 Years Later*. Cincinnati: Anderson Publishing Co., 1994.

Cronin, Thomas E., Tania Z. Cronin, and Michael E. Milakovich, *U.S. v. Crime in the Streets*. Bloomington: Indiana University Press, 1981.

Cunningham, William C., John J. Strauchs, and Clifford Van Meter, *Private Security Trends, 1970–2000: The Hallcrest Report II.* Boston: Butterworth-Heinemann, 1990.

Davidson, Osha Gray, *Under Fire: The NRA & the Battle for Gun Control.* New York: Henry Holt, 1993.

Diaz, Tom, *Making a Killing: The Business of Guns in America.* New York: The New Press, 1999.

Dickenson, Mollie, *Thumbs Up: The Life and Courageous Comeback of White House Press Secretary Jim Brady.* New York: William Morrow, 1987.

Dickey, Walter J. and Pam Stiebs Hollenhorst, *"Three Strikes": Five Years Later.* Washington, D.C.: Campaign for an Effective Crime Policy, 1998.

Duke, Stephen B., and Albert C. Gross, *America's Longest War.* New York: G. P. Putnam's Sons, 1993.

Falco, Mathea, *The Making of a Drug-Free America.* New York: Times Books, 1992.

Feeley, Malcolm M., *Court Reform on Trial; Why Simple Solutions Fail.* New York: Basic Books, 1983.

Feeley, Malcolm M., and Austin D. Sarat, *The Policy Dilemma: Federal Crime Policy and the Law Enforcement Assistance Administration, 1968–1978.* Minneapolis: University of Minnesota Press, 1980.

Fenno, Richard F., Jr., *Learning to Legislate: The Senate Education of Arlen Specter.* Washington, D.C.: CQ Press, 1991.

Fleisher, Mark S., *Dead End Kids: Gang Girls and the Boys They Know.* Madison: University of Wisconsin Press, 1998.

Forst, Martin L., and Martha-Elin Blomquist, *Missing Children: Rhetoric and Reality.* New York: Lexington Books, 1991.

Frankel, Marvin E., *Criminal Sentences: Law Without Order.* New York: Hill and Wang, 1973.

Friedman, Lawrence M., *Crime and Punishment in American History.* New York: Basic Books, 1993.

Goldstein, Herman, *Problem-Oriented Policing.* Philadelphia: Temple University Press, 1990.

Harris, Richard, *Justice.* New York: Avon Books, 1970.

Heide, Kathleen M., *Young Killers.* Thousand Oaks, Calif.: Sage Publications, 1999.

Hudzik, John K., *Federal Aid to Criminal Justice.* Washington, D.C.: National Criminal Justice Association, 1984.

Kaminer, Wendy, *It's All the Rage: Crime and Culture.* Reading, Mass.: Addison-Wesley, 1995.

Kelling, G. L., T. Pate, and C. E. Brown, *The Kansas City Preventive Patrol Experiment.* Washington, D.C.: Police Foundation, 1974.

Kelling, George L., and Catherine M. Coles, *Fixing Broken Windows.* New York: The Free Press, 1996.

Kleck, Gary, *Point Blank: Guns and Violence in America.* New York: Aldine de Gruyter, 1991.

Kleck, Gary, *Targeting Guns: Firearms and Their Control.* New York: Aldine de Gruyter, 1997.

Kopel, David B., *The Samurai, the Mountie, and the Cowboy.* Buffalo: Prometheus Books, 1992.

Krajicek, David J., *Scooped!* New York: Columbia University Press, 1998.

Kramer, Rita, *At a Tender Age: Violent Youth and Juvenile Justice.* New York: Henry Holt, 1988.

La Free, Gary, *Losing Legitimacy: Street Crime and the Decline of Social Institutions in America.* Boulder, Colo.: Westview, 1998.

Lardner, George, Jr., *The Stalking of Kristin.* New York: Atlantic Monthly Press, 1995.

Loeber, Rolf, and David P. Farrington, *Serious & Violent Juvenile Offenders.* Thousand Oaks, Calif.: Sage Publications, 1998.

Lord Windlesham, *Politics, Punishment, and Populism.* New York: Oxford University Press, 1998.

Lott, John R., Jr., *More Guns, Less Crime.* Chicago: University of Chicago Press, 1998.

Mahoney, Barry, "The Politics of the Safe Streets Act, 1965–1973: A Case Study in Evolving Federalism and the National Legislative Process." Ph.D. diss., Columbia University, 1976.

Massing, Michael, *The Fix.* New York: Simon & Schuster, 1998.

Mauer, Marc, *Race to Incarcerate.* New York: The New Press, 1999.

McGee, Jim, and Brian Duffy, *Main Justice.* New York: Simon & Schuster, 1996.

Metaksa, Tanya K., *Safe, Not Sorry.* New York: HarperCollins, 1997.

Miller, Jerome G., *Search and Destroy.* Cambridge: Cambridge University Press, 1996.

Moore, Mark H., Susan R. Estrich, Daniel McGillis, and William Spelman, *Dangerous Offenders.* Cambridge, Mass.: Harvard University Press, 1984.

Morris, Norval, and Gordon Hawkins, *The Honest Politician's Guide to Crime Control*. Chicago: University of Chicago Press, 1970.

Morris, Norval, and Michael Tonry, *Between Prison and Probation*. New York: Oxford University Press, 1990.

Murphy, Patrick V., and Thomas Plate, *Commissioner: A View from the Top of American Law Enforcement*. New York: Simon & Schuster, 1977.

Musto, David M., *The American Disease: Origins of Narcotic Control*. New York: Oxford University Press, 1993.

The President's Commission on Law Enforcement and Administration of Justice, *The Challenge of Crime in a Free Society*. New York: Avon Books, 1968.

Rand, Michael R., *Carjacking*. Washington, D.C.: Bureau of Justice Statistics, U.S. Department of Justice, March 1994.

Reiss, Albert J., Jr., *The Police and the Public*. New Haven, Conn.: Yale University Press, 1971.

Reiss, Albert J., Jr., and Jeffrey A. Roth, eds., *Understanding and Preventing Violence*. Washington, D.C.: National Academy Press, 1993.

Rosenbaum, Dennis P., Arthur J. Lurigio, and Robert C. Davis, *The Prevention of Crime: Social and Situational Strategies*. Belmont, Calif.: West/Wadsworth, 1998.

Scheingold, Stuart A., *The Politics of Street Crime*. Philadelphia: Temple University Press, 1991.

Schichor, David, and Dale K. Sechrest, *Three Strikes and You're Out: Vengeance as Public Policy*. Thousand Oaks, Calif.: Sage Publications, 1996.

Sherman, Lawrence W., *Policing Domestic Violence*. New York: The Free Press, 1992.

Shields, Pete, *Guns Don't Die—People Do*. New York: Arbor House, 1981.

Silberman, Charles E., *Criminal Violence, Criminal Justice*. New York: Vintage Books, 1978.

Skogan, Wesley G., *Disorder and Decline*. New York: The Free Press, 1990.

Skogan, Wesley G., and Susan M. Hartnett, *Community Policing, Chicago Style*. New York: Oxford University Press, 1997.

Stith, Kate, and Jose A. Cabranes, *Fear of Judging: Sentencing Guidelines in the Federal Courts*. Chicago: University of Chicago Press, 1998.

Strazzella, James A., reporter, *The Federalization of Criminal Law*. Washington, D.C.: American Bar Association, 1998.

Sugarmann, Josh, *NRA: Money, Firepower, Fear*. Washington, D.C.: National Press Books, 1992.

Surette, Ray, *Media, Crime, and Criminal Justice*. Belmont, Calif.: Wadsworth, 1998.

Tonry, Michael, *Sentencing Matters*. New York: Oxford University Press, 1995.

Twentieth Century Fund Task Force on the Law Enforcement Assistance Administration, *Law Enforcement: The Federal Role*. New York: McGraw-Hill, 1976.

Walker, Samuel, *Taming the System: The Control of Discretion in Criminal Justice, 1950–1990*. New York: Oxford University Press, 1993.

Weed, Frank J., *Certainty of Justice; Reform in the Crime Victim Movement*. New York: Aldine de Gruyter, 1995.

Wilson, James Q., *Thinking About Crime*. New York: Basic Books, 1975.

Wilson, James Q., ed., *Crime and Public Policy*. San Francisco: Institute for Contemporary Studies, 1983.

Wilson, James Q., and Joan Petersilia, *Crime*. San Francisco: Institute for Contemporary Studies Press, 1993.

Wise, Charles R., *The Dynamics of Legislation*. San Francisco: Jossey-Bass, 1991.

Wolfgang, M., R. M. Figlio, and T. Sellin, *Delinquency in a Birth Cohort*. Chicago: University of Chicago Press, 1972.

Zimring, Franklin E., *American Youth Violence*. New York: Oxford University Press, 1998.

Zimring, Franklin E., and Gordon Hawkins, *The Search for Rational Drug Control*. Cambridge: Cambridge University Press, 1992.

INDEX

ABC News, 246
Abraham, Spencer, 127
Abramson, Jerry, 181
Adraktas, Stephanie, 205
Agnew, Spiro, 28
Agopian, Michael, 97–98
Ailes, Roger, 216
Aimee's Law, 245
Allen, Ernest, 32
Allen, George, 194
Ambrose, Myles, 111
American Bar Association, 64, 66, 72, 80
American Correctional Association, 211
American Probation and Parole Association, 209
American Youth Work Center, 246
Anderson, David C., 215, 263
Anslinger, Harry, 109
APBNews.com, 268
Arcara, Richard, 74
Armed Career Criminal Act, 67, 86
Arrestee Drug Abuse Monitoring (ADAM), 256
Assault–style weapons, 150, 171, 228–229, 231–236, 238–241
Atlantic Monthly, 160–161

Baker, Bill, 199
Baker, James, 139
Ballasiotes, Diana, 190
Ballasiotes, Ida, 190–191
Barr, William, 97, 168
Basu, Pamela, 68–69
Basu, Sarina, 68

Battaglia, Lynne, 81
Baum, Dan, 66, 110–112
Bayh, Birch, 30, 84–85
Beck, Allen, 208, 210
Beckett, Katherine, 269
Behan, Neil, 140, 142
Bell, Griffin, 34–38, 43, 47
Bennett, William, 123–124, 192
Benson, Russell, 206
Bertram, Eva, 123, 130
Biaggi, Mario, 139
Bias, Len, 119
Biden, Joseph, 37, 45–49, 57, 66, 70, 122–123, 127, 146–148, 169, 174–176, 179–181, 221, 224, 226–227, 229–231, 234, 236, 240–243
Biderman, Albert, 10, 12
Bilchik, Sheldon (Shay), 98, 104, 276
Blueprints for Violence Prevention, 260
Blumstein, Alfred, 12–13, 210, 274
Boggs, Hale, 27
Boland, Barbara, 255
Bond, Christopher, 137
Bonior, David, 232, 241
Bourne, Peter, 111–112
Bouza, Anthony, 140, 142
Boxer, Barbara, 272
Boyd, Richard, 140, 142
Boys & Girls Clubs, 246
Bradley, Bill, 164
Brady Act, 136, 143–50, 171, 228–229, 233
Brady, James S., 143–144, 233
Brady, Sarah, 143–145, 147–148, 233
Branch Davidians, 80, 224

Brann, Joseph, 182, 185
Bratton, William, 167, 178, 182
Breaking the Cycle program, 258
Brewster, Kingman, 8
Breyer, Stephen, 60, 122
"Broken Windows," 161
Brookings Institution, 271
Brooks, Jack, 146, 165–166, 175, 179, 221, 225, 230–242
Brown, Edmund, 194
Brown, Jerry, 194
Brown, Kathleen, 194
Brown, Lee, 124–125, 140, 163, 169
Brzonkala, Christy, 70
Bureau of Alcohol, Tobacco, and Firearms, 63, 67, 77–78, 80, 137, 139, 240
Bureau of Justice Assistance, 180, 246, 276
Bureau of Narcotics and Dangerous Drugs, 110–111
Burger, Warren, 262
Bush, George H. W., 77, 117, 119, 121, 123–124, 131, 136, 164, 168, 170, 172, 213, 215–216, 223, 255
Bush, George W., 126, 186, 202
Business Week, 196
Byrd, Robert, 45, 166, 227
Byrne, Brendan, 30
Byrne, Garrett, 8
Byrne Program, 168

Cabranes, Jose, 60
Cahill, Thomas, 8, 10
Califano, Joseph, 7, 13, 250
Campaign for an Effective Crime Policy, 207, 211, 271
Campbell, Ben Nighthorse, 229
Caplan, Gerald, 5, 14
Carjacking, 68–69
Carlson, John, 189–192, 194, 196, 205
Carrington, Frank, 43
Carter, Jimmy, 28, 34–35, 38–39, 41, 43–44, 46, 79, 85, 91, 111–113, 115, 159, 162, 226
Casey, Joseph, 140, 142
Cassidy, Warren, 142
Cato Institute, 212
Ceasefire Initiative, 252
Celler, Emanuel, 19, 31
Centers for Disease Control, 274
Cerda, Jose, 173–177
Chandler, Otis, 8
Chernoff, Harry, 196, 224, 230
Chesapeake & Potomac Telephone Company, 12
Chicago Tribune, 96
Chiles, Lawton, 118, 120
Chiricos, Ted, 268
Church, Frank, 45
Cikins, Warren, 271
Civiletti, Benjamin, 38
Clark Foundation, 267

Clark, John, 270
Clark, Ramsey, 14–15, 20–22, 31, 213
Clark, Tom, 14
Clinton, Bill, 19, 74–75, 77–79, 97–8, 104, 123–125, 127, 146–147, 149, 152–153, 164–166, 168–177, 180–186, 189, 195–196, 213, 220, 223–226, 229, 237–239, 241–243, 245–247, 256–257, 274
Clinton, Hillary Rodham, 104
Coburn, Daniel, 263
Cohen, Mary Louise Westmoreland, 142
Columbia Journalism Review, 267
Columbine High School, 100, 153, 266
Communities That Care, 259
Community Oriented Policing Services program (COPS), 172, 178–186, 243, 276
COMPASS program, 265
Congressional Black Caucus, 121, 230–231, 234–235, 237–238
Congressional Quarterly, 141
Conner, Roger, 262
Conservative Opportunity Society, 52–53, 200–201
Conte, Silvio, 55
Contract With America, 181
Conyers, John, 38, 47, 49, 222, 235
Cook, Philip, 150
Cop–killer bullets, 138–141, 143
Correctional Association of New York, 207
Corrections Compendium, 216
Corrections Corporation of America, 269–270
Coster, Clarence, 23, 25
Couper, David, 160
Craig, Larry, 228
Crime Prevention Through Environmental Design, 256
CrimeStrike, 152, 191, 197
Criminal code, federal, 44
Criminal Justice Institute, 211
Criminal Justice Journalists, 267
Criminal Justice Policy Council (Texas), 201
Cronin, Thomas, 26, 83
C–SPAN, 53–54, 221
Culver, John, 84
Cuomo, Mario, 163, 194
Curfews, 104
Curtis, Richard, 108

D'Amato, Alfonse, 69–70, 225, 272
Danforth, John, 231
Danziger, Martin, 28
Darman, Richard, 164
Davidson, Marshall, 268
Davidson, Osha Gray, 142, 144
Davis, Gray, 207
Davis, Richard Allen, 192–193, 199–200
Davis, Robert, 252
Day, Doris, 76
DeConcini, Dennis, 228
Democratic Leadership Council, 166, 224
Deukmejian, George, 90

Dewey, Thomas, 7
Dickey, Walter, 211
Dickinson, Mollie, 144
Diegelman, Robert, 39
DiIulio, John, 99, 217, 262–263, 271
Dingell, John, 68–69
Dodd, Thomas, 134–135
Dogin, Henry, 36, 38
Doi, David, 136, 139–140, 142, 145
Dole, Bob, 120, 147–148, 166, 241–242, 257
Domenici, Pete, 88, 231
Dorgan, Byron, 241
Dornan, Bob, 165–166
Drinan, Robert, 47, 52
Drug Abuse Resistance Education (DARE), 272
Drug courts, 129
Drug Enforcement Administration, 46, 66, 78,
    111, 113–114, 119–120
Drug Use Forecasting (DUF), 256
Duffy, Brian, 77
Duffy, John, 141
Dukakis, Michael, 123, 164, 170, 215–216, 223
Duke, Stephen, 124
Dyson, Roy, 138

Early, Joseph, 37
East Bay Public Safety Corridor Partnership,
    253
Eastland, James, 19
Eck, John, 160
Edelman, Peter, 85, 105–106, 225, 231
Edwards, Don, 49, 222, 232, 234
Edwards, Keith, 213
Ehrlichman, John, 27
Ellingwood, Herbert, 87
Elliott, Delbert, 260
Emanuel, Rahm, 104, 125, 149
Espy, Mike, 232
Evans, Courtney, 18

Fabelo, Tony, 201
Fagan, Jeffrey, 117, 119, 266
Falwell, Jerry, 87
Family Research Council, 97
Families Against Mandatory Minimums, 213–
    214
Farrell, John, 81
Federal Bureau of Investigation, 6–7, 12, 13, 18,
    28, 46, 71, 76–81, 113–114, 144–145, 150, 244,
    249
Federal Bureau of Narcotics, 109
Federal Prison Industries, 262
Fehr, Larry, 191–192
Feinberg, Kenneth, 33, 38, 59, 61
Feinblatt, John, 254
Feinstein, Dianne, 228–229, 232
Feldman, Daniel, 212
Ferguson, Colin, 195
Fiederowicz, Walter, 35–37
Firearm Owners Protection Act, 138

Fitzgerald, Peter, 272
Flanagan, Timothy, 269
Fleisher, Mark, 103
Fletcher, Ernest, 272
Florio, James, 263
Foley, Thomas, 176, 231, 236–238, 241
Fong, Matt, 272
Ford, Gerald, 33–35, 46, 85, 232–233
Ford Foundation, 141, 160, 267
Forfeiture, 57–58
Foster, Jodie, 143
Foster, J. Price, 149
Frank, Barney, 165
Frankel, Marvin, 58–59
Franklin, Benjamin, 268
Frazier, Thomas, 185–186
Freeh, Louis, 72, 76, 78
Friedman, Lawrence, 199
From, Al, 224
Furloughs, 215–216
Furman, James, 94–96

Gates, Daryl, 22, 140, 164–165
Gearan, Mark, 238
Gelacek, Michael, 127
Geller, William, 186
Gell–mann, Murray, 94
General Accounting Office, 26, 46, 107
Gephardt, Richard, 166, 176, 240–241
Gergen, David, 176
Gibbons, Don, 271
Gingrich, Newt, 52–53, 131, 165, 201, 231, 236,
    240, 246
Gist, Nancy, 246, 276
Gitenstein, Mark, 47
Giuliani, Rudolph, 114, 163, 168
Glass, Stephen, 273
Goldsmith, Stephen, 256
Goldstein, Herman, 158, 160, 167, 177, 183
Goldstein, Paul, 118
Goldwater, Barry, 5, 65
Gore, Al, 104–106, 173, 176, 202, 215, 246
Governing, 102
Gramm, Phil, 69, 227
Green, Scott, 57
Greenberg, Reuben, 163, 169
Gregg, James, 20, 34–35
Gregg, Judd, 202
Gregory, Hayden, 120
Griffin, Jeff, 185
Griset, Pamala, 203
Gun Control Act, 135, 137, 144
Gun–Free School Zones Act, 70
Gurule, Jimmy, 168, 177

Haldeman, H. R., 27
Hallcrest Systems, Inc., 269
Handgun Control, Inc., 133, 136, 139–149, 228,
    232, 240–241
Hannaford, Peter, 144

Harmon, Clarence, 182
Harrell, Adele, 260
Harris, Jo Ann, 196
Harris, Richard (*Justice*), 21
Harris, Richard (Virginia), 24, 26
Harrison Act, 109
Harshbarger, Scott, 72
Hastert, Dennis, 246
Hart, John, 183, 185
Hart, Philip, 22
Hatch, Orrin, 62, 122, 202, 214, 222–223, 229, 231, 235, 241, 243, 246
Hawkins, Gordon, 69
Hawkins, J. David, 259
Heck, Robert, 90–91, 97
Heritage Foundation, 217
Herrington, John, 50
Herrington, Lois, 50–52
Heston, Charlton, 237
Heymann, Philip, 66, 79, 105, 213, 224–226
Hilley, John, 227
Hinckley, John, 54, 143
Hollings, Ernest, 22, 57, 234
Holsclaw, Kevin, 54
Hoover, J. Edgar, 6, 12, 14, 18, 20, 109, 178, 186
Horton, William (Willie), 123, 215–216
Howell, James C., 103
Hruska, Roman,19, 135
Hubbell, Webb, 105, 175, 180, 225–226
Hughes, William, 46–47, 56–57, 66, 68, 115, 118–121, 138, 165, 222, 225
Hungate, William, 137
Hyde, Henry, 54, 66, 232

Inciardi, James, 129
Indiana Avenue, 17–18, 22, 25, 32–33, 35, 37, 85, 180
Integrated Criminal Apprehension Program, 90
International Association of Chiefs of Police, 97, 140, 142–143

Jackson, Jesse, 123
Jacob, Herbert, 162
Jacobs, Andrew, Jr., 233
Jaworski, Leon, 32
Jeffery, C. Ray, 273
Jensen, Lowell, 50
Johnson, Lyndon Baines, 5, 9, 13–14, 18, 29–30, 43
Jones, Bill, 204
Jones, Paula, 75
Jordan, Michael, 174, 219
Just Say No campaign, 116
Justice For All, 244
Justice Policy Institute, 204, 207
Juvenile Accountability Incentive Block Grant, 101

Kanka, Megan, 244
Kasich, John, 172

Kassebaum, Nancy, 106, 147
Katzenbach, Nicholas, 7, 10, 14, 18, 21
Kelley, Clarence, 76
Kelling, George, 160–161, 167, 256
Kelly, Bill, 202
Kelly, Christopher, 196, 224, 230
Kennedy, David, 92, 252
Kennedy, Edward, 33, 36–39, 45, 58–59, 61, 122, 137, 164–165, 174, 215, 222–223
Kennedy, John F., 134, 226
Kennedy, Robert, 7, 14, 18, 21, 134–135, 161, 164
King, Martin Luther, Jr., 134–135
King, Rodney, 172
Klaas, Joe, 207
Klaas, Marc, 193–195, 199
Klaas, Polly, 192–193, 195, 199, 207, 219, 267
Klain, Ronald, 169, 181
Kleck, Gary, 150–151
Kleiman, Mark, 257–258
Kleindienst, Richard, 22, 28
Kolender, William, 140
Krajicek, David, 266, 268
Kramer, John, 127
Kramer, Rita, 89
Krisberg, Barry, 259
Kroger, John, 169, 196, 224, 230
Krogh, Egil, 27, 110
Krol, John, 76
Kunin, Madeleine, 105
Kurlander, Lawrence, 163

LaCourse, David, 191, 205
LaFree, Gary, 261
Lamar University, 236–237
Lanier, Bob, 169
LaPierre, Wayne, 139, 142–143
Lapp, Katherine, 210, 212
Lauer, Charles, 88–89
Law Enforcement Assistance Administration, 20–39, 46, 50, 52, 75, 83, 86–87, 135, 159, 162, 167–168, 180–182, 186, 243, 246, 263, 276
Law Enforcement Coordinating Committees, 76
Law Enforcement Education Program, 159
Law Enforcement Steering Committee, 141
Lawn, John, 119
Lawrence *Eagle–Tribune*, 215
Laxalt, Paul, 56, 89
Lehman, Joseph, 264
Leonard, Jerris, 25–30, 34–36
Levi, Edward, 33–36
Lewinsky, Monica, 75, 185, 274
Lewis, John, 238
Lindsey, Bruce, 170
Lineberry, Robert, 162
Local Law Enforcement Block Grants, 182, 243
Los Angeles Times, 107, 150–151, 206–207
Lott, John, 151
Lowry, Mike, 191
Ludwig, Jens, 150–151

Lugar, Richard, 30
Lungren, Dan, 52–57, 119, 121, 201, 204
Luntz, Frank, 230–231
Lurigio, Arthur, 252
Luttig, Michael, 71
Lynch, James, 200
Lynch, Thomas, 8
Lynchner, Pam, 244

MacArthur Foundation, 94–96
MacCoun, Rob, 122
Madden, Thomas, 22, 27
Mansfield, Mike, 20
Marcus, Stanley, 70
Markus, Kent, 181
Martinez, Bob, 124
Martinson, Robert, 198
Massing, Michael, 110, 115
Mattingly, Marion, 87–88
McBride, Andrew, 97
McBride, Thomas, 162
McCaffrey, Barry, 123, 125–131
McCain, John, 246
McClellan, John, 19–20, 31
McClure, James, 137
McClure–Volkmer bill, 137–141, 144–145
McCollum, Bill, 104, 106, 222
McConnell, Robert, 57
McCurdy, Dave, 166
McGee, Jim, 77
McGovern, George, 29, 110
McGregor, Clark, 23
McGruff the Crime Dog, 249, 269
McIntyre, James, 38
McNamara, Joseph, 142, 163
McNulty, Paul, 106
Meese, Edwin, 43, 48–50, 66, 77, 79, 86–87, 95, 116, 168
Meese, Ursula, 50
Megan's Law, 244–245
Metaksa, Tanya, 139, 229, 233, 240
Metzenbaum, Howard, 90, 142, 147, 228
Michel, Bob, 52, 55
Michel, Paul, 39
Midtown Community Court, 254
Milk, Harvey, 228
Miranda v. Arizona, 32
Mitchell, David, 127
Mitchell, George, 166, 224, 226–227, 241–242
Mitchell, John, 21–23, 25–27, 30, 33
Molinari, Susan, 74–75
Monagan, John, 26–27
Moore, Mark, 79
Morris, Norval, 36, 38, 94
Moscone, George, 228
Moseley–Braun, Carol, 272
Mott Foundation, 160
Murphy, Jerry, 111
Murphy, Patrick, 18, 20–22
Murray, Donald, 25

Musto, David, 109
Myers, Dee Dee, 230

Nadelmann, Ethan, 271
Nadol, Jack, 180–181
National Academy of Sciences, 29, 211
National Advisory Commission on Criminal
   Justice Standards and Goals, 29
National Aeronautics and Space
   Administration, 10, 12
National Association of Counties, 25
National Association of Criminal Defense
   Lawyers, 213
National Association of Police Organizations,
   165, 170, 238
National Association of Retail Druggists, 66
National Center for Missing and Exploited
   Children, 52
National Center on Institutions and
   Alternatives, 217
National Conference of State Legislatures, 69
National Crime Information Center, 145
National Crime Prevention Council, 269
National District Attorneys Association, 48, 168
National Institute of Justice, 275–276
National Journal, 271
National Legal Aid and Defender Association,
   64, 121
National Narcotics Intelligence Consumer
   Committee, 116
National Opinion Research Center, 198
National Organization for the Reform of
   Marijuana Laws, 111–112
National Organization for Victim Assistance,
   245
National Organization of Black Law
   Enforcement Executives, 163
National Research Council, 211
National Rifle Association, 101, 133–153, 155, 191–
   192, 197, 228–229, 232–237, 239–240, 242, 273
National Science Foundation, 274
National Transportation Safety Board, 20
Newman, Oscar, 256
New Republic, The, 273
Newsweek,196
Nixon, Richard, 12, 14, 22, 25, 27, 30–33, 35, 52,
   110–112, 124
Nunn, Sam, 45

Office of Drug Abuse Law Enforcement, 111
Office of Justice Programs, 2, 180, 243, 275
Office of Juvenile Justice and Delinquency
   Prevention, 84–85, 87–88, 96–98, 101–104, 106
Office of Law Enforcement Assistance, 18
Office of Management and Budget, 38
Office of National Drug Control Policy, 113
Ohlin, Lloyd, 9, 10, 12
Omaha World–Herald, 267
O'Neill, Thomas (Tip), 56, 119, 139
Operation Exile, 152

Operation Night Light, 253
Operation Scrap Iron, 252
Operation Triggerlock, 77
Oswald, Lee Harvey, 134
Ounce of Prevention Council, 104–106
Owen, Deborah, 56

Paisner, Susan, 245
Palumbo, Dennis, 102
Pam Lynchner Act, 244
Paparozzi, Mario, 209
Parent, Dale, 59
Parents' Resource Institute for Drug Education, 112
Partnership for a Drug-Free America, 96
Pataki, George, 210–211
Pate, Antony, 172
Peel, Sir Robeert, 167
Percy, Charles, 111
Peterson, Russell, 30
Philadelphia Inquirer, 249
Pitchess, Peter, 30
Pittman, Karen, 105–106
Pitts, Bill, 55
Police Executive Research Forum, 141, 163, 177–178, 261
Police Corps, 161–166, 168–176, 179
Police Foundation, 140, 160, 162
Pomeroy, Wesley, 21–22
Potter, Tom, 182
President's Commission on Model State Drug Laws, 255
Project Achilles, 67, 77
Pryor, Richard, 116
Public Interest, 198

Quartel, Rob, 164, 169

Racial Justice Act, 230, 234–236
Rangel, Charles, 123–124
Rayburn, Sam, 181
Reader's Digest, 97, 216
Reagan, Nancy, 90, 114, 116, 123
Reagan, Ronald, 41, 43, 48–54, 56, 76–77, 86–90, 93, 95, 113, 115–116, 119, 123, 129, 136, 143–145, 170, 201, 232–233
Reed, Bruce, 104, 169–170, 173–177, 179, 224, 232, 243
Regan, Donald, 144
Regier, Gerald, 97
Regnery, Alfred, 89–90, 96
Rehnquist, William, 30, 69
Rendell, Ed, 152
Reno, Janet, 72, 77–79, 81, 98, 104–105, 107, 126–127, 129, 131, 173, 175–178, 180–182, 213, 216, 224, 234, 264–265, 274
Research Triangle Institute, 272
Restorative justice, 264
Reuter, Peter, 116, 122, 128
Reynolds, Kimber, 193

Reynolds, Mike, 193–195
Richards, Ann, 202
Richardson, Elliot, 22
Riggs, Frank, 104
Riveland, Chase, 192
Rizzo, Frank, 28
Robertson, Pat, 50–51
Robinson, Laurie, 216, 274–275
Robinson, Paul, 60
Rockefeller, Nelson, 111, 119, 198–199, 211
Rodino, Peter, 47, 49, 53–54, 137–138, 228
Rodriguez, Matt, 178
Rogovin, Charles, 22–25, 27–28, 162
Rooney, John, 18, 21
Rosenbaum, Dennis, 252
Roth, Jeffrey, 184
Rubenstein, Jonathan, 163
Rudman, Warren, 164
Ruth, Henry, 6, 8–9, 13, 23

Sabol, William, 200
Safe and Drug-Free Schools and Communities Act, 107
Safe Streets Violent Crime Initiative, 78
SafetyTips.com, 268
Saland, Stephen, 72
Salk, Jonas, 94
Sampson, Rana, 177–178
Sanders, Jerry, 178
Santarelli, Donald, 30, 32–33
Sasser, Jim, 164, 166
Sawyer, Harold, 46–47, 54
Schichor, David, 207
Schmidt, John, 180, 183
Schmults, Edward, 163
Schumer, Charles, 68–70, 166, 169, 176, 179, 184, 222, 224–225, 232–233, 236–237, 239–241, 272
Schwartz, Ira, 85
Scott, Hugh, 28
Scully, Robert, 165, 171–172, 186
Secrest, Dale, 207
Sensenbrenner, James, 222, 230
Sentencing guidelines, 53–54, 58–61
Sentencing Project, 271
Serious Habitual Offenders Criminal Apprehension Program, 91, 97
Serious Habitual Offenders, Drug Involved program 91
Sessions, Jeff, 77, 104
Shalala, Donna, 105
Shapp, Milton, 28
Shaw, Bernard, 216
Shaw, Clay, 123, 126
Sherman, Lawrence, 150, 185, 274, 276
Shields, Pete, 133, 143
Shorstein, Harry, 65, 71, 100
Shrum, Robert, 130
Silver, Isidore, 7, 9–10, 14, 30
Simon, Paul, 214
Simpson, O. J., 193, 219, 266–267

Singer, Max, 116
Siu, Ralph, 21–22
"60 Minutes," 26, 159
Skoler, Daniel, 18–19, 21
Smith, D. Brooks, 63, 75
Smith, Neal, 37, 57, 124
Smith, William French, 43, 89, 95, 163
Soler, Mark, 276
Specter, Arlen, 28, 48–49, 57, 67–68, 86, 88–90, 98, 101, 103, 152, 164–165
Spelman, William, 160, 211
Sperling, Gene, 174
Sposato, Jody, 228
Sposato, Stephen, 228
Stallone, Sylvester, 87
Stein, John, 245
Stephanopoulos, George, 240
Stephens, Darrel, 167, 177–178
Sterling, Eric, 120
Stevens, Ted, 107
Stewart, James K. (Chips), 94–95, 163, 166–168
Stewart, Jeff, 212
Stewart, Julie, 212–214
Stith, Kate, 60
Stockman, David, 51
Stokes, Dewey, 142
Stuart, Julia, 7
Sugarmann, Josh, 140
Sweet, Robert, 97

Teeter, Robert, 164
Ten Point Coalition, 253
Thomas, Clarence, 221
Thompson, Jim, 43, 47
Thompson, Mike, 193
Thornburgh, Richard, 95, 97, 168
Thurmond, Strom, 45, 48–49, 53, 60, 68, 122, 214
Time, 196
Toensing, Victoria, 58
Tonry, Michael, 217
Townsend, Kathleen Kennedy, 164, 172
Treatment Alternatives to Street Crime program, 258, 263
Trojanowicz, Robert, 160
Truth in sentencing, 201
Turner, Carlton, 116

Uchida, Craig, 168, 175, 180–181, 183–184, 186
Underwood, James, 162
U.S. Conference of Mayors, 170
U.S. v. Lopez, 70
U. S. News & World Report, 106, 117, 167, 186, 196
University of Maryland crime prevention study, 103, 272, 274
Urban Institute, 183–184

Vaughn, Jerald, 142
Velde, Richard (Pete), l4–15, 19–20, 22–23, 25, 29–31, 33–36, 135
Vera Institute of Justice, 267
Vicchio, Stephen, 117
Victims of crime, 50–52, 58, 263–264
Violence Against Women Act, 70, 226, 244
Violence Policy Center, 140
Viramontes, Maria Theresa, 253
Virginian Pilot, 267
Volkmer, Harold, 137–138, 228
Vorenberg, James, 7–8, 13, 18

Wackenhut Corporation, 270
Wagner, Robert, 8
Walinsky, Adam, 161–166, 168–174, 176
Walker, John, 139
Walker, Robert, 146–148, 228, 232–233, 241
Wallace, Mike, 26–27
Wallace, Scott, 64, 121
Walsh, Adam, 51
Ward, Benjamin, 167
Warren, Earl, 8
Washington Citizens for Justice, 191
Washington Council on Crime and Delinquency, 191
Washington, Craig, 231
Washington Post, 61–62, 245
Weaver, Vicki, 80
Webb, Jack, 158
Webster, William, 76–77, 80, 114–115
Weed and Seed program, 97
Weicker, Lowell, 88–89
Weiner, Robert, 123
Welch, Neil, 163
Wetterling, Jacob, 244–245
Weyrich, Paul, 165
Wicker, Tom, 14
Wickersham Commission, 6
Widom, Cathy Spatz, 264
Wilkins, William, 60–61
Willard, Aimee, 245
Wilson, James Q., 43, 161, 250, 256, 271, 274
Wilson, John, 98, 101, 102
Wise, Charles, 49
Witkin, Gordon, 117–118
Wolfgang, Marvin, 92–93, 98
Wootton, James, 90–91, 96
Work, Charles, 31
Wormeli, Paul, 34–36
Wright, Leo, 265

Yassky, David, 240
Young, Whitney, 7
Youth Today, 246

Zimmer, Dick, 244
Zimring, Franklin, 69